AS EASY AS IT GETS!

Meditation

by Domyo Sater Burk

ALPHA
A member of Penguin Random House LLC

Dedicated in the memory of Kyogen Carlson, a brilliant Zen teacher and a great fan of interfaith dialogue.

ALPHA BOOKS

Published by Penguin Random House LLC

Penguin Random House LLC, 375 Hudson Street, New York, New York 10014, USA • Penguin Random House LLC (Canada), 90 Eglinton Avenue East, Suite 700, Toronto, Ontario M4P 2Y3, Canada (a division of Pearson Penguin Canada Inc.) • Penguin Books Ltd., 80 Strand, London WC2R 0RL, England • Penguin Ireland, 25 St. Stephen's Green, Dublin 2, Ireland (a division of Penguin Books Ltd.) • Penguin Random House LLC (Australia), 250 Camberwell Road, Camberwell, Victoria 3124, Australia (a division of Pearson Australia Group Pty. Ltd.) • Penguin Books India Pvt. Ltd., 11 Community Centre, Panchsheel Park, New Delhi—110 017, India • Penguin Random House LLC (NZ), 67 Apollo Drive, Rosedale, North Shore, Auckland 1311, New Zealand (a division of Pearson New Zealand Ltd.) • Penguin Books (South Africa) (Pty.) Ltd., 24 Sturdee Avenue, Rosebank, Johannesburg 2196, South Africa • Penguin Books Ltd., Registered Offices: 80 Strand, London WC2R 0RL, England

International Standard Book Number: 978-1-61564-886-3
Library of Congress Catalog Card Number: Available upon request

18 17 16   8 7 6 5 4 3 2 1

Interpretation of the printing code: The rightmost number of the first series of numbers is the year of the book's printing; the rightmost number of the second series of numbers is the number of the book's printing. For example, a printing code of 16-1 shows that the first printing occurred in 2016.

Printed in the United States of America

Note: This publication contains the opinions and ideas of its author. It is intended to provide helpful and informative material on the subject matter covered. It is sold with the understanding that the author and publisher are not engaged in rendering professional services in the book. If the reader requires personal assistance or advice, a competent professional should be consulted. The author and publisher specifically disclaim any responsibility for any liability, loss, or risk, personal or otherwise, which is incurred as a consequence, directly or indirectly, of the use and application of any of the contents of this book.

Most Alpha books are available at special quantity discounts for bulk purchases for sales promotions, premiums, fund-raising, or educational use. Special books, or book excerpts, can also be created to fit specific needs. For details, write: Special Markets, Alpha Books, 345 Hudson Street, New York, NY 10014.

Publisher: *Mike Sanders*
Associate Publisher: *Billy Fields*
Acquisitions Editor: *Jan Lynn*
Development Editor: *Kayla Dugger*
Cover Designer: *Laura Merriman*

Book Designer: *William Thomas*
Indexer: *Brad Herriman*
Layout: *Ayanna Lacey*
Proofreader: *Monica Stone*

Contents

Appendixes

Introduction

Do you fall into any one of the following three categories?

- You want to know why everyone's talking about meditation, and what the heck it actually is.

- You're ready to start meditating, so you need to choose a type of meditation and find out how to get started.

- You already practice a form of meditation and wonder what all those *other* kinds of meditation are about.

No matter which one applies, this book is for you. I'm in the last category myself, and I found the research for this book quite fascinating because I got to learn what other Buddhists, yogis, Christians, Jews, Sufis, and others were doing when they meditate!

Meditation is a passion of mine, and I'm thrilled to be able to offer you an accessible and thorough introduction to a practice that can change your life. I like to think of meditation as a fundamental, natural human activity. I'm fond of comparing it to exercise; meditation benefits your mind—mentally and emotionally—while exercise benefits your body. (Of course, mind and body are not actually separate, so exercise can benefit the mind, and meditation can have physical benefits. But still ….)

My main point is this: meditation is not a special, extra activity you do in order to experience something unusual. Instead, it's an amazingly simple but profound thing any human being is capable of, and it's a huge support to your everyday mental health and well-being.

This book is unique in that it contains entire chapters devoted to nine very different kinds of traditional meditation, each containing a practice you can try. It also offers over 25 additional meditation exercises, including ones incorporating movement, activity, and emotional work, and some meditations that will appeal to children. I feel confident that you'll find a meditation practice described in these pages that sounds interesting, accessible, and appropriate to you. If you don't already meditate, I sincerely hope this book will inspire you to start.

What You Will Learn in This Book

This book is divided into six parts that take you on a journey through the amazing human experience of meditation:

Part 1, The Basics of Meditation, defines what meditation is and what it does *to* you and *for* you. You learn about how meditation developed over the course of human history, the many different forms it can take, and the scientific research on the benefits of doing it. This part also gives you basic instructions for how to start any kind of meditation practice. It covers meditation postures, how to meditate comfortably, and how to best start a meditation practice of your own.

Part 2, Meditation for Enlightenment, contains four chapters, each devoted to a traditional form of meditation focused on your spiritual development: Kriya Yoga, Vipassana, Zen, and Vajrayana. Each chapter covers the larger spiritual tradition in which the form of meditation developed, the importance of meditation within the tradition, and the basic theory behind the method. In each chapter, you also find meditation instructions for beginners, including a practice you can do and tips for improving your meditation. Finally, I offer a vision of the ultimate goal of meditation and spiritual practice in each of these traditions.

Part 3, Devotional Meditation, also contains four chapters, each focusing on a spiritual tradition in which devotion to God or the Divine is central: Judaism, Christianity, Sufism, and Native American religion. You learn how meditative practices have been part of these traditions since their beginnings and the role such practices play in the larger context of the spiritual practice. In each chapter, you find instructions for a basic practice you can do and advice for how to deepen your meditative practice over time. Again, I wrap up each chapter with a section on the ultimate goals of each form of meditation and spiritual practice.

Part 4, Secular Meditation, introduces a number of forms of meditation that are completely secular. You find a whole chapter devoted to meditation in the context of modern-day mindfulness practice, including an explanation of the practice, the role meditation plays in it, a practice you can do, and instructions for further developing your meditation. You also find a chapter devoted to a number of other basic, accessible secular meditation practices developed over the last 50 years for relieving stress and improving mental and physical health. For each meditation technique discussed, I offer a practice you can try.

Part 5, More Ways to Meditate, covers over 25 additional forms of meditation to which I couldn't devote entire chapters. You learn about other traditional forms of meditation, including silent Quaker worship, Bahá'í meditation, Taoist meditation, and Transcendental Meditation. In this part, you also learn how to make walking, running, working out, bowing, and simple work into meditation. I then explain how to make any activity meditative and introduce five traditional meditative activities: chanting, hand copying texts, using beads in meditation, performing a ritual, and expressing yourself artistically. You also find a chapter in this section with meditations you can do to address specific life challenges and a chapter on meditation you can do with children.

Part 6, Taking It Deeper, gives you guidance for how to keep up a meditation practice over time, advice for how to deepen and develop your meditation, and tips for dealing with common challenges in meditative practice. I wrap things up with a description of the four different reasons you might want to adopt a meditation practice and how each is valuable: 1) meditating to improve your everyday life; 2) seeking to live more authentically and deeply; 3) gaining greater insight into the nature of reality or God; 4) reuniting with the Ultimate.

At the end of the book, there's a glossary that defines any specialized terms used in the book. There's also an appendix with resources, including books and articles cited, recommended reading, and useful websites.

Extras

Throughout the text, you'll see four different kinds of sidebars. These are meant to clarify the subject matter being discussed, give you additional tips and warnings, or offer further information that might be of interest to you.

DEFINITION

In these sidebars, I offer definitions of any terms used in the text that you may not know or that may have a specialized meaning in the context of the discussion.

POINT OF CLARIFICATION

In these sidebars, I offer additional explanations related to the text that you may find useful.

WATCH OUT

In these sidebars, I discuss potential misunderstandings or traps you'll want to watch out for.

CONTEMPLATE THIS

In these sidebars, I share concepts, ideas, and information that will enrich your reading and give you additional things to think about.

But Wait! There's More!

Have you logged on to idiotsguides.com lately? If you haven't, go there now! As a bonus to the book, we've included audio versions of some of our meditations you'll want to check out, all online. Point your browser to idiotsguides.com/meditation, and enjoy!

Acknowledgments

Deep gratitude to the many people who generously took the time to share their meditation traditions with me, including Nayaswami Daiva Glazzard (Kriya Yoga), and Renee and Rolf Erickson (Transcendental Meditation). Special thanks to Abby Gail Layton, who went above and beyond by not only helping me understand Jewish meditation, but by creating the meditation exercise featured in that chapter. It was a delight learning from people who deeply treasure their traditions and with whom I could relate on many levels. Many of these people read the chapters they inspired, and I greatly value their feedback and ultimate approval.

Thanks also to my Zen community, Bright Way Zen, for their support of my writing, their patience as I neglected Zen center work in order to write, and for continuing to walk their spiritual path with me. They are my inspiration and my teachers. Special thanks to Lorna Simons, who copy edited chapters; Bella Jhunjhunwala, who delivered delicious dinners to me and my husband when I got really busy; and Ellen Shoketsu Carlin, for dog sitting.

Acknowledgment must always go to my Zen teachers, Gyokuko and Kyogen Carlson, who first shared the Dharma with me almost 20 years ago and who taught me everything I know about the Essential Matter. Kyogen passed away in September 2014 at much too young an age, and I dedicate this book to him. I hope he would be proud; he always had a deep appreciation for interfaith dialogue, so I like to think he'd be fascinated by the chapters on different traditions.

Personal gratitude goes, as always, to my parents, Greg and Diane Sater, who planned and sacrificed in order to provide me with an excellent education and who have always been thrilled with my writing. Gratitude also to my husband, John; just about everything he does is to support me and my Dharma work, and he's simply my best friend. Thanks also to my parrots, Isaac and Ursula, for their stimulating and entertaining companionship, and to my dogs, Curly and Sukha, for all the cuddles and for being my greatest fans, even though they can't read.

Trademarks

All terms mentioned in this book that are known to be or are suspected of being trademarks or service marks have been appropriately capitalized. Alpha Books and Penguin Random House LLC cannot attest to the accuracy of this information. Use of a term in this book should not be regarded as affecting the validity of any trademark or service mark.

The Basics of Meditation

In the first part of this book, I get you up to speed on meditation in general, and I tell you all you need to know in order to try it for yourself. First, I describe meditation's fascinating history, from prehistoric times—when humans sat around their campfires and were lulled into meditative states—up through the twentieth-century development of secular techniques for use in medical and psychotherapeutic settings. All major religious and spiritual traditions have included meditative practices in one form or another, and I provide an overview of these, as well as offer a simple definition of meditation based on what all these forms have in common. I also cover the scientific research on meditation and discuss the benefits of meditating.

Second, I provide instruction for basic meditation postures. While some forms of meditation don't require a particular posture, many do, so you may want to refer back to the information on posture in this part depending on what form of meditation you choose to try. The posture information may also be useful to you if you struggle with some physical discomfort while meditating.

Finally, I offer tips for how best to prepare yourself for meditation and how to get started with a meditation practice. With the right attitude and a supportive lifestyle, you improve your chances of finding meditation rewarding and effective. I discuss how to choose a type of meditation that's right for you, cover the best time and place for meditating, let you know when you might need to consult a meditation teacher, and offer encouragement for actually getting started.

What Is Meditation?

In the last 50 years or so, meditation has gradually made it into mainstream Western culture. It has become widely recognized as an accessible and beneficial practice for just about anyone, appearing in one form or another on national magazine covers, in the lives of celebrities, in widely accepted psychological treatment programs, and in regimens used to reduce stress in settings ranging from corporations to the military. The techniques used for meditation vary widely, as do the goals of the practice and reported results.

What *is* meditation, anyway? There are obviously big differences between the meditation practices of a devout monk in a Tibetan monastery, a student of Transcendental Meditation, and people spending a few minutes in corpse pose in a yoga class. In this chapter, I briefly describe the history and development of meditation as it has appeared in various cultures and traditions throughout the millennia. I also discuss what meditation is—that is, the defining characteristics shared by all meditative practices—and talk about the benefits of doing it yourself.

In This Chapter

- When and how meditation developed over the centuries
- Meditative practices appearing in spiritual traditions
- What all meditative practices have in common
- The two ways meditation affects your mind
- The benefits you might experience from meditating

A Brief History of Meditation

It has been suggested—in publications such as Matt Rossano's article in the *Cambridge Archaeological Journal* called "Did Meditating Make Us Human?"—that one of the critical points in the evolution of humans occurred when *Homo sapiens* developed the ability to deliberately focus their attention. If you think about it, it's remarkable to be able to *choose* what you want to pay attention to and for how long. Imagine having your attention drawn here and there based only on what seems most potentially rewarding or threatening at the moment or on instinctual drives. (Of course, it may feel like this is the way your mind works much of the time, but if you can read this book, you're able to deliberately focus!) Still, whenever (and however) humans first experienced *meditative* states, it seems likely they've been exploring alternative ways to use their minds since they developed the ability for conscious thought.

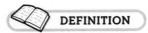 **DEFINITION**

Meditation is a practice of deliberately directing your mind in a particular way for a period of time for the purpose of affecting the mind itself—either your mental or emotional experience, or the way you relate to or use your mind.

The Evolution of Meditative Practices

Most indigenous cultures across the world developed traditions of deliberately inducing altered states of consciousness at certain times. This was done a number of different ways, including the use of rhythmic and repetitive dance or song, fasting, breathing techniques, psychoactive drugs, and the performance of feats or quests that couldn't be successfully completed without tapping into alternative ways of operating. It was common for cultures to have a significant rite of passage into adulthood that involved some of these methods, highlighting how important they believed it was to be at least somewhat familiar with different states of consciousness. In many societies, a religious figure would become adept at entering states of trance or ecstasy in order to gain healing powers or insight on behalf of her people.

The oldest references to meditation in the historical record are probably those in the *Rig Veda*, an ancient text dating from around 1500 B.C.E. (transmitted orally for about 1,000 years before being written down). It originated in India and mentions meditative practices such as priests "harnessing their minds," although it doesn't describe in detail any meditation methods. Similarly ancient references to states, abilities, and insights that probably resulted from meditative practices can be found in the Jewish Torah, which dates as far back as 1300 B.C.E. In the Torah, the teachings of the prophets, particularly Moses, feature centrally. In his book, *Jewish Meditation: A Practical Guide*, Jewish scholar Rabbi Aryeh Kaplan writes, "From the literature, it seems evident that a prophet would almost always experience his first prophetic experience while in a meditative state."

Meditation as a Specific Discipline

The first explicit and detailed references to meditation as a discipline—complete with methods, a philosophical basis, and prescribed goals—appeared around 500 B.C.E. The meditative approaches of practitioners in the ancient Vedic tradition of India (which later evolved into Hinduism) were recorded in parts of the newer Vedic scriptures, the *Upanishads.* Around the same time, meditation featured centrally in the new Indian religions of Jainism and Buddhism, as well as in particular schools of Judaism in the Middle East. About 300 B.C.E., records of Taoist meditation began to appear in China, and about 500 years later the Indian sage Patanjali composed a short text known as the *Yoga Sutras,* a classic exposition of meditation techniques and philosophy.

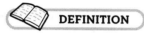 **DEFINITION**

> The **Rig Veda** (*Veda* means "knowledge") is an ancient Indian religious text, dating from as far back as 1500 B.C.E., that formed the basis of the Vedic tradition of religious practice in India. The **Upanishads** are the most recent part of the Vedic literature and consist of a number of texts composed somewhere between 800 B.C.E. and the beginning of the Common Era.

All of these meditation disciplines—Vedic, Jain, Buddhist, Taoist, and Yoga—are still practiced today. Their methods are technical, specific, and experiential. In a very general sense, these forms of meditation are all intended—one way or another—to mature, enhance, and extend the insight and abilities of their practitioners. The basic idea is that meditation and spiritual practice are necessary for you to fully develop your potential as a human being (merely making it into adulthood isn't enough). They also all tend to emphasize a means of directly accessing truth (or closeness to the Divine) through a mode of awareness below or beyond thought (more on that later, under the section "Cultivating Insight").

Meditative Practices as Part of Spirituality and Religion

Almost all spiritual and religious traditions have included some kind of meditative practice from early on in their development. These practices include contemplative prayer, ritual silence, and meditative chanting. Sometimes these meditative forms were known and practiced by only a small subset of the tradition's practitioners—mystics or monastics—but their mastery was often considered to represent an ideal of deep spiritual attainment. In other cases, the meditative forms were also done by ordinary adherents to a tradition.

For example, meditation has been used and valued in various mystical movements in Judaism over the centuries, and there has always been a Jewish ideal of praying and performing other religious observances with a special sense of concentration and devotion. In Christianity, there has been the silent and repeated use of the Jesus Prayer in a meditative way, divine reading of scripture, and the silent worship of Quakers. Another Christian tradition of contemplative prayer was inspired by a classic fourteenth-century mystical text, *The Cloud of Unknowing*. In Islam, the meditative practice of "remembrance of God"—involving repeated recitations of short prayers, phrases, or the names of God—has been a central practice for many Muslims since Islam arose in the seventh century.

Twentieth-Century Developments

As the flow of information and travel increased in the twentieth century, more westerners encountered the formal and explicit meditation practices of Eastern religions. Teachers of these forms of meditation also became interested in attracting Western students; they either invited westerners to come study with them in Asia or traveled to the Americas and Europe to share their tradition.

CONTEMPLATE THIS

The spread and cross-pollination of meditation practices in the twentieth century mean you have an incredibly wide range of traditions, styles, and methods to choose from if you want to begin meditating. In fact, the challenging part might be picking which kind of meditation to try. This book should help you with that by going into detail about a number of the forms most widely practiced and giving you exercises to try. I also discuss how to decide on a kind of meditation to explore in Chapter 3.

This cultural exchange of meditative practices led to three significant results:

- Many westerners began practicing Eastern religions, some of them even converting or eventually becoming meditation teachers themselves.

- Jews, Christians, and Muslims were inspired to make more accessible and explicit the meditative practices in their own traditions.

- Meditation became increasingly viewed as a legitimate means of reducing stress and maintaining mental and physical health.

In order to make meditation attractive for a wider audience and more appropriate for practice in clinical settings, secular and relatively simple meditation methods were developed and popularized. These include Transcendental Meditation, the relaxation response, and mindfulness-based stress reduction.

Meditation Defined

What do all these kinds of meditation have in common? Think of it like this: meditation is a category of human activity, like exercise. There's clearly something going on in meditation that's common to all forms of it, just as there's something going on in all forms of exercise (namely, energetically moving your body in a way that improves your physical fitness and health). There are countless types of exercise that vary widely in how strenuous they are, whether you do them alone or in a group, and what aspect of your physical health they most affect. Similarly, there are countless forms of meditation—some are elaborate practices that require special training, while others are very simple and accessible; some are usually done in the context of a rich religious tradition, while others are practical and secular.

What's common to all forms of meditation is this: *meditation involves a conscious direction of your mind for a period of time in order to affect the mind itself.* You might say meditation is a little like exercise for the mind, except it can be restful and restorative, as well as improve your mental fitness. Let's break down each of the pieces of this definition of meditation.

Conscious Direction of Your Mind

For the most part, meditation requires a conscious effort. On occasion, you may find yourself in a somewhat meditative state spontaneously—when feeling especially calm, aware, or appreciative, for example—but usually such an experience will involve a natural increase in your level of consciousness about your state of mind (when, for example, a beautiful sunset inspires you to breathe deeply and appreciate the moment). Unless you make an effort to continue that consciousness (that is, make an effort to keep your mind on the experience), however, the moment will fade. Naturally occurring meditative moments are usually brief and dependent on your surroundings.

CONTEMPLATE THIS

Some researchers have suggested early humans were first drawn into meditative states while sitting around their campfires at night. The fires kept them safe, so they could let go of their constant vigilance against danger, and staring into the flames for hours induced a meditative state.

Incredibly though, it seems the simple act of consciously directing your mind toward an object of meditation induces a beneficial physical and mental state unlike any other. Herbert Benson, MD, has done many physiological studies of people while they were doing simple forms of meditation. In his classic book *The Relaxation Response,* Benson describes how, after only a few minutes of meditation, your body enters a unique, wakeful, restful state. Your breathing slows down because your body starts using oxygen at much lower rate than it does even in deep sleep. This meditative state also differs from sleep in terms of your brain waves and how quickly the decrease in oxygen consumption occurs (it takes many hours of sleep to produce the same decrease). The "relaxation response" caused by meditating isn't seen in people who are relaxing in typical ways like listening to music, daydreaming, or reading a novel.

For a Period of Time

No matter where you direct your mind in meditation, it becomes meditation when you continue to do it for a period of time. This period may be anywhere from a few minutes to many hours. In any case, it's much longer than you would naturally be inclined to concentrate on something, unless it was an engaging task or something entertaining. You may find yourself paying momentary attention to something you could, theoretically, meditate on, such as your breathing or the sound of a waterfall. For a moment, you may feel more calm or contented, but then your mind will wander off to something else.

If you consciously try to keep your mind on something fairly simple for more than a few moments—even if it's very beautiful, inspiring, or pleasant—you'll find it's quite difficult. Fortunately, meditation can still have a very beneficial effect on you even if you can't seem to concentrate for long. It seems it's the *effort* to direct your attention that's most important. Over the course of your meditation, as you realize your mind is wandering and you recall the object of your meditation, you're continually drawn back into the state of restful wakefulness.

In Order to Affect the Mind Itself

Meditation is done for a variety of reasons, including the maintenance of mental health, the development of useful skills, the insight gained in alternative states of consciousness, the cultivation of devotion to God, and sometimes for the pleasure of the experience itself. In general, the goal of meditation is some kind of positive effect on your mind—either on your mental and emotional experience or on how you use your mind. Changing how you use your mind includes gradually influencing how you *tend* to use your mind (changing habits), as well as developing new skills and abilities.

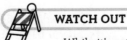

WATCH OUT

While it's natural to have things you want to get out of meditation, beware of trying to make it productive in some subtle (or not-so-subtle) way. The effort to get particular results usually only gets in the way of your meditation. Fortunately, it seems to work if you let yourself be motivated and inspired by what you hope for *before* you meditate. But *while* you're meditating, forget about attaining results and just focus on your meditative method.

What makes meditation effective is how or where you choose to direct your mind while you're doing it. Meditative objects or techniques are never productive or useful in and of themselves. Something beneficial may arise from the whole process, but you aren't achieving anything tangible by directing your mind toward your breathing, God, the space within which thoughts arise, a word you silently repeat, a slow stretch in a yoga pose, or a visualization. You aren't getting any work done, you aren't figuring anything out (at least in your usual way), and you won't have anything to show for your meditation afterward—except, perhaps, subtle differences in your behavior or health because of how meditation has affected your mind.

Meditation's Two Main Functions

Meditation has two basic functions: calming the mind and cultivating insight. Most people are familiar with the idea that meditation helps you calm down, but you may not be as familiar with the use of meditation in a contemplative way. Basically, the idea behind contemplation is that once your mind is calm, you can enter a different state of consciousness. This isn't necessarily a dramatic experience, but it allows you to see things more clearly and perhaps even gain significant insights. Most forms of meditation include both calming and contemplative functions, although some are primarily meant to calm the mind.

Calming the Mind

The normal activities you do to take care of your life are inevitably stressful to some extent. They require you to turn your attention outward and scan the environment constantly. Even if you're just pondering things in your mind, it's usually in order to be better prepared for the future. Let's call this your "normal mode" of operating. It isn't bad—in fact, it's necessary and useful—but if that's the only way you know how to operate, it can get very exhausting and stressful and have negative effects on your health and well-being. If you're always in your normal mode of operation, your life can end up feeling out of balance, or like you're constantly caught in the "rat race."

In order to step outside your normal mode of operating, you have to let go of your efforts to be productive, figure stuff out, and plan for the future. When you do this, you begin to relax. You're probably used to relaxing by putting your work aside and engaging in leisure activities you enjoy, but even this level of activity prevents you from settling into the restful state induced by meditation. Dr. Herbert Benson suggests the act of meditation allows you to turn off your anxious fight-or-flight mode of being in a very direct and effective way. The ability to induce this relaxation response in yourself at will, he says, may very well be a beneficial adaptation in human beings to mitigate the negative effects of constant stress!

POINT OF CLARIFICATION

It's important to realize a calmer mind does not necessarily mean a mind without thoughts. You may experience fewer thoughts—or even a complete cessation of thoughts—in meditation, and that's usually a pleasant experience. However, you may find your mind continues to generate thoughts, but as your mind calms down, you're able to relate to them differently. Thoughts end up seeming like less of a big deal—less real. Their emotional impact decreases, and you tend to feel less of an imperative to act on or react to them. Thoughts come and go, but without disturbing your underlying sense of calm.

By their very nature, meditative objects require you to let go of your planning, thinking, and worrying. As you keep bringing your mind back to a very simple object or technique, you send the message to your body and mind that you aren't in danger. (Or else you'd be running around dealing with it, right?) This calms the mind at an unconscious level, and eventually at a conscious level. With enough meditation experience, you can experience a profound level of inner silence and stillness.

Cultivating Insight

Meditation helps you access alternative ways of perceiving and knowing. These are only alternative ways in the sense that they're not the ways you usually use. In general, you use your physical senses (sight, hearing, smell, taste, and touch) to perceive what's happening and your intellect—or left-brain function—to analyze the information you receive. At times, you may make decisions based more on your emotional preferences than your rational analyses, but you usually understand those preferences are individual and don't reflect some greater truth about the world. For most people, the closest they come to alternative ways of perceiving and knowing is when they recognize something arising out of their intuition or when they go into a different mode for the purposes of artistic expression or the performance of a well-practiced skill.

In contemplative meditation, you deliberately enter a state where the intellect and all of its manifestations—words, abstractions, linear analyses, and so on—become much less important. You've probably spent countless hours engaging those aspects of your mind with any given question or problem and have reached the limits of their power for now. Looking for something else, something deeper, you settle into a subverbal awareness. This makes you receptive to more subtle sources of experience and insight—both outside yourself and within.

It's possible to perceive something and know it to be true without using your physical senses or your intellect. For example, you may gain insight in your meditation about things in your everyday life. With sudden clarity, you "see" what's been going on or the best way to respond to something. Often, the subject about which you're gaining insight is one you've thought about a great deal. You may have analyzed it, talked about it with others, tried to guess what caused the problem, and even experimented with solutions, to no avail. Then, in the quiet space of meditation, without trying to figure it out, you perceive the truth, as clear as day.

Insight in meditation can be about anything, from the mundane to the profound, from the individual to the universal. It can arise spontaneously—even if you're just meditating to calm your mind—or it can be consciously cultivated and sought. Insight may be something you can qualify as understanding, but it may also be entirely experiential, defying verbal description. In some forms of meditation, you're primarily looking for a greater understanding of the way your mind works in order to gain perspective on your thoughts and emotions. In other types of meditation, the ultimate insight you're seeking is about the deeper nature of reality because such insight has been found to be healing and liberating. In still other kinds of meditation, you're seeking a direct, experiential insight into the nature of God and your relationship to Him.

CONTEMPLATE THIS

In his book *Riding the Ox Home: A History of Meditation from Shamanism to Science*, Willard Johnson describes how early forms of meditation were disciplines you undertook in order to be able to achieve a particular end. As opposed to other kinds of efforts to perfect an art or a skill, however, "meditation does something completely different in that it reverses [your] outward, sensory orientation, directing the meditator to calm the body, to regulate the breath and, by temporarily closing the eyes and shutting off other senses, to turn attention inward, exploring another dimension of consciousness."

The Scientific Research on Meditation

It can get confusing pretty fast if you delve deeply into the research on the benefits of meditation! The mainstream media frequently lists all the ways meditation can help you physically, mentally, and emotionally, and thousands of peer-reviewed scientific studies back up these claims. At the same time, many of the studies on meditation have serious limitations, and plenty of studies also suggest meditation doesn't particularly help, at least no more than other kinds of treatments or activities. On rare occasions, research has even suggested meditation can have negative effects for some people (see Chapter 3). Despite the limitations of research on meditation, however, there's a great deal of evidence suggesting different kinds of meditation can have positive effects on your mental and physical health and sense of well-being.

The Challenges Faced by Researchers

Scientific studies on the benefits of meditation vary widely in quality and rigor. Because of limited funding, sample sizes (the number of people studied) are often small, and most of the studies are relatively brief (typically one day to a few months long). The comparisons between meditators and nonmeditators or of people before, during, and after meditation, are often based on self-reports about various symptoms and experiences. Self-reports are generally the simplest and least expensive way to document changes, but they're limited in value. Something such as a meditation exercise may actually cause a certain change in you, or it may simply make you more aware of something or more likely to mention it on your questionnaire! Another problem with self-reporting is bias; if you're hopeful that meditation has helped you or if you're a devoted long-term meditator, you're more likely to perceive and report positive effects associated with meditating.

Many research studies on the benefits of meditation are based on physical measurements, but even this has limitations. For example, you may have heard about the remarkable studies using functional magnetic resonance imaging (fMRI) that have proven both temporary and lasting changes in the brain associated with meditation. While this is exciting stuff, what those changes actually mean to you and your life (how helpful they really are) is still poorly understood. Also, even when the measurement of changes are objective (such as changes in blood pressure or performance on tests), critics point out that researchers don't actually know precisely *what* meditating subjects are doing in their minds or how well they're doing it.

Perhaps one of the biggest limitations on meditation research is the fact that studying how long-term meditators compare with nonmeditators is not ideal. You'd expect to see the greatest benefits in people who have lots of experience with meditation and do it regularly, and plenty of studies suggest this is the case. But long-term meditators are a self-selected group, which means they might be different from nonmeditators for other reasons. Maybe they just tend to be more mentally stable, happy, or health-conscious people to begin with!

 POINT OF CLARIFICATION

> If you want to decide for yourself how valid the claims about meditation's benefits are, you can access primary sources (the professional articles published about the details and results of each study) at the website for the National Center for Biotechnology Information (ncbi.nlm.nih.gov). Search there for articles using the terms *meditation* or *meditation benefits*.

Current Scientific Conclusions

The most rigorous studies of the benefits of meditation randomly assign a group to a short meditative exercise or to some kind of meditation course lasting anywhere from a few hours to a couple months. The meditators are then compared to a control group who hasn't meditated. The meditation courses most often used in research have been Transcendental Meditation or mindfulness-based stress reduction, primarily because such courses are standardized. Many—but not all—of these randomized studies demonstrate small but statistically significant improvements in the subjects who have meditated. If you think about it, this is pretty remarkable considering they have only done a brief meditation exercise or have only been meditating for a few weeks or months.

The benefits of meditation are becoming more and more widely accepted in the scientific establishment simply because of the sheer number of studies that indicate at least modest benefits from the practice (and rarely, if any, negative effects). For the most part, medical and mental health professionals feel very comfortable suggesting meditation as a complementary treatment. That is, for most medical and psychological conditions, standard interventions such as surgery, medication, and psychotherapy are still recommended, but meditation may complement these methods by increasing their effectiveness and aiding the healing process.

The Benefits of Meditation

As I describe the benefits of meditation in this part of the chapter, I'll be relying not only on the relevant conclusions of the scientific establishment, but also on the subjective reports of meditators throughout the world. If a particular benefit is supported by the research, I'll mention it—but, as described previously, there are still many limitations in terms of the research. For one thing, there have been studies based on measurable benefits to your mental and physical health, but some benefits of meditation are subjective and experiential and may never be able to be measured.

As you read through these benefits, keep in mind you may not experience all of them. Also, the way a particular benefit may manifest depends on things like your personality, life experience, how often you meditate, and the kind of meditation you do. (In each chapter of this book that focuses on a specific form of meditation, I'll also describe a few benefits associated with that particular practice.) While the best thing is to simply try meditation and see for yourself what kinds of effects it has, you can take some encouragement from the fact that meditation has been practiced widely for thousands of years, and countless people swear they have benefited from it.

Mental Health

Many studies have suggested meditation can alleviate some of the symptoms and severity of both clinical and nonclinical mental health issues. Conditions and behaviors that may be positively impacted by meditation include anxiety, depression, post-traumatic stress disorder (PTSD), schizophrenia, eating disorders, and substance abuse. While many documented improvements are based on self-reports, there's also evidence that meditation decreases activity in areas of the brain associated with anxious and negative thinking, as well as decreasing levels of hormones in the body associated with worry and rumination (getting stuck in repeated loops of thought). Other potential benefits suggested by the research include improvements in the ability to regulate and deal with emotions, tolerate discomfort, concentrate, find satisfaction in relationships, and manage the symptoms of chronic illness.

WATCH OUT

Meditation doesn't make you into a perfect person—always calm, collected, patient, kind, and capable. Even if you meditate a lot, you'll still experience negative emotions, thoughts, and reactions. The important thing is how meditation helps you relate to these experiences in a more stable, objective, and positive way.

Subjectively, most meditators report positive changes in the way their mind works—and not just while they are meditating, but in their daily lives. For instance, during or after meditation you may notice things generally don't upset you as much. You seem to have more freedom of choice in how you respond to situations and people, as if meditation allows your behavior to become more conscious instead of reactive. Even when you're experiencing negative states like anger or anxiety, you're more aware these states won't last forever and don't define who you are. Instead of being drawn relentlessly into trains of thought around worries and resentments, you're better able to focus your attention on the present—and therefore be more effective in dealing with your life.

Physical Health

Most positive physical effects of meditation are probably related to its ability to induce a state of relative relaxation and relieve stress. I described this state earlier in this chapter (see the section "Calming the Mind" earlier in this chapter), and how it's essentially the physiological opposite of the stress response (which involves increased metabolism, respiration, and levels of stress hormones in the body, among other things).

Research shows that stress causes or worsens all kinds of physical problems and ailments, including high blood pressure, heart disease, irritable bowel syndrome, premenstrual syndrome, chronic pain, psoriasis, and insomnia. It's probably not surprising, then, that meditation is associated with decreases in symptoms or severity for all of these sorts of problems. It also seems to enhance immune function and to increase rates of healing.

Subjective reports of increased physical health don't tend to feature centrally in most meditative traditions. Exceptions to this include forms of meditation that involve very specific methods of working with your breath or body, such as Kriya Yoga. Part of the strength of such meditation traditions is their attention to both body and mind in a holistic program of health. However, most types of meditation are understood to affect physical health indirectly—by dealing with the mind—and it's understood that you'll do other things to focus more directly on your physical health and fitness.

Spiritual Health

Meditation is intended to—and generally does—improve your mental health. It also improves your spiritual health, if you consider that an important aspect of yourself. By *spiritual health*, I am referring to improving your understanding of, and relationship to, what Huston Smith calls the "more" in his book *Why Religion Matters: The Fate of the Human Spirit in an Age of Disbelief*:

> "[T]he finitude of mundane existence cannot satisfy the human heart completely. Built into the human makeup is a longing for a 'more' that the world of everyday experience cannot requite. This outreach strongly suggests the existence of the something that life reaches *for* in the way that the wings of birds point to the reality of air ..."

For you, the "more" may be God, the Divine, the compassionate nature of the universe, or a just a sense of gratitude and awe for life. Whatever it is, it's what helps make your life seem meaningful in some way or helps you put your problems and projects in proper perspective. It's easy to get caught up in the activities of life and lose touch with what is most important to you. When this happens, life can become very challenging. You may end up feeling depressed, unsatisfied with your life, or simply lost or numb. Alternatively, you may never have felt inspired by a sense that there is more than your everyday, mundane experience.

POINT OF CLARIFICATION

There are plenty of forms of meditation you can practice if you have no interest in things that are spiritual. Although the teachings in Yoga and Buddhism have what you might call spiritual aspects, the meditation in those traditions can be practiced without any special beliefs. There are also purely secular forms of meditation including mindfulness meditation and the relaxation response.

Throughout the millennia, most humans have practiced meditation primarily—or at least, ultimately—for their spiritual health. (Of course, this spiritual aspect of your being is intimately related to your mental and physical health, so these three benefits of meditation are actually never entirely separate.) As I described earlier in this chapter, one of the functions of meditation is to help you cultivate insight by opening you up to alternative ways of perceiving and knowing. In the space of meditation, you end up more receptive to what theistic traditions call "the still, small voice of God." Generally speaking, the "more" tends to be pervasive but subtle and gets drowned out by the hubbub of daily life. Meditation can help you reconnect with the "more"—or allow you to experience it for the first time.

The Least You Need to Know

- Meditation is a practice of directing your mind in a deliberate way for a period of time. Unlike most other activities you pay attention to, meditation is done for the sake of your mind itself—to improve your mental and emotional experience or to help you use your mind more effectively.

- It's likely that human beings have been experimenting with and using meditative states since they first developed the capability to consciously direct their attention.

- The first records of meditation being practiced as a discipline—complete with explicit methods—appear around 500 B.C.E., in several different religions.

- Meditative practices appear in all the world's major religions, and in the twentieth century, a number of secular methods were developed.

- Meditation works by calming your mind and opening you up to alternative ways of perceiving and knowing.

- Scientific research and the subjective reports of meditators suggest meditation can benefit your mental, physical, and spiritual health.

Basic Meditation Postures

When you hear the word *meditation,* do you think about slim, flexible people sitting on the ground with their legs neatly folded into pretzel shapes? Don't let that image stop you from meditating! Very few forms of meditation require you to sit on the floor. Most simply recommend a comfortable position in a chair, and even when a type of meditation has traditionally been done seated on the floor, you're encouraged to sit on a meditation bench or a chair if that works better for you.

Generally speaking, your posture in meditation is important because you want to be able to remain fairly stable and still while you concentrate on your meditation technique. If you're in pain or constantly fidgeting, you'll probably find it difficult to focus, whereas any stillness you're able to cultivate physically tends to help your mind settle down as well. In this chapter, I explain how to position your body for comfortable and alert seated meditation whether you're going to sit on the floor, a bench, or a chair.

In This Chapter

- The most essential aspects of good meditation posture
- The best ways to sit on the floor for meditation
- Meditating in a chair
- How to deal with physical discomfort while meditating
- Standing, walking, and lying down for meditation

The Essentials of Good Meditation Posture

Before I go into detail about different postures, I'm going to describe what all good meditation postures have in common. Using these guidelines, you can find an effective position regardless of your physical flexibility or whether you're going to sit on the floor, a bench, or a chair. You're likely to find these posture essentials are just common sense—if you think about it, it's a good idea to practice them whenever you're trying to bring your attention and best effort to something.

Staying Comfortable but Alert

The most important thing in a meditation posture is for you to remain comfortable but alert. Ideally, your body shouldn't be the center of your attention in a negative way. For example, if you're squeezing yourself into full *lotus position* and spending your time struggling with excruciating pain, you're missing the point of meditation! On the other hand, you shouldn't be too comfortable, or you're likely to get sleepy or dull. For example, leaning back in an overstuffed chair isn't very likely to be conducive to meditation or to concentrating on anything other than a good book.

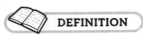 **DEFINITION**

> The **lotus position** is a meditation posture in which you sit cross-legged on the floor or a small cushion and rest the outsides of your feet on your thighs. Few westerners are flexible enough to find this position possible or comfortable. Some people are able to do the half-lotus position, where you rest only one of your feet on the opposite thigh.

Generally speaking, you'll be able to stay more alert in a posture that requires some energy for you to maintain it. This is why traditional postures don't involve leaning against anything, such as the back of a chair. If you need to lean on something in order to support your back, go ahead and do so, but make an effort to sit up straight and see if you can avoid resting your entire weight against the chair.

The Proper Spinal Position

You'll find an upright, aligned spine is essential for effective seated meditation for several reasons. In the long run, it will be the most comfortable way to hold your body. Slouching, bending your spine, or leaning to the side will eventually cause discomfort or restlessness. Such a position may feel more comfortable momentarily, but watch and see how long you actually want to stay that way! Sometimes the designation "comfortable" is only relative; for the purposes of meditation, you're comfortable if you're able to remain more or less still without actual pain.

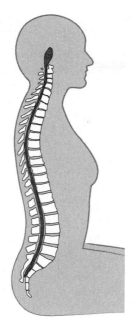

The ideal position of your spine during meditation.

A good spinal position in meditation also allows the smooth flow of oxygen, blood, and energy throughout the body. This will, in turn, let your body function at its best. In addition, an upright, balanced posture affects your mind, as well as your body. There's a reason your parents and teachers told you to sit up straight as a child (besides making sure you grew up straight and tall)! An upright posture tends to encourage you to be aware of and deal with the present (as opposed to leaning back, away from what's going on, or forward, toward what's going to happen in the future). It fosters a sense of centeredness, strength, and balance—all qualities that will support calmness and clarity in your meditation.

The spine should also be slightly "elongated" in your meditation posture. This is a fairly subtle instruction about how to hold your spine; it's not about stiffening the spine in order sit up even taller (definitely a bad idea in meditation—your back will start to hurt pretty quickly). Instead of doing that, take a full, deep breath and feel your chest, back, neck, and spine naturally expand.

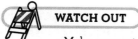 **WATCH OUT**

Make sure not to shrink, hunching inward, when breathing out. Try to maintain that gentle sense of energetic expansiveness throughout your meditation, renewing it with a deep breath whenever you need to.

Unrestricted Breathing

While unrestricted breathing during meditation is related to your spinal posture, it's worth mentioning separately. The ability to breathe deeply lets you take in more oxygen, which keeps you more alert and awake, but just as important, your breath is your main connection between your conscious mind and your unconscious processes. You keep on breathing even when you're completely unaware of it, at which point it's an automatic process that's not under your control. However, if you want to, you can consciously breathe—you can make your breathing deeper or shallower, or simply become aware of it.

Because of this unique relationship between your consciousness and your breath, in some forms of meditation learning to control your breathing is seen as critical to unifying body and mind or the unconscious and the conscious. In other types of meditation, you don't control your breath, but it still features centrally either as an object of meditation or as a touchstone of sorts—you return your awareness to your breathing when you mind has wandered. Let your breath flow freely by sitting up straight, opening up your chest, and slightly relaxing the muscles in your abdomen. Usually, if you become aware of your breathing even for a moment, you automatically take a deep breath and straighten up a little.

Sitting on the Floor

Sitting meditation on the floor—if you can do so comfortably and keep the essentials of a good meditation posture—tends to be a very stable and grounded position. This is why it has been favored by Eastern meditation traditions for thousands of years. Many people report a greater ability to settle their mind and energy if they are in contact with the ground. Again, it's better for you to have good posture in a chair than for you to sit on the floor with bad posture, but if you're physically up to it, you may want to try sitting on the floor.

The Value of a Meditation Cushion

Even on the floor, you're aiming for the nice, upright spine discussed in the previous section. This generally requires your hips to be tilted slightly forward and for your knees to end up lower than your hips. To understand for yourself why this is, try sitting cross-legged flat on the floor without using any kind of cushion or support. If you relax and let gravity take over, you'll find yourself falling over backward. This means that in order to sit up straight, your back muscles will be doing a lot of work. They'll eventually get tired and sore, and then you'll either slouch or feel uncomfortable.

Regular meditators sit on small, specially designed cushions—usually round—in order to elevate their hips and tilt them ever so slightly forward. The cushions are anywhere from 3 to 6 inches high, and the idea is for your knees to touch the floor in front of you when you're sitting on one. This allows you to easily maintain the proper spinal position. Ideally, if you rock slowly backward and forward, as well as side to side, you'll find a nice, upright posture somewhere in the middle that's almost effortless to hold.

Meditation cushions are usually very firm, and are stuffed with either a dense, cottonlike material or buckwheat hulls. Their round shape provides stable support without pressing against the backs of your upper thighs (which can restrict blood supply to your legs and make them fall asleep). You can buy a meditation cushion online for around $50 to $60. If you don't have or want to purchase a meditation cushion, you can try sitting on a firm pillow folded in half or on a pile of blankets; just make sure the support is high enough and stable.

Various Things to Do with Your Legs

Once you've positioned yourself on nice, stable cushion or stack of blankets on the floor, what do you do with your legs? Ideally, your knees end up on the floor so they're slightly lower than your hips and provide a basis of support for your posture. You may or may not have enough flexibility for this to happen. (It helps if you wear loose clothing.) If your knees are sticking up in the air, you can try putting additional cushions or blankets under them. This will help you relax into the posture, and eventually you may find your flexibility increasing.

 WATCH OUT

If your knees stick up too far when sitting on the floor, you won't be able to maintain the proper spinal posture while seated on the floor. To counteract this, you should try sitting on a bench or a chair.

While you have a number of ways you can position your legs when seated on the floor, you generally want to make sure one leg (or ankle, or foot) isn't stuck underneath your other leg. The top leg will end up pressing down on the bottom leg, and the bottom leg will probably end up falling asleep if you meditate for longer than 5 to 10 minutes. In the traditional lotus or half-lotus postures, the top leg is actually resting on your thigh, which can handle the weight so the lower parts of your body don't go to sleep. Many people lack the flexibility for the lotus postures, however, particularly in their ankles and hips. A great alternative is the Burmese posture in which you place one calf in front of the other. In the Burmese position, your knees are on the floor and no parts of your legs are tucked underneath you.

Sitting cross-legged in the Burmese position.

Using a Meditation Bench

The meditation bench is a wonderful invention for meditators who want to sit on the floor but aren't comfortable in cross-legged positions. Meditation benches are about 18 inches wide and vary in height but are typically about 5 to 8 inches high in the front and a couple inches higher in the back. You kneel with your legs together and place the meditation bench over your ankles, with the shorter edge of the bench closer to your knees. You then sit down and, voilà, perfect posture!

If you aren't handy enough to make your own bench, they are available online starting at around $40. If you don't have a bench, you can also sit in the same basic meditation posture by straddling a firm pillow (placing it on the floor between your calves and then sitting down on it).

Sitting on a meditation bench.

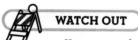 **WATCH OUT**

Keep in mind that everyone's body is different, especially as people get older. What works for someone else may not work for you. Take into account any physical limitations or injuries you may have, and be gentle with yourself. It *is* possible to hurt yourself by staying in a meditation posture that isn't right for you—even though you're just sitting there! Backs, ankles, and knees are especially delicate, so watch for discomfort, numbness, or pain that might indicate you're overextending them or keeping them in a particular position too long.

Sitting on a Chair

Chances are you're going to be fairly comfortable meditating in a chair, but it may require a little extra effort to focus on your meditation. This is simply because you're used to sitting in a chair, as opposed to sitting in some special position on the floor just for meditation. Fortunately, you have ways to tell yourself "I'm meditating now," even while sitting in a chair.

Meditating in a chair.

For one, you can always sit in the same chair for meditation, and choose one that makes you sit up nice and straight. You can put the chair in a particular place, cover it with a nice blanket, or hold your hands in a particular way. You may also find it helpful to meditate in a chair but sit only on the front edge and not lean against the back of it. You might even want to put an extra cushion on the chair so, once again, your knees end up slightly lower than your hips and your spine ends up in the ideal position.

If you need support for your back, choose a chair that lets you sit up as straight as possible. It can help to place a cushion between the middle of your back and the chair because almost all chairs invite you to lean back a little. Even a slight lean can make you less alert and energized during meditation.

 POINT OF CLARIFICATION

Even if you meditate in a chair, you're probably not used to sitting there as still as you can for prolonged periods. Assuming you want to be able to sit still for longer, the best approach is to experiment and push yourself a little bit at a time. If you're comfortable sitting for 10 minutes, try 12. Once you're used to 12 minutes, try 14.

What to Do with the Rest of Your Body

Some forms of meditation recommend particular positions for your eyes, mouth, and hands, while others don't specify. In the chapters of this book that focus in detail on different types of meditation, I'll give you the instructions specific to a particular form, if there are any. Here, I just discuss some options and give you the basis for making your own choices.

In many kinds of meditation, you keep your eyes closed. People generally find this helps them turn inward and focus and even makes them feel calmer. However, sometimes closing your eyes makes it more likely you'll get sleepy or drawn into fantasies. If either of these things is a problem for you, you may want to try meditating with your eyes open. Keep your gaze soft and unfocused as opposed to staring intently at one spot; ideally, let your gaze rest on a wall or the floor about 4 feet in front of you. At first, it may feel like keeping your eyes open makes you more vulnerable to distraction, but it's possible to work with this and eventually be able to achieve calm and focus even with your eyes open.

If you're able to breathe freely through your nose during meditation, that's ideal (but not required). Keep your lips gently closed, your teeth slightly apart (as opposed to clenched together), and the tip of your tongue lightly touching the back of your front teeth. If you need to breathe through your mouth, just let the lips part a bit.

Unless you're doing a form of meditation that uses a special hand position, you can simply place your hands where they're comfortable and keep them still. It helps your state of mind if you choose the position of your hands deliberately, rather than just casually resting them wherever they end up. You can place them palms up or down on your thighs, or neatly folded in your lap.

Dealing with Physical Discomfort

Physical discomfort during meditation is one of the main reasons people resist trying it or stop doing it. This is unfortunate because you can usually alleviate some or all of your discomfort by changing your meditation posture. Of course, depending on your physical condition, there may always be *some* discomfort associated with meditation if you're doing a kind that requires you to sit still for prolonged periods. As long as you aren't injuring yourself or making existing physical ailments worse, you may want to put up with some discomfort and meditate anyway. Many people do and feel the benefits of meditation are well worth it.

Restlessness

If you're doing seated meditation, you may find it difficult to simply sit still. This restlessness often has nothing to do with pain, although it's physically uncomfortable in its own way. Despite your intention, you may find yourself moving your hands, scratching itches, shifting your posture, or even looking around. You probably correct your posture and tell yourself you'll sit still—but then find yourself moving again or at least wishing you could.

WATCH OUT

If you suffer from physical restlessness in meditation, you may be inclined to stop meditating (or at least avoid doing it with others). Try to remember that everyone who meditates experiences restlessness! You can't tell from the outside because most people primarily experience *mental* restlessness.

Restlessness is just a physical manifestation of habitual energy. You're used to staying busy, working, getting places, and keeping up with activities of daily life. When you sit still, your mind and body don't know what to do with themselves. Try to be patient with this fact. The most important thing is the effort you put into meditation; it will have positive effects on you, even if you can't stay perfectly still. Simply notice when you move (or really want to) and then bring yourself back to your meditation technique with a minimum of fuss. Chances are your restlessness will decrease over time if you don't try to fight it too hard.

Legs Falling Asleep

It's usually not a big deal if your legs fall asleep occasionally in meditation—just be careful standing back up! However, if your legs *regularly* fall asleep, this isn't healthy and you need to adjust your posture. One of the most common reasons for numb legs in meditation is that one of your legs is pressing down on the other; when people are asked to sit cross-legged, what they usually do is tuck one leg under the other. If you're going to sit cross-legged in meditation for more than a few minutes, this isn't ideal. Try one of the positions I described earlier in this chapter for sitting meditation on the floor.

Another reason legs fall asleep in meditation is that whatever you're sitting on is pressing into the back of your thighs. There are major blood vessels and nerves in this area that you don't want to restrict. Try sitting farther forward on your cushion, bench, or chair, so the bottom of your pelvic bone is supported but the upper part of your legs aren't touching anything. Alternatively, add a soft cushion to the top of your meditation support to reduce the pressure on your legs (a dense foam cushion is ideal).

Pain

Pain in meditation can be tricky. If you've followed all the advice in this chapter but still have significant pain in meditation, you may want to consult a meditation or yoga teacher. Everyone's body is different, and a teacher may have some advice specific to you. Exercise and good self-care can help, too, of course, but it's possible you'll always have some pain during prolonged seated meditation. Sometimes the physical stillness aggravates existing injuries, conditions, or weaknesses.

 CONTEMPLATE THIS

It may inspire you to know that in deep meditation many people experience moments when their pain disappears completely or when it recedes in importance. However, they reach this place only because they haven't let pain stop them from meditating.

If you want the benefits of meditation despite experiencing some pain while you're doing it, you can learn to make pain part of your meditation. There are many ways to do this, such as the following:

- Breathe into the pain, acknowledging it while encouraging yourself to relax around it.

- Investigate the pain, asking yourself exactly where it occurs, what qualities it has, and whether it comes and goes.

- Bring your awareness to areas of the body that don't hurt.

All of these approaches can reduce your resistance to the pain, which is a good thing because resistance usually just makes pain worse. Nothing should hurt to the point of distraction, and you shouldn't have any lasting pain after you get up from meditation. If you keep this in mind, you can gradually increase the length of time you sit in meditation without injuring yourself.

Alternatives to Seated Meditation

Don't despair if you find yourself unable to do seated meditation comfortably or if it holds no appeal for you. There are forms of meditation you can do in the midst of thoughtful, deliberate movement. These include mindful yoga (see Chapter 12), body practices like Qigong (see Chapter 14), and meditative activities like chanting and ritual (see Chapter 16).

It's also possible to walk very slowly, stand, or even lie down while doing any of the forms of meditation that are usually done while seated. These positions aren't generally recommended because they can make it harder for you focus (if you're walking), relax (if you're standing), or avoid getting drowsy (if you're lying down). However, with some extra effort these alternative postures can work just fine, especially if physical limitations will otherwise prevent you from meditating.

Whatever position your choose, keep in mind the need to balance comfort and calmness with alertness. To meditate while walking, take small, slow steps coordinated with your breathing. Walk back and forth or in a circle within a relatively small area that contains minimal distractions (see Chapter 15 for more on walking meditation). If you want to stand during meditation, place your feet shoulder-width apart, bend your knees slightly (avoid locking them), and hold your arms in some kind of deliberate way (instead of just letting them dangle).

To meditate while lying down, lie on your side with a small pillow under your head and your legs slightly bent, one on top of the other. Bend your lower arm so your hand ends up near or under your pillow, and keep your upper arm straight, resting it on top of your body. Variations on this theme are fine, but this is a traditional lying meditation posture that helps keep you focused. If you need to lie on your back, it can be challenging to stay alert. If this is a problem for you, try placing a small cushion or object on your chest and then lightly holding it there, keeping your hands on either side of it but not resting on it.

 WATCH OUT

Try not to be stubborn and insist on sitting meditation on the floor even if you don't have the flexibility for it or if it hurts. It's much more important that your meditation posture meets the guidelines discussed earlier in the chapter than that it looks like the classic images you've seen of cross-legged meditating monks. Sitting on the floor with a slouched back or a screaming pain in your knee is going to compromise your meditation.

The Least You Need to Know

- Many forms of meditation don't require any special kind of posture at all, and none of them require you to sit on the floor if that's not comfortable for you.
- In seated meditation, the essential aspects of posture are being able to remain comfortable but alert; a straight, upright spine; and unrestricted breathing.
- Seated meditation posture can be achieved by sitting on a cushion on the floor, using a meditation bench, or sitting in a chair.
- When trying different meditation postures, listen to your body. It may take some time to get used to something new, but in general, don't use postures that hurt so much you can't concentrate or that cause you to experience pain after meditation.
- There are ways to deal with the various kinds of physical discomfort that might occur during meditation. Talk to a meditation teacher or try a different body position, including standing, walking, or lying down.

Getting Started with Meditation

Generally speaking, beginner's meditation techniques are straightforward and easy to try—not much preparation is required. In fact, sometimes the hardest part of starting a meditation practice is simply *starting*, so it's a good idea not to get too caught up in preparations. Still, it can be helpful to know how to make meditation a regular part of your life, get the maximum amount of benefit out of it, and make it easier to do.

This chapter helps you understand the best attitude for approaching meditation. I also briefly describe other ways of supporting your physical and mental health that are usually associated with meditation practice, and give general instructions for finding the best time and place in your life for meditation. Even if you have already started to meditate, you may find things in this chapter to aid you in strengthening and stabilizing your practice.

In This Chapter

- The best attitude for approaching meditation
- Things you can do to make your experience easier and more positive
- How to choose a type of meditation that works for you
- The role and value of meditation teachers
- Tips on when and where to get started on your meditation

All You Need for Meditation

All you really need for successful and enjoyable meditation is the right attitude. Sure, good posture and a meditation cushion might be useful, too, as I described in the previous chapter. But now it's time to focus on how to prepare your mind and heart for meditation. After all, most of the benefits of meditation have to do with changes in your mental or emotional experience and then with physical changes related to the body-mind connection. How can you make yourself receptive to the positive mental and emotional changes meditation can offer?

Willingness and a Beginner's Mind

A huge part of the right attitude for meditation is simply being willing to try it and then stick with it for a while to see what happens. The thought of doing something that could change the way you think and feel may be a little daunting. This is because you tend to be identified with the way you think and feel; even if you tend to be stressed, irritable, or depressed, at least this is the "devil you know." Fear of the unknown can be inhibiting, even if people are telling you the unknown is better than where you are now.

CONTEMPLATE THIS

In his classic book *Zen Mind, Beginner's Mind,* Zen teacher Shunryu Suzuki reminds us, "In the beginner's mind there are many possibilities, but in the expert's there are few."

In order to engage in meditation with willingness, you may find it helpful to know that the Zen tradition recommends a "beginner's mind" in meditation, no matter how long you've been meditating. Beginner's mind is an attitude of open curiosity where you admit to yourself you don't know what's going to happen next. (Even if you're an expert, you don't really know what's going to happen next, either; you just think you do.) With the beginner's mind attitude, you also don't have any problem with the fact that you don't know because, well, you're a beginner! It's possible to keep this receptive attitude long past the point where you're technically a beginner, and it makes you much more receptive to meditation because you're focused on the here and now instead of holding on to what you think you already know.

Intention

Like others who decide to practice meditation, you're willing to engage the meditative process because you have some kind of intention—to improve your health, reduce stress, achieve some inner peace, and so on. When you find your meditation practice flagging, it may be helpful to remind yourself of your deeper aspiration. It may also be useful to allow your intention or aspiration to change over time; sometimes, the original reason you started meditating becomes less important, but you discover a new benefit that really inspires you to keep doing it. Remind yourself of your intention as you begin your meditation, and use it to bring yourself back when your mind has wandered. You can allow it to inspire you and motivate you to devote yourself wholeheartedly to whatever meditative approach you're using.

However, there may also be times when focusing on your intention gets in the way of your meditation. You'll notice this is the case when you start to feel frustrated or when your meditation becomes a new source of stress. Sometimes when you get too fixated on a particular outcome, you close yourself off to the process that's actually happening—and the process that's actually happening might be beneficial in a way you haven't anticipated. If you find yourself frustrated or stressed about your meditation, you might try letting go of your intention. Imagine meditation is simply a maintenance activity like brushing your teeth; keep doing it without concern for remarkable outcomes.

Reasonable Expectations

Setting reasonable expectations is another way to cultivate a receptive attitude in meditation. The important thing is to realize there's no objective definition of *reasonable* when it comes to expectations. Basically, if you constantly find yourself falling short of your own expectations, they aren't reasonable for you. While this can be difficult to accept, learning to recognize and set reasonable expectations for your meditation is a great way to make sure it remains a positive aspect of your life.

Expectations about meditation fall into two categories. The first category consists of your plans for how often and how long you're going to meditate. While some people manage to set expectations for themselves and then meet them more or less perfectly, those people are rare. Most of us set a goal such as "I will meditate for 30 minutes in the morning before work at least five days a week," but then find ourselves struggling to do it. When we end up only meditating once in a whole week—and then only for 15 minutes—we typically feel frustrated or disappointed. The trick is to set a goal you can actually keep, like "I will meditate at least once a week." When you meditate once in a week, you can then appreciate how even that is great. The positive reinforcement may even inspire you, eventually, to meditate twice a week!

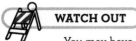 **WATCH OUT**

You may have had positive meditative experiences in the past where all thinking dropped away and you were left with a sense of spacious peace and relief, or maybe you've only heard about this kind of experience and you're hoping to achieve it. Either way, you end up forming an expectation: If you try hard enough, such-and-such will happen. This kind of expectation only gets in the way of the meditative process because part of your mind will always be stuck in a kind of self-interest. Therefore, it will be very beneficial if you can let go of past experiences and open up to new ones.

In the other category of expectations around meditation are all of your hopes for how your meditative experience will go. Depending on the meditation technique you choose, you may enter your meditation with the expectation of keeping your awareness centered on your breathing or an inspiring word. It's difficult not to feel disappointed or frustrated when instead of meditating and settling into a place free of thoughts, you find yourself worrying incessantly about a project at work or, even worse, reciting inane advertising jingles in your mind. In this case, a reasonable expectation about your meditation can focus on your effort instead of the outcome, such as "I will diligently return my awareness to my meditation object each and every time I notice I'm thinking." While this may not seem like much, simply returning to whatever practice you're trying to do is the essence of meditation. Ultimately, your effort is all you have control over anyway.

Patience and Commitment

Patience is incredibly useful if you want to develop a meditation practice. It's tempting to want to learn how to meditate and then do it "correctly." For instance, people new to meditation will often ask, "Am I doing this right?" While you can improve your meditation in definite ways, it's important to realize this improvement happens over a lifetime.

Beginners often find it helpful when I compare meditation to the martial arts. When you train in karate or aikido, you make an effort to learn the art correctly; however, it's clear the process of mastery takes time. Understanding intellectually what you're supposed to do is only the first step. You have to practice the art over and over to learn it with your body. Along the way, you'll have insights about what is obstructing your progress, and you'll learn to face those challenges. Even after you attain a black belt and presumably know what you're doing, there will always be at least one practitioner around with a level of mastery that makes you feel like a beginner. And yet, that doesn't demean you as a new black belt *or* as a beginner; instead, the various levels of mastery simply point to how profound and deep the martial art is. Likewise, meditation is a process that's learned over a long period of time and requires patience to practice.

Exercising patience in your meditation practice doesn't have to be passive or boring. If you engage the practice energetically, as you would a martial art, you can bring all kinds of determination to the effort. In this case, patience is about taking a long view and committing to a process of growth and development. Instead of expecting meditative bliss tomorrow or losing interest in meditation because it doesn't give you the results you want within a few months, you can try to inspire your commitment to the method by looking at people who have mastered meditation more than you have. Do you want what they have? Chances are, if you follow their instructions and keep on meditating, you'll taste some of those benefits for yourself.

Supports for Effective Meditation

Most of the forms of meditation presented in this book are taught and practiced within a larger context designed to increase or maintain your health and well-being. In other words, in most traditions meditation is only one of many tools in your spiritual toolbox, and you don't expect to be able to solve all of your problems with only that one tool. Taking care of your life in other ways, such as the following, tends to support your meditation, allowing it to become deeper and more effective. Note that you certainly don't have to wait until you've got all of these things squared away before you meditate! While they support your meditation, meditation can, in turn, support your other efforts to take care of your life.

Basic Moral Behavior

You may get your morals from your religion, your family, or your own internal sense of right and wrong. In any case, appropriate behavior is an important part of calming your mind and becoming receptive to the benefits of meditation. The classic illustration of this invites you to imagine trying to meditate right after you rob a bank. It's very unlikely you're going to be able to focus on any kind of meditation—chances are you won't even be able to sit still!

 POINT OF CLARIFICATION

> While concern about the appropriateness and skillfulness of your own behavior is necessary, it can also become an obsession. If you find yourself sitting in meditation mulling over whether something you did was right or wrong, you can use your meditation technique to disrupt your critical or defensive train of thought and return to the present moment. This isn't a way to avoid facing your conscience; instead, it helps you gain some emotional distance from the situation so you can see things more clearly.

A typical list of behaviors that interfere with meditation (and your spiritual well-being as a whole) includes killing (primarily people, but any thoughtless or unnecessary killing is considered agitating), stealing, misusing sexual energy, lying, abusing intoxicants, engaging in malicious gossip, and unleashing anger on people. These kinds of activities tend to have troubling consequences either for you or for others. Even if someone else has apparently borne the brunt of the negative consequences of your action, you'll probably find thoughts and feelings about the whole situation appearing repeatedly in your meditation because of your empathy or conscience. Alternatively, you may find yourself spending lots of time and energy constructing elaborate justifications for your choices. Whatever the case, even if basic moral behavior isn't an aspiration of yours in and of itself, it's highly recommended as a support for your meditation.

Stable Life Circumstances

It's not that you shouldn't meditate if your life is in a state of transition or chaos; it's just that you should recognize that meditation is going to be more challenging at such times. In order to focus on meditation, you need to let go of worrying and planning for a while. When lots of things are going on in your life that you actually need to be thinking about and taking care of, it will probably be difficult for you to set thinking aside and concentrate on meditation.

It's still worth a try! Even a few moments of calm will be beneficial. However, if you really want to deepen your meditation over the long term, you may want to take stock of your life and see if there are ways you can make it simpler or more stable. It doesn't have to be boring, just a little less demanding of your attention in terms of making decisions and adapting to constant change. For example, you may find that on a regular basis, you get dissatisfied with your job, quit, find another job, and have to get used to a new work environment. This may be due to restlessness that you can learn to put aside for a while in order to stick with one job for at least a year (or two, or three) and minimize the disruption in your life.

Physical and Mental Health

A basic level of physical and mental health is naturally supportive of your meditation practice. While you may think this goes without saying, sometimes people expect meditation alone to take care of certain problems when a holistic approach to health would be better. For example, you may try meditation to mitigate stress-related chronic pain. While meditation may indeed help, therapy or exercise might also contribute to a reduction in symptoms. This, in turn, will help you settle into your meditation more deeply.

 WATCH OUT

Nan Fink Gefen offers some good advice in her book, *Discovering Jewish Meditation: Instruction & Guidance for Learning an Ancient Spiritual Practice:* "[M]editation is not appropriate for people who are in extreme mental health crises. Anyone who is contemplating suicide, or who is clinically depressed or psychotic, or who cannot function in daily life should stay away from the practice." Meditation can sometimes encourage isolation, and what you need at times of crisis is the support of others and active practices. Once your life has stabilized, you can start meditating again.

As for maintaining your mental health, it's smart to do whatever it takes and not just rely on meditation. While meditation has been shown to relieve stress, decrease anxiety, and generally increase happiness, sometimes meditation isn't enough. Consider all of the following ways to improve your health and well-being, and remember they may actually improve your meditation as well:

- Therapy

- Medication

- Exercise

- Eating well

- Getting enough sleep

- Maintaining positive social connections

- Taking time to enjoy yourself

A Positive Worldview

Finally, the way you view the world has an enormous effect on your experience of it and therefore on your experience of meditation. If you see human beings as basically selfish and life as inherently meaningless, your daily life will have a very different character than it would if you saw people as ultimately good and life as an opportunity for spiritual growth. A negative worldview is inevitably going to affect your meditation, making it restricted, guarded, and potentially even depressing instead of curious, open, and inspiring.

Of course, this raises the question, "How do you sincerely change your worldview?" For the most part, the process of meditation isn't about creating or maintaining a positive worldview. It's usually about settling the mind so you can more clearly perceive the way things really are. However, in most meditation traditions this process is recommended because *the way things really are* is much more positive and hopeful than many of us tend to think. No form of meditation is recommended because you'll ultimately arrive at a negative worldview. Instead, all forms of meditation are inherently optimistic: settle into reality, and you'll find things get better.

Of course, most meditative traditions have a whole set of teachings about the worldview they hope you can wake up to and actualize through your own meditation. Such teachings range from simple descriptions of how mindfulness helps you develop a healthier relationship to your own thoughts, to complex teachings on how your existence is inherently complete and precious. If you don't already have a positive worldview, you may want to explore the teachings around your chosen form of meditation in order to reframe your life and the role meditation plays in it.

Choosing a Type of Meditation

This book gives you an introduction to many kinds of meditation, including meditation exercises for you to try. You may want to read about all the forms of meditation that interest you before deciding on one to try, or you may want to try a number of them. It's important to remember that you may need to stick with a particular kind of meditation for a while—at least a few sessions, maybe a few weeks, or even longer—before you'll start to understand what it's about or taste its benefits.

CONTEMPLATE THIS

The spread of meditation traditions all over the world in the last century has pre-sented us with an opportunity our ancestors never had: to study and try many and varied forms of meditation. You have the option of shopping around among traditions you would never have been able to encounter even 50 years ago. But this can also be a challenge—instead of applying themselves diligently to the practice at hand, some people just keep shopping.

In choosing a meditation to commit yourself to for a time, read the description of the tradition in which the meditation is embedded, including the theory behind the method used. Look for a tradition that makes sense to you because this will help you trust the process. Are you inspired by the ultimate goals of the meditation tradition? Is the meditation compatible with your life and beliefs?

Knowing whether a form of meditation is right for you once you've started practicing it can be a little more difficult. Most kinds of meditation can be challenging at times. You may not see obvious benefits, you may wonder if you're doing the meditation right, or it may get a little boring after a while. Beware of simply dropping a particular meditation for these kinds of reasons in order to move on to something that looks like it might be easier or offer quicker payoffs. In order to experience the long-term benefits of meditation, you generally have to work through some challenges, even with a kind of meditation that is well-suited to you.

The Time and Place for Meditation

Now that you have a sense of how to prepare your mind and life for meditation, as well as how to pick a type of meditation to investigate, let's consider the activity of meditation itself. If you've never done meditation before, you may encounter some resistance to actually setting aside some time and doing it. It won't be long, however, before it feels like a fairly normal activity that fits into your life like exercise, cleaning your house, or taking the dog for a walk.

When to Meditate

There are no hard-and-fast rules about when to meditate. Generally speaking, you should choose a time that works for you. First of all, you need to be able to fit it into your schedule, so that alone may determine when you meditate. Some people are able to wake up early and do it before starting their day, some find a slot where they can fit it in midday, and others meditate in the evening. You may need to get creative and take advantage of spare moments to meditate throughout the day—perhaps in an empty room at work.

If you have some options in terms of when you meditate, pick a time when you tend to experience a good balance of alertness and relaxation. At certain times of the day, you may find you're either too alert (and can't concentrate or settle) or too relaxed (so you get dull or sleepy). It's inevitable that you'll struggle with a wandering mind or sleepiness at certain times, no matter what time of day you meditate. However, try different times to see if there's one that's easiest for you.

How Long and How Often to Meditate

For the most part, it's up to you how long you meditate. Some types of meditation come with recommended session lengths, and I'll indicate if that is the case in the chapters that focus on particular meditation traditions. You'll find that most meditation instructions suggest 20 to 30 minutes for a period of formal meditation, but almost all acknowledge that shorter periods can also be beneficial. If you find yourself unwilling or unable to meditate for more than 5, 10, or 15 minutes, just meditate for as long as you can. Your experience may be positive—especially if you aren't pushing yourself too fast or too far—and it may inspire you to meditate more.

 POINT OF CLARIFICATION

> If you're trying to do a fairly still and silent form of meditation, part of the process is learning to stay present with your discomfort instead of seeking something to distract you from it. Discomfort in meditation can be physical, mental, or emotional, and it can make you want to fidget, daydream, or end your meditation. While you shouldn't force yourself to sit there until you're miserable, you might try meditating for *just a little longer* than you want to. This helps you gradually increase the length of time you can sit and increases your tolerance for mild discomfort in all areas of your life.

The most important thing is to make meditation a fairly regular habit. Meditating for 5 minutes 3 days a week is usually better than doing it for 40 minutes every once in a while. Working meditation into your routine helps build it in as a habit; the habit gains its own momentum and becomes easier to keep up over time. Each session of meditation also tends to be rewarding in some way, so doing it regularly helps you not lose touch with your reasons for meditating in the first place. Finally, each day with a little meditation in it tends to feel more manageable and worth appreciating, so the more days you do it the better!

Where to Meditate

While some of the meditations presented in this book involve particular settings or activities, most of them are things you do on your own in relative silence. The ideal place for silent (or quiet) meditation is a place that's fairly free of visual and auditory distraction. While background noise from something like traffic or flowing water isn't a problem (complete silence isn't necessary), it will be almost impossible to meditate if you can overhear conversations, television, or sounds from activities that draw your interest or concern.

If you have the space, it can help to designate a particular place or room in your home for meditation. Try to keep it uncluttered, and maybe even leave a meditation cushion out so you'll be reminded about the practice every time you pass it. Ideally, you'll be able to find a space (or time) where you're unlikely to be interrupted during your meditation; this will help a great deal with your concentration. (You won't be alert to every sound, waiting for the moment someone is going to disturb you.) If you don't have much space and you live with others, you might try laying claim to the bathroom for a half hour. You could also try meditating behind the wheel of your car during your lunch break—wherever you can find a little space and quiet.

Removing Barriers to Getting Started

You may be inclined to put off the moment you actually sit down and meditate. You may procrastinate, or decide you need to do some more reading, or simply notice that you never end up meditating despite your interest in the concept. If this is the case, two things may be helpful to keep in mind.

First, your initial (or second, or third) meditation session doesn't have to be a big deal. No one else even has to know you tried it. You don't have to experience something great right away in order to make the effort worth it; in fact, whatever benefits you receive from meditation will probably be fairly subtle. On the other hand, you might end up being surprised how profound an apparently simple meditation really is—but then again, don't worry if nothing strikes you as profound. The meditation will still be working on you, and it will still be effective.

Second, you don't have to meditate more than once. In other words, you don't have to decide to "start meditating"; you only have to decide to meditate this one time and see how it goes. Your subconscious is much less likely to put up resistance to trying meditation if you frame your intention in this more lighthearted way. Just quietly shut yourself in a room, review your meditation instructions, decide how long to meditate, and try it!

CONTEMPLATE THIS

You may feel some resistance to starting a meditation practice because when people find out, they'll suddenly expect you to conform to the stereotype of a meditator: someone without too much passion, who never gets angry, judgmental, anxious, or depressed. It's true; if they know you meditate, sometimes people will notice you lose your temper and ask, "Don't you meditate?" Of course, you can respond, "Yes, I do, and this is why."

A Disclaimer About Meditating on Your Own

You've probably encountered the disclaimer offered with just about any exercise program: "Always consult your physician before beginning a new exercise routine." The vast majority of meditation teachers will similarly advise you to consult a qualified teacher if you want to develop a meditation practice, especially when you're first learning. As is the case with the disclaimer about exercise, you're free to ignore the advice to get input from a professional based on your own common sense.

You may decide that you're physically, mentally, and emotionally stable enough to give meditation a try on your own or even to continue meditation indefinitely without getting advice from anyone outside of a book. You're probably right, especially if you're doing the kind of basic meditation practices offered in this book. On the other hand, it may be helpful to know why—and when—you might want look for a teacher.

The Value of Meditation Teachers

Some forms of meditation are very simple, and you may find you need little or no instruction from a trained teacher to be able to do them and benefit from them. Other forms are more complex and are never taught outside a carefully considered training program led by someone qualified to do so. Teachers of these more complex (or subtle) forms of meditation are skeptical about the possibility of learning to do their type of meditation effectively without personal instruction, and if you try to do so, you run the risk of seriously misunderstanding or misapplying the approach. I have not featured any of these complex forms in this book, and if you're interested in them, you'll have to meet a teacher in person to learn them.

Even in the case of relatively simple and straightforward styles of meditation, however, interacting with a teacher can be useful. Earlier, I compared learning meditation to training in a martial art; the value of having a living, breathing human instructor is another area where the two disciplines are similar. As teachers of Transcendental Meditation are fond of saying, "Would you try to learn a golf swing from a book?" Meditation involves and affects your whole body and mind. You have to try it, make mistakes, try again, and allow the lessons you learn along the way to sink in. It ends up being a very personal process, so it can be valuable to get personalized instruction from someone who can observe you, get to know you, and answer your particular questions.

> **CONTEMPLATE THIS**
>
> In almost all traditional forms of meditation, you have a choice about how and to what degree to engage with a teacher. You may simply want to attend a workshop to get an introduction. You may want access to a teacher only when you have specific questions. You can also establish a longer-term relationship with a teacher so she can get to know you better and make her advice to you more personalized and appropriate. A teacher can be especially helpful when you're facing challenges, either in your meditation itself or in finding better ways for meditation to support the rest of your life.

When to Get Some Help

I sincerely hope this section does not scare you off from meditation any more than the disclaimer "consult your physician before beginning any exercise routine" scares you off from exercise. While chances are the things I mention here won't apply to you, as a meditation teacher it's my responsibility to fully inform you about the process and some of the things that *can* happen in connection with meditation.

In recent decades, meditation has often been presented as a simple, easy, side effect–free way to relieve stress and increase satisfaction. The vast majority of the time, it is. Occasionally, however, it can have unintended results—some of them simply surprising:

- **The arising of strong emotions, memories, or images:** Sometimes, you've been suppressing these things and now have the opportunity to look at them. Other times, they just pass away without you needing to understand them.

- **Visual, auditory, or olfactory hallucinations:** These are relatively uncommon, but also not something to worry about. They usually go away with time and are just an interesting (or annoying) side effect.

- **Involuntary physical movements:** Occasionally people find they twitch during meditation, and in some cases, the twitch can be somewhat dramatic. This phenomenon is fairly rare, but it can be disturbing when it happens. Generally speaking, it's best just to accept or ignore such movements; they usually subside with time.

If you experience some of these unusual but generally harmless effects of meditation, you may want to consult a teacher for moral support or for guidance in how to understand or integrate your experiences into your life.

More serious effects of meditation require the support of a professional—a meditation teacher, experienced yoga teacher, trained practitioner of Chinese energy work, therapist, psychiatrist, or doctor. Please note that it's extremely rare to experience these side effects of meditation unless you're meditating a lot—that is, for hours each day. Try not to let fear of these kinds of experiences stop you from meditating; that would be a little like not exercising because there's always a tiny chance you could fall and break something. If you experience any of these things, just get some help and you'll be able to deal with them:

- **Greater depression or anxiety:** Sometimes meditation isn't able to break the feedback loop of these conditions. A meditation teacher may be able to suggest a better technique for you, and therapy, medication, or exercise may serve as a complement to your meditation practice.

- **Disruptive physical or energetic phenomena:** On very rare occasions, meditation triggers otherwise inexplicable pain, illness, or disturbing sensations that feel like energy or electricity coursing strongly through the body. Get help from professionals trained in bodywork that acknowledges and works with energy flow.

- **Radical shifts in consciousness or perspective:** Usually such shifts happen only after many years of meditation practice. When they happen quickly, particularly outside of the context of a tradition and without a teacher, they can be profoundly disorienting. Definitely discuss your experience with a meditation teacher.

 WATCH OUT

> People who meditate sometimes experience a remarkable insight or a sudden change in their perspective on the world. While these experiences—called *openings* in some traditions—are usually valuable and provide great opportunities for learning, concluding they are "enlightenment" isn't helpful. Any opening, no matter how dramatic, is partial. Seek perspective from a meditation teacher, and understand that it generally takes time and effort to integrate your insights into your life.

Pay attention to how meditation is affecting you, and trust your intuition. The unpleasant or negative side effects of meditation almost never appear suddenly, full-blown and unmanageable. You can generally sense something's amiss. Checking with a meditation teacher may put your mind at ease simply because their response is often "Oh, that's normal. Nothing to worry about." On the other hand, they may be able to help you get through a challenge in a way that contributes to your strength and understanding in the long term.

The Least You Need to Know

- The most important things you need for meditation are an open, curious mind; a willingness to be reasonable in your expectations; and patience with what can be a subtle and long-term process of growth.

- You'll find it easier to meditate if you follow basic moral principles, lead a relatively stable life, take care of your physical and mental health, and cultivate a positive worldview.

- All forms of meditation can be challenging at times; choose a form of meditation that appeals to you and then commit to doing it for a while.

- It's pretty much up to you when and where you meditate and how often. The most important thing is to get started and make it a regular habit.

- Sometimes meditation has unforeseen effects, some of which may be surprising, disorienting, or even harmful. While these side effects are rare, it's good to seek professional help if something arises in meditation that troubles you.

Meditation for Enlightenment

In this part of the book, I feature four classic meditation disciplines—Kriya Yoga, Vipassana, Zen, and Vajrayana. These were specially designed to help you move toward enlightenment, which is really just a fancy word for a deeper understanding of ultimate truth and the realization of your full human potential. All four of these forms of meditation have been practiced for 1,500 years or longer. Kriya Yoga developed in India and is based on ancient Indian texts and teachings. Vipassana, Zen, and Vajrayana are all forms of Buddhist meditation, but with very different flavors and approaches. While these meditation disciplines are usually associated with particular teachings and philosophies about the nature of reality, practicing them doesn't require belief (or disbelief) in any deity or acceptance of any dogma.

You find an entire chapter on each form of meditation, including a brief history and description of the spiritual tradition in which it was developed, and the philosophy behind the meditative approach. After a general introduction to the meditation tradition as a whole, I focus on a particular style of meditation within that tradition in order provide more detail and give instructions for a basic practice you can do. I also offer advice about how to deepen your meditation, and how to find out more about each tradition.

Yoga Meditation

Meditation has featured centrally in the spiritual traditions of India for thousands of years. Since long before recorded history (approximately 500 B.C.E.), spiritual seekers in that area of the world have been struggling with questions about the nature of life and death, the best way to attain lasting happiness, and the true limits of human potential. Their approaches included mythology and philosophy but focused primarily on methods—such as meditation—that bring about positive change or transformative insight.

In this chapter, I introduce you to the Yoga tradition, which originated in India but has spread throughout the world. I describe the philosophical underpinnings of the tradition and give you a sense of the richness and complexity of this spiritual path. I then share a type of Yoga meditation, give you an exercise you can try, and explain how you can deepen your meditation. To put everything in context, I end by shedding some light on ultimate goal of meditation within the context of Yoga.

In This Chapter

- Yoga as an ancient religious tradition
- Yoga's goal of union with God consciousness
- Practical benefits of Yoga meditation
- The relationship between awareness, breath, and energy
- Other Yoga practices to deepen your meditation

Overview of Yoga

When you hear the word *Yoga*, you probably think of stretching and holding particular postures with your body. This physical practice is actually *Hatha Yoga*, which is only one aspect of a traditional Yoga practice. Typically, Yoga is a holistic approach to spiritual development that also includes philosophical teachings, guidelines about moral behavior and diet, cultivation of positive energy flows in the body, and meditation. In many cases, it even incorporates devotion to God, rituals, prayers, mantras, and reverence for spiritual teachers.

 **DEFINITION**

Hatha Yoga is one type of practice within the Yoga tradition and involves moving your body through a series of traditional postures. While some Yoga traditions focus largely on Hatha Yoga, most also include practices to cultivate devotion, self-discipline, selfless action, insight, and meditative concentration, among other things.

The origins of Yoga are most likely very ancient, but in the historical record it appeared in a recognizable form by around 500 B.C.E. (Within the tradition itself, Yoga is viewed as having been passed down through the millennia since the last "high age" 14,000 years ago, when common people intuitively understood profound teachings.) Mentions are made of Yoga and meditation in Indian scriptures, including the Upanishads and the *Mahabharata*. Yoga continued to develop over the centuries, until Patanjali wrote the *Yoga Sutras* around 400 C.E. His writings are considered the first codified presentation of Yoga as a separate and complete spiritual discipline (more about the *Yoga Sutras* of Patanjali later).

The Idea of Spiritual Development

Many of the native religious traditions of India—including Yoga, Vedanta, Jainism, and Buddhism—recognize the value of a path of intensive spiritual development. This path is for individuals who have sufficient aspiration and isn't generally viewed as a requirement for the average person (that is, even a little bit of spiritual practice is considered beneficial). However, these traditions typically consider it likely that if you live out your whole life without personally exploring a path of spiritual development, you'll end up less fulfilled.

What does spiritual development entail in Yoga? Basically, you work to unlock your full potential as a human being, which is probably much greater than you realize. However, this isn't a path of self-improvement as much as it's a path of self-transcendence. This is the spiritual aspect of the development, essentially pointing toward that which is beyond you in a small, personal sense or isn't immediately obvious to you.

Central to most Yoga traditions is the idea that it's possible—and extremely desirable—to directly experience reunion with the Infinite Unity from which all things arose. This Unity may be called God, or Brahman, or left without a name, but experiencing yourself as part of this larger, undifferentiated reality is extremely healing and liberating. In fact, the word *Yoga* means "union" or "to connect," and the goal of Yoga is to reconnect you with the Infinite. Because of our habits, delusions, and self-interest, human beings tend to cling to our individuality, so we need a path of spiritual development like Yoga to allow us to awaken to our unity with all of life.

Yoga as a Lineage Tradition

It's very difficult to generalize about Yoga because traditions that identify in some way with the term are incredibly diverse. This is because the native religions of India have typically developed organically and are usually *lineage* based. There have been few (if any) centralized institutions that have sought to define or control a particular religious sect or school or that claim to have an exclusive handle on the truth.

 **DEFINITION**

A spiritual **lineage** is a tradition passed from teacher to student through the generations. Lineage is emphasized in spiritual traditions in which someone's practice or realization has to develop to certain level—and be confirmed as sufficient by an existing teacher—before he can teach the tradition himself.

Rather than religion in India developing in the context of large institutions, it has centered on remarkable spiritual teachers who have appeared periodically throughout the ages. These teachers have learned and mastered the traditions available during their lifetimes and then offered something new. When enough people conclude a master has something valuable to offer, a new lineage is formed and the teachings get passed through the generations from teacher to student (the student eventually becoming a teacher). Each new spiritual movement builds on the old, even if it claims to correct or improve it, resulting in an evolution of many diverse paths that nonetheless share similarities because they have some roots in common.

Two particular lineages of Yoga have a significant presence in the West. The first lineage was brought to the United States, England, and Europe by Swami Vivekananda (1863–1902) in the late 1800s and is typically known as Advaita Vedanta (although schools of Advaita Vedanta exist that have nothing to do with Vivekananda). Vivekananda was a student of Ramakrishna (1836–1886), a popular and charismatic religious leader in India who taught that God realization should be the ideal goal of all beings and that all religions are valid and true to the extent that they lead toward this goal. Ramakrishna saw worldly concerns as keeping people trapped in lower realms of consciousness, while spiritual practice helped them cultivate positive forces in their lives and allowed them to experience higher types of consciousness—and ultimately, to experience their oneness with God.

Vivekananda helped establish the Ramakrishna order of monks after Ramakrishna's death, as well as Vedanta societies in the West. He is credited with much of the increasing respect and attention the West began paying to Eastern spiritual traditions in the early twentieth century. A famous quote from his commentary on the *Yoga Sutras* of Patanjali summarizes his teaching beautifully (found in *The Complete Works of Swami Vivekananda*):

> "Each soul is potentially divine. The goal is to manifest this Divinity within, by controlling nature, external and internal. Do this either by work, or worship, or psychic control, or philosophy—by one or more or all of these—and be free. This is the whole of religion. Doctrines, or dogmas, or rituals, or books, or temples, or forms, are but secondary details."

WATCH OUT

If you aren't familiar with Eastern contemplative spiritual traditions, you might get the impression they are focused on your development in a self-absorbed or self-interested way. While the ultimate goal is always transcendence of self-concern, this is achieved by turning inward and exploring your own body, mind, and experience. This works because you're part of, or a reflection of, that which is greater than yourself. The idea then is always to offer yourself in service to greater humanity through what you've discovered.

The other Yoga lineage you're likely to encounter in the West is the one that comes through Paramahansa Yogananda (1893–1952), author of the classic book *Autobiography of a Yogi* and founder of the Self-Realization Fellowship. Yogananda lectured, taught, and wrote in the West from the time he first arrived in 1920 until his death, widely disseminating his teachings and leaving many students to carry on his lineage. He presented Yoga as a scientific approach to spiritual development and encouraged his students to test all of the teachings and practices for themselves rather than simply believing them.

Yogananda taught that we are already one with the omnipresence of God and simply need to awaken to that fact, something he called *Self-realization* (*self* being capitalized because it refers to your higher self as opposed to ego). He also taught that the fastest (but not the only) way to Self-realization is the path of Kriya Yoga. Kriya Yoga is a method of meditation that focuses on the spine and on mastering the flow of energy in the body so it's directed upward, decreasing the soul's identification with matter and individuality while increasing its ability to merge into the Infinite.

The Essence of Yoga

The fundamental premise of Yoga is there's an underlying unity to all of existence, and lasting happiness and peace come only from training yourself to perceive and live in harmony with that unity. All manifestations in the world, including people, are like waves in the ocean: although in a sense they can be said to exist, they aren't actually separate things. Human ignorance and suffering arises because we believe we are, in reality, separate from the rest of existence. We become identified with our bodies and individual lives and filled with self-concern about our survival and well-being—forgetting that, in truth, we are just waves in the infinite ocean of existence. If we can become more identified with the ocean than with our limited, temporary manifestation, we can attain a deep sense of peace and freedom.

From Egoism to an Experience of Unity

According to the cosmology of Yoga, everything in the universe arose out of pure consciousness, which is the subtlest kind of manifestation. The vast, single, universal consciousness may be called God, Brahman, or the Infinite, but it's seen as a creative force to which everything owes its existence. To create the universe, God simply thought things into being. The thoughts became energy, and then energy became matter—and thus all the myriad individual manifestations came about.

In order to create the universe, God also had to create the negative forces that pull beings toward individuality and away from unity with Him. These negative forces include our self-interest; hatred; desire for worldly pleasure and power; and willingness to harm others to get what we want by lying, stealing, and violence. Although ultimately, these forces are also from—and part of—God, they keep us bound to egoism and a sense of separateness that eventually will be unfulfilling (if it isn't already).

 CONTEMPLATE THIS

While the Yoga tradition is a contemplative tradition, it's also focused on achieving happiness and peace in your life. Swami Kriyananda (1926-2013, also known as J. Donald Walters), founder of the Ananda tradition of Yoga, wrote in his book *The Art and Science of Raja Yoga: Fourteen Steps to Higher Awareness,* "The essence of religion is not its ceremonies, nor even its talk of a life hereafter, but its emphasis on an inner life here and now and on the lasting peace that accompanies this inner life once it is discovered."

Fortunately, human beings have a choice about how we participate in the world, such as the following:

- We can choose to cultivate positive forces in our lives, such as kindness, insight, and generosity.

- We can work to decrease our attachment to our individuality by engaging in spiritual practices like devotion, service, self-discipline, and meditation.

- We can view as undesirable anything that obscures the truth of our oneness with all of life and view as desirable anything that helps reveal it to us.

A Science of Spiritual Development

The teachings and practices of Yoga are the result of over 2,000 years of spiritually motivated humans experimenting with their own bodies and minds. Seeking a direct and personal realization of unity with God, yogis have discovered countless ways to facilitate that process. Yoga includes recommendations about your conduct in everyday life, diet, relationships, exercise, cultivation of devotion, performance of rituals, and meditation, among other things!

Although you're encouraged to test all aspects of Yoga for yourself, there's a general path of development that's viewed as common to all people. In his *Yoga Sutras,* Patanjali explains eight "limbs" of Yoga practice, which are stages you need to go through, as well as practices you need to maintain throughout your spiritual development. This development involves decreasing identification with your physical body and individuality and increasing identification with pure consciousness or awareness (underlying, undifferentiated unity) by:

1. Breaking free of the grossest level of attachment to your individuality through external discipline and refraining from harmful actions.

2. Adopting internal discipline in order to transcend your self-interest in a positive way by cultivating positive qualities and virtues.

3. Turning your attention to maintaining appropriate posture with your mind *and* body—centered, grounded, balanced, and stable. (This stage is associated with Hatha Yoga but isn't limited to physical postures.)

4. Learning to regulate the flow of energy in your body, particularly as associated with your breathing, so you can still your mind and direct your energy toward the Divine.

5. Learning to direct the mind inward toward its own experience and processes, instead of outward toward the world (where you're always looking for rewards for the self).

6. Cultivating concentration, or learning to deliberately focus your mind on something for a prolonged period.

7. Mastering meditative absorption, or learning to enter deeper and deeper meditative states where your ego consciousness starts to fall away.

8. Experiencing the complete dissolution of ego consciousness in the Infinite.

 POINT OF CLARIFICATION

The idea is to approach your spiritual development in a scientific way by testing for yourself whether something has a positive effect on you or not. If a practice helps you feel calmer and more connected, or encourages spiritual virtues in you, it works for you. You observe carefully within yourself the effects of each thing you do. But of course, you have to make this observation in a clear and objective way, like a scientist observes an experiment, in order for your observations to be useful. It's not enough to ask whether you like or enjoy a particular practice; you need to be honest with yourself and look for positive results over time.

The Role of Meditation in Yoga

Although Yoga contains many different practices, many of them considered supplemental or complementary, meditation is generally considered to be essential—that is, if you want to awaken to oneness with the Infinite. Meditation is thought to inform and guide your other practices and also to most directly address the issue of your attachment to individuality. After all, the error of egoism starts in your mind: thoughts give rise to energy, and energy coalesces into habits and patterns that keep you bound to egoism. So if you study your own mind and learn to direct it properly, you can cut the problem off at the source.

In Yoga, the process of meditation is about making your mind more and more still—or alternatively, *allowing* it to become more and more still. The idea is that all the stuff in your mind—thoughts, plans, desires, worries, and so on—is related in some way to your self-concern and obscures the pure consciousness that is your divine Self within. The other practices of Yoga can be seen as preparatory—calming your life down and settling your body so your mind can become as still as possible. It's only in the state of consciousness beyond thought that it's possible to become completely receptive to reality. The Yoga process of meditation is (or can be) an involved lifelong path of refining your ability to calm your mind and thereby attune yourself to the subtle reality of the Infinite.

Three Benefits of Yoga Meditation

Fortunately, as you practice Yoga you experience many benefits along the way before you attain the ultimate goal of complete dissolution of ego consciousness. The theory behind this is that the more you live in harmony with Ultimate Reality (all things are one even if they appear separate, like the waves in the ocean), the healthier and happier you'll be. Sometimes Yoga practices are called *living in harmony with the rules of nature;* when you live in harmony with the deeper reality of unity, you allow your body and mind to function in the healthiest way possible. Whatever the case, the following are three benefits you may find from doing Yoga meditation.

Better Physical and Mental Health

Yoga focuses a great deal on the flow of energy in the body. It's thought that energy tends to flow toward wherever you're directing your awareness. So if your mind tends to be full of self-interest and negative concerns (out of harmony with deeper reality), your energy will also be out of harmony with the laws of nature. This leads to ill health and negative psychological and emotional states. On the other hand, if you direct your awareness in positive ways, your energy will increase and flow more easily and in more healthful ways—and your mood will also improve.

 WATCH OUT

Although Yoga associates successful practice with good health and an increased ability to heal, it doesn't deny the influence of causal factors on your health besides your spiritual practice (genetics, environment, or even chance). Practitioners aren't blamed for their physical or mental problems, but rather encouraged to deepen their practice to maximize their capabilities for healing and long-term health.

Meditation is the way you engage in self-study or introspection, a process that allows you to notice and eventually control where you're directing your awareness. You also begin to be able to discern the flow of energy in your body and learn to direct that flow. This kind of self-study isn't geared toward figuring out more about your personality and opinions or clarifying your likes and dislikes. Instead, it's about first becoming aware of the processes within your own mind and body and then finding ways to make beneficial choices about those parts of the process you can influence. While we often think the quality of our life is dictated more or less by our external circumstances and our emotional reactions to those circumstances, in reality we have many points of choice regarding our internal processes.

Decreased Bondage to Ego Concerns

Through the process of Yoga meditation, you "still" all the stuff in your mind—all those self-concerned thoughts, plans, desires, worries, resentments, and so on. You learn that the stuff of the mind comes and goes and is actually only present at the most superficial level of consciousness. Even if it's only for a few moments during your meditation, you can experience a deeper kind of consciousness in which you're alert and energized (as opposed to asleep or distracted) and yet not fixated on your usual thoughts and feelings. This is a powerful lesson because you essentially learn at a deep level that your self-interested mind stuff isn't real. Sure, the thoughts and feelings probably start up again after your meditation, but you're now familiar with the silence underneath all that static.

Essentially, the more you become identified with universal, undifferentiated unity (or God), the less identified you become with your personal manifestation—your body, thoughts, personality, life circumstances, and so on. As long as you're alive, you'll still inhabit this personal manifestation. But once you realize that you're just a wave in the big ocean of universal consciousness, it's easier to let go of attachment to your ego concerns. It's not that you stop taking care of your life—you just do so without a sense of panicked imperative, because you know at a deeper level your existence doesn't depend on the details.

Greater Appreciation and Awareness

We're usually caught up in the activities and concerns of daily life, and therefore subject to emotional ups and downs based on how things are going for us. For instance, you may feel great because you just got to go on a nice vacation, you enjoy your job, or you're looking forward to a pleasant dinner with friends. While there's nothing wrong with any of these sources of happiness, we tend to rely on such external sources of contentment exclusively. When things change and we're deprived of what we enjoy or face unpleasant circumstances, we struggle to maintain our positive frame of mind. This also means that even when things are going well and we're happy, we're always a little bit worried about the future.

 CONTEMPLATE THIS

While it may seem ironic that giving up all desire would bring greater happiness, contemplatives throughout the ages say it's true. For example, Swami Vivekananda wrote, "This meditative state is the highest state of existence .... It is only to the soul that has attained to this contemplative state that the world really becomes beautiful. To him who desires nothing, and does not mix himself up with them, the manifold changes of nature are one panorama of beauty and sublimity." (From *The Complete Works of Swami Vivekananda, Volume 1, Chapter VII.*)

In the course of Yoga meditation, you turn your awareness toward more and more subtle levels of existence—and your experience of these levels is extremely enjoyable and rewarding. You learn to be still, to give up all extraneous thoughts and feelings, and to discover it's deeply satisfying to just *be*. The pleasures of meditation are always available to you regardless of the fortunes of your life, and knowing this makes you less dependent on external things. Therefore, you can actually appreciate external things even more because you're not depending on them for your ultimate happiness or inner satisfaction.

Kriya Yoga Meditation

As you learned earlier in this chapter, Paramahansa Yogananda taught a particular form of Yoga meditation called *Kriya Yoga*. *Kriya* means "action" or "rite," and *Yoga*, as you know, refers to "union or connection with the Infinite." So Kriya Yoga is bringing about this union through an active process. It's a meditative method that involves directing your awareness, breathing, and energy flow in a very deliberate way. It's centered on your spine and the various energy centers, or *chakras*, located there. Yogananda described Kriya Yoga as a "scientific" method of attaining union with the Infinite, meaning it has been discovered, tested, and proven to be effective. In fact, he said this method is so effective it will allow you to develop spiritually at a much faster rate than any other technique.

General Description of the Method

The full technique of Kriya Yoga is only taught to you after you've done many preparatory practices and established a relationship with a *guru*, or teacher (more on guru devotion later in the chapter). However, the preparatory practices are themselves powerful and consistent with the overall Kriya Yoga approach. Each exercise builds on the last, encouraging relaxation, interiorization (turning your focus and energy inward), concentration, and increased control of the flow of your life energy.

The most basic practice begins with concentrating on the point between your eyebrows, which is your "spiritual eye" and one of the body's chakras. Beginning meditations can be very simple, such as imagining you're sending energy to your spiritual eye and that peace and calmness are spreading out from there throughout your whole body. Like most forms of meditation, part of the initial challenge is learning to keep your mind on your meditative object (in this case, the spiritual eye) and letting go of any thoughts and feelings that intrude.

 **DEFINITION**

> **Chakras** are the seven energy centers of the body. They are located along the spine (just in front of the physical spine) at the base of the spine; at the levels of the sacrum, navel, heart, and throat; at the base of the skull and between the eyebrows (two poles of one chakra); and at the top of the head. A **guru** is a qualified spiritual teacher with whom you've established a committed teacher-student relationship.

Concentration and your ability to focus inward are further developed with meditative breathing exercises. As an example, one exercise involves inhaling slowly for a certain number of seconds, holding your breath for the same amount of time, and exhaling for the same amount of time. The breath is connected closely to the flow of energy and gives you a tool for starting to connect with and influence that flow.

Later meditative exercises associated with Kriya Yoga, like the one shared in detail later in this chapter, may involve the silent "chanting" of particular sounds, concentration on energy centers in the spine, and visualizations of energy flow within your body. When the meditation involves visualization, the technique is usually not the construction of elaborate visual images in the mind (as happens in some other meditative traditions). Instead, you essentially move your awareness through your body in certain ways, inviting your breath and energy to follow that awareness.

The Theory Behind the Meditation

Yogananda wrote in *Autobiography of a Yogi* that in ordinary life, "the flow of life energy is toward the outward world; the currents are wasted and abused in the senses. The practice of Kriya reverses the flow; life force is mentally guided to the inner cosmos and becomes reunited with subtle spinal energies." This energy is then encouraged to flow up the spine using breathing and visualization exercises. Ultimately, the practitioner's life energy merges with the Infinite through the energy center at the very top of the head, but only after a long and careful process.

The basic idea is that matter and the negative forces drawing you toward individuality tend to pull your energy downward. If you do no spiritual practice and just let life unfold, your energy centers tend to be oriented downward and much of your energy will flow into your lower centers (associated with material security, sexuality, and power). This causes you to remain caught up in egoism and attached to your physical manifestation, and both of these things impede your spiritual progress.

According to Yoga, you need to work on decreasing your identification with matter or form by reversing the downward flow of energy in your body. Through the practice of putting your awareness on the energy center at your spiritual eye and employing other Kriya Yoga techniques, you can reorient your energy centers upward. The energy will then flow upward toward energy centers higher in the body associated with love (a place in your spine near your heart), calmness (opposite your throat), divine surrender (the base of the skull), and soul consciousness (the point between your eyebrows). Eventually, your breath slows or stops, your mind becomes alert but beyond thought, and you enter a state of consciousness that's part of the Infinite and no longer identified with your body or the material world.

Beginner's Meditation Instructions

Don't let apprehension about what it would mean to merge with the Infinite stop you from trying basic Yoga meditation. Remember, you're supposed to try each practice for yourself, and only keep doing it if you prove to yourself it's beneficial and effective. Even simple preparatory meditations can have very positive effects, as described earlier in this chapter. Here, I share a very common Yoga meditation used in the Ananda tradition that centers on following your breath—one taught to beginners but also used regularly by seasoned Yoga practitioners.

Setting and Posture

The goal of Yoga meditation is to turn your awareness inward, so the best setting for this kind of meditation is very quiet and private. If you don't have a place to meditate that's quiet enough, you can use earplugs or noise-reducing headphones. For energetic reasons, yogis recommend that you face east, if you can (to line up your body's magnetism with that of Earth), and that you sit on a wool or silk blanket or cloth (to insulate yourself from the magnetic forces of Earth, which tend to draw your energy downward).

POINT OF CLARIFICATION

One aspect of Yoga is recognition that because everything is made of energy, it also has magnetic qualities—including your own body. You can find Yoga teachings about all kinds of energetic or magnetic influences on your meditation, including those exerted by Earth, other planets and stars, food, and materials like natural fibers or metal.

A number of postures are appropriate for Yoga meditation. Any of the seated postures presented in Chapter 2 will work, although if you sit in a chair, you should try to sit forward in the chair so there's nothing pressing up against your spine. There's very strong emphasis in Yoga meditation on the spine and the energy flow through it, so a straight posture is considered essential. Sit with your chest extended and your shoulders back—not in a rigid or uncomfortable way but in a way that encourages an elongated spine. Keep your chin parallel to the floor and rest your hands on the tops of your thighs, palms up and pulled in close to your body.

Basic Practice

Yoga meditation is supposed to be practiced in a state of deep relaxation. This is why it's often preceded by Hatha Yoga postures. You might want to spend a few minutes before meditation doing Hatha Yoga or doing some other kind of simple, gentle stretches. One Yoga posture, the corpse pose, is physically very simple if you want to try it: Simply lie down on the floor on your back with your legs slightly apart. Place your arms by your sides with the palms of your hands turned upward. As you lie there, close your eyes and try to relax every part of your body as completely as you can.

Once you feel relaxed, get into your seated meditation posture and follow these steps (you can find an audio version of this meditation on idiotsguides.com/meditation):

1. Close your eyes. Take a few deep breaths, trying to relax your body completely as you do so.

2. The space between your eyebrows is one of your body's important energy centers; it's sometimes called your "spiritual eye." Concentrate your attention there. Don't physically tense the area; just let your attention and energy gather there. Concentrating on your spiritual eye also brings your gaze upward, even though your eyes are closed. Remain concentrated on your spiritual eye and maintain this upward gaze throughout the meditation.

3. Become aware of your breathing. Breathe through your nose if you can. Notice the coolness of the breath as it comes in and the warmth of it as it goes out. If you can, keep your awareness on the breath itself, rather than the physical movements involved in breathing. However, if it's easiest for you to remain aware of the movements, go ahead and do so. On the inhalation, notice the coolness of the air on your skin. On the exhalation, notice the warmth of the air.

4. As you inhale, imagine the sound "hong" (rhymes with *song*). Imagine the breath itself is producing the sound as it comes in and that the sound lasts exactly as long as the inhalation. Work on this practice for a few breaths, each inhalation causing the sound "hong" to resonate within you. (This sound is used not because of its meaning but because of the beneficial effect of the sound itself.)

5. Continue practicing "hong" with your inhalations, but add a silent sound to your exhalations as well. As you exhale, imagine the breath makes the sound "sau" (rhymes with *saw*) for exactly as long as the exhalation lasts. On the inhalation, "hong"; on the exhalation, "sau."

6. Continue with the hong-sau meditation for the next several minutes. Don't try to control the breath in any way. It can be helpful to watch your breath as if it belongs to someone else.

7. Remember to keep part of your attention on your spiritual eye, even as you breathe "hong" as you inhale and "sau" as you exhale. When your mind wanders, simply bring it back to awareness of the breath and the sounds of hong-sau.

8. Try to deepen your concentration if you can. Your awareness of your breath might be at the tip of your nose; bring awareness of it higher and higher in the nasal passages until the awareness merges with that of your spiritual eye. Become completely absorbed in the breath so there's no longer a sense of you being aware—only breathing and the sounds of hong-sau.

9. For the next several minutes of your meditation, let go of practicing any technique and simply sit in silence. Allow any changes, benefits, or sense of relaxation to permeate your consciousness. If your mind wanders, simply notice it and relax. Remember that whatever benefits you get from this meditation, they're something you simply have to be open to and receive.

10. Take three deep breaths and open your eyes. (If you want to, say a short prayer; it's traditional to say a prayer as you finish, so this effort doesn't become another tool of ego.)

While this meditation is beneficial even if you only do it for a few minutes, the benefit increases the longer you spend at it and the more effort you put into it. For instance, even experienced Kriya Yoga practitioners spent part of their meditation sessions doing hong-sau meditation. In *Autobiography of a Yogi*, Yogananda noted that a beginner might want to start by doing 14 to 24 cycles of hong-sau breathing twice a day. For anyone who wanted to become a master at Yoga, he recommended doing it for two hours a day.

Additional Guidance and Encouragement

In Yoga, meditation is a serious discipline. Instructions are very specific, and there's a great deal of guidance available from teachers to help you learn to meditate and deepen your meditation. Still, fundamentally, the hong-sau meditation is very simple; additional guidance is primarily to encourage you to make a strong, concentrated effort while simultaneously learning to relax completely.

Concentration Through Relaxation

Until you actually practice meditation for a while, it may not make sense to you that deep concentration is also a matter of deep relaxation. In your daily life, these two modes usually seem to be opposed to one another. When you concentrate, you have to work hard, and when you relax, your mind wanders. But you're definitely meant to concentrate in Yoga meditation! Ideally, you become completely absorbed in your meditative object to the point that all thought ceases and even your sense of self—your ego consciousness—falls away. Clearly, Yoga meditation is not just a matter of sitting around and letting your mind wander.

CONTEMPLATE THIS

Concentration can also be thought of as wholeheartedness or single-mindedness—doing whatever you're doing completely. As Yogananda explains, "The trouble with most people is that when they are performing an action they are thinking about something else. They don't know how to concentrate on what they are doing when they are doing it. You should learn to think of one thing at a time with all the power of your mind. Your whole attention should be there" (From *Man's Eternal Quest: Collected Talks and Essays on Realizing God in Daily Life.*)

It might help if you think of making a strong effort to relax. There's a certain kind of self-discipline involved in real relaxation when you realize that mind wandering isn't actually relaxing. In fact, a wandering mind is usually fairly agitated and self-concerned, even if only at a subtle level. You're usually planning ways to gain satisfaction or ways to avoid distress. To cultivate real relaxation, you deliberately set these concerns aside, inviting your deeper self to take charge—the deeper self that knows real happiness is only to be found within. You then find yourself concentrated but not through striving.

Receptivity Instead of Achievement

On a related note, it helps your Yoga meditation to remember you're simply trying to attune yourself to a deeper reality that's already there—as opposed to achieving some special state by making a big, admirable effort. You *do* have to make an effort, but Yoga practitioners tend to get around the trap of making their effort egoistic by thinking of themselves as cultivating receptivity to the Infinite. In a sense, the Divine realizes itself through them, if they just get out of the way and learn to listen.

Because it's so important to remember your effort is about attunement or receptivity to something greater than yourself, Yoga tends to include many devotional elements, such as prayers to God and to gurus. You may or may not feel comfortable with this devotional aspect of Yoga; if you don't, recall the reason for it (cultivating receptivity and letting go of egoistic concerns), and see if you can put your Yoga practice in context using your own idea of God, the Divine, or something greater. You'll find the concept of God in Yoga very fluid, formless, and compatible with almost any other religious or spiritual tradition.

Deepening Your Yoga Meditation

All the practices in Yoga are designed to support each other. In order to deepen your meditation, you can certainly spend more time at it, and put all of your will into concentration and meditative absorption. You can also investigate the other practices of Yoga, and you'll probably find your meditation deepening as a result. I cover a few supplemental practices here; see Swami Kriyananda's *The Art and Science of Raja Yoga* for more information on how your Yoga meditation can be deepened through Yoga, Hatha Yoga, diet, physical healing, positive thinking (affirmations), visualizations, prayers, and exercises to energize the mind and body.

Following the Moral Principles of Yoga

In Yoga, moral principles are strongly emphasized. The goal of Yoga meditation—union with the Infinite—requires a profoundly deep stilling of the mind, and there's no way to achieve this while acting in selfish or sloppy ways in your daily life. A clean conscience brings peace of mind. In addition, the whole point is that you're trying to awaken to the reality you're not actually separate from anything in the universe; if you keep acting as if you are, you'll inhibit that awakening. Your actions will keep you attached to your body and individuality.

The moral principles of Yoga were presented by Patanjali in his *Yoga Sutras* around 400 C.E. They're divided into two groups, one being the don'ts (things you refrain from doing), and one being the dos (positive qualities you cultivate in your life). The moral principle groups are as follows:

Dos	Don'ts
Cleanliness	Violence
Contentment	Lying
Austerity	Stealing
Introspection	Attachment to sensual pleasure
Devotion to God	Greed

Acting according to the moral principles of Yoga puts you in harmony with the deeper reality of oneness. So even if you haven't personally experienced oneness yet, you're preparing yourself to do so by following the dos and avoiding the don'ts.

Keeping Good Company and Guru Devotion

Yoga teaches that you're deeply affected by the world around you—your environment, what you eat, what you wear, what you read or watch, and even the movements of the planets. What affects you the most, however, is the human company you keep. If you're surrounded by positive people who are living moral lives and devoting themselves to spiritual development, you'll be profoundly affected and supported in your own efforts. This is why Yoga strongly recommends keeping good company. This generally refers to other Yoga practitioners but also includes other positive and supportive people in your life.

POINT OF CLARIFICATION

The term *guru* has ended up associated with some negative connotations based on past abuses of power. But it's important to note that while gurus are revered in many forms of Yoga, your relationship with one is entirely voluntary, and whatever reverence you give a guru is actually reverence for God or the Infinite, not the guru himself. Gurus simply give you a basis for faith that self-realization is possible because they have achieved it themselves and conduct themselves in a moral, loving, and generous way. They provide individualized guidance because each person's spiritual path is different. So as long as you keep your wits about you and avoid cults of personality, finding a guru may be something you want to explore.

No positive person is thought to exert as beneficial an influence on your Yoga practice as a teacher who has practiced diligently for many years and achieved an experience of unity with the Infinite. This is why there's a strong emphasis on the guru, or a self-realized teacher and personal guide, in Yoga. In most schools of Yoga, you can only be initiated into deeper levels of the practice if you find and commit yourself to a guru (after careful consideration). It's thought that until you find a teacher you trust enough to follow with complete faith, you can't master or safely try the most complicated and subtle practices. If you study in a traditional Yoga lineage, you'll encounter teachers who are empowered to fulfill the guru role with students. Before committing to one of them, study with them over time to make sure you trust them and that their teaching style is useful to you. Each lineage will have its own process for subsequently formalizing the guru-student relationship.

Learning More

Keep in mind that your local Yoga center probably focuses on Hatha Yoga. Of course, most Hatha Yoga traditions also value the teachings of Patanjali, and some offer quite involved yoga teacher trainings, which last three months or more and require many hours of study and practice each week. In such trainings, you'll encounter some of the other (non-Hatha) aspects of Yoga, such as guidelines for moral behavior, yoga philosophy, and meditation.

If you want to explore a traditional Yoga practice more deeply, both the Vivekananda and Yogananda traditions offer lots of resources and have many practice centers you can visit. To learn more about the practice established by Swami Vivekananda, explore the website of the

Ramakrishna Mission (belurmath.org), which lists affiliated practice centers all over the world, or the website of the Vedanta Society of Southern California (vedanta.org). For publications, see the online Vedanta Press catalog (vedanta.com).

To learn more about the Yoga tradition of Yogananda—including resources and the locations of practice communities and groups—visit the website of the Self-Realization Fellowship (yogananda-srf.org). And to further explore the Ananda tradition founded by Swami Kriyananda, a disciple of Yogananda who founded his own organization called the Ananda Sangha Worldwide, visit their website (ananda.org).

Yoga Meditation Over a Lifetime

There's definitely enough in the practice of Yoga meditation to keep you busy for a lifetime. You can go as deeply into it as you want with meditation retreats, advanced courses of study, residential communities, and in some traditions monastic orders. Within Yoga, while it's generally accepted that any amount of meditation and practice will be beneficial for you, it's also true that mastery is recognized and highly valued.

In fact, it's understood that there are two different levels of mastery. Usual levels of mastery are the kinds that allow someone to teach Yoga and function as a guru for students. Unusual levels of mastery, on the other hand, are those found about once every generation. People with this unusual level of mastery—such as Ramakrishna, Vivekananda, and Yogananda—are highly revered to the extent they are considered to be able to act as guru to living students, even though they themselves can no longer be found in a living body. While ordinary folks don't expect an unusual level of mastery, remarkable spiritual masters serve as an inspiration and as a reminder to all practitioners of what's possible.

"Ideal" Yoga Meditation

Mastery of Yoga meditation means you're able to control your mind and the flow of life energy in your body. Of course, the word *control* isn't entirely appropriate because it makes you think dualistically of "controller" and "that which is controlled." As discussed earlier, you actually achieve mastery through profound relaxation rather that ego-based striving. Still, the end result is that you have complete freedom of choice—at least in the course of your meditation—about where your awareness is resting, and where your life energy is directed. Eventually, control of your life energy, connected to your breathing, allows your breathing to slow down and sometimes even cease altogether for periods; this allows the greatest stillness of mind.

 **WATCH OUT**

The experiences of advanced Yoga meditation may sound like they're worth pursuing for their own sake because, for example, they're fascinating, blissful, or exotic. Be very careful not to push your way into deep Yoga meditation with essentially egoistic motivation; if you do, you may indeed have some unusual experiences, but they won't be the measured and selfless surrender that's the goal of Yoga.

In Yoga, mastery also means you've learned to make your energy flow upward toward spiritual union with God, rather than downward into the forces that keep feeding your drive toward individuality. At least in Kriya Yoga, this means you've become intimate with and cleared obstructions out of your energy centers. This allows energy to flow freely, so you can safely unlock the body's deepest reserve of primal energy. This then travels up the channel of the spine and out the top of your head, literally uniting your energy with that of the universe. (Note that attempting this stage of meditation is highly discouraged in Yoga unless you have the close, personal guidance of a qualified teacher; the techniques are subtle and can be easily misunderstood, and the energy involved is powerful enough to do damage if it isn't directed properly.)

The Ultimate Goal

Yoga is fairly up front about the ultimate goal of meditation from the outset: a complete dissolution of the ego consciousness into the pure consciousness that is God. This is described as indescribably blissful and liberating. Extremely devout Yoga practitioners strive to release themselves from attachment to their individual material manifestation in any way they can, making all of their life choices—practical and spiritual—with an eye toward living in greater harmony with the reality of universal unity.

However, the goal is not a selfish one aimed at the spiritual release or attainment of the practitioner. Instead, according to Swami Kriyananda, "The closer one's consciousness is to the divine ocean, the more he senses the inner unity of all things, and the more naturally therefore he lives at peace with the universe." Therefore, successful Yoga practitioners are not only identified more and more with pure consciousness, they're also naturally inspired to conduct themselves in a moral way and be of service to others and—through them—to God. They create supportive communities; foster peace within their own families; and bring a calm, loving attitude into their work. You can quickly recognize someone who "senses the inner unity of all beings"; they are attentive and loving to everyone with whom they come in contact.

The Least You Need to Know

- The basic premise of Yoga is that everything in the universe arose out of pure, undifferentiated consciousness, or God—and that the ultimate goal of human life is to seek reunion with God.

- Yoga meditation involves making your mind more still, concentrated, and energized, until you experience consciousness beyond thought and become attuned to the Infinite.

- The many practices and teachings in Yoga—involving physical postures, diet, devotion, chanting, and more—are meant to calm the mind, decrease your attachment to your physical body and material life, and increase your identification with the Infinite.

- While advanced Yoga techniques generally require initiation and a relationship with a guru, even simple beginner's techniques can be very beneficial.

- The ultimate goal of Yoga meditation is the complete dissolution of your ego consciousness into the pure, universal consciousness. Long before you attain the ultimate goal, however, you can have a deeper sense of unity with all of life.

Insight Meditation

While Insight Meditation is grounded in Buddhism, you can practice it regardless of your religious affiliation or lack thereof. The basic premise of Insight Meditation is that you have choice about many aspects of your life, including how pain and difficulty affect you; how much extra stress and suffering you create for yourself; and which kinds of thoughts, emotions, and habits dominate your experience. While it's inevitable your life will be challenging at times, it's possible through conscious and deliberate practice to gain insight into what *really* makes your life better and what doesn't. You can then make wiser decisions about where to put your energy.

In this chapter, I give you a brief introduction to basic Buddhist ideas about the natures of human dissatisfaction and happiness. I also explain the essential role meditation plays in the process of seeing your life more clearly, letting go of the things that cause you suffering, and cultivating the things that makes you truly happy (as well as making you calmer and more compassionate). In addition to a beginner's practice you can try, I offer advice about how to keep developing an Insight Meditation practice over time and the benefits you might experience.

In This Chapter

- What Insight Meditation is and how it relates to Buddhism
- The relationship between mindfulness, concentration, and meditation
- Why insight is important and transformative
- How you can let go of dissatisfaction and suffering
- Achieving inner peace through Insight Meditation

Overview of Insight Meditation

"Insight" is a modern translation of the Buddhist term *Vipassana*, which can also be translated as "clear-seeing"; Vipassana refers specifically to clearly seeing the nature of reality. Clearly seeing reality in a transformative way is what a man named Siddhartha Gautama is believed to have done over 2,500 years ago in India. A spiritual seeker, Gautama wanted to find a way to address the suffering human beings had to face, including pain, illness, old age, death, loss, and having to endure difficulty. Was there anything that could be done?

According to the Buddhist story, Gautama found a way. Through meditation and spiritual practice, he awakened to the true nature of reality and saw how we could be liberated from much of the suffering we experience. Once this happened, he was referred to as Shakyamuni Buddha. (*Shakyamuni* means "sage of the Shakya clan," while *Buddha* means "awakened being.") He taught others the method he had discovered, and this became Buddhism.

Over the millennia, Buddhism spread throughout India and eventually to the rest of Southeast Asia, as well as Nepal, Tibet, and China. From China, the religion was transmitted to Korea and Japan, and over the last century or so, it has spread from all of the countries already mentioned to North and South America and Europe. Insight Meditation traces its origins to *Theravada* Buddhism, or "the way of the elders," which is the form of the religion as it developed in Southeast Asia. Theravada is generally considered the most traditional form of Buddhism in the sense that it most closely resembles how the practice looked at the time of Shakyamuni Buddha.

 **DEFINITION**

Vipassana means "insight" or "clear-seeing," and refers both to a method of meditation and a movement within Buddhism that employs that method. A **buddha** is a being who has awakened to the true nature of reality and thereby attained freedom from suffering. **Theravada,** or "way of the elders," is the most traditional school of Buddhism. It's practiced in Southeast Asia and is the source of modern Insight Meditation.

In the 1960s and 1970s, a number of Americans—including Jack Kornfield, Joseph Goldstein, Ruth Denison, and Sharon Salzberg—went to Southeast Asia to study with Theravadin masters. Some of them even got ordained as monks or nuns and spent time in monasteries there. After their course of study, they returned to the West to share Insight Meditation with others. They founded a number of practice centers that thrive to this day, including the Insight Meditation Society in Massachusetts and Spirit Rock—An Insight Meditation Center in California. Currently, hundreds of meditation groups and practice centers in the West identify themselves as teaching either Vipassana or Insight Meditation.

The Essence of Insight Meditation

So what did the Buddha discover in meditation that can be done about the inevitable suffering we face as human beings? In the midst of deep meditation, which let him see reality clearly, the Buddha saw the incredibly important role your mind plays in creating your experience. He observed within himself that if he used his mind in certain ways, or cultivated certain thoughts or qualities, it would lead to negative results like stress, anger, or dissatisfaction. On the other hand, there were ways to use his mind, and thoughts and qualities he could cultivate, that led to positive results like inner calm, insight, or compassion.

The Nature of Suffering or Dissatisfaction

You might say the Buddha was the ultimate pragmatist who conducted scientific inquiry into his subjective experience and found valuable ways to influence it. One of the most surprising things he discovered was that painful things like illness, death, and loss are really not all that terrible in and of themselves. They can be unpleasant and distressing—even excruciating. But you can add an extra layer of suffering on top of your experience, depending on how you relate to it (that is, how you perceive and deal with things in your mind).

This extra layer of suffering is what the Buddha called *dukkha*, or dissatisfaction. It's sometimes simply translated as "suffering," but that implies dukkha is always a dramatic or acute experience, when it can actually be quite subtle. It's basically your sense of "this isn't right" or "this isn't the way things should be." It may not sound like a big deal but it is. For example, let's say you're driving your old car and you get into a minor accident that damages it. You're insured but very inconvenienced. This is an example of the kind of difficulty you typically encounter in life. While it's not pleasant or easy, maybe you can console yourself with the thought that you were planning to get a new car within the next couple years anyway.

 **DEFINITION**

> **Dukkha** can be translated as "dissatisfaction" or "suffering," and is a Buddhist term referring to the extra distress you add to your experience when you resist the reality of this moment and wish things were different.

Now instead, imagine you've just gotten a shiny and beautiful new car—one you carefully considered buying for a long time and have been anxiously anticipating—and you get into a minor accident that causes damage. Even if you're insured and the damage will be fixed, it's pretty much inevitable that you're going to be more upset than you would be if you were driving an old car. What's the difference between the two situations? Simply how you view them in your mind. In the case of the new car, you're much more likely to add dukkha to your experience by resisting it and thinking "This isn't the way things should be!"

Letting Go of What Causes Suffering

The Buddha's insight didn't end there. He saw not only how you make things much worse by wishing they were different, he also saw how you can learn to change your own mind. You can meditate, practice, and study in order to find out how to let go of wishing things were different. As you probably know, it isn't enough just to think letting go is a good idea or to try to make yourself do it. It takes time and effort to learn more about your own mind and how it works. It takes practice to identify dukkha and learn how to let go.

When you do let go and choose a different course for your mind, the results can be profound. You've probably experienced this for yourself. Think of a time when you were all worked up about something, but then suddenly your thinking changed and there was a great release of extra stress and resistance. Maybe you were worried that someone was avoiding you and then you found out they had been sick. Maybe you were certain someone stole your wallet, but then you found it on the floor where you dropped it. Whatever the scenario, the difficulty of a situation shifted abruptly based on how you were viewing it.

The Path of Practice

Another part of the teaching of the Buddha is a detailed path of practice—instructions for how to study your mind and shift your perspective in a fundamental and wholesome way. It includes teachings about the nature of reality—how we tend to misperceive or misunderstand reality and cause problems for ourselves and others. I've already discussed how we resist the way things are and therefore cause extra anguish for ourselves. Another pivotal misunderstanding is thinking there's a permanent, independent, enduring self-essence inside us somewhere—some "I" who experiences and acts. Instead, your life is actually a boundaryless flow of causes and conditions. When you see this clearly, you can meet each moment more freely and without so much concern about "I," "me," and "mine."

 WATCH OUT

It's easy to assume that not resisting difficult or painful things means just giving up and not trying to make positive changes in your life or in the world. This isn't what is meant by the Buddhist teachings. It's entirely possible to energetically work for change or deal with problems *and* give up any sense that "this isn't the way things should be." That resistance to the reality of the situation just causes dukkha, saps your energy, and distracts you from what needs to be done.

Another teaching central to Insight Meditation is the importance of cultivating mindfulness. Mindfulness is awareness of the present moment without judgment or commentary; it's awareness without thinking. This is the only way for you to see reality directly—without the filters of your concepts and self-concern—and thereby learn how to work with your own mind and make choices that result in less suffering and more happiness. (Note: Mindfulness as discussed in this chapter is essentially the same practice as the secular mindfulness covered in Chapter 12 but with a different practice context. In fact, secular mindfulness arose out of the Vipassana tradition, but tends to be taught free of the more in-depth Buddhist teachings discussed in this chapter.)

Once you have a basic level of concentration and mindfulness built up, you proceed to examine many different aspects of reality in a deep and thorough way. The important objects for your direct mindful contemplation are known as the Four Foundations of Mindfulness:

- **Body:** This includes your physical sensations, movements, bodily functions, aging, illness, and eventual passing. Mindfulness practice starts with the body because it's always available as an object of awareness, and it's grounded in the present moment.

- **Feelings:** Specifically, this refers to your automatic judgments of like, dislike, or neutrality with respect to every experience you have; in this sense, feelings are distinct from more complicated emotions. Noticing your feelings is an important first step in letting go of resistance.

- **Mind states or mental factors:** These are divided into skillful factors that lead to positive results (such as faith, conscience, trust, generosity, and loving-kindness) and unskillful factors that lead to negative results (such delusion, greed, shamelessness, hatred, envy, and regret).

- **Mind objects:** These are the core Buddhist teachings that can lead to insight, including the five hindrances to practice (sensual desire, ill will, sloth, anxiety, and doubt) and the seven factors of enlightenment (mindfulness, investigation, energy, joy, tranquility, concentration, and equanimity).

While the Four Foundations of Mindfulness serve as focal points for your mindfulness, they are also like lenses through which you examine your experience. All of your insight comes, as did Shakyamuni Buddha's, through direct observation of your own mind and life. The resulting insights aren't intellectual understandings of abstract concepts; rather, they're personal and experiential, which result in real changes in how you relate to the world.

The Role of Meditation in Insight

Hopefully it's clear by now how important it is from the Buddhist point of view to see reality clearly. As I mentioned previously, you do this by cultivating mindfulness, or awareness of the present moment without the filter of thinking. The primary way you do this is through meditation. You can certainly try to be mindful at other times, and this is a big part of the practice in Insight Meditation. However, you need to practice mindfulness and concentration during meditation in particular in order to develop the stability of mind to see clearly.

Mindfulness helps you bring your mind back to the present moment, and concentration allows you to hold your awareness on something and look at it deeply without getting distracted. You're probably not used to doing this in a conscious or deliberate way in your daily life, unless you happen to be doing something that naturally holds your interest. You need the space of meditation to contemplate the Four Foundations of Mindfulness in a way that's going to be transformative.

 CONTEMPLATE THIS

> In Vipassana meditation, you basically learn by watching very, very closely and carefully what happens within your own experience. Arinna Weisman and Jean Smith describe this in their book *The Beginner's Guide to Insight Meditation:* "When we meditate, we can see how the mind works and how we react—such as the insight that by pushing away and avoiding discomfort we close down our hearts. Joseph Goldstein's teacher once told him, 'If you want to see how the mind works, sit down [meditate] and watch it.'"

For example, it's not enough to momentarily ponder your feelings of like, dislike, or neutrality; you need to develop sensitivity to them and familiarity with them, so at any given moment you can identify what you're feeling. You need to keep your awareness on your feelings long enough to see them come and go or change. You also need to explore your feelings until you notice a way to acknowledge them while holding a larger perspective, so you aren't pulled around by them. This intensive kind of investigation happens in meditation.

Three Benefits of Insight Meditation

In a sense, you never know what benefit you might get from doing Insight Meditation because you never know what kind of insight you'll end up getting. It could be mundane, such as suddenly seeing clearly why you still let your sister get to you after all these years (which opens up a possibility of working out your unresolved stuff). Alternatively, it might be fairly universal or profound, such as seeing the transformative power of compassion in a clear, vivid, and real way. Here, I share three categories of potential benefits from Insight Meditation.

Liberation from Suffering

In order to gain greater freedom from your sense of dissatisfaction or suffering (dukkha, as discussed earlier), you need to see it more clearly, so you can do something about it. This actually happens in two steps:

1. Seeing that you're feeling dukkha

2. Seeing what's causing you to feel that way

Simply noticing how you're feeling is a significant thing for some people! It can be difficult to acknowledge dukkha as well; either you want other people to think you're feeling great, or you want to believe you're feeling great. Despite any resistance, however, the first step to addressing dukkha is simply to notice it and accept the fact that you're feeling it.

The second step of seeing dukkha more clearly is tracing it back to its source. While your first thought is probably going to be that something external is causing your dukkha, this is incorrect. Something external may be causing you pain and trouble, but dukkha is the extra suffering you layer on top by resisting the reality of the situation. So your dukkha is coming from inside. It usually arises from some idea or expectation you're holding on to, such as "I'm a nice person! They shouldn't treat me that way," or "I take care of my health; I shouldn't be sick." Once you see what's causing your dukkha, you have a choice: either hold on to the cause or let it go. Often, your dukkha will dissipate in a puff of smoke when you finally see the real cause of it—because why would you continue to cause yourself suffering?

The wonderful thing about using Insight Meditation to look at and address your suffering is that as soon as you start the process, you'll already feel some relief. The moment you turn your awareness toward dukkha in a mindful way, you become slightly less identified with it. Your awareness is bigger than your discomfort or unhappiness, and it simply reflects dukkha like a mirror. Just this basic level of objectivity about what you're feeling can be very helpful.

Unconditional Happiness

Insight Meditation helps you personally gain understanding of another fundamental Buddhist teaching: there's no lasting happiness to be gained from the "things of the world." While the phrase *things of the world* may sound disparaging, it really just refers to all the things you can see and touch. All of these things will eventually change or disappear, so you can't count on them forever. It's also the nature of life that you aren't permanently satisfied by sensual or material things.

> **POINT OF CLARIFICATION**
>
> While all aspects of Insight Meditation practice are aimed at increasing your happiness, this isn't a selfish kind of happiness based on pleasure. Instead, it's the kind that naturally makes you a more content and generous person. To quote the Buddha: "All experience is preceded by mind, led by mind, made by mind. Speak or act with a corrupted mind, and suffering follows as the wagon wheel follows the hoof of the ox. All experience is preceded by mind, led by mind, made by mind. Speak or act with a peaceful mind, and happiness follows like a never-departing shadow." (From *The Dhammapada: A New Translation of the Buddhist Classic with Annotations,* by Gil Fronsdal.)

For example, let's say you buy the most comfortable chair in the whole world. You've saved up for it, and you've never before experienced such comfort. When you finally get it, you happily settle into the chair and contemplate the years of comfort ahead of you. You're so content you stay in the chair for hours. After several hours, you actually feel a little uncomfortable. If you stay sitting there for 24 hours, you'll be *very* uncomfortable. And if you stay there for days or weeks, you'll actually end up doing physical damage to yourself. It's not that there's anything wrong with the chair—it's just that you can't rely on it for your happiness.

Likewise, we all tend to look outward for things to make us happy—relationships, money, influence, and pleasurable activities—and wonder why we're eventually left feeling hollow inside. The Buddha said this is because all things are impermanent and can't ultimately be grasped. Things are constantly changing, including us. So if you want to be truly happy, you have to understand and accept this fact. You can then relax into the flow of life and meet each thing as it comes without trying to hold on or find permanent satisfaction in anything external. This actually brings great joy and happiness—an unconditional happiness that comes simply from being alive.

Greater Skillfulness in Your Life

In his book *Insight Meditation: The Practice of Freedom,* Joseph Goldstein explains, "Skillful, in the Buddhist sense, refers to that which leads to happiness, to freedom, and unskillful to that which leads to suffering." If you're like many of us, while you probably do many things in your life that could be considered skillful, you probably also do other things that are unskillful. You mean well, but despite yourself, you continue with actions, speech, or ways of thinking that end up causing problems for yourself or others.

Insight Meditation can help you see more clearly what you're doing and what the effects of your choices are. Sometimes before turning toward your life with mindful awareness, you may be oblivious of certain patterns of behavior you have or of the negative effects you're having on others. Of course, just because you see a problem doesn't necessarily mean it will go away. If it doesn't, it means you need to keep looking at it. When you can eventually trace the string of causes back far enough, you'll find some point in the chain where you can make a different choice and act with more skillfulness.

WATCH OUT

While meditation and mindfulness can sometimes allow you to make substantial changes in your life and behavior, this isn't a process that lends itself to being controlled. If you set out with an agenda to change some particular thing, it's probably not going to happen. However, if you pay attention with an open mind, you'll very likely find things you *can* change for the better.

For example, maybe you get easily triggered into heated arguments with your significant other. With further mindfulness, you may recognize she starts the process by implying you're stupid, and in response you get angry and defensive. Looking even deeper, you may realize your partner's tendency to bait you springs from her own sense of inadequacy, and suddenly a possibility occurs to you: when she implies you're stupid, you can summon a sense of compassion for her and try to communicate in some way that you respect her. While this may not always work, you may have found the one point in the behavioral cycle where you could do something different and break the pattern.

Modern Insight Meditation

Insight Meditation can take many forms, depending on your experience level with meditation and the purpose of the meditation. However, keep in mind that this kind of meditation is done in a very open-handed way, usually without a clear agenda. While greater mindfulness, concentration, and insight are always general goals, it's more like you settle into a state of calm, direct perception, as opposed to striving to figure out something during your meditation. An insight may occur, or it may not. Your greatest insight might even be about your own impatience or desire for understanding or change.

General Description of the Method

In Insight Meditation, you choose a meditative object and then keep your awareness on that object throughout your meditation as closely as you can. When your mind wanders, you simply bring your awareness back to your chosen object. Throughout this effort to concentrate, you maintain a mindful attitude and simply observe whatever is happening in your meditation without judging or analyzing it and without getting caught up in the stories you're likely to tell about your experience.

In order to do this kind of meditation in a deep and effective way, you need both mindfulness and concentration. Mindfulness allows you to notice when you're caught up in thinking and to shift your awareness back to your present reality. Concentration is the power behind your meditation; it allows you to focus in on a particular object, observe it at a deeper level than a superficial one, and keep your attention there for a sustained period. Some of the things you'll be contemplating as part of the Four Foundations of Mindfulness, such as the presence or absence of anxiety in your mind, are fairly subtle and will probably require more concentrated awareness than you're used to employing.

The Theory Behind the Meditation

To develop mindfulness and concentration in Insight Meditation, you go through a systematic process of training by using various objects in your meditation. The process of development usually starts by meditating on your breathing. This is a rich practice that can teach you a great deal, and it's very grounding. You then proceed through other meditations based in the body. Once you've achieved a certain level of stability of mind doing this, you'll move on to feelings and the other objects within the Four Foundations of Mindfulness. It's not necessary for you to study them all in order, and you might end up with an insight about your emotions or about the Buddhist teachings at any time—even early in your meditation practice.

 POINT OF CLARIFICATION

The insights you get through Insight Meditation aren't intellectual. Instead, they're perceived intuitively through your direct mindful experience of the present moment. Essentially, you can look within for insight into all important spiritual questions because you're part of the universe and connected to all other beings. Your sense that you're a separate, independent self is partly an illusion (one about which you can gain insight through meditation). So the Buddhist theory goes, you can explore universal questions—such as the nature of suffering or compassion—within the "laboratory" of your own body and mind.

Generally speaking, however, you progress through the Four Foundations—body, feelings, mind states, and mind objects—because each one gets a little more challenging and presents more of a temptation to involve your discriminating mind. The point is to observe reality from a still, mindful state in which you simply reflect what's going on without analyzing it, judging it, or commenting on it. This is difficult enough to do when you're concentrating on your breathing; it gets more challenging when you're meditating on your mental state (which you'll be tempted to judge or change) or on something like tranquility (which you're supposed to examine in your own experience rather than think about in an abstract way).

Beginner's Meditation Instructions

The path of Insight Meditation is a fairly flexible one, so you're encouraged to find out what works for you. If you're trying something—a posture, a particular meditation, or an approach to concentration—and it doesn't seem to be effective, go ahead and adjust it. Basically, if something helps you stay present and concentrate, that's great. In fact, paying close-enough attention to your own mind that you can tell what works for you is also strengthening your mindfulness.

As a beginner, you may want to listen to guided meditations at first, like the one included online at idiotsguides.com/meditation. Guided Insight Meditations tend to be very simple and basically just walk you through a meditation you could do on your own. Many people find listening helps them stay focused and gives them a sense of what meditative stillness feels like. Eventually, however, if you want to keep developing your mindfulness and concentration, you probably want to try meditating on your own.

Setting and Posture

In order to aid in concentration, it's best to meditate in a quiet place where you won't be interrupted. However, if you can't escape some noise, that's fine—just include it in your meditation as another thing to be aware of in the present moment. If you can designate a special place for meditation, it can help you get into the mindset but it isn't necessary.

Any of the seated postures described in Chapter 2 will work for Insight Meditation. While you should be comfortable enough that you can relax, take a position where you can also stay awake and alert. However you position your body, try to keep your back nice and straight; don't lean back on anything unless you really need to. You can then place your hands neatly on your lap. Lightly close your eyes to help minimize distraction from your surroundings; however, if you're drowsy, you can meditate with your eyes slightly open but angled downward toward a spot about 3 feet in front of you on the wall or floor.

Basic Practice

To help focus your meditation and gather energy for it, you may want to make a statement of intention before you begin your meditation. You might say something to yourself like "I take this time to settle into my life and see things clearly" or "May my practice awaken great compassion in me."

If you aren't familiar with this meditation, you may need to read part of the instructions, pause to follow them, and then read a bit more. Alternatively, you can listen to the guided meditation included along with this book at idiotsguides.com/meditation. Get into your meditation posture, take a few deep breaths, and follow these instructions, taking your time with each one to explore it fully:

1. Become aware of your breathing. Notice whether your inhalations and exhalations are short or long, without trying to change your breathing in any way.

2. In time with the motions of your breathing, say silently to yourself, "Breathing in, I breathe a long breath. Breathing out, I breathe a long breath." If a particular inhalation and exhalation is short, however, say "Breathing in, I breathe a short breath. Breathing out, I breathe a short breath." Make these observations as gently and objectively as you can.

3. Observe your breathing in this way for the next five minutes (or longer, if you want to). Watch your breathing as if it were someone else's, and try to let go of judgments about your breath or your meditation. Continue to say silently "Breathing in, I breathe a long (or short) breath. Breathing out, I breathe a long (or short) breath."

4. If your mind wanders, simply turn your attention back to your breathing. See how deeply you can relax, so your breathing is natural and free. Observe your tendency to want to make your breath longer or shorter. But don't fight with that impulse; just observe it. Simply watching your breath is a very simple activity, and your mind will want to leap away from doing it. Try to allow yourself to be very simple.

5. Let go of your verbal observations and take note of all the places in your body where you feel sensations related to breathing. Notice the coolness in your nose or mouth as air enters and the warmth as it exits. Also notice sensations of stretching or energy in your chest, abdomen, shoulders, neck, arms, and lower body. Notice the changes throughout your body as you breathe.

6. For the next several minutes (or longer, if you want to), make breathing something you're doing with your whole body in an open, experiential way. Feel how there's actually no boundary around your awareness of breathing.

7. If you notice your mind wandering, try to take interest in your breathing and in your living experience of the present moment. When you need to return your awareness to your breathing, do so as gently as possible. Minimize any internal judgment or reaction, and simply let your breathing fill your awareness. Notice how complex the process of breathing really is, and try to observe it so closely you don't miss anything about it.

8. For the last few minutes of your meditation, see if you can let go of your sense of an "I" who's separate from your breathing. Don't worry about whether you're meditating correctly because this only brings up a sense of "I." Breathing is the most natural thing in the world, so just allow it to happen. Just breathe wholeheartedly, as if it's the most satisfying and interesting activity in the world.

It's best to set some kind of pleasant-sounding timer to end your meditation (unless you're listening to a guided meditation, of course). If you use a timer, you won't be as likely to think about what time it is while you're meditating, and you won't be deciding at each moment how long you want to meditate. During whatever length of time you've decided on (10 to 30 minutes is recommended), just relax into the meditation as best you can.

Additional Guidance and Encouragement

Many people find meditation to be an enjoyable thing to do. Others always find meditation challenging but continue to do it because of the positive benefits it has. Regardless of whether you find meditation pleasant or not, it's not always easy. You may find it frustrating to follow the meditation instructions and wonder whether you're meditating well enough to make any difference. You may also find your mind wanders relentlessly, constantly turning to thoughts of the past, future, or things going on elsewhere. Fortunately, there are established ways of dealing with these challenges because you're definitely not the first person to experience them.

Not Trying to Make Things Different

In Insight Meditation, your goal is to perceive reality directly with mindful awareness. You want to reflect it like a mirror without biasing your perception with extra thinking and analysis and without trying make things different. Your typical mode of operation is to grasp after the things you like (or you think are good or right) and try to get rid of things you don't like (or you think are bad or wrong). It's easy to bring this same approach into meditation with you and start trying to make your meditation into what you want it to be or think it should be. Ironically, if you want to meditate well, you have to let go of consciously, willfully trying to make your meditation different from what it is.

 **WATCH OUT**

Be patient with yourself. It takes time to build up mindfulness and concentration, and it's common for beginners to be unable to closely follow even one full breath (inhalation and exhalation) without their mind wandering! Eventually, you'll find yourself settling into a stability of mind where thoughts and feelings come and go within your field of awareness and don't disturb you so much.

Instead of striving to make your meditation better, simply include whatever is going on—a wandering mind, anxiety, restlessness, physical discomfort—in your awareness. Rather than trying to get rid of a problem or ignore it, actually turn your mind toward it and examine it with mindful curiosity. Note I said *mindful*. This isn't about analysis of what's wrong so you can fix it; this is about seeing more clearly. If your mind is wandering, where is it going—the future or the past? Don't get involved in the content; just notice. If you're experiencing pain, where is the pain? Is it intense, dull, or throbbing? Do you feel it in a small or large area? Can you relax around the pain? Often, when you turn the light of awareness on whatever is "wrong" in your meditation, it loses its ability to distract you.

Realizing Not All Insights Are Pleasant

It can help you stay committed to the process of meditation if you remember that some of the insights you gain from it can be humbling or even—at least temporarily—distressing. Sometimes new meditators wonder if the practice isn't working for them because instead of feeling happier, wiser, and calmer, they seem to feel more agitated, dissatisfied, and stuck in habits. Of course, it's not that meditation has made things worse; it's just that the new meditator has become more aware of what's actually been going on for some time.

While facing difficult truths about your life and the world is never an easy or pleasant process, it's the first step toward change. In Insight Meditation, the biggest things that interfere with your ability to achieve deeper spiritual insight and happiness are called the five hindrances: desire (making your happiness dependent on things you don't yet have), ill will, sloth or torpor, restlessness, and doubt. When you discover these hindrances in your meditation or in the rest of your life, it's an opportunity to see more clearly what's going on and potentially find a way to make positive changes.

Deepening Your Insight Meditation

The practice of Insight Meditation can be lifelong. As is the case with most forms of meditation, you can benefit from doing it occasionally. Alternatively, you can intensively train to deepen your meditation and insight or do anything in between casual and intense practice. Insight Meditation is also part of the Buddhist tradition; if you prefer, you can practice it without engaging with Buddhism much at all. But if you're so inclined, you can explore the teachings and practices that have been associated with Insight Meditation for over 2,000 years.

Other Supportive Practices

One of the main supportive practices in Insight Meditation is keeping to the five precepts or moral guidelines. The precepts are very practical; the idea is that you create disharmony in your life when you break them. This not only causes suffering for you and others, it agitates your mind and makes it more difficult to cultivate mindfulness and concentration. So Insight Meditation students generally agree to do their best to refrain from killing (this doesn't necessarily mean not eating meat but rather cultivating a reverence for all life), stealing (practicing nonharming and generosity instead), false speech, sexual misconduct (treating others with respect), and heedless use of intoxicants.

> **POINT OF CLARIFICATION**
>
> Part of the reason morality is an important part of Buddhist practice is that it reflects the behavior of a buddha, or an awakened being. When you gain insight into the nature of reality, you realize you're not actually separate from anyone else. (You're an individual *and* part of something greater at the same time, like a leaf on a tree.) Therefore, when you act in ways that benefit yourself at the expense of others, you're reinforcing your sense of separation rather than preparing your mind for deeper insight into the way things really are.

Other effective ways to deepen your Insight Meditation are to practice with a community and find a teacher. The importance of having the positive moral support of others in your practice has been acknowledged since the time of the Buddha 2,500 years ago. Getting meditation instruction from a teacher can also be valuable, especially when you can ask questions and get personalized advice. In Insight Meditation, a teacher is considered a spiritual friend—someone with more experience than you who can provide some perspective and encouragement as you walk your own path.

Attending Meditation Retreats

The most common way to deepen your Insight Meditation is to sit more often and for longer periods of time. A challenging and effective way to do this is to attend a formal meditation retreat. People usually find meditation retreats to be daunting and difficult but also deeply rewarding. At the very least, you have a chance to work on your meditation in very concentrated way!

Meditation retreats last from 1 to 10 days but are more typically 5 to 7 days. Most retreats are residential and conducted in almost complete silence with a 24-hour schedule. Everyone keeps the schedule, and each day includes about eight hours of meditation, an hour or two of silent work practice, time to listen to teachings, silent communal meals, and short breaks. You can look online to see if any meditation retreats are being held near you, but keep in mind that many practitioners travel some distance to attend them.

Learning More

If you live in a major city, chances are good there's an Insight Meditation or Vipassana center or group near you. Even if you don't intend to practice with a community for a prolonged period, you may be able to attend a workshop or meeting where you can learn more about Insight Meditation and how to do it. Such groups will usually also have teachers or senior students who can refer you other resources or tell you where to attend a retreat. The Buddhist Insight Network (buddhistinsightnetwork.org) maintains a searchable listing of Insight Meditation and Vipassana groups that you may find useful.

You can also learn more about Insight Meditation through the Insight Meditation Society (dharma.org), or read one or more of the following books: *The Beginner's Guide to Insight Meditation* by Arinna Weisman and Jean Smith; *Insight Meditation: The Practice of Freedom* by Joseph Goldstein; or *A Path with Heart: A Guide Through the Perils and Promises of Spiritual Life* by Jack Kornfield.

Insight Meditation Over a Lifetime

The goal of Insight Meditation is to steadily practice throughout your life and continually develop into a happier, better-adjusted person. While this may sound simple, the implications of it are profound. When you're happier—and your happiness arises from a deeper, unconditional source, as discussed earlier in this chapter—you're naturally more at peace and more generous, patient, and kind. When you're well-adjusted, it means you know how to live your life effectively without causing suffering for yourself and others. When you can do this, you're going to tend to be more successful in everything you do.

"Ideal" Insight Meditation

Over time, your Insight Meditation can become more and more concentrated. While that doesn't mean it will *always* be deep or focused, you'll find you're able to settle into a state of open, alert, and mindful awareness more easily and more often. The more you meditate, the more likely this stability of mind is going to develop. However, it's also important to remember that this concentrated meditative state isn't necessarily free of thoughts. Ideally, you become centered in attentive receptivity, where all phenomena can arise and fall without causing you to react or get drawn into thinking about them—including physical sensations, thoughts, and emotions.

 WATCH OUT

It's tempting to think that a successful meditation practice will mean you're always calm and happy. Even after you've become very familiar with mindful awareness and gotten a fair amount of insight into your life, you'll still experience things like anger, disappointment, pain, and grief. However, this is not as bad as it sounds; you end up relating to your experiences in a way that allows you to "go with the flow" with an overarching grace and equanimity. The storms of life tend to pass more quickly.

Deeper insight usually happens when you can not only sustain mindful awareness but also concentrate to some extent. Again, while this doesn't usually mean an absolute absence of thoughts or distractions, it does mean you can direct your mind where you want to and then keep it there long enough to see more clearly and deeply. And whatever you're contemplating—from something as personal and mundane as your troubles with a coworker, to something as universal as the nature of lasting happiness—you can then discern the truth at a deeper level than you could with your ordinary, discriminating mind.

The Ultimate Goal

Ultimately, Insight Meditation becomes a way you live, not just a practice you do. The spirit of inquiry can be brought into every aspect of your life, making all of it part of your spiritual journey. While formal meditation always remains important, ideally you become more able to function with mindful awareness at any time. This allows you to see everything and everyone more clearly and therefore live more in harmony with the truth. Because you don't want to suffer, when you see clearly that something you do causes suffering, you naturally want to stop doing it. You're actually not separate from anything or anyone, so when they suffer, you suffer—meaning compassion and generosity arise naturally.

At the deepest level of insight, you recognize in a very personal, transformative way that you don't have to grasp after the things you want and push away the things you don't. You see clearly how this causes you stress, anguish, and suffering. You know an alternative: allowing everything in your life, whether pleasant, unpleasant, or neutral, to arise and pass away. You also discover how to act effectively and freely as you take care of yourself and your responsibilities without resisting reality. A great joy arises simply in being alive, and you live with a growing equanimity and acceptance.

The Least You Need to Know

- While there are many difficult things in life you can't do anything about, you *can* do something about your own mind. Whether you feel suffering or happiness depends largely on how you view your experiences and relate to your thoughts and emotions.

- The tradition of Insight Meditation, grounded in Buddhism, contains countless teachings and practices about how to work with your mind so you can live your life more skillfully and happily.

- If you simply see reality clearly, you'll notice when you're causing suffering for yourself or others, and you'll naturally want to change.

- Another important thing to see clearly is the fact that there's no lasting happiness to be found in external things. While you can certainly enjoy them while you have them, it's possible to find an unconditional source of joy and happiness within.

- The key to seeing clearly is developing mindfulness and concentration so you can perceive reality without the filters of self-concern and discriminative thinking. These abilities are developed primarily through meditation.

Zen Meditation

Meditation is central in the Zen Buddhist tradition. In fact, *Zen* actually means "meditation," because meditation is considered the primary method by which you achieve peace of mind, deeper understanding of yourself, and transformative insight into the nature of reality. If you're reading the chapters of this book in order, all of this may sound familiar! In the last chapter, I introduced you to Insight Meditation, another form of Buddhism in which both meditation and insight are considered essential. In this chapter, I focus on teachings, approaches, and practices that are particular to Zen. Although all of the Buddhist meditative traditions have a great deal in common, they differ significantly in flavor and emphasis.

One of the neat things about Zen is the actual process of Zen meditation is very simple. Although this kind of meditation doesn't involve complicated instructions or techniques, those who practice it regularly report that it has a profoundly positive effect on their lives. This chapter gives you everything you need to know in order to try Zen meditation.

In This Chapter

- How Zen meditation leads to liberation
- Accessing greater calm and perspective
- Instructions for "just sitting" meditation
- Tips for settling your mind in meditation
- The Zen goal of a wholehearted life

Overview of Zen

Zen is a kind of Buddhism that arose around the sixth century in China. (An overview of Buddhism in general can be found in Chapter 5.) By the time Zen arose, a number of forms of Buddhism existed in which teachers emphasized the study of scriptures, rituals, chanting, and bowing, among other things. The founders of the Zen school wanted to return to the basic form, at least as they saw it: meditation. After all, they reasoned, that's how Shakyamuni Buddha attained enlightenment. In China, this new school of Buddhism was called *Ch'an,* and it eventually spread and became well-established in Korea, Vietnam, and Japan.

CONTEMPLATE THIS

While different schools of Zen throughout the world are called by various names, they are all translations (or transliterations) of the ancient pre-Buddhist Pali word for meditation, *dhyana.* In China, this became *Ch'an;* in Korea, *Seon;* in Vietnam, *Thiền;* and in Japan, *Zen.*

Zen eventually traveled to Europe and North America with Asian immigrants, but an event of note was the formal introduction of Zen to westerners by Soyen Shaku at the World Parliament of Religions in Chicago in 1893. After this, a fair number of people started exploring Zen who had not been born into the religion. However, it wasn't until the 1950s and 1960s that major Zen centers were established in the West that were primarily for convert practitioners. Now, there's at least one Zen center in most major cities in the United States, and many practice places have been established throughout North, Central, and South America, as well as in Europe.

The Essence of Zen

Like all forms of Buddhism, Zen has freedom from suffering as its ultimate goal. However, as discussed in Chapter 5, it's important to note that while *suffering* can refer to obvious, acute distress in Buddhism, it can also refer to subtle, pervasive dissatisfaction, such as a vague sense of meaninglessness in your life.

From the Buddhist point of view, you can't do much to avoid pain in this life because you will inevitably experience loss, difficulty, old age, illness, and death. However, it turns out that pain is not as terrible as you might think. Typically, you add an extra layer of suffering to your pain because of how you react negatively to it. (See "The Nature of Suffering or Dissatisfaction" in Chapter 5 for more discussion of this phenomenon.) While all forms of Buddhism share this view of suffering, what follows are particularly Zen takes on the nature of human life and the path to greater happiness.

The Emptiness of Self

According to Buddhist teachings, your primary reason for reacting negatively to things is your self-concern. You not only end up wanting to defend your own well-being and that of your loved ones, you also worry quite a lot about taking care of everything you identify with in some way. This provokes endless stress.

 WATCH OUT

The Zen concept of emptiness can be easily misunderstood. When you read that "everything is empty," it may sound like Zen is teaching that all things (and people) are ultimately meaningless, hollow, or mechanistic—or, even worse, that nothing really exists. What the teaching of emptiness is really saying is that all things are empty of inherent, enduring, independent self-nature. Things and beings still exist in a vibrant and very real way, just without any inner, unchanging essence.

In Zen practice, while you need to make a conscious effort to be less self-concerned and to minimize your negative reactions, the primary means of liberation from self-concern is gaining personal, experiential insight into the fact that everything—including you—is impermanent and interdependent with everything else. Who you are constantly changes over the course of the day and your life, so there's really no unchanging essence you can identify within yourself and hold on to. You're only who you are because of your relationships with everything else—the air, the earth, your parents who gave birth to you, and so on—and therefore the state of your life is intimately tied to the state of everything around you. Therefore, there's no inherent, independent "you" to protect; there's just an unfolding of circumstances in your life you can either meet wholeheartedly and thoughtfully or not. The experience of real insight into this frees you from bondage to self-concern and gives you much greater equanimity and compassion in your daily life.

Liberation Through Insight

Zen has been called a tradition passed from generation to generation "outside the scriptures." This essentially means that, while Zen has many teachings, your liberation from suffering— your enlightenment—isn't dependent on knowing those teachings (although they may help). All you actually need to do is wake up to reality; the answers you need are already there in your own experience. Your tendency is to search for happiness or resolution to your problems either by trying to change your circumstances or by trying to figure things out with your discriminating mind. While sometimes this works, as discussed in Chapter 1, it's possible to perceive deeper truths in a direct, intuitive way that doesn't depend on ordinary thinking.

However, even though the answers are right in front of you, you still need to do some kind of spiritual practice, because "waking up to reality" isn't so easy. A classic Buddhist image is that your true nature is like a clear sky obscured by clouds. The clouds are of your own making, consisting of things like your preferences, delusions, preconceptions, habits, and reactions. In Zen practice, you don't fight with these clouds to get rid of them. Instead, you pay close attention to your life and learn to see your preferences, delusions, preconceptions, habits, and reactions for what they really are—phenomena in your life, without any inherent, enduring reality to them. After a time, you're able to see past these "clouds" in order to perceive reality directly.

The Role of Meditation in Zen

In Zen, meditation is revered as the practice through which you wake up to reality and see clearly. This may sound dramatic—and at times it can be—but most of the time you're simply waking up to this moment, and then the next moment, and then the next. You might experience a particular moment as blissful, boring, exciting, dull, mundane, remarkable, annoying, or pleasant. The point isn't to attain some kind of preferable state but to become aware of what's actually happening. Seeing clearly can lead to a big insight ("My self-nature is actually empty!") or a small one ("Hmm … I think I'm a little depressed today.")

Zen meditation techniques are primarily about helping your mind to settle and then to focus. It's like your mind is a pail of muddy water; with Zen meditation, you hold it still so the mud can gradually settle out of the water until it's completely clear and you can see straight to bottom. The goal is to uncover or recognize what's already there, as opposed to making a deliberate effort to improve or change yourself. While you may at times work very hard in Zen meditation, ultimately it's more about *not doing* than it is about *doing* anything.

Three Benefits of Zen Meditation

The Zen school of Buddhism isn't fond of listing the benefits of meditation, especially not as a way of encouraging you to meditate. This is because the effort to achieve a particular benefit generally gets in the way of your very important effort at *not doing*, which was mentioned as a good description of Zen meditation. However, this reticence about pointing out the benefits of Zen meditation doesn't mean Zen lacks any!

 WATCH OUT

As you should when doing any form of meditation, take care of yourself. If something powerful or troubling arises in your meditation, seek support from friends, counselors, or meditation teachers. This doesn't mean you shouldn't meditate; it just means you may need to take some time to process or integrate something meditation helped uncover.

A Greater Sense of Calm

You're likely to find that after sitting Zen meditation, you feel calmer, and for many people this effect lasts throughout the day. You'll probably feel less triggered and reactive in the face of challenges. It's like meditation gives you greater sanity or increases your ability to function in a healthy and rational way.

Some people describe the calm that results from Zen meditation as arising from the ability to take a greater perspective. For example, when your toddler dumps his food on the floor, instead of getting swept up in anger or frustration because of the mess, you might end up seeing the episode as a minor annoyance in your mostly rewarding journey as a parent. This calm perspective-taking isn't an intellectual exercise; it's a spontaneous response grounded in a recent experience of meditation.

Opting Out of Dysfunctional Patterns

In Zen meditation, you dedicate time to letting go of mental elaboration and commentary in order to return your awareness to what's going on right here, right now. When you practice doing this over and over, you develop more freedom of choice when it comes to what your mind is doing. You learn how to disrupt stressful, repetitive, or dysfunctional trains of thought. You become more familiar with basic awareness of here and now, and you learn to notice and appreciate what's actually going on in your life.

If even one time you manage to let go and step out of a particularly compelling or habitual cycle of thoughts or emotions, you are forever changed. Part of you knows the cycle isn't mandatory; you have some choice about whether to participate. For example, you might occasionally become overwhelmed with irrational jealousy and feel twisted up inside with insecurity and self-doubt. With some experience in meditation, however, you may be able to step outside the pattern for a moment and observe, "Oh, that again! That just hurts and rarely ends up being justified." One day, you might simply refuse to take the next step in the cycle, and be free from it.

Deeper Knowledge of Yourself

After hours spent in Zen meditation, you end up getting pretty familiar with your own mind. You won't always like or enjoy what you see there, but generally speaking, it's always better to know the truth than to walk around in ignorance! You'll learn whether you resist sitting still, where your mind goes (past, future, or fantasy), what you're anxious about, who you're resentful of—the list is endless. If you can simply notice these things about yourself with a minimum of judgment, a possibility opens up for you to learn to live your own life more skillfully. You might notice when you're starting to get depressed and be able to take measures to mitigate the depression. You might also recognize your level of worry about your intimate relationship and then devote some time and energy to taking care of it.

At a deeper level, the space and silence of Zen meditation can sometimes allow things to arise and manifest in surprising ways. If there's something you've been denying or suppressing, chances are it will try to find its way into your consciousness in meditation at some point, although perhaps not in an obvious way. For example, you may have been denying a deep sense of grief within yourself and then suddenly find yourself—apparently inexplicably—crying during your meditation. (If you keep exploring such a phenomenon, you'll usually find out what's behind it.) It's worth remaining open to what you might learn about yourself in meditation and trying to have confidence that a path of growth will open up if you simply shine the light of awareness on what you've discovered.

Meditation in the Soto Zen Lineage

In this chapter, I focus on *shikantaza,* or themeless Zen meditation. This is the main type of meditation in the *Soto* lineage of Zen, which arose in China in the ninth century and is the largest Zen sect in Japan. Shikantaza is a fairly straightforward type of Zen meditation to try on your own.

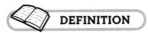 **DEFINITION**

Shikantaza is a kind of Zen meditation known as themeless meditation or "just precisely sitting." The **Soto** school of Zen Buddhism is the largest sect of Zen in Japan and traditionally employs themeless meditation.

General Description of the Method

All you're trying to do in Soto Zen meditation is be completely present with exactly what's happening this very moment. One literal translation of the Japanese term *shikantaza* is "just precisely sitting." When you're doing shikantaza, all you're doing is sitting there. You're not trying to get anything done, figure anything out, or achieve anything. The point is to do this extremely simple activity with energy, attention, and wholeheartedness. You're not just sitting around the way you usually do; you're just sitting *precisely.*

If this sounds confusing or vague, don't worry. Learning what it *really* means to just precisely sit—or just precisely do anything in your life—is part of the whole process of Zen meditation. There are techniques to help you. However, it's important to know from the outset that perfect Zen meditation isn't a special skill. Instead, it's the basic human condition of being present and aware, and is instantly available to you at any time. If I ask you to be aware of your hand, you are. No problem! Problems only arise because you don't know how to recognize, rest in, or be satisfied with your simple, direct experience of life.

The Theory Behind the Meditation

There's a Buddhist teaching about the nature of your mind that's very useful when learning to do Zen meditation. It says you have three different levels of mental activity. The first is pure perception; the second is naming and categorizing; and the third is elaboration, commentary, and abstraction.

I'll illustrate with an example. At the level of pure perception, your mind registers a sound. Your mind quickly jumps to the second level of activity when you identify the sound as that of a barking dog or as your neighbor's barking dog. Typically, you then enter the third level of mental activity as you think, "That's annoying; I'm trying to meditate! I should say something to my neighbor. Maybe I should get on the neighborhood committee, but I'm too busy. My job is so stressful right now. Maybe I should get a different job, but I really can't afford to ...."

You're probably very familiar with how long your mind can stay on a train of thought in the third level of mental activity! You may spend much of your day caught up in elaboration, commentary, and abstraction of various kinds. It's rare for people to spend prolonged time in the first and second levels of pure perception and simple naming and categorizing, even though that's where they're directly experiencing what's going on in their life at the moment. Motivations like fear and excitement tend to inspire you to analyze the past and anticipate the future instead of paying attention to the here and now.

In Zen meditation, you devote time to letting go of the third level of mental activity in order to return to the level of pure perception, or the second level of very basic naming or categorizing. This allows your mind to settle somewhat because it isn't being pulled around by long trains of thought. At a deeper level, this gives your poor mind a rest and allows you to get more in sync with what's actually going on around you.

Beginner's Meditation Instructions

You don't need any special equipment or preparation to try themeless Zen meditation. All you have to do is sit in a way that allows you to be comfortable but alert and then allow yourself to *be*. Still, you can increase your chances of enjoying your meditation if you keep the following suggestions in mind.

Setting and Posture

Traditionally, Zen meditation is done facing a wall or an open space large enough to allow your gaze to rest on the floor about 3 or 4 feet in front of you. Otherwise, to find a good place to sit, follow the suggestions for a good setting for silent meditation found in Chapter 2.

Zen meditation is also traditionally done in a seated position. In fact, Zen meditation is usually referred to as *zazen,* or "seated meditation." A comfortable seated position is preferable in order to keep your body as still as possible. Physical stillness helps your mind to settle down because the mind tends to follow what the body does. While you don't need to force yourself into stillness in a rigid way that causes discomfort, you should try to resist minor urges to fidget. Rather than scratching the slightest itch or rubbing your hands together to relieve restlessness, it helps to watch the urges to move arise and pass away without acting on them. It can be liberating just to realize this is possible.

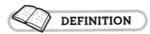 **DEFINITION**

Zazen, created out of the Japanese characters *za* (meaning "seated") and *zen* (meaning "meditation"), simply refers to seated Zen meditation.

Any of the seated postures described in Chapter 2 will work. You can sit cross-legged on the floor, on a meditation bench, or in a chair. If you get drowsy or experience pain, it's also possible to stand (again, staying as still as possible), although a seated position is generally more stable and grounded.

Keeping Your Eyes Open

It helps to learn how to do Zen meditation with your eyes open. Many people find this challenging, at least at first, but it's worth persevering in the effort until you get used to it (and you will). While it can feel calming to close your eyes, this tends to compromise your alertness. It also encourages you to draw your awareness inward and create a stronger sense of self (there's "you" inside your body and "the rest of the world" out there). One of the goals of zazen is to decrease the sense of separation between yourself and the world, so it helps to keep your eyes open if you can.

Your eyes should be directed downward at an approximately 45-degree angle, your eyelids should be relaxed, and your gaze soft and somewhat unfocused (as opposed to staring fixedly at one point). Ideally, wherever your eyes rest should be visually neutral; avoid looking at books, landscapes, or elaborate patterns while meditating.

Basic Practice

Dedicate a certain length of time for zazen. Thirty minutes is good for allowing your mind to settle, but any amount of time can be beneficial. Sit for anywhere between 5 and 40 minutes, depending on the time you have available and your willingness. You may want to set a timer (one with a pleasant sound) to indicate when the meditation period is over, so you don't have keep looking at the clock. With your time set, you can use the following steps as a general guide-line for your meditation (you can find an audio version of this meditation on idiotsguides.com/meditation):

1. Become aware of the here and now. This is very easy to do. It's not a special skill; it's completely natural. What's not necessarily easy is staying aware of the here and now. Once you realize nothing special is going on, your mind will want to leap away into the past, future, or abstraction. In this meditation, you'll want to keep your awareness in the present. To do this, gently settle your awareness on something you can perceive directly.

2. You may want to cultivate an awareness of your breathing without trying to change your breathing in any way. Simply notice your inhalations and exhalations. Alternatively, you may want to cultivate awareness of sounds. Notice all of the sounds around and within you; let them arise and pass within your field of awareness without commenting on them.

3. You can also become aware of whatever is in your visual field, noticing light, shapes, textures, and any subtle movements. Or you can bring awareness to your physical presence.

4. Whatever you're paying attention to, simply rest in your experience of the present moment. This is all you'll do throughout this meditation. You're aiming to be fully present for your life.

5. Notice when you've gotten caught up in the third level of mental activity (commentary, elaboration, or abstraction). Simply notice without adding any judgment of or reactivity to this fact. As soon as you become aware of such mental activity, you're already aware of the present moment. Take a second or two to feel grateful about this.

6. Encourage yourself to stay in the present by gently shifting your awareness to something you can perceive in your body or in your environment. Notice your tendency to dismiss your current, simple experience as boring or unimportant. Remind yourself that you've never experienced this moment before, and you'll never experience it again.

7. Continue practicing awareness of your present experience and watch your desire to think about something exciting or pleasurable instead. Or notice your compulsion to worry about something that isn't actually happening right now. Give yourself permission to let go of all thoughts and concerns and simply rest.

8. Each time you notice your mind has wandered off again, you're already back in the present moment. The present moment includes your thoughts and emotions, how you feel about your meditation, and any restlessness or drowsiness you may be experiencing. Just allow these things to be as they are.

9. Notice whether you feel any resistance to this meditation, because you want to be doing something useful. That's a natural desire, but the value of meditation is that it invites you to set aside all agendas for the time being. Let yourself be completely useless for the remainder of this meditation.

10. Let your awareness of your chosen meditation subject—breathing, sound, sight, or your physical presence—deepen. Observe it closely and carefully, as if it's infinitely complex and interesting. If you find it difficult to focus on one meditation subject, let your awareness be as wide open as possible. Simply notice whatever is most salient—sound, light, warmth, coolness, or even a thought. Try not to miss anything.

11. Continue with whatever method of staying present works for you. Focus your awareness on something that's happening here and now, letting go of everything else, or keep your awareness as wide open as possible. Over and over, bring your awareness patiently back to the present moment.

Do this basic practice over and over for the length of your meditation. That's it! The very simplicity of this activity is a large part of why it's effective at reducing stress and calming the mind.

Additional Guidance and Encouragement

Zen meditation techniques are about counteracting the habit of your mind to get caught up in elaborative thinking, such as rumination, planning, fantasizing, evaluation, and commentary. It's essential to remember that what you're aiming for is the basic human condition of being present and aware, and you can instantly be that way at any time. Zazen is not about getting good at any particular technique or achieving some kind of special state of concentration. Still, it helps immensely to have some guidance to help you let go of your tendency to dwell in mental elaboration, commentary, and abstraction.

Concentration vs. Expansive Awareness

You may find the conscious effort to concentrate only agitates your mind further. Don't give up right away; some degree of concentration is a valuable skill. However, it isn't the main point of Zen meditation. If you find it difficult or frustrating to concentrate on a single object, it may help you to know that you can use any object of meditation in a concentrated way or in a gentler, more expansive way.

> **POINT OF CLARIFICATION**
>
> In zazen it's possible to be aware of your thoughts and emotions in the same detached but receptive way that you are aware of your breathing, sounds, or other sensations. Observing thoughts and emotions in the stillness of zazen lets you notice how changeable they are, and you start to identify less with the content of your mind and more with the space through which the content moves. However, it is not recommended that you use thoughts and emotions as objects in your zazen when you are first beginning your practice, because it's easy to get caught up in them when you're not yet familiar with the still, observing function of your mind.

For example, if you're bringing your awareness back to your breathing, you can use concentration by trying to cultivate an intimate awareness of the whole breathing process: inhalation, a little pause at the end of the inhalation, exhalation, a little pause at the end of the exhalation, and repeat. Some people even count their exhalations from 1 to 10 and then start back at 1. You can become so absorbed in an object of meditation that there ceases to be any sense of separation between you, the act of perception, and the object of perception.

Alternatively, you can use your breathing (or any meditation object) as an anchor in a more expansive awareness practice. While keeping a portion of your awareness on your breath, open your senses to everything going on around you as if you want to be ready to perceive anything that happens, no matter how small. When you find your mind has wandered, rather than bringing it back to a single meditation object, notice your awareness has closed down during the episode of mind wandering and then open your awareness back up. This ends up having the same effect as concentration in that you're letting go of elaborative thinking and commentary in order to return to your present experience.

Not Judging Your Meditation

You may find zazen difficult, or wonder whether you're doing it wrong. You're not alone! While most meditators look calm or blissful from the outside, many of them are struggling to some degree despite appearances. Struggle is actually a valuable part of the process, although not a part anyone particularly looks forward to. It's well worth working through challenges and resistance and discovering for yourself what on Earth "just precisely sitting" really involves.

The most important reason not to judge your meditation is that it's simply counterproductive. It may seem like evaluating and critiquing your meditation will let you improve it, but as soon as you start the evaluative process, you have leapt into the third level of mental activity and left your meditation far behind. The most helpful thing you can do when you notice your mind is wandering or you're spacing out is to feel grateful you noticed and then just start over. Part of the goal of Zen meditation is to be present with what is—and that gives you a clean slate every moment.

Deepening Your Zen Meditation

The best way to deepen your Zen meditation is simply to keep doing it. Sitting every day, or at least a few days a week, will be informative in and of itself. The learning process is very organic and individual, so there's no predicting what your experience will be like or how it will change over time. It's an inner adventure that may take you to surprising places, or it may simply allow you to find more calm and perspective in your daily life. If you're interested in developing your Zen meditation in a deliberate way, however, the Zen tradition has established ways for you to do this.

Finding a Zen Teacher

One way to work on your meditation is to work with a trained Zen teacher. You can engage teachers at different levels. At the most basic level, you can find a teacher and ask him questions about your meditative experience and any challenges you're facing. He may have helpful suggestions for practices or teachings you could explore, or he may simply help you clarify what your questions are and advise you about how to find the answers for yourself. Your questions can be about meditation, Zen teachings, or how to practice Zen in your everyday life.

If you develop a relationship with a teacher over time, he will become more able to guide you in a way that's appropriate to your needs and character. Many serious Zen students formally commit to a particular teacher and invite that person to guide their Zen practice indefinitely. (This is always entirely optional, and no Zen teacher should ever pressure you to study with him.) It can be very valuable and meaningful to have a "companion" of sorts on your spiritual path long term—a witness who can provide moral support, as well as compassionate (and fairly objective) feedback.

Attending Meditation Retreats

Typically, if you really want to deepen your Zen meditation, you'll attend a meditation retreat. Most practitioners find there's a limit to how still and deep their meditation can get in the midst of daily life, so a retreat is like a total immersion course in meditation that can teach you an enormous amount about what's possible. You can then carry what you've learned back into everyday life, as well as your daily meditation.

Zen retreats are much like Insight Meditation retreats, which I described in Chapter 5, and differ only in flavor and emphasis. The schedule tends to be similar, with most (but not all) Zen retreats tending to place a little more emphasis on silent work practice and communal rituals like chanting or meal ceremonies. When it comes to meditation, however, both Zen and Insight retreats will give you an opportunity to meditate a lot—so if you're interested in Zen but can only find an Insight retreat nearby, go ahead and attend it.

Practicing Zen Meditation with Koans

In some traditions of Zen, most notably the *Rinzai* school, students practice *koan* introspection. Koans are traditional stories that typically describe the exchange between a teacher and a student. There are hundreds of them, each one presenting a different aspect of Zen teaching for the student to wrestle with. A classic koan is "What is the sound of one hand clapping?" (This question is presented within a larger story.) A teacher assigns a student an appropriate koan, and the student proceeds to work with it in (and outside) his meditation until he resolves or understand it in a personal, authentic way. The student then presents that understanding to the teacher and may or may not "pass" the koan and move on to another one.

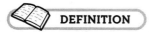 **DEFINITION**

Rinzai is a sect of Zen Buddhism that often employs contemplation of koans in meditation. **Koans** are traditional stories of interactions between Zen teachers and their students that are meant to convey an important aspect of Zen teaching.

The process of working with a koan isn't about intellectual consideration. In his book *Sitting with Koans: Essential Writings on Zen Koan Introspection,* Zen teacher Daido Loori explains, "In order to see into a koan we must go beyond the words and ideas that describe reality and directly and intimately experience reality itself. The answer to a koan is not a fixed piece of information. It is one's own intimate and direct experience of the universe and its infinite facets. It is a state of consciousness." The insights you achieve through koan work aren't about some kind of abstract, transcendent, or philosophical truth outside of yourself. Instead, koans invite you to wrestle in a very personal way with the fundamental truths of your life. Therefore, your insights will be experiential and transformative, and not something you can fully describe in words.

Clearly, Zen meditation with koans requires the guidance of a teacher, especially when a student is first learning what koan introspection involves. Many of the Zen centers in the West are in koan lineages, so if you're interested in this practice, you can contact one near you and ask about the kind of meditation they teach.

Learning More

While meditation is the central practice in the Zen tradition, it typically takes place within a rich context supportive of personal growth, deeper understanding, and greater compassion. While you don't have to engage with these other aspects of Zen in order to do themeless Zen meditation, most Zen practitioners will recommend you at least investigate them and see if they help support you.

For instance, you may want to meditate and study Zen with a community. Like-minded practitioners offer moral support to one another and provide opportunities for discussion. Zen puts a strong emphasis on sitting with others, so you may be able to find opportunities to do this in your area. Visiting a Zen center or sitting group is a great way to find out more about Zen and Zen meditation. Almost all Zen centers are open to the public, at least during their regular programs, and most are used to people showing up who are new to the practice. Just search on the web for "Zen meditation." You might also visit sweepingzen.com for a searchable directory of Zen centers all over the world.

You may also want to read and study Buddhist or Zen teachings; these offer ways to understand your spiritual experiences, give advice about how to deal with challenges, and suggest additional things you may want to investigate.

If you're going to choose between reading and meditating, the Zen advice will always be to meditate. However, reading can be very valuable support to your practice at times. My favorite basic Zen books are *Zen Mind, Beginner's Mind* by Shunryu Suzuki and *Everyday Zen: Love and Work* by Charlotte Joko Beck. You may also want to check out *Idiot's Guides: Zen Living*, in which I cover just about everything I believe is essential to Zen practice.

Zen Meditation Over a Lifetime

Even with years of practice, the method of themeless Zen meditation remains more or less the same. However, your experience of it can change profoundly over time as you become less identified with the content of your mind and more identified with the space through which the content moves. An example of this is recognizing the presence of angry thoughts and feelings within the larger context of your experience, as opposed to being completely caught up and consumed by anger (just sitting there *being* angry).

 **WATCH OUT**

> It's easy to get attached to certain pleasant, blissful, or remarkable experiences or insights in Zen meditation. Actually, if you end up having them, a certain level of attachment is kind of inevitable, so don't beat yourself up too much if you find yourself longing to repeat a certain experience or state. Just notice that the effort to hang on to or repeat something almost never works. Try to open yourself up to what comes next and trust there will be more rewarding meditation and insights in the future.

At times in Zen meditation, you may sink into a more or less thoughtless, spacious state of pure awareness. This is more likely to happen if you meditate often or for prolonged periods, but some people access this state fairly easily. While such an experience can be pleasant and allow for certain insights, it isn't the goal of Zen meditation to willfully bring about thoughtless or blissful states. Instead, the idea is to allow pleasant or spacious states to arise and pass away with a minimum amount of grasping after them. Ironically, if you *can* just let pleasant states go, they will be more likely to occur again.

"Ideal" Soto Zen Meditation

Over a lifetime of Zen meditation, your practice will keep growing and changing, and your experience of meditation won't be exactly the same as someone else's. As mentioned earlier, the important thing is to be fully present with your experience, whatever it is—something even a complete beginner can do perfectly (in theory).

With that caveat, it may still be helpful to know what themeless Zen meditation is "supposed" to be like. Essentially, an experienced meditator practicing themeless meditation is really, truly going to be *just sitting*. You just sit, without trying to grasp after anything or push anything away. Your sense of time tends to slow down so you can notice each thing that arises in your experience—including thoughts, which you watch bubble up, take form, and then pass away without them disturbing the stillness of your meditation.

It may sound like "just sitting around" would be supremely boring, but it's not. It actually has a very active, vibrant feeling to it. You're open and ready, perceptive and willing. Instead of evaluating your life or your present experience in terms of what you still want to obtain or achieve, you can be intimately aware and appreciative of life just as it is. Everything can seem very luminous and precious without denying any of the hard realities of the world. No one experiences every moment of their meditation like this, no matter how experienced they are, but even a taste of this spacious and silent way of being can sustain and inspire you for a long time.

The Ultimate Goal

It may seem ironic, but a Zen master is seen as someone who has "reached the goal of goallessness." While there's plenty of room in Zen for making a strenuous effort, it's like a strenuous effort to return home (or more accurately, to wake up to the fact that you're already home). According to Zen, you already have everything you truly need, so striving for ideals or emulating Zen masters is taking a detour on your spiritual path. Still, it may be a detour you have to make because there *is* such a thing as mastery. Until you master the goal of goallessness, you've just got to keep trying.

There's a classic Zen story of a spiritual seeker going off in search of an ox. The ox stands for enlightenment, and at first the seeker is just following footprints through the forest. Eventually he sees the ox, catches it, tames it, and is able to ride it. While you might think this would be the end of the spiritual process (not only attaining enlightenment but developing a working relationship with it), it's not. The process continues when the spiritual practitioner leaves the ox behind and returns to the village—or normal, everyday life—where he blends in easily with all beings and tries to be of service. Ultimately, both ox and seeker disappear as all dualities are transcended.

POINT OF CLARIFICATION

Even when you practice Zen diligently and end up embodying some of the ideals described here, the goal is to do so without being self-conscious and proud of it. You should come to realize that these ideals describe everyone's true nature (not just the nature of special or advanced people) and that people have only to discover and uncover that true nature for themselves.

In practical terms, this means the ultimate goal of Zen—and thus the meditation methods it employs—is to personally and directly experience the sense in which you and your life are complete and precious just as they are. You then inhabit your life wholeheartedly without fear, and are no longer compelled to grasp after happiness outside yourself. You're even more able to enjoy and appreciate life and relationships because you engage them without the filter of self-concern. You're naturally more compassionate because you've seen through the delusion that there's a sharp boundary between self and other.

The Least You Need to Know

- In the Zen view, insight leads to lasting liberation—particularly insight into the emptiness of self, which allows you to engage life with less self-concern.

- The purpose of Zen meditation is to wake up to reality and see clearly.

- In themeless Zen meditation, you can use simple objects of meditation, such as breath or sound, but these simply counteract your habit of getting lost in thought.

- In "perfect" themeless Zen meditation, you really are just sitting there. Although this sounds simple, it's a surprisingly profound and beneficial experience.

- The ultimate goal of Zen is to wholeheartedly and authentically inhabit your life.

Vajrayana Meditation

There are hundreds—if not thousands—of meditation techniques in the Vajrayana Buddhist tradition. For this reason, it's sometimes called the *method tradition*. The idea is that you can approach any problem or limitation in your mind as an ill for which there's a remedy, so the meditation you choose to do depends on what's going on for you and what you need to work on.

Vajrayana includes almost all of the practices and teachings of other kinds of Buddhism, but it has many elements not found elsewhere. So in this chapter, I introduce you to Vajrayana Buddhism and explain how it relates to other forms of Buddhism already mentioned in this book (Insight Meditation and Zen). I then discuss various kinds of Vajrayana meditation, offer a basic practice you can try, and tell you how you can deepen your meditation.

In This Chapter

- What Vajrayana is and how it relates to other kinds of Buddhism
- The real meaning of tantric practice
- The importance of being motivated by compassion
- A simplified exercise inspired by a tantric meditation
- The goal of buddhahood and what that means

Overview of Vajrayana Buddhism

Vajrayana Buddhism developed in the Tibetan cultural region, and is therefore commonly referred to as *Tibetan Buddhism*. The religion spread to Tibet from India in the ninth and tenth centuries, and therefore reflects later developments in Indian Buddhism more than other traditions like Theravada or Zen. In particular, Indian Buddhism by this time had become dominated by the use of *tantric* texts and practices, and these also became well-established in Vajrayana.

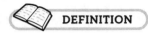 **DEFINITION**

> A **tantra,** at the most basic level, is an instruction manual. In religious contexts, it refers to texts containing teachings, rituals, and practices that are considered esoteric, or difficult to understand and therefore taught to a limited number of people.

Contrary to the popular conception that they focus primarily on sexual practices, Buddhist tantric texts teach highly developed meditations and techniques believed to be extremely effective for spiritual development. In their flavor, they're reminiscent of various approaches used in Indian Yoga (see Chapter 4): initiation into higher practices requires the guidance of and commitment to a guru, and it often involves the manipulation of subtle energies in the body for spiritual purposes. (In fact, many of the tantric practices are called *Yogas*.) Because of its reliance on tantras, Vajrayana is considered one of several forms of Tantric Buddhism.

Vajrayana developed for centuries in a unique Tibetan style, eventually splitting into four main schools, and dominated the Tibetan religious landscape. In the 1950s, however, China invaded and occupied Tibet and began to suppress and persecute the practice of Buddhism, particularly because the leader of the Vajrayana religion in Tibet—the Dalai Lama—was also the temporal leader of the country. The Dalai Lama was exiled, and hundreds of thousands of Tibetans fled the country.

As a result, Vajrayana Buddhism has spread throughout the world along with Tibetan refugees. Many Vajrayana monks and teachers started practice centers in other countries and attracted Western students. One of the more well-known (and innovative) Tibetan teachers was Chögyam Trungpa, who founded Naropa University in Colorado, wrote a number of popular books, and established the Shambhala training method. Among his students is nun and author Pema Chödrön. More traditional teachers who have established practice lineages in the West include Kalu Rinpoche, Sogyal Rinpoche, Lama Thubten Yeshe, and Lama Zopa Rinpoche.

The Essence of Vajrayana

Vajrayana includes and values the Buddhist teachings described so far in this book (see Chapters 5 and 6). One of those teachings is that your mind plays a significant role in creating your experience, and it's possible to change the way your mind works in order to decrease suffering for yourself and others. Another is that you suffer from the problematic delusions of having an inherent, independent, enduring self-essence and believing you can find lasting happiness in external things.

Here, I focus on several additional aspects of Vajrayana that are essential to its unique flavor and practice. While two of these teachings are also very important in other forms of Buddhism—the ideal of the *bodhisattva* and the emphasis on letting go of your idea of an inherently existing self-nature—I present them here with a distinctly Vajrayana flavor.

 **DEFINITION**

> A **bodhisattva** is someone who commits to doing whatever is required to attain buddhahood (full awakening and liberation) for the sake of all beings, even if the process of awakening takes many lifetimes.

Rebirth

A central teaching in Vajrayana is that we are subject to rebirth, which means that—unless we achieve spiritual liberation—we will be reborn in another form (human or otherwise) after we die. Basically, as long as you remain caught up in delusion and subject to craving and aversion for the world, your life energy will not completely dissipate after death, but instead will be drawn toward another life. The kind of parents, body, and circumstances you're drawn to in the next life are dependent on your actions of body, speech, and mind in this life (and previous ones).

From the Buddhist point of view, which has its origins in ancient India, being reborn in another life is not a positive outcome. This is because, even if your next life is mostly fortunate and pleasant, eventually you'll end up experiencing the typical human sufferings and be reborn in difficult and painful circumstances. The whole process of birth, death, and rebirth is seen as endless and ultimately dissatisfactory. We get stuck in it because we keep on hoping something outside ourselves will bring us permanent refuge and happiness, but this will never happen (see Chapter 5 for more on the Buddhist view of the nature of dissatisfaction).

The Bodhisattva Path

If, however, you devote yourself to intensive spiritual practice and transformation, it's possible to change the course of your trajectory through the cycle of rebirths. Through renunciation of your attachment to the world and emulation of enlightened beings, you can purify your mind and body of negative causes and delusions. It's even possible to practice so diligently that you achieve buddhahood, or complete, perfect awakening and liberation. At this point, you'll have transcended the dualistic thinking that differentiates self from other, and you will naturally embody compassionate concern for all living things.

Those who aspire to buddhahood for the sake of all beings are considered to be on the bodhisattva path. At lower levels of practice, bodhisattvas may still be largely motivated by relieving their own suffering or seeking their own happiness. Eventually, however, they awaken to no self and feel more and more love and compassion for all beings. The traditional definition of a fully realized bodhisattva is someone who has attained the possibility of buddhahood (and therefore won't be drawn into rebirth) but *chooses* to be reborn in order to continue working for the welfare of all beings.

In Vajrayana, the bodhisattva path toward full buddhahood is the ideal. While it's acknowledged that few of us will achieve this in our lifetime, because of rebirth, you can rest assured that any efforts you make on the bodhisattva path won't go to waste. Instead, they will impact your next birth and help bring all beings closer to enlightenment and liberation.

 POINT OF CLARIFICATION

Firm belief in literal rebirth is part of Tibetan culture and continues to be a significant force in modern Vajrayana Buddhism. For example, it's by influencing the process of rebirth with their spiritual strength that revered Vajrayana teachers are "reborn" (and their successors identified) so they can continue their teachings throughout another life. While modern Vajrayana practitioners vary in terms of how literally they believe in physical rebirth, this teaching is the basis for many other approaches and practices in the religion.

The Tantric Vehicle

The bodhisattva path is a long one. Even in Vajrayana, the first part of the path is very similar to that presented in Insight Meditation and Zen: it begins by developing an intention to find a better way to live than simply being dragged around by circumstances and by your desires and aversions. You then develop clarity and insight through mindfulness and meditation. In particular, you need to start seeing how cause and effect operate in your life (so you can make wiser choices), as well as challenge your delusions about your inherent self-nature and about the possibility of obtaining lasting happiness from the things of the world.

Eventually—when your mind is steady, your character is grounded in ethical behavior, your selfishness is transcended, and your aspiration is strong enough—you can be initiated into the tantras, which are viewed as the most effective way to approach buddhahood within your lifetime. The idea is that your habits and delusions—particularly your belief in an inherently existing, independent, enduring self—are very strong after countless lifetimes of reinforcement. It takes potent methods such as using tantras to counteract these strong habits, which are reflected in your body and energy, as well as in your mind.

The Role of Meditation in Vajrayana

Like most other forms of Buddhism, Vajrayana views meditation as a way to understand reality at a deeper level—a level which leads to transformation and change, as opposed to a merely intellectual understanding. Vajrayana therefore incorporates meditation into your practice at all stages. Initially, you practice simple meditations on your breathing or some other meditative object in order to calm your mind and increase your ability to concentrate. When various agitations arise that interfere with your meditation or other aspects of your spiritual practice—such as anger, craving, or restlessness—you do particular meditations as antidotes for each problem. In order to gradually influence your mind and life in a positive direction, you do meditations that help you cultivate compassion or let go of self-cherishing.

When you're ready—and only if you want to—you can ask to be initiated into tantric meditation practices, which will employ the skills you've developed in simpler meditations. There are many, many different tantric meditations. While they vary in terms of their complexity and purpose, generally speaking, they involve ritual, visualization, and symbolism and are intended to bring about a positive change in your mind or body. In his book *A Concise Introduction to Tibetan Buddhism*, John Powers describes this change as *cognitive transformation*. Basically, rather than merely gaining insight into deeper truths about reality and gradually letting those insights change your life (which may take many lifetimes), you actively practice becoming one with those deeper truths.

Three Benefits of Vajrayana Meditation

To clarify, while I'm calling a meditation *Vajrayana* here because it's associated with and taught within the tradition, practitioners typically call only tantric meditations Vajrayana meditations. Other meditations are typically called by specific names, such as calm-abiding meditation, loving-kindness meditation, or meditation on emptiness. In any case, the three benefits I share here are general enough to apply to just about any kind of meditation taught in the Vajrayana tradition, including both preparatory and tantric ones.

Development of Bodhicitta

The thread that ties all Vajrayana practice together from beginning to end is the emphasis placed on *bodhicitta*. While bodhicitta has many meanings, two are most important to our discussion. First, bodhicitta is your aspiration for enlightenment, or buddhahood, which will not only liberate you from suffering but allow you to help others do the same. Second, bodhicitta is the state of mind and heart that causes you to have the aspiration for buddhahood—namely, sincere love and compassion for all living beings, without discrimination.

 **DEFINITION**

Bodhicitta is the motivation of a bodhisattva, including both the aspiration for complete enlightenment and buddhahood in order to benefit all beings and infinite, unconditional love and compassion for those beings.

Through Vajrayana practice and meditation, you deliberately try to cultivate bodhicitta. You do chants and visualizations that require you to act as if you're motivated by bodhicitta even if you don't yet feel it. This has an effect on you over time, and you inevitably actually start feeling greater warmth and compassion for beings, including yourself. Eventually, you work on extending such love and compassion toward beings for whom it's more difficult, such as people who have hurt you or who you don't respect. This not only increases your bodhicitta, it also challenges your self-concern, which would prefer to extend positive feelings only toward certain beings based on your preference.

Learning to Transform Qualities of Mind

Vajrayana is full of meditations designed to counteract negative habits of the mind and cultivate positive qualities instead. Of course, you first have to notice and acknowledge your selfish and harmful thoughts, emotions, and limitations. This happens by learning to observe your own mind through meditation and mindfulness. Once you notice something in you that impedes your progress on the bodhisattva path—such as anger, stinginess, fear, low self-esteem, judgment, desire, or shame—you find a way to transform it. If you want to find out more about these kinds of meditations, you can find traditional as well as improvised ones in Vajrayana texts, and an experienced teacher can recommend some to you.

Transformative meditations tend to take an otherwise negative experience—one you might berate yourself for—and turn it into an opportunity for spiritual growth. For example, when you notice you're feeling aversion toward someone, you meditate on how all beings have led countless lives in the past, and how in a previous life, this being may have been your mother. Potentially, a moment of judgment becomes a moment to cultivate gratitude and compassion. In another example, if you're feeling small and limited, you visualize yourself as a bodhisattva of compassion, radiating kindness out to all beings in the world. Such an image is the opposite of a self-critical or self-absorbed one, and helps awaken positive qualities within you.

Greater Equanimity

Equanimity is achieved through Vajrayana meditation in two complementary ways. First, over time, your mind becomes more focused and disciplined. Hundreds of hours of meditation practice plus the effort to be mindful in daily life help you become able to direct your mind at will. When you become upset by something, you're better able to choose your response. Do you react and set off a habitual pattern? Or do you turn your mind toward the internal cause of your upset in order to discern what's really going on? And then once you see what's going on, do you apply an appropriate antidote? Greater equanimity comes not through a rigid refusal to react to things but rather through a pliancy of mind that allows you to respond more skillfully.

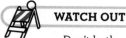 **WATCH OUT**

Don't bother trying to pretend you feel equanimity before you actually do. This can actually be harmful and counterproductive because it invites you to suppress emotions and thoughts. Pretending also causes you to turn away from what's going on just when you need to look more closely at it. You're welcome to do your best to refrain from acting on or expressing your reactive feelings, however—as long as you admit to yourself that you're experiencing them.

The second source of equanimity comes from a growing insight into the empty nature of all phenomena. This primarily comes from meditation, which allows you to investigate closely your assumption that there's something inherently real about yourself and the things you encounter. When something upsets you, you can learn to recognize how certain conditions are causing other things to arise, and how all of it is a play of phenomena instead of a drama that's true in some absolute sense. For example, instead of getting drawn into a story about how your boss is being unfair and how you need to respond with defiance or sacrifice your self-respect, you can take note of your perceptions and thoughts for what they are: empty of inherent reality, and therefore (although definitely part of your experience) not something you're compelled to believe or act on.

Chenrezig Meditation

It's tricky to give you a taste of a uniquely Vajrayana meditation, given the instructions for tantric meditations are generally secret until you receive them from a teacher who feels you're ready for them. However, one exception to this rule is *Chenrezig* meditation. Chenrezig is one of many Buddhist cosmological figures representing some important aspect of reality—in this case, compassion. These figures are sometimes portrayed as idealized, fully realized bodhisattvas or sometimes as deities of some kind. Whatever the case, they aren't believed to exist separately from the meditator or practitioner. The apparent contradiction—a universal principle or aspect of reality not separate from you, but portrayed as a separate being anyway—is a teaching tool in and of itself. The full truth of the matter can't be conveyed either by the concept of an ideal principle or an embodied being, so both are employed. You're challenged to go beyond concepts to discover what's actually true.

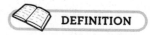 **DEFINITION**

> **Chenrezig** is a male, deity-like figure in Vajrayana Buddhism who symbolizes the manifestation of perfect compassion informed by perfect wisdom, or insight into emptiness. In other Buddhist traditions, this figure is known as Avalokiteśvara, Kuan Yin, Kannon, or Kanzeon, and is sometimes portrayed as female.

Practiced in its entirety, Chenrezig meditation is a tantric meditation that requires preparation, initiation, and the guidance of a teacher. However, simplified versions of the full practice are widely recognized as still being beneficial and—more importantly—not dangerous. Other tantras are considered potentially dangerous in that, if you aren't prepared for them and don't have correct guidance in them, you can easily misunderstand them and potentially encourage negative things in yourself (such as pride, self-attachment, fear, desire, and so on) instead of the meditation furthering you on your bodhisattva path. Because Chenrezig meditation is all about encouraging love, compassion, and devotion, it's seen as a rare Vajrayana practice that can be shared publicly (although there are still aspects you're advised not to practice without a teacher).

General Description of the Method

The full Chenrezig meditation is a fairly long, elaborate ritual. In a somewhat abbreviated version, you begin with the mindful repetition of a prayer in which you "take refuge" in the three essential aspects of Buddhism (the possibility of awakening, the teaching, and the community) and try to arouse bodhicitta. There may also be other preparatory prayers, offerings, or prostrations.

You then enter the "phase of creation" in which you visualize the bodhisattva Chenrezig in great detail about an arm's length or a body's length in front of you. Detailed drawings and paintings of Chenrezig are available to help you with this; just search on the internet for "Chenrezig." Sometimes he's portrayed as having 1 head and 4 arms, but at other times, he's visualized as having 11 heads and 1,000 arms. Visualization is aided by the recitation of a text that describes

Chenrezig, including his luminosity, the position of his body and hands, what he's wearing and holding in his hands, and how he emits rays of light from various places.

The meditation proceeds as you recite various prayers to Chenrezig, asking for his support and blessing, and recite his *mantra,* "om mani padme hum." His compassion and energy flow into you in the form of light, and you imagine him purifying you of all negative habits, energies, and attachments. If you've been initiated into the Chenrezig meditation, you would then continue with a process of imagining yourself as Chenrezig (this is called *self-generation,* as opposed to front-generation, or visualizing Chenrezig in front of you). If you don't have initiation into the meditation from a teacher, you would instead imagine absorbing the light and energy of Chenrezig into your mind and body. In either case, you close with dedications and prayers.

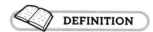

DEFINITION

A **mantra** is a syllable or series of syllables recited silently or audibly for positive spiritual effect. Mantras are usually based on ancient Sanskrit syllables and have accepted meanings and effects but are rarely translatable.

The Theory Behind the Meditation

The point of Chenrezig meditation is never to imagine Chenrezig as a separate entity, or supplicate him with prayers so he can give you something you don't already have. The Vajrayana idea is that Chenrezig represents the potential for perfect compassion and wisdom that resides within you. That potential has been obscured by negative and selfish actions and habits of mind in your current life, as well as in many past ones, so your own perfection is often difficult to access. This is why you imagine Chenrezig as having a beautiful and benevolent form outside of you—so you can imagine him turning his unconditional love and compassion toward you, despite what you think about yourself.

Beginner's Meditation Instructions

Here, I give a very basic meditation exercise you can try that contains elements of the Chenrezig meditation. (Even a simplified version is too long to include here!) Search for a picture of Chenrezig online to aid in your visualization. I suggest beginning with the 4-armed version rather than the 1,000-armed version, just for simplicity's sake. Keep in mind it's much less important that you achieve a detailed or stable visual image than that you feel the presence of perfect compassion, love, and equanimity. Chenrezig is the ultimate nature of mind, or your highest aspiration.

Setting and Posture

The attitude with which you engage in Chenrezig meditation is important. It may be helpful to take a few minutes to clean the area where you're going to meditate, so the space feels more sacred and conducive to concentration. You may also want to try one of the traditional preparatory practices associated with Vajrayana meditation, such as setting up an altar with a buddha image on it (or even better, a picture of Chenrezig) and making an offering of incense or fresh flowers.

In a space with minimal distractions, sit in a comfortable position. Any of the seated postures described in Chapter 2 will work. Make sure your back is straight, regardless of whether you're sitting on a cushion on the floor or in a chair. Put your hands in your lap close to your body. Place your right hand on top of your left, with your thumbs touching so your hands form a sort of triangle. Keep your eyes slightly open but your lids lowered, so they let in some light but close out distractions.

CONTEMPLATE THIS

Part of the reason for the emphasis on ritual in Vajrayana and other spiritual traditions is it involves your body in whatever practice you're doing. Ritual activities like chanting, doing prostrations, or creating altars help you absorb a spiritual message—such as compassion, equanimity, letting go, or devotion—at a deeper level than if you just thought about these things. (Note that the meditative technique of visualization, while it doesn't engage the body, is not just "thinking about" something but, in a sense, is a kind of ritual activity of the mind.)

Basic Practice

Until you've memorized these instructions, you can stop to read them periodically and then go back to the meditation. You can also listen to the audio version of these instructions on idiotsguides.com/meditation. Recitations during the meditation can be done silently or out loud as you prefer. When you're ready, set aside at least 10 minutes or longer for your meditation, settle into your meditation posture, and follow these instructions:

1. Recite to yourself silently or out loud three times, "Until enlightenment, I'll rely on the potential for awakening, beneficial teachings, and supportive people. Through the merit I create by practicing generosity and other perfections, may I attain awakening for the sake of all beings."

2. Spend the next couple minutes allowing your body and mind to become calm. Become aware of your breathing. Whenever your mind wanders, simply bring it gently back to awareness of your breathing. Be as gentle as possible when bringing your mind back to the present; you want your mind to become calm.

3. Imagine Chenrezig becomes literally present, floating in the air 3 to 5 feet in front of you. At first, his features may not be clear, but you should feel his warm, compassionate presence. Because you're not trying to see Chenrezig with your eyes, allow mental images to arise in your mind as his form is described; however, don't worry if images don't arise or don't remain clear. Your visualization should be made of light—transparent, illusionlike, and not solid.

4. Visualize Chenrezig's body as being composed of white light. He's seated in a cross-legged posture on a white lotus flower. He has a youthful, beautiful form and is wearing flowing garments and adornments of jewels and flowers. His face is round and moonlike, radiant, calm, kind, and compassionate. You've never seen such a beautiful and loving face. His hair is long and black and falls in curls over his shoulders. He wears an intricate crown of gold and jewels.

5. Imagine Chenrezig's four arms. Two arms come together in front of him; his hands hold a shining, wish-fulfilling gem in front of his heart. Chenrezig's other hands are held up near his shoulders, with the palms facing you. In his right hand, he holds a crystal rosary; in his left hand, he holds a white lotus flower by the stem.

6. Picture Chenrezig's compassionate gaze focused toward you. His lips are held in a slight smile. You've never before experienced such complete and unconditional love and faith. Chenrezig clearly recognizes himself in you. Continue visualizing Chenrezig, making him as real as you can (repeating the visualizations in steps 4 and 5), while he looks at you with a personal gaze of infinite compassion.

7. Recite the Chenrezig mantra "om mani padme hum" while you visualize him sending white light out from his body throughout the universe, purifying everything it touches.

8. To end your meditation, allow the Chenrezig visualization to dissolve and recite, "Through the merit of this practice, may I realize perfect compassion and help all other beings do so as well."

Although the meditation instructions may seem detailed, don't get stuck in trying to make your experience technically perfect. Keep a sense throughout of the deeper reason for doing this meditation: awakening your awareness of profound compassion, and recognizing that compassion within yourself.

Additional Guidance and Encouragement

Depending on how your mind works, you may find Chenrezig practice easy and rewarding or quite challenging and bewildering. If you find it difficult, your skill at concentration may need to be built up through simpler forms of meditation first. However, visualization can be challenging even if you've learned to concentrate in other kinds of activities or meditations. It's important to try it a number of times and question your assumptions about the technique.

Understanding Visualization

The technique of visualization may be hard to grasp and takes practice, so be patient. It's important to remember that you're not trying to imagine a solid form in front of you. Instead, you can think of your visualization as being made of light and therefore translucent. The visualization is also something occurring in your mind. It's not self-induced hallucination; it's a mental image.

 POINT OF CLARIFICATION

Visualization is what spontaneously happens when, for example, someone asks you to picture your mother or your house. You suddenly have a visual or a picture in your mind's eye. In a visualization meditation, you simply learn to focus in on that picture and fill it in with more detail.

In the beginning, you'll probably find you can concentrate on only one detail of the visualization at a time. For example, as you try to imagine Chenrezig's smile, the position of his body gets fuzzy, and then when you picture his hands, his face gets fuzzy. This is okay; allow your mind to move around to different aspects of the visualization without worrying too much about maintaining the whole thing. The ability to do this will come with time. Alternatively, you can concentrate on the image as whole, trying to make it more stable and real; this also calms your mind.

Gaining Confidence

Perhaps the most important part of Chenrezig practice is recognizing Chenrezig's perfect, awakened, compassionate nature in yourself. If you're like most people, this is not how you view yourself at all. Even imagining Chenrezig's complete and unconditional love and compassion coming your way may be difficult enough, let alone imagining you're capable of the same kind of compassion—or as more advanced versions of the practice require, imagining you *are* Chenrezig! (Keep in mind that when you're Chenrezig, you radiate infinite love and compassion toward all beings without discrimination.)

Of course, this is part of the transformative nature of Chenrezig meditation. He represents your higher or deeper nature—a nature you share in common with all beings. When you find yourself resisting a certain aspect of this practice, it's very useful to investigate the reason for that resistance. Sometimes it's lack of self-esteem, and sometimes it's a belief you're too small and limited to be capable of unconditional love and compassion. Fear of losing your sense of self or of being taken advantage of may also arise. Treat these as opportunities to deepen your practice and turn toward compassion anyway—and see what happens.

Deepening Your Vajrayana Meditation

Like many of the meditative traditions presented in this book, Vajrayana is a practice you can spend a lifetime developing. While even a little bit of practice and meditation will be beneficial, you can also make it into a major part of your life or even aim for buddhahood itself! There are too many other aspects of Vajrayana to go into here—teachings, meditative techniques, and rituals—so I'll just mention a few of the most fundamental ones.

Other Supportive Vajrayana Practices

You're likely to get lost trying to navigate the many different Vajrayana practices, teachings, and meditation techniques on your own. This is why a qualified teacher—called a *lama* in Vajrayana—is considered so important; she acts like a doctor in prescribing you appropriate practices, antidotes, and approaches. If you go deeply into Vajrayana and want to explore tantric practices, your teacher becomes more than a guide. As part of your practice, you adopt the teacher as your guru and work on seeing her as a buddha (or as Chenrezig). While this doesn't mean everything the teacher does is right, you learn to recognize buddha nature as manifested in a real person.

 **DEFINITION**

> **Lama** is the Vajrayana Buddhist term for someone who has been empowered to teach Vajrayana, including the tantras, and to function as a guru in the student-teacher relationship.

Also similar to other Buddhist traditions, meditation retreats are an important part of deepening your Vajrayana meditation. (See a description of a Buddhist meditation retreat in Chapter 5.) Vajrayana actually takes meditation retreats to an even more involved level with the ideal one being three years, three months, and three days long. While few people are able to do such a retreat, of course, most Vajrayana teachers have done at least a one-year retreat. During a prolonged Vajrayana retreat, you're completely cloistered and work intensively on tantric practices.

Such retreats are only undertaken under the guidance of a lama in a monastery setting designed for them and after many years of preparatory practices.

Learning More

Practicing with community is considered very important in Buddhism, and Vajrayana is no exception. In fact, it's particularly essential to Vajrayana practice because the tradition is so rich. You may have a Vajrayana practice center near you where you can learn more; search online for "Vajrayana" or "Tibetan Buddhism," or visit websites that list their affiliated centers, including the Foundation for the Preservation of the Mahayana Tradition (fpmt.org), Kadampa Buddhism (kadampa.org), and the Kagyu Lineage (kagyu.org).

For more on Vajrayana in general, see John Powers's book *A Concise Introduction to Tibetan Buddhism*. To learn more about Chenrezig meditation specifically, read *Chenrezig, Lord of Love: Principles and Methods of Deity Meditation* by Bokar Rinpoche or *Cultivating a Compassionate Heart: The Yoga Method of Chenrezig* by Thubten Chodron. You can also find more about this form of meditation, including an image of Chenrezig and commentary on the practice, by going to the Kagyu Lineage site (kagyu.org) and searching for "Chenrezig."

Vajrayana Meditation Over a Lifetime

The depth of Vajrayana meditation you experience over a lifetime depends primarily on how much time and effort you put into it. However, sometimes it's a matter of working smarter rather than harder. It's easy to misunderstand a particular practice or technique, or fail to realize in what ways you're impeding your own progress. The guidance of a meditation teacher is essential for exploring these deeper levels of Vajrayana meditation.

"Ideal" Vajrayana Meditation

Eventually, it's possible to become so experienced with concentration and calming your mind that it becomes much easier, even effortless. At the same time, this concentration isn't grim or rigid. Instead—in part because it's easier—your mind also develops a bright, energetic, perceptive quality. Once you reach this stage of development, called *physical and mental pliancy,* you feel light, clear-headed, and blissful.

Being able to rest in a state that partakes of both mental stability and pliancy allows you to undertake more analytical or elaborate meditations. At some point, you develop an ability to perceive something—a physical object or a mental one—directly, without the slightest obscuration. While this allows deep insight, at another level, the meditation itself begins a process of purification. Negative habits, energies, and views built up over many lifetimes permanently disappear. You become able to access the pure nature of mind, which is clear, luminous, and without the slightest conception of inherent existence.

The Ultimate Goal

The ultimate goal of Vajrayana Buddhism, of course, is buddhahood, but what does that really mean? In short, it's an ideal very few of us are going to reach in our lifetimes. But on the other hand, it's a goal worth spending your lifetime approaching. Buddhas are completely awakened beings, and what they have awakened to is reality itself. They have seen there's no inherently existing, enduring self-nature in themselves or in anything else—and not only have they realized this in their minds, they have purified themselves of all delusions. Every action and word of a buddha manifests perfect wisdom and compassion.

In the meantime, before attaining buddhahood, devoted practitioners don't worry about whether or not they're buddhas or how long it's going to take to attain that state. They just continue practicing with the goal of relieving suffering and bringing true happiness to all beings. In a sense, this is also manifesting perfect wisdom and compassion. It's not about your personal experience or attainment—instead, it's a continual labor of love.

The Least You Need to Know

- The ultimate goal of Vajrayana meditation is achieving complete enlightenment and liberation (buddhahood) for the sake of all beings.
- You might want to consider the Vajrayana path because it claims to offer the fastest route to Buddhahood. You might be able to achieve buddhahood and benefit beings in *this* lifetime, instead of being reborn again and again and having to start your practice over each lifetime.
- The especially fast and effective route to enlightenment is the practice of tantras, which are prescribed ritual meditations (and only include sexual imagery in the most advanced stages of the practice).
- It's believed that through tantric practice, you not only achieve insight, but you also recondition your whole mind and body to overcome lifetimes of bad mental and physical habits.
- Any amount of practice in Vajrayana is thought to be beneficial and noble because it moves you closer to eventual buddhahood, a state that maximizes your ability to help all beings.

Devotional Meditation

This part of the book focuses on meditative practices within the devotional spiritual traditions of Judaism, Christianity, Sufism, and the indigenous people of North America. In these traditions, the central point is cultivating devotion and connection to God or to the spirit world. Therefore, meditative practices are designed and used for this purpose, rather than as a method of self-development or enlightenment. At the same time, there really isn't such a big difference between devotional mediation and meditation for enlightenment. Over the course of devotional practice, you're going to mature and gain insight, and after meditating for self-development, you're going to strengthen your connection to something greater than yourself.

I provide a whole chapter on each spiritual tradition, introducing you to the history and teachings of the tradition and explaining how meditative practices have featured in it over time. Within each chapter, I then focus on a particular kind of meditative practice within the larger tradition, giving you a description of the method and a practice you can do. I also offer a vision of the ultimate goal of each spiritual tradition and how meditation helps you reach it, as well as instructions for how to explore a particular form of meditation further.

Jewish Meditation

Judaism has had a rich tradition of meditative practices since its beginning. Throughout the millennia, Jews have looked for ways to deepen and intensify their sense of closeness to God. While all Jewish practices—including prayer services, ritual observances, and putting aside one day a week for rest—are essentially aimed at developing a relationship to God, meditation has been valued by the mystical movements within Judaism as an especially potent tool for directly experiencing closeness to God.

Despite the meditative threads in Judaism, you might get a quizzical look from some Jews if you ask them about "Jewish meditation." The thing is, until recently, the meditative practices in Judaism have rarely been called *meditation* or been identified as some kind of Jewish corollary of Eastern styles of meditation. Instead, Jewish meditation typically takes the form of prayers or observances done with especially focused devotion; contemplation done to achieve higher states of consciousness; and practices of seclusion or turning inward, sometimes called *self-isolation*. Fortunately, Jewish scholars over the last 30 years have called attention to the meditative practices of Judaism and made many of them accessible to anyone who's interested, and you learn about those in this chapter.

In This Chapter

- A brief history of Judaism and Jewish meditation
- The importance of seeking "closeness to God"
- How Jewish meditative practices can enrich your life
- Engaging in Jewish contemplative prayer
- Ways to deepen your sense of connection and devotion

Overview of Judaism

Judaism traces its roots back to around 2000 B.C.E. It developed as the religious tradition of a group of people living in the region of Canaan (the general area of the present-day nation of Israel and the Palestinian territories). This group of people consisted of many tribes, but collectively they called themselves the *Israelites*.

> **POINT OF CLARIFICATION**
>
> There are an estimated 14 million Jews in the world today, but that number may be misleading to anyone not familiar with Judaism. While there's some disagreement about definitions, generally speaking, someone is considered Jewish if his mother was Jewish or if he has undergone the formal process of conversion to Judaism. Both of these categories include people who actively practice Judaism (called *observant*) and people who don't practice and may not even know much about Judaism (called *nonobservant* or *secular*). Of course, most Jews fall somewhere along the spectrum between devoutly observant and completely secular.

Judaism was originally—and continues to be—closely tied to the land of Canaan, which according to Jewish scripture was the "land of milk and honey" promised to the Jewish people as a homeland by God himself. The Israelites lived and practiced their religion primarily in their homeland until around 135 C.E., when the Romans defeated them militarily and took control. This caused the Diaspora, in which Jews dispersed all over the world. At many times and in many places, Jews have been persecuted, the most notable example being the Holocaust that occurred during World War II. The majority of Jews still live outside their historical homeland, even though they regained control of the area in 1948 with the establishment of the state of Israel.

The Essence of Judaism

Although Judaism is sometimes seen as part of a cultural or national identity, it's also a rich religious tradition that can be valuable and inspiring to anyone. In most Jewish communities, you'll be welcome to practice and study (although you won't be considered a Jew unless you go through the official process of conversion, which involves lots of study, an exam, and a formal commitment). While it's difficult to distill out the most essential aspects of this rich and ancient tradition, I've tried to provide you with some particulars.

The Jewish View of God

Central to all of Judaism is its view of God as being beyond all definitions, permeating all existence, and being the most important thing there is. Everything exists because of God, and all things—whether they are apparently good or apparently bad—are of God.

Judaism goes to great lengths to remind you, over and over, of the transcendent nature of God. God has no form, so "He" is neither male nor female. Even conceiving of God as an "It" or a universal principle is incomplete. He is usually referred to by indirect titles like Lord or the Name. Some Jews avoid writing or speaking any reference to God whenever possible, and when it's thought to be necessary, terms are abbreviated, as in "G-d." Perhaps the most profound teaching device is the use of four Hebrew letters to represent the unpronounceable name of God: YHVH (in Roman letters). In order to refer to God, you simply speak the four letters (transliterated from the Hebrew *Yod-Hei-Vav-Hei*), reminding yourself that you can't even name what you're speaking about, let alone conceive of it. Human beings rely on thought and language, so we describe different attributes of God using these tools; however, they are always inadequate to the task.

Honoring, serving, remembering, and connecting to God is the essence of Judaic practice. Putting Him first and above all—without getting distracted by selfish concerns—is the primary goal and is seen as a reward in and of itself. Note that *honoring, serving, remembering,* and *connecting* are all verbs; in Judaism, what you do is much more important than what you believe. While Jews throughout time have contemplated questions about the nature of good and evil, the meaning of human life, or what happens after death, for the most part, no Jewish dogmas have been established about these matters.

The Torah

Also essential to Judaism is the *Torah,* which is traditionally held to be the word of God as given to Moses, a Jewish patriarch born around 1400 B.C.E. The Torah contains five books—Genesis, Exodus, Leviticus, Numbers, and Deuteronomy (the same ones that make up the first five books of the Christian Bible)—that basically describe how a Jew should honor, serve, remember, and connect to God. However, because most Jews believe the Torah was received directly from God, it's revered as a tangible manifestation of God Himself, and therefore much more than an instruction book.

The Torah contains 613 commandments about how Jews should fulfill their duty to God. In the *Talmud,* another sacred Jewish book that contains authoritative interpretations of the Torah, it becomes clear that many of these commandments only apply to people in special locations and roles. Still, observant Jews follow dozens of rules in their daily life, covering everything from prayer, to diet, to sex. In most cases, these codes of behavior are followed as practices meant to be done reverently in order to deepen a connection with God (as opposed to rules that have to be followed out of a sense of grudging obligation or fear of retribution).

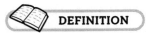

DEFINITION

The **Torah** is the most sacred scripture in Judaism, traditionally viewed by Jews as being the word of God as communicated directly to the prophet Moses over 3,000 years ago. The **Talmud** is an ancient book of commentary on and interpretation of the Torah, and it is also widely revered and relied upon in Judaism.

There are three movements within modern Judaism, which are defined in large part by how they view the Torah. (Note: These are very general categories that don't fully reflect the complexity of Jewish practice.) They are identified as follows:

The Orthodox movement: This movement generally believes the Torah was given literally and directly to Moses in its current form and that all of its commandments are binding.

The Reform movement: For the most part, this movement doesn't believe the Torah was literally written by God, but was instead gradually compiled by various practitioners in ancient times. Reform Jews generally don't regard it as imperative to follow all of the Torah's commandments, but they value the general ethical and spiritual teachings of Judaism.

The Conservative movement: This movement falls somewhere between Orthodox and Reform, holding the belief that while the Torah was received from God, it's meant to be adapted as appropriate in response to cultural changes and needs.

If you're going to try Jewish meditation, it's helpful to know these movements, as how a particular Jewish community views meditation—and the appropriateness of sharing it outside the context of a commitment to Judaism—may depend in part on whether it identifies as Orthodox, Conservative, or Reform.

The Role of Meditation in Judaism

It appears that very early in Jewish history, many Jews were involved in intensive programs of meditation aimed at experiencing transcendent closeness with God. Studying in these programs involved strict regimens dictating diet and behavior, and required self-discipline, commitment, and the guidance of masters of that particular type of meditation. This strenuous training is reported to have eventually offered practitioners the transcendent experiences they were seeking—up to and sometimes including the prophetic visions that have heavily influenced the development of Judaism.

According to *Rabbi* Aryeh Kaplan, the prominent role of intensive meditative practice changed around the time Jews began dispersing from their homeland. Jewish leaders were concerned that practitioners far from home and isolated from proper guidance would end up misunderstanding the rather mystical meditation practices or might get frustrated with how difficult the practices were and end up turning to other religions. Simplified meditations and prayers were codified for the masses, and restrictions were placed on teaching the more esoteric methods (they had to be taught to one person at a time, and that person had to be male, over 40 years old, and have completed his study of the Torah and Talmud). After this, references to meditation tended to become veiled in what Kaplan calls "allusion and allegory."

Over the centuries, however, there have been periodic revivals of explicit meditation practice in Judaism, including in the Kabbalah teachings that arose in the twelfth century. Generally speaking, meditation in a Jewish context involves cultivation of a direct and personal experience of closeness with God, so the practice often seems to have arisen as an antidote to engaging Judaism in an overly (or exclusively) intellectual way. One prominent example of such a revival was the *Hasidic* movement in the 1700s, which emphasized both mysticism and meditation.

 **DEFINITION**

> A **Rabbi** is a Jewish teacher sufficiently educated in Jewish law and practice to guide a Jewish community. **Hasidism** is a movement within Judaism that gained popularity in the 1700s and continues to this day; it tends to emphasize the immanent divine in all things, the value of piety and fervor in all activities, and a reverence for spiritual leaders who are considered to be especially righteous and spiritually powerful.

Starting somewhere in the 1800s, explicit Jewish meditation went more or less underground. This was due in part to reactions against Hasidism in mainstream Judaism; although the Hasidic movement continued, it developed a somewhat antimystical stance and stopped emphasizing meditation. It wasn't until the 1970s and 1980s that Jewish meditation experienced another renaissance. Inspired in part by the growing number of Jews exploring meditative practice in other religious traditions, Rabbi Aryeh Kaplan and other Jewish scholars revitalized interest in Jewish meditation by demonstrating how it has featured centrally in Judaism all along and by making meditation instruction available in books. Subsequently, many other practitioners and teachers of Jewish meditation have made it more accessible and widely practiced, including rabbis David Cooper, Jeff Roth, and Sheila Weinberg.

Three Benefits of Jewish Meditation

Meditation—like any practice in Judaism—is primarily about drawing closer to God. Some Jews would also add the goal of making themselves more fit and able for the sacred work of "repairing" the world, in which Jews are partners with God in an effort to bring about an eventual state of complete peace and perfection on Earth. Therefore, any benefits you might experience personally are typically put in a larger context of devotion and service.

Understanding and Control of Your Mind

All teachers of Jewish meditation recognize the positive effects meditative practice has on the way your mind works and on the way you relate to your thoughts and emotions. This is usually not presented as the goal in and of itself, but rather as a way to mature yourself and to improve your relationship with God and His creation.

As you purposefully direct your mind in meditation, you end up becoming much more familiar with how it works and its contents. In turn, this familiarity lets you become more skillful with how you use your mind, and how you relate to your thoughts and feelings. You gain perspective on your "childish" tendencies, such as self-centeredness and envy. You don't necessarily have to struggle against them; they simply lose much of their power over you. In addition, as you return your mind to the object of your meditation over and over—whether it's the sound of a Hebrew letter, a visualization, or a prayer—you also increase your powers of concentration. This is beneficial for all kinds of activities in your daily life.

CONTEMPLATE THIS

Kabbalah has traditionally been practiced within the context of various Jewish traditions and doesn't constitute a sect or school in and of itself. It includes many meditation techniques and what you might consider mystical practices, and they are what most people think of when they hear the term *Jewish meditation*. The Jewish Kabbalah teachings recommend meditation as a way to help you transition from the mentality of childhood to the mentality of adulthood. This transition, unfortunately, doesn't necessarily happen just because you get older!

Enhanced Awareness and Receptivity

Usually your mind is like a radio tuned to a particular station but also producing lots of static or even faintly playing another station or two at the same time. Using this analogy, you could say meditation is learning to tune your "mind radio" more precisely. This leads to less static, and the station you're trying to tune into—whatever it is you want to pay attention to—starts to come in loud and clear. You end up with a heightened awareness of and receptivity to what's going on both inside and outside you. Many people report that meditation makes everything a little brighter and more beautiful, which in turn inspires greater appreciation for life.

One of the results of enhanced awareness and receptivity is an increased ability to perceive the spiritual dimension of things and people. The "immanence" (or in-dwelling) of God in all of His creation is often subtle and difficult to see because of your reactivity, preconceptions, and self-concern (the static on your mind radio). The more focused and receptive your mind becomes, the more often the spiritual or divine aspects of life shine through. An increased sense of community and connection with other people usually follows as well. You might even end up seeing God reflected in the most annoying person in your life!

An Experience of Closeness to God

The ultimate benefit of Jewish meditation is an experience of greater closeness to God. The Jewish term for this is *devekut,* which is translated in a variety of ways, including "cleaving to the Divine" or "closeness to God." Once you've tasted some of the benefits of Jewish meditation I've already described—increased understanding and control over your own mind, and enhanced awareness and receptivity—you may find yourself opening to this deeper level of spiritual experience, alternatively described as a higher state of consciousness.

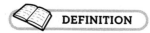 **DEFINITION**

Devekut is a Jewish term meaning "cleaving to the Divine" and refers to either the practice of holding God's presence in your mind at all times or the transcendent experience of closeness to God.

Closeness to God is nearly impossible to describe, but if you've felt it, you'll probably recognize references to the experience in all kinds of places—poetry, music, literature, and a variety of spiritual teachings. A deep experience of devekut requires great openness and devotion. You recognize the presence of God as pervading all things outside you, but also as residing deep within. Despite the fact that all things are *of* God, you still exist as an individual and can therefore have a relationship *to* God—one of intimate and intense love. While a personal experience of devekut is of course rewarding in and of itself, it also puts your life into perspective. This experience can also have many positive effects, including a greater devotion to God, more inspiration for spiritual practice, and greater equanimity (because the troubles of your life seem small compared to God).

Jewish Prayer as Meditation

There are many different kinds of Jewish meditation. Some of them are fairly explicit forms of meditation with roots in ancient Jewish texts and teachings, including the visualization of specific Hebrew characters and Kabbalistic practices. Other Jewish meditations you may encounter are fairly recent improvisations of teachers who combine Jewish content and intent with more modern approaches to meditation inspired by Buddhism and mindfulness. Such meditations can be very accessible and useful, such as repeating the Hebrew word for "Here I am" in silent meditation, coordinated with your breathing, as suggested by Nan Fink Gefen in her book *Discovering Jewish Meditation: Instruction and Guidance for Learning an Ancient Spiritual Practice.*

Here, I'm going to focus on a form of Jewish practice that's traditional, familiar to all Jews, and can be used as a profound form of meditation: Jewish prayer. The essence of meditation is directing your mind in a deliberate way, and this can definitely be done during prayer. While it's entirely possible to perform prayers in a rote way that isn't meditative, throughout Jewish history, devout practitioners have sought to pray in a way that's meaningful and allows the prayer to affect their mind and heart. This is prayer with *kavanah*, a Jewish word that refers to directing your consciousness in a deliberate, focused, and devotional way.

General Description of the Method

Observant Jews pray four times a day: morning, afternoon, evening, and before bed. Prayer is woven into the fabric of each day to ensure you never forget about God for long. Daily prayers involve a set liturgy, with particular verses and blessings performed in a prescribed way and order. Texts of these prayers can be found in the standard Jewish prayer book, and some of them, along with instructions for how to do them, can be found online (for example, at chabad.org).

 **WATCH OUT**

As you read Jewish prayers and other writings, you're probably going to encounter lots of names, terms, and imagery that are unfamiliar to you. This may turn you off if you assume such language refers to something that's only of interest to someone who is technically Jewish or deeply observant. You usually don't have to look far into Judaism before you can find a scholarly explanation of the meaning and symbolism of every significant name, term, or image—and the meaning is often universally applicable, despite how it may appear at first.

Making your prayer meditative requires intention, or kavanah, as mentioned earlier. Your intention may take different forms at different times. Sometimes you may simply want to take a restorative break from your stressful life. At other times, you may seek to deepen your experience of God or open yourself up to being affected and informed by the act of prayer. Whatever your explicit, conscious intention, it requires you to concentrate on the prayer as best you can. When you find your mind wandering, you bring it back to the prayer. You try to put everything you have into the prayer (instead of doing it halfheartedly while thinking of something else). Ideally, the prayer occupies your body and fills your whole consciousness.

The Theory Behind the Meditation

In the Jewish view, God is naturally the most important thing in the universe. Of course, as described earlier, He isn't a thing, a being, or a principle, but is formless, indivisible, and eternal. God is also the creator of the universe from which all things arise. He is just, merciful, holy, and perfect. Consequently, if you have a deep personal conviction that God is real, present, and exactly as described here, you naturally want to make your whole life about God. A desire to praise, honor, serve, contemplate, and cleave to God is simply part of the natural order of things. Prayer and meditation are ways to remember, express, and fulfill that desire.

The efficacy of using Jewish prayers in meditation has a lot to do with the fact that most of the prayers Jews regularly use are 1,000 years old or more and were carefully designed by learned and experienced Jewish teachers and leaders. Every aspect of the prayer—the sound of the syllables in Hebrew, the meaning of the words, the order in which prayers are done, and so on—are thought to have deep significance and power. Therefore, it's very valuable to experience the prayer fully, giving it your full attention and energy and letting it affect you at both conscious and unconscious levels.

Beginner's Meditation Instructions

One of the most valued and well-known Jewish prayers is the *Shema,* one of the religion's primary declarations of faith. The Shema is traditionally recited three times a day: morning, evening, and before bed. The full Shema is about 27 lines long, but the first line is sometimes used by itself. While you're saying the first line, you try to arouse extra concentration and devotion. Here, I present how you can recite the first line of the Shema as a meditation.

 **DEFINITION**

> The **Shema** is a very old, traditional Jewish prayer recited at least twice a day. The first line, "Sh'ma Yisraeil, Adonai Eloheinu, Adonai Echad," is often a focus of special concentration and devotion and can be translated as "Listen, Israel: the Lord our God, the Lord is One."

Setting and Posture

To recite the Shema, choose a time and place where you'll be relatively free from distraction and interruption. You should also be in a setting that's appropriate for the contemplation of the Divine—somewhere clean, without unpleasant odors. It's a good idea to choose a particular place with some care out of respect for God and for your own effort. Recite the Shema only while seated; a chair will work just fine. While praying, you'll want to "turn inward," so a physical posture that reflects this is best: close your eyes, bow your head slightly, and even allow your back to bend a little.

During the prayer, cover your eyes with your right hand to further encourage yourself to focus on the prayer. As you do so, keep in mind an observant Jew would be wearing a prayer shawl at such a time and would gather the fringes at each of the four corners of the shawl into his left hand and hold this hand over his heart. This action represents bringing together the "four corners of the world" in the act of prayer; without a shawl, you may want to contemplate for a moment how your prayer, even though it's private and internally focused, affects and is part of the greater world.

Basic Practice

The following is a simple practice in which you slowly recite out loud the first line of the Shema and pause as long as you want to after each word to allow its sound and meaning to sink in. (Note that the Shema is usually preceded by introductory prayers and followed by closing prayers; I'll briefly describe abridged versions of these prayers later, in the section "Additional Guidance and Encouragement," so you can add them to the meditation practice if you want to.) While it's considered preferable to use the Hebrew words (or transliterations of them), you can use the English, if you prefer (you can find an audio version of this meditation on idiotsguides.com/meditation):

1. Sit comfortably and recite "Bring us in peace from the four corners of the world." For a moment, bring to mind your connection to and concern for the whole world.

2. Recite out loud the first word of the prayer: *Sh'ma*, which means "hear" or "listen." Listen inwardly so you can hear the still, small voice of God. (Each time you recite a word of the prayer, pause to contemplate as long you want to, but move on if your mind starts wandering.)

3. Recite *Yisraeil*, or "Israel." In Hebrew, this means "one who wrestles with God." As you recite and contemplate this word, arouse the part of yourself that seeks to have a conversation with or relationship to the Divine.

4. Recite *Adonai*, or "Lord." In Hebrew, this part of the prayer is actually YHVH, or *Yod-Hei-Vav-Hei*, four letters that stand for the name of God but can't actually be pronounced. As you recite and contemplate this word, call to mind the vast and formless nature of God.

5. Recite *Eloheinu*, or "our God." This refers to the personal nature of God, who cares for you as the beloved and with whom you can have an intimate relationship. As you recite and contemplate this word, call to mind the loving and personal aspect of God.

6. Recite *Adonai*, or "Lord," again. As you recite and contemplate this word, again bring back into your mind and heart the vast, formless, indefinable nature of God.

7. Recite *Echad*, or "One." (If you're using Hebrew, place an emphasis on the *d*, and pronounce the *ch* as a particularly breathy *h*.) As you recite and contemplate this word, allow your meditation to be a moment of oneness, when you as subject, you as object, and all that's yours become one with God.

Because the Shema is considered such a significant prayer in Judaism, you're only supposed to do one recitation at a time (as opposed to repeating it over and over). If you'd like, however, you can remain seated after you've finished the prayer and sustain the devotion you've cultivated for a short period of time—or, as described in the following section, you can add a closing prayer.

Additional Guidance and Encouragement

Although I've talked a lot here about how you should feel during this kind of meditative Jewish prayer, don't get discouraged if you don't feel the way you think you're supposed to. The important thing is to try. The whole process is informative and affects you. Keep in mind that in Judaism, prayer and all other important practices are done because they're commandments. This means God has commanded they be done, so doing them—even if they don't feel particularly inspiring or special on a given day—improves your relationship with Him.

Your experience of reciting the first line of the Shema as a meditation may be deepened by performing the prayer in a more traditional way—that is, in the context of a prayer service, as follows:

- **First prayer:** Blessed are you, Adonai (Lord) our God, who forms light and creates darkness, makes peace and creates all. You who illuminates the earth and those who dwell upon it with compassion, and in Your goodness renews daily, perpetually, the work of creation.

- **Second prayer:** Holy, holy, holy is Adonai, the whole world is filled with Your glory.

- **Third prayer (just before Shema):** With an eternal love have You loved us, Adonai, our God.

- **Closing prayer (just after Shema):** Adonai our God is true.

The Shema can be the part you focus on specifically as a meditation by taking your time and concentrating as hard as you can. The preceding and closing prayers can be said more quickly, although it's still best if you give them your full attention and say them with devotion.

These opening and closing verses are parts of longer prayers, as is the first line of the Shema itself, so you may want to investigate the complete prayers on a website such as jewfaq.org, or in Rabbi Zalman Schachter-Shalomi's book *Sh'ma: A Concise Weekday Siddur for Praying in English*.

Deepening Your Meditative Jewish Prayer

Generally speaking, the more determined you are to experience devekut—closeness to God—in meditative Jewish prayer, the more likely you are to be able to do so. This determination amounts to a kind of longing, like the longing you might feel to be close to someone you've fallen in love with. When you're in love, no obstacle is too great to overcome when you're trying to get close to your lover. In the case of devotional prayer or any other Jewish practices, you may face obstacles to devekut in the form of boredom, dullness, emotional defensiveness, resistance, anger, and so on. If you continue to engage the practice anyway, sooner or later you can find your own way around these obstacles (and learn a lot about yourself in the meantime). You can also try practices that complement your meditation, explore other kinds of Jewish meditation, learn more from reading, or find a community to study and practice with.

Other Supportive Jewish Practices

Most, if not all, Jewish practices are meant to make you more mindful of God, aware of His presence in all creation, and spiritually open to Him. All of these benefits will, in turn, prepare you for a deeper experience of meditation. So I'll briefly describe two Jewish practices here you may want to investigate in order to deepen your meditation and potentially gain these benefits.

As mentioned earlier in this chapter, observant Jews pray at least three times a day: morning, afternoon, and evening. At these times, they do an established set of prayers in a particular order, in prescribed ways. All of the prayers, like the Shema introduced in this chapter, have important meanings and functions in spiritual practice. Interspersing prayer with the activities of your daily life can help you feel very grounded and inspired. Even if you aren't interested in the rigor of established prayer services or praying three times a day, you might want to try something like taking time to do this chapter's Shema meditation twice a day—once in the morning and once in the evening.

Perhaps the most important practice in Judaism is the ritual observance of *Shabbat*, a day of rest beginning at sunset on Friday and ending after sunset on Saturday. During Shabbat, creative work (work that produces something or is an effort to control your environment) is set aside. Time is devoted to things like prayer, Torah study, spending time with family, and enjoying leisurely meals. While you aren't supposed to drive, shop, or use the television or computer during Shabbat, those who observe it report these restrictions feel more freeing than limiting, and they anticipate and relish their day of rest. Note that Jews vary widely in how strictly they observe Shabbat, but any effort to simplify your life like this for a day tends to help you remember what is most important in life.

Learning More

Once you've done meditation using the Shema, you may want to explore many other forms of Jewish meditation. The most accessible kinds can be found in books on the subject published in the last 20 to 30 years (see the section "The Role of Meditation in Judaism" for a few reading options). Some of the meditations they offer are taken directly from traditional Jewish sources, while others are improvisations that give you techniques for engaging Jewish practices and content in meditative ways. Meditation techniques you can find in other books include mantralike repetitions of Jewish prayers and syllables, visualizations of Hebrew letters, and contemplation of the names of God.

If you want to take things to the next level and find a meditation teacher or community, try calling your local synagogue. They may offer training or opportunities for group practice of meditation or at least know who to refer you to. You can also check out the website of the Awakened Heart Project for Contemplative Judaism (awakenedheartproject.org) for upcoming workshops and retreats being offered in various parts of the United States.

Jewish Meditation Over a Lifetime

You may experience a number of positive states and feelings in Jewish meditation—peace, relief from stress, devotion, love, or closeness to God. Over many years of practice, the challenge is to sustain and deepen those experiences instead of letting meditation and prayer become rote, automatic, or something given low priority in your life. The idea is to allow the love and joy of prayer to spread into all areas of your life, so you always feel close to God. While it's a high ideal, it's worth a lifetime of effort.

"Ideal" Jewish Meditation

There's no better or "more evolved" place to be in your Jewish meditation. Whatever your experience, you're doing your best and your meditation or prayer is an offering to God. In fact, the first required daily Jewish prayer services were established over 2,000 years as a way for people in exile to make an "offering of their lips," because they couldn't make tangible offerings in their homeland's temple. While it's great to have a transcendent experience or deep feelings, a sincere offering in the form of meditative prayer is more important.

Of course, there *is* an experience of connection and transcendence that many people long for. In Jewish meditation, this is none other than devekut, as you learned a little about earlier. In devekut, you're conscious of being one with all that is. This is a transcendent consciousness, in that it's beyond your usual small sense of self, but it's also *inclusive* of everything, including your individuality. Judaism teaches that God is formless and beyond space and time but at exactly the same time immanent in (dwelling within) everything. In devekut, you experience this directly and know yourself to be intimate with God. You experience this as extreme love between yourself, God, and all of His creation.

The Ultimate Goal

Jewish mysticism offers a very lofty goal for your practice of meditation: *tikkun olam,* or repairing the world. This aspiration is part of a very optimistic view of the future presented in traditional Judaism in which, eventually, a sort of heaven on Earth will be established. In that world to come, all the ills like suffering, injustice, violence, and conflict will cease. Everyone will understand the nature of God and love Him, so everything will fall back into its natural order.

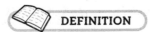 **DEFINITION**

Tikkun olam is a Hebrew term meaning "world repair," and refers to a Jewish responsibility to fix what's wrong with the world.

Those who commit to Judaism share responsibility for making this perfection on Earth come about. As you go about the task of repairing the world, you may be called to undertake many things. Part of your work may be to learn to let go of your anger so you can open more fully to God and be a better instrument of His will. You may devote yourself to supporting your family so all of its members will be healthy and able to do spiritual practice. Repairing the world involves all kinds of positive activities, including generosity, study, taking care of people, and ritual observances that help you maintain an appropriate relationship to life. In the Jewish view, meditation is part of a larger effort to take care of the world.

The Least You Need to Know

- The Jewish view of God is that He is formless (and therefore neither male nor female), indivisible, and outside space and time. However, He also dwells in all creation and is just, merciful, and loving.
- The primary function of Jewish meditation is to give you a way to experience closeness to God.
- Jewish meditation can be esoteric and mystical, or very simple and devotional— and everything in between.
- In the Jewish view, while there's value in performing acts of prayer, meditation, and other spiritual practices regardless of how you feel about them, it's better if you engage in them with an intentional spirit of focused devotion.
- Any benefits you achieve through Jewish meditation are meant to help you be a wiser and more generous, compassionate person as you fulfill your responsibility to help address the problems in the world.

Christian Contemplative Prayer

Throughout the 2,000-year history of Christianity, contemplatives have practiced, taught, and advocated for a deep kind of meditative prayer. While the terms *contemplation* and *meditation* have meant different things in Christianity than they have in other traditions, Christian contemplative prayer has at least two essential features in common with the other meditative traditions discussed in this book: it requires you to set aside your usual engagement in thinking, and it's meant to give you access to a deeper, intuitive, more direct way of knowing.

In this chapter, I give you a brief overview of Christianity and how contemplative prayer fits into the tradition. Because Christians who do contemplative prayer make important distinctions between their practice and Eastern kinds of meditation, I also describe those distinctions and why they're significant. Finally, I give you a practice you can do, advice about how to take your contemplative prayer further, and what it might look like if you did this practice over a lifetime.

In This Chapter

- The development of Christian contemplative prayer over the millennia
- How contemplative prayer differs from a meditative technique
- Letting God pray through you
- How to do Centering Prayer
- Deepening your relationship with God

Overview of Christianity

Christianity is a monotheistic religious tradition that arose in the first century c.e., originally as a sect of Judaism, in and around Jerusalem. The religion is based around the life and teachings of Jesus, who was seen as fulfilling the messianic prophecies in the Jewish scriptures. The religion grew and spread from the Middle East, continually gaining new adherents despite repeated persecutions. In 380 c.e., it became the official religion of the Roman Empire and proceeded to gain prominence throughout Europe and the Near East. It split into a number of significant sects over the millennia, including the Roman Catholic, Eastern Orthodox, and Protestant churches.

The growth of Christianity—the largest religion in the world, with over 2 billion followers—is due in part to the fact that Jesus himself gave instructions that the religion be spread to all nations (Matthew 28:16–20, Holman Christian Standard Bible [HCSB]). With colonialism, the tradition spread from Europe throughout the world. According to the Pew Research Center, as of 2011, while the United States still had the highest number of Christians (247 million), only one European country (Germany) was among the other top-10 countries in terms of Christian population. The remaining countries on the list (in decreasing order in terms of numbers of Christians) were Brazil, Mexico, Russia, the Philippines, Nigeria, China, the Democratic Republic of Congo, and Ethiopia.

The Essence of Christianity

There are so many kinds of Christianity, and they vary so widely in beliefs and practices, it's very difficult to summarize the essence of the tradition in general. However, all types of Christianity have in common the belief in an all-powerful, omniscient God who created the world. There's also agreement that God cares about His creation, including us human beings. The following takes you through those and other beliefs that make up the essence of Christianity.

The Father, the Son, and the Holy Spirit

Sometimes God is described as being pure love, but when this love manifests, in many ways it's like that of a father. He's concerned for the long-term well-being of His children and has a much greater perspective and wisdom than they have, which means His actions—while always loving and appropriate—are sometimes mysterious to us. God the father is beyond form and description and is present everywhere.

Sadly, God's children often turn away from Him, His love, and His wisdom. They become absorbed in their own selfish concerns and views, and act in harmful (or "sinful") ways. In order to draw His children closer to Him and redeem them, God sent His son, Jesus, to be born in human form. Jesus served as a religious leader and teacher and then accepted his fate of martyrdom in order to be resurrected by God three days later, thereby demonstrating to mankind God's power and benevolence. Jesus is the tangible evidence of God's love for limited human beings, and by most Christian sects, he's seen as having been both entirely human and entirely divine.

A third aspect of God, the Holy Spirit, completes the mystical phenomenon that Christians call the *Trinity*. God sent the Holy Spirit to Earth after Jesus was resurrected, and this divine animating force—the invisible spirit of truth—abides in the world with us, even though the physical form of Jesus returned to heaven to be with God the father. (However, Jesus also abides with us in spirit.)

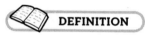

DEFINITION

> The **Trinity** is the Christian view of God as consisting of three people: God the father (ineffable, omniscient, and omnipresent), Jesus Christ (the son of God, who was born as a human, died, and was resurrected), and the Holy Spirit (the invisible spirit of truth, sent by God to abide in the world).

While there has been much debate in the history of Christianity about the exact nature of the Trinity (it has been the cause of some religious schisms), generally speaking, all three aspects of God are seen to be God in His entirety, even though they can manifest separately.

Accepting God's Love as Salvation

It may seem ironic that God is present everywhere and in everything, and yet you can still turn away from Him. Of course in reality you can't. He—along with Jesus and the Holy Spirit—are always with you. However, it's one of the mysteries of God's creation that He made us capable of choice, and that we can reject His love. While that rejection doesn't injure Him in any way or change the underlying reality of His presence, it can profoundly affect the nature of your own experience of life. It can also affect whether after physical death you end up reunited with God in heaven or you end up separated from Him.

The redemptive possibility of accepting God's love and surrendering to His guidance is always available to you. Like a loving father, God will joyfully accept your return at any time. Of course, we human beings tend to be stubborn and stuck in our ways, so sometimes acceptance and surrender aren't easy. Your own ideas, agendas, desires, and fears dominate your experience in such a way that the presence of God in your life is obscured. It's said he speaks with a "still, small voice." Therefore, much of Christian spiritual practice is learning to set aside self-absorption and listen for God's voice, which can be heard within you, as well as through all of His creation.

The Role of Meditation in Christianity

Contemplative prayer is an example of a Christian meditative practice meant to help you listen deeply to God. Throughout the 2,000 years of Christianity's existence, there have always been contemplatives inspired by the words of Jesus, who instructed his followers, "[W]hen you pray, go into your private room, shut your door, and pray to your Father who is in secret. And your Father who sees in secret will reward you." (Matthew 6:6, HCSB) Contemplatives interpret this passage as a reference to turning inward in a meditative way rather than, necessarily, physical solitude.

 CONTEMPLATE THIS

Explicit Christian contemplative practices were first recorded in written form with the sayings of the desert fathers and mothers. These monastics lived in communities in the deserts of Egypt in the fourth and fifth centuries and inspired the Eastern Orthodox practice of *hesychasm,* or internal silence and continual prayer. Hesychast prayer was—and still is—done with the eyes closed and the mind empty of thoughts but receptive to the presence of God.

Christian contemplatives have also sought to cultivate the "mind of Christ" according to the instructions of one of Jesus' disciples, Paul, who said, "Make your own attitude that of Christ Jesus." (Philippians 2:5, HCSB) The attitude, or mind, of Christ isn't a matter of holding on to certain ideas or values. Instead, it's a nonconceptual, experiential form of faith in which you open yourself to God. Over the history of Christianity, it was often monks and nuns—referred to as "mystics"—who went deeply into contemplative prayer. These mystics included the anonymous author of *The Cloud of Unknowing,* St. Teresa of Avila, St. John of the Cross, Hildegard of Bingen, Bernard of Clairvaux, and Ignatius of Loyola.

In the last 50 years or so, modern contemplatives like Thomas Merton have brought more public attention to this Christian practice through their writings. Others, like Thomas Keating, William Meninger, and Basil Pennington, have helped popularize contemplative prayer by adapting ancient approaches to make them more accessible and relevant to modern lay Christians. One way these three monks in particular did this was by creating a method called *Centering Prayer* based on the instructions found in the fourteenth-century classic *The Cloud of Unknowing;* you'll learn more about this method later in the chapter.

Three Benefits of Contemplative Prayer

Like all meditative practices, contemplative prayer can have physical, psychological, and emotional benefits. Because of the recent increase in public interest in meditation, such prayer is beginning to be studied to learn more about such benefits. However, teachers of contemplative prayer emphasize that any utilitarian or practical rewards of this practice are *not* the point of doing it. Instead, it's a way of cultivating a deeper relationship with God. In that spirit, I share three benefits of contemplative prayer that are directly related to that ultimate goal.

Less Self-Attachment

You have many opportunities for decreasing your self-attachment as you practice contemplative prayer. Like all the meditative practices discussed in this book, it requires you to give up your attachment to thinking. Whatever method you're using, you refrain from indulging in thoughts about the past and future, fantasies, and analyses; thoughts will still arise, but you stay focused on your meditation anyway. In the context of contemplative prayer, the deep silence, stillness, and pure awareness underneath all of your thoughts is identified with God or at least with being open and receptive to Him. Over time, you become less identified with your thoughts—which always reflect your sense of existing separately from God—and more identified with Him. You become less attached to your thoughts, emotions, and sense of separateness.

POINT OF CLARIFICATION

In Christian practice, you're not trying to cultivate less self-attachment in order to be happier or to become a good person. These are still self-centered concerns. Instead, you seek selflessness in order to be of benefit to others and to drop what gets between you and God.

Another, even deeper opportunity for decreasing your self-attachment comes later in the meditative process. At some point, in order to make any further progress, you have to give up your attachment even to your desire for spiritual experiences. Ultimately, you're seeking to open yourself completely to God—to let God take over and pray through you. As long as there's a sense of you feeling one with God, your prayer is still limited and somewhat self-centered. The process of deepening your contemplative prayer can be challenging, and acceptance of this (your prayer experience not being how you'd like it to be) is yet another opportunity to release self-attachment.

Greater Surrender to God

The process of contemplative prayer gradually makes you more comfortable with the process of surrendering to God. As long as this act remains a mere ideal you hold in your mind, it's unlikely to actually happen. You know you should give up your own agenda and small-minded effort and trust in God, but what does that really mean? Your body and mind learn a little bit about what surrender really means every time you let go of your thinking and settle back into the silence of contemplative prayer. When you stop trying to figure things out for yourself and focus on listening for the still, small voice of God, this is in itself an act of faith.

Christian contemplatives emphasize that deep prayer isn't something you do. Rather, it's something you allow by getting out of the way. After all, God is already present within and around you, so all you have to do is wake up to that fact. The effort you make in contemplative prayer is more about "giving up doing" than it is about doing anything special or developing any kind of concentration or particular skill.

To illustrate, David Frenette writes in his book *The Path of Centering Prayer: Deepening Your Experience of God,* "To reach true transformation in Christ, you surrender into his sacrificial life within. The mystery of sacrificial love … is inscribed in time through his passion, death, and resurrection, when Jesus gave his life in self-emptying love to the Father for all humankind." In contemplative prayer, you try to enact the same kind of "self-emptying" that Christ did in his ultimate act of love.

God as a Living Reality

Contemplative prayer invites you to experience God in a more direct way. While there's value in belief, or an intuitive faith that God exists, these kinds of relationships to God are more open to doubt than a conviction based on your own personal experience. The deeper your conviction, the more willing you'll be to set aside your worldly concerns in order to listen to His will. The more you feel bathed in God's love, the more open and generous you'll be toward others. Therefore, ideally, the intention to deepen your experience of God isn't based on a selfish motivation.

CONTEMPLATE THIS

Experiencing God as a living reality is a natural outcome of surrendering to Him. At some level, before you let go of your effort and ultimately your self-consciousness, you fear what will happen. When you manage to let go completely through practice, however, you find He's there supporting you and your life (as He was all along).

Contemplatives and mystics throughout history have reported experiences of direct encounters with the Divine, achieved through contemplative prayer and similar meditative exercises. Of course, it isn't that they encountered a deity who exists outside of them, but rather that they allowed themselves to become subsumed within God, who is everywhere. Sometimes these experiences are dramatic—even including visions. Most of the time, however, they are simple, quiet, and take place within.

Centering Prayer

In this chapter, I focus on the type of contemplative prayer developed by Thomas Keating and others from *The Cloud of Unknowing* called *Centering Prayer.* To clarify, Centering Prayer is actually seen as a precursor to contemplative prayer; in contemplative prayer, you simply open your mind, heart, and being to God beyond any thoughts or effort. Contemplative prayer is a gift God may or may not give you at any given time. Essentially, you work on preparing yourself for contemplative prayer using methods such as Centering Prayer.

General Description of the Method

In Centering Prayer, you sit comfortably with the intention of giving consent to God. You invite Him into your life and experience. You consent to allow Him to make your prayer however He wants it to be. You also agree to give up your attachment to your thinking (your effort to figure things out) and settle into the silence within, where He dwells. The most important aspect of Centering Prayer is this intention and consent; while it's the instruction given to beginners, it's also the touchstone to which experienced contemplatives return in order to deepen their prayer.

To focus your intention, you choose a one- or two-syllable word that symbolizes for you the consent you're offering to God. This is called a *sacred word,* and it can be something like *God, Jesus, amen, trust, mercy, love, peace,* or *kindness.* As you sit in prayer, whenever you find yourself distracted by thoughts, emotions, or sensations, you gently introduce your sacred word as a symbol of your consent. The point isn't to concentrate unwaveringly on the word, or to repeat it to the exclusion of thoughts. Instead, this is supposed to be a process of inviting God into your experience rather than achieving connection with Him through a technique.

The Theory Behind the Meditation

The practice of Centering Prayer is intended to remove the obstacles you have to receiving the gift of contemplative prayer. Your self-attachments and habits of mind get in the way of your open-hearted acceptance and surrender. The direct experience of God's presence happens in the space of pure awareness, beyond thinking and conscious effort. So the practice of gently remembering to let go of thinking and give your consent gradually affects you; over time, the attitude necessary for true contemplation gets stronger in you.

 **WATCH OUT**

As is the case whenever stages of meditation are described (such as relying on a sacred word in meditation, as opposed to being able to let go of it), be careful of getting caught up in evaluation, comparison, and impatience. While it's useful at some level to know about the arc of development in a spiritual practice, concern about where you are on that arc only gets in the way of your prayer or meditation.

Eventually, you can let go of the activity involved in Centering Prayer—returning to your sacred word—in order to see how the word arises out of a deeper stillness from God Himself. You can then drop your word in favor of listening for God's voice Itself. This is when you may be visited by the gift of true contemplative prayer, in which God is a partner.

Beginner's Meditation Instructions

Centering Prayer is a very simple, accessible practice you can easily try on your own and even make a regular part of your life. If you find yourself feeling stuck, you may want to consult a teacher or book on the subject. But for the most part, if you just do it, the prayer itself will gradually affect and teach you. It's recommended you practice Centering Prayer for 20 minutes at a time, twice a day. Of course if you can't commit to that much time, any amount is beneficial.

Setting and Posture

It's best to pray in a clean, private place where you can focus on God without worrying about being interrupted by people, phones, or other electronic signals that mean someone wants something from you. Dedicate the period of your meditation to God alone, and close your eyes in order to turn your attention inward.

Take a comfortable seated posture that encourages alertness. Your physical posture before God will affect your "mental posture," so sit in a way that communicates attentiveness and respect. Although the seated postures in Chapter 2 will work, you may choose to sit in a chair instead of in a special cross-legged posture on the floor. Sometimes people find taking a special posture just for prayer promotes a sense you're engaging in a technique meant to achieve some particular effect, instead of simply opening to God just as you are.

Using a Sacred Word

While I've gone over this briefly already, I think additional instruction in the use of a sacred word will be helpful here. Don't worry too much about choosing your word. It's not the word that counts; it's the attitude with which you return to it. If a word naturally inspires you, that's fine, but once you pick a word, don't change it—at least during a given period of meditation. However, it's advisable to stick with the same word whenever you practice. Thinking too much about what word to use only encourages a sense of striving in your prayer, as if you're trying to achieve some particular state or experience by using your word. Instead, in your prayer, allow your word to arise whenever you realize your mind has wandered. It's simply a tool to remind you of your deeper intention: consenting to God's presence and action within and growing more still so you can hear Him.

It's okay if your intention doesn't always feel clear. You may have no idea what you think God is, or what a deeper experience of Him means. Part of what you consent to in the process of Centering Prayer is moving into the unknown. As you silently return to your sacred word, you strengthen your intention to open up to whatever comes and to accept whatever is happening.

Rather than thinking about what your sacred word means or trying to connect with some feeling it has once given you, simply let the word remind you to become more receptive, willing, accepting, and open.

> **POINT OF CLARIFICATION**
>
> While it's most typical to start your Centering Prayer practice by using a sacred word, two other ways of focusing your prayer may be more suitable for you. You can practice awareness of your breathing instead, or make a quick "inward glance" toward the Divine Presence within (this may involve a mental image of some kind). In either case, these meditative objects are used as symbols, just like a sacred word. You gently become aware of them in your prayer when your mind has wandered, but then you let them go; you don't concentrate on them.

Basic Practice

By way of preparation, you may want to spend a few moments calling to mind however God is manifesting most clearly for you in your life. This may be a sense of mystery, omnipresent support, or Christ's selfless love. If nothing arises for you, you can call to mind God as the unknown. You then follow these instructions (you can find an audio version of this meditation on idiotsguides.com/meditation):

1. Choose a one- or two-syllable sacred word that for you symbolizes your consent to God. This is called a *sacred word*, and can be something like *God, Jesus, amen, trust, mercy, love, peace,* or *kindness.* Don't worry too much about choosing your word. It's not the word that counts; it's the attitude with which you return to it. Once you pick a word, don't change it during the meditation.

2. In the midst of your prayer, allow your word to arise whenever you realize your mind has wandered. You don't need to concentrate unwaveringly on the word or to repeat it to the exclusion of thoughts. When you need to, say it inwardly one time, using it as a tool to remind you of your deeper intention—consenting to God's presence and action within—and growing more still so you can hear Him.

3. Spend a few moments calling to mind however God is manifesting most clearly for you in your life. This may be a sense of mystery, omnipresent support, or Christ's selfless love. If nothing arises for you, call to mind God as the unknown.

4. Allow your sacred word to arise silently in your prayer. Say it inwardly one time and then offer your consent to God's presence and action within you.

5. Sit silently in openness, willingness, curiosity, and love. Whenever you find your mind wandering from your prayer, gently return to your sacred word. Sustain a sense of openness and willingness toward God as long as possible.

6. Say your sacred word inwardly, inviting God into your experience with as much sincerity as possible. If your intention or sense of God feels unclear, that's fine. You may have no idea what you think God is or what a deeper experience of Him means. Part of what you consent to in the process of Centering Prayer is moving into the unknown.

7. As you silently return to your sacred word, strengthen your intention to open up to whatever comes and to accept whatever's happening. Let your word remind you to become more receptive, willing, accepting, and open.

8. At the end of your prayer period, let go of your sacred word and any effort.

These four steps in Centering Prayer are traditional. Each one has significance and can be explored further as a way to deepen your prayer. You can work to clarify and connect with your intention, pay closer attention to how your posture affects your prayer, examine what gentleness and noneffort really mean in your experience, and learn how to carry the effects of your prayer into your daily life.

Additional Guidance and Encouragement

Whatever happens during your Centering Prayer, you're doing it correctly as long as you're trying! Your mind may wander over and over, and you may wonder if this is useful at all because you never have a "felt sense" of God's presence. You may fall asleep or constantly critique your ability to stay present. On the other hand, you may have pleasant experiences or feel like you're developing a deeper relationship with God. No matter what seems to be happening, your job is to let go of both your positive and negative experiences and consent to the next moment.

Letting Go of Rigidity

According to Centering Prayer practitioner and teacher David Frenette, "The primary obstacle to deepening Centering Prayer in the first years of practice is rigidity. Rigidity develops unconsciously, especially when you are caught in the attitude that Centering Prayer is something that you are doing on your own. There is an important difference between a technique and prayer." It's very easy to approach contemplative prayer the way you approach most things in daily life: there's a task in front of you, so the faster and harder you buckle down and do it, the faster it will be accomplished. You strategize about how best to finish the task and feel good or bad depending on whether your goal has been achieved.

 **WATCH OUT**

There's only one way you can learn the difference between rigidly trying to do Centering Prayer on your own and learning to participate in it with God: trial and error. Considering different approaches intellectually is of limited use. Ultimately, you simply have to keep trying, sometimes getting too rigid and sometimes getting too slack, until you happen upon a way that works.

Centering Prayer is a very different kind of task. Of course, it's not really a task at all. It might be more helpful to think of it as an offering in which you offer yourself up to God (or at the very least, you offer up 20 minutes of your life). Having made the offering, God can then do with you whatever He wills. This can be tricky, of course, because it's possible to become dull, sleepy, and complacent, figuring God will do all the work. In this case, the metaphor of offering breaks down; it's then more useful to think of contemplative prayer as something you do with God, as partners. If you don't participate in a wholehearted way, the process can't unfold—even if God's doing His part.

Energetic Consent

Despite your best efforts, your Centering Prayer experience may not be what you would like it to be. Or, if it is how you'd like it to be, eventually it's going to change (this can be even worse, if you feel like you've lost a sense of connection to God or a source of meaning in your life). How do you deal with these disappointments? If you want to keep deepening your Centering Prayer, it's important to let go of attempts to make your experience anything other than what it is. You fold your experience—whatever it is—into your prayer, and practice accepting it and consenting to it.

However, consenting to something like a wandering mind or the loss of sensing God's presence doesn't mean you go passive and resign yourself to your prayer staying that way forever. Consent is an active, energetic act of love. Whatever is happening in your life and prayer, this is what God is asking you to deal with. If you turn toward obstacles in your prayer without trying to change them, consenting to whatever God has in store for you, your attention and willingness may allow you to receive the lesson inherent in the obstacles. Change may happen, but it does so because you consented to the process and not because you managed to gain control of the situation.

Deepening Your Contemplative Prayer

The best way to deepen your Centering Prayer, and thereby open yourself up to the gift of contemplative prayer, is to practice it regularly. As mentioned earlier, it's recommended you spend two 20-minute periods doing Centering Prayer each day. You can also develop and deepen your prayer significantly simply by opening yourself to each of the four steps of Centering Prayer more completely—trying to be more consenting, more relaxed, more gentle, and more restful.

Other Supportive Contemplative Practices

As is the case with many other meditative traditions, a tried-and-true way of deepening your contemplative prayer is to attend an intensive, residential retreat. These provide an opportunity to spend lots of time in prayer, receive instruction, and explore other supportive practices (such as *Lectio Divina*). Contemplative prayer retreats range anywhere from a weekend to 21-day intensives, and can be a transformative experience.

 **DEFINITION**

> **Lectio Divina** means "divine reading." It dates back to monastic practices in the fifth century and involves contemplative reading of, reflecting on, responding to, and resting in a passage of scripture, as if you're in a conversation with Christ. The practice of Lectio Divina complements and supports contemplative prayer.

Contemplative prayer is meant to be completely compatible with—and complementary to—other Christian practices. Traditionally, deep contemplative prayer takes place within a greater religious context that includes such things as bible study, attending church services, and practicing generosity in your community. In addition, your contemplative prayer will be strengthened by whatever you can do in your life to cultivate a receptive, open attitude and reverence for God.

Learning More

To learn more about Christian contemplative prayer in general, as well as more about Centering Prayer, read Thomas Keating's *Open Mind, Open Heart: The Contemplative Dimension of the Gospel* or David Frenette's *The Path of Centering Prayer: Deepening Your Experience of God*. Both of these books contain great advice for beginners, as well as guidance for people with an established practice who want to deepen their prayer experience.

You can also locate Centering Prayer groups in many major cities, and most of them are small and informal; essentially, they consist of practitioners coming together to mutually support and inspire one another. You can find links to local groups, as well as many great videos, reading materials, and recommended books, on the Contemplative Outreach website (contemplativeoutreach.org). Contemplative Outreach is the organization started by Thomas Keating and others to support people in their contemplative prayer practice. Their website lists different upcoming events, including contemplative prayer retreats of various kinds (not limited to Centering Prayer). You can explore an alternative modern approach through the World Community for Christian Meditation (wccm.org); their website has links to many local meditation groups throughout the world, as well as possibilities for participation with a group online.

Contemplative Prayer Over a Lifetime

The early years of a practice of contemplative prayer can be challenging at times as you learn to deepen your meditation without becoming rigid and learn how to orient your mind and body in the appropriate attitude of prayer. Eventually, it gets easier and begins to feel more relaxed and natural. If you continue, chances are you'll have some direct and profound experiences of God's presence or action within you. These may be brief, and at first they are temporary. While they can provide you with much inspiration for your practice, they can also end up being a source of frustration, because when they go away, your attempts to recapture them could be difficult. Over time, however, these experiences are not so remarkable or temporary, and there ends up being less of a difference between your contemplative prayer and the rest of your life.

"Ideal" Contemplative Prayer

Once you've practiced an approach like Centering Prayer for a number of years, you may find yourself doing less and less in the midst of prayer. You can let go of symbols, mantras, and techniques, and simply rest in pure awareness—still with your orientation completely toward God. You can listen carefully in the great inner silence without any impatience and end up with a sense that you're resting in the space of contemplative prayer. God has taken over and proved He's there. At times, you may feel overwhelmed by love or have some other kind of ecstatic experience, but in some sense simply resting in God is more intimate than that—it's quiet, complete, and almost ordinary.

> **POINT OF CLARIFICATION**
>
> With all this talk about ultimately having to give up your awareness of your spiritual experiences, it may sound like you need to somehow become unconscious in order to experience unity with God. This is not the case. Although you're conscious in the deepest experience of contemplation, you're not self-conscious—there's only God. Part of God is a conscious you, so while there *is* consciousness, awareness of separateness falls away.

Eventually, in order to surrender into God's hands in the space of contemplation, you give up any awareness of your self. As nice as it is to rest in God, there's still a sense of separation there (you are resting in something that's not you). The final stages of dropping even your awareness of having a spiritual experience can be very challenging. Ultimately, of course, it once again requires surrender, because you can't get rid of *you*. You simply allow God to take over—this time completely, by letting go of even the subtlest effort.

The Ultimate Goal

It's said the fruits of contemplative prayer are realized outside the context of prayer in daily life. Ideally through your contemplative practice, you end up grounded in a deep, personal conviction of reality, presence, and love of God. Because of the acceptance you've had to practice along the way, you recognize how all the stuff of life—including things like thoughts, desires, and struggles—are part of God and embraced by Him. In a practical sense, this makes you more patient and compassionate with yourself and others. Ultimately, you see all things are God, and because you've learned to be one with God, you're also one with all things.

You can always awaken to the reality of God at deeper levels, and eventually you can see this as an invitation to a joyful, lifelong spiritual journey rather than as an indictment of whatever level of spiritual development you happen to feel you're at. Part of your journey is to extend your conviction of God's presence and infinite love to all people, all things, and all experiences. This isn't easy! However, the attainment of perfection isn't the point; all along the way, it's a labor of love.

The Least You Need to Know

- In Christianity, the redemptive possibility of accepting God's love and surrendering to His guidance is always available to you.
- Contemplative—or meditative—prayer opens up the possibility of experiencing God's presence directly in a nonconceptual, personal way.
- The deepest kind of contemplation isn't something you do; it's a gift from God. It's more about God's action than yours and is essentially receptive.
- In order to prepare yourself for contemplative prayer, you can cultivate greater receptivity and inner stillness through methods like Centering Prayer.
- Ultimately, it's a deep spiritual practice of surrender to simply do your best and accept whatever happens in your contemplative prayer.

Sufi Meditation

Sufism arose out of Islam, and meditative prayer has been an integral part of Islam since the religion began with the prophet Muhammad (c. 570–632 C.E.). Over the centuries, the Sufis particularly emphasized the importance of meditative prayer, and also established various methods of introspective meditation intended to facilitate a union with God. Most Sufi practices are geared toward the experience and cultivation of divine love.

In this chapter, I give you a basic introduction to Sufism, including its central teachings and meditative practices, how Sufism fits in the larger context of Islam, and how it's sometimes taught separately from orthodox Islam in a way that's meant to be compatible with any religion. I also provide basic instructions that will allow you to try a simplified version of the most ancient form of meditative prayer in Sufism—the remembrance of God through mindful recitations of His name—and explain how you can explore Sufi meditation further.

In This Chapter

* The basic teachings of Sufism and its relationship to Islam
* The importance of meditation in achieving reunion with God
* Sufism as a path of love
* The practice of dhikr or remembrance
* Balancing the inner world of oneness with the outer world of multiplicity

Overview of Sufism

Sufism began as a particular way of practicing Islam, and for most Sufis in the world, this is still the case. Islam is a monotheistic religious tradition that's considered an Abrahamic faith, meaning it shares some common roots with Judaism and Christianity. Muslims believe God has sent many prophets to aid humankind over the millennia, including Jesus Christ, but that He sent his final prophet Muhammad to reveal the definitive version of His teaching. This ultimate message from God is articulated in the *Qur'an,* the Islamic holy book.

Subsequent Islamic scholars have interpreted the Qur'an and other scriptures in order to compile orthodox Islamic law, or *sharia.* This form of law governs all aspects of a Muslim's life, including prayer, family life, and business. Part of the Islamic tradition is the idea that there are three areas of emphasis for a devout Muslim:

- What one should do (the focus of sharia)

- Why one should do it (the focus of scholars and theologians)

- One's intention or attitude while doing it

 **DEFINITION**

The **Qur'an** is the holy book of Islam, believed to have been revealed by God to his prophet Muhammad and to contain God's definitive teaching and instructions. **Sharia** is Islamic law—a set of rules carefully derived from the Qur'an and other important Islamic scriptures—governing the public, private, religious, and secular lives of a Muslim.

While all Muslims try to cultivate the appropriate attitude and devotion, Sufis are seen as emphasizing this third aspect above all others (although most Sufis throughout history have also kept the external form of Islam through observance of sharia). Because of the Sufi emphasis on internal experience, they are often called the mystics of Islam. In addition to their intensive practices aimed at cultivating the right attitude in religious devotion and observance, they teach it's possible to attain reunion with God in this lifetime, rather than having to wait until after death and the eventual resurrection foretold to all devout Muslims. Sufis also tend to view all religious paths as sharing the same ultimate aim, so they're generally tolerant and accepting of diverse approaches to spiritual practice.

The Development of Sufism

Sufism traces its roots back to the beginning of Islam because there have always been mystics in the tradition. For a long time, it didn't identify itself as a separate or definable practice. Eventually, however, around the year 1000 C.E., written manuals describing Sufi practices and teachings began to appear. At times, Sufism was persecuted and suppressed by orthodox Islam, but the writings of the great scholar Al-Ghazali (c. 1058–1111 C.E.) helped people understand and accept Sufism as an aspect of mainstream Islam.

Around the same time as Al-Ghazali was writing, students of Sufism began to gather around particular teachers who then established lineages or orders. Each order, or *tariqa*, maintains its own set of teachings and practices, which are transmitted through the generations from teacher to student. Every order has a head teacher called a *shaykh*, and many practices require initiation and a commitment to a teacher. This accounts for the wide variety of Sufi practices, with no order claiming to be the only way to ultimate truth.

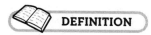 **DEFINITION**

> A **tariqa** is a Sufi order, doctrine, or path. Tariqas trace their lineage back to a highly realized founding teacher who established the particular practices and emphases of the order. **Shaykh** means "leader"; within Sufism, the head of a tariqa is often referred to by this term.

Sufism in the World Today

Generally speaking, wherever you find Islam, you find Muslims who identify or practice as Sufis. While the exact number of Sufis in the world is difficult to estimate, Stephen Schwartz, author of *The Other Islam: Sufism and the Road to Global Harmony*, estimates that over half of the world's Muslims also practice Sufism or have been significantly influenced by it. In addition, many Muslim countries acknowledge the significant contribution that Sufi scholars and poets, such as Jalaluddin Rumi (1207–1273 C.E.), have made to their literary heritage—especially as those writings have been translated and appreciated worldwide.

A number of Sufi orders have also spread to the West over the past 100 years, where new students don't generally come from a Muslim background. Some of these orders (such as the Shadhiliyya and Nimatullahi orders) include the observances of basic Islamic practices, such as performing formal prayers five times a day. Other orders (such as the Naqshbandi and Mevlevi orders) strongly emphasize traditional Islamic teachings but don't require you to adopt any Islamic practices, apart from the Sufi ones associated with the order. Another order, Sufi Order International, was founded by Hazrat Inayat Khan; it's sometimes also called *Universal Sufism*, because Khan taught the unity of all religions. In this order, it's mostly the teachings of Khan—a voluminous writer—and his successors who are studied.

The Essence of Sufism

Whether or not Sufism is practiced along with Islam, it arose out of Islam and therefore shares that religion's view of God and humankind's relationship to God. Sufism's unique contributions include its emphasis on how you were originally one with God and how that original nature of unity resides within you, waiting to be reawakened. Sufism also emphasizes how your longing to return to God is experienced as love and longing for Him and how meditation is the most effective path to achieving reunion with God, the Beloved, in this lifetime.

Surrendering to God

Sufism includes the Islamic view of God as being utterly incomprehensible, perfect, all-powerful, all-knowing, and outside of time and space. All of God's names are simply descriptions and evocations because His true being is beyond conception or definition. (This is also why God is also never portrayed in images in Islam or Sufism.) God is the creator of all things, and He made human beings so they could know and worship Him. In the Qur'an, for instance, God explains to the prophet Muhammad that He addressed the earliest people—the offspring of the "children of Adam"—and asked them "Am I not your Lord?" They replied "Yes, we bear witness." (Qur'an 7:172, Haleem 2004) This exchange is viewed by Sufis as man's covenant with God.

Therefore, worship of God is your primary purpose in life, and "perfect worship" should be your goal. Depending on your religion or circumstances, perfect worship may include following codes of conduct like sharia. It also requires you to act morally, responsibly, and in a way consistent with God's will. At an even deeper level, you need to cultivate a deep inner faith and devotion to God such that you would be willing to sacrifice everything and surrender to Him in an instant if He asked.

Remembering Original Unity

In the Sufi view, you're only temporarily separated from God, and in a sense—because God is everywhere and in everything—even that separation is an illusion. You have an original inner nature or state of being that's completely directed toward God or unity. This state is associated with various positive aspects of humanity, including compassion, intelligence, and perfect worship. Over your life, this inner state of purity, or *fitra,* becomes obscured because of your ego and involvement with worldly concerns. All you have to do is remove those obscurations and allow your original nature to manifest. In the state of fitra, you're motivated purely by the love of God, not by hope of reward or fear of retribution.

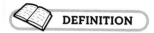 **DEFINITION**

Fitra is an Islamic term meaning "nature" or "instinct." In Sufism, it refers to your original, pure nature, which is inclined toward goodness and oriented toward God.

Our original inner orientation toward God, and toward unity with Him, is part of the natural order of the universe. While He created separation and difference so there would be beings who could know and relate to Him—and so He could be known—we also long to return to Him. For example, in his book *Sufism: The Transformation of the Heart,* Llewellyn Vaughan-Lee suggests God calls to all things to return to Him, meaning "every particle of creation desires to be reunited with the Creator. His call is at the core of creation; without it, the world would disintegrate. It is the centripetal pull which balances the centrifugal, expansive energy of creation."

To heed the call of God, all you have to do is remember Him. In Sufism, *remembrance* refers to anything you do that affirms unity and helps you return to your original state of oneness with God. He's already one with you, and your original nature is already oriented toward Him. You came from God, and your destiny is to return to Him. Nothing in the universe is random; He has planned everything carefully, and He only waits for you to remember your true state.

Walking the Path of Love

Sufis view your relationship with God as a love affair and say the fastest route to reunion with Him (or surrender to Him) is through cultivating love. The first step in this process is awakening to your separation from God. Your original nature knows oneness with God, so you're able, at some level, to remember intimacy with Him. Although ultimately all things are of God, you're separated from him as if by a veil. You experience a longing to know God and to be reunited with Him, and this longing can be painful. Rumi describes the pain of this separation in this excerpt of his poem "The Reed Flute's Song" (translated by Coleman Barks):

> Listen to the story told by the reed,
> of being separated.

> Since I was cut from the reedbed,
> I have made this crying sound.

> Anyone apart from someone he loves
> understands what I say.

> Anyone pulled from a source
> longs to go back.

If you want to be reunited with God as Beloved, Sufis consider it essential that you open up to the pain of longing, for only then do you realize the great love you feel for God. Your lifelong journey to remove the veil between you and God eventually becomes motivated purely by love—even the desire to be free of the pain of longing becomes unimportant. Just as romantic love between people provides the inspiration for heroic courage, patience, devotion, and action, divine love inspires you to let go of your attachment to your illusion of separation from God. You strive to become more and more selfless, passionate, and wholehearted in your love, and by doing so, you purify yourself and open up to the discovery of God within.

The Role of Meditation in Sufism

It's through meditative practices that you recondition yourself and return to the state of fitra—your original, pure self who knows unity with God. Mere intellectual contemplation or willful struggle will never allow you to connect with the deep inner truth of unity or to see past the veil that separates you from God. In a sense, the false self—the one who holds onto the illusion of separation and balks at surrender to God—can't liberate you. Because the illusion of separation is maintained by your mind, the only way to enact surrender to God is to still the mind, withdraw from the senses, and lose yourself in a meditative devotion on God.

POINT OF CLARIFICATION

In Sufi meditation, it's not that you meditate in order to understand *how* to surrender to God, or in order to attain the transcendent ability to do so. Rather, in your meditation, you *practice* surrendering to God. Giving up your sense of separation and self-concern becomes an act of devotion or love (as opposed to a technique employed in order to achieve a particular outcome).

Meditation and meditative practices in Sufism go by many names. Some of these practices involve reciting the names of God while cultivating deep devotion, and others involve deliberate introspection. While different sects and orders teach and emphasize different practices, in general, Sufi meditation is about going deeply within in order to connect with and awaken your deep love for God. By repeatedly turning toward Him with as much devotion as possible, you eventually transform yourself until God is always foremost in your mind and heart.

Three Benefits of Sufi Meditation

Sufi meditation is done purely for the sake of God—to worship Him and to draw closer to reunion with Him. Reunion first requires the purification of the false self, which results in a relinquishment of selfish actions and habits. Through the process of cultivating divine love, you also awaken your own true heart and reacquaint yourself with the experience of unconditional love—both giving and receiving it. Ultimately, your growing sense of connection to God provides you with a stable foundation for your life and a relief from the pain caused by the illusion of isolation. Let's take a look at each of these benefits.

Purification of the Lower Self

The biggest obstacle to your reunion with God is the ego, or your conviction that you are, in reality, a separate and independent self. While your being contains fitra, it also contains what Sufis call the *nafs*, or lower self. There are different levels of the nafs, and the lowest reflect your instinctual tendencies in the opposite direction of God toward things like selfishness, anger, judgment, and greed. In order to return to a state of fitra, you need to purify yourself of these selfish and negative impulses.

 **DEFINITION**

> **Nafs** is an Arabic word for "self," "ego," or "soul"; in Sufism, the word tends to refer in particular to the lower aspects of self that keep you separated from God.

While many Sufi practices are aimed at helping you free yourself from the lower aspects of your nature, none are viewed to be as effective as meditative devotion. After all, in a sense, these baser, selfish impulses arise because of the illusion of separation and because you've forgotten your love for God. You reconnect with that deep love through meditative practices that take you beyond the level of thinking. Your remembered love naturally inspires in you the desire to renounce that which separates you from God. Every time you set aside time for prayer and meditation, and every time you let go of thoughts in order to concentrate on God, you enact the renunciation of selfishness in favor of God. Over time, this has a transformative effect.

Cultivating Greater Love

In Sufi meditation, you get plenty of practice cultivating love. You try to feel it and learn to notice when you are limited in your ability to do so. You seek for sincere love within, and in the process explore what such love really is. You intimately inhabit your human experience of loneliness and separation, and allow longing for God as Beloved to arise. Eventually, you recognize the biggest obstacle to reunion with God is your inability to accept His love or to realize the Divine that's already within you.

All of this requires you to expand your heart—to practice loving, and consequently continue learning to love more deeply, more fully, and more unconditionally. The more you awaken to the reality of God, the more you see He's in all beings and all things. This means your abundant love for Him naturally extends to His creation. Finally, your love for God becomes so deep that you're willing to allow yourself to be "annihilated" in God—any distance between you and God becomes too much, and you surrender out of love.

Deeper Experience of Connection

All devout Muslims anticipate reunion with God, at least after death and the final judgment when all souls are resurrected. Sufis aim to realize this reunion in this lifetime, particularly through their meditative practices. Like most of the meditative traditions covered in this book, Sufism teaches that meditation gives you access to a different way of knowing and experiencing. It takes you beneath the surface of things—dominated by your thinking mind—and opens you up to direct contact with deeper realities.

Through Sufi meditation, you bring back to consciousness your original state of unity with God. The bond you share with Him is timeless and eternal, so it's always available to you. Gradually, your experience of this bond becomes more and more real, alive, and intimate. At times, you feel God's companionship, and this deepens your love and conviction. At other times, you may not feel so much of a connection. Out of love, you then call to Him and praise Him. Because of your growing love, it becomes less important to you exactly how intensely you're experiencing God's presence at any given time—your connection with Him is sustained at all times through your love, which only manifests because you came from Him and will, inevitably, return to Him.

The Practice of Dhikr

While there are silent, introspective practices in Sufism called *meditation,* here I concentrate on the most central meditative practice of Sufism: *dhikr,* or "remembrance." Dhikr (pronounced with a heavy *d* sound that makes the word sound like *zikker*) easily fits our working definition of meditation; by practicing this, you're deliberately directing your mind in a particular way for a period of time with the purpose of affecting it.

General Description of the Method

While dhikr can take many different forms, at its most basic it involves reciting the holy names of God in a concentrated, devotional way in order to remember Him and your connection to Him. The term *dhikr* can also refer in a more general way to remembering God no matter what you're doing; however, the actual practice of reciting God's names (which can be done silently or out loud) is considered an essential part of Sufi practice. While God can't actually *be* named in Islam, there's a traditional list of 99 reverent ways to address God or refer to Him. The most common of His names is Allah (meaning simply "The God"), but the list also includes Ar-Rahman, "The All-Merciful"; As-Salam, "The Source of Peace"; Al-Khaliq, "The Creator"; and Al-Khabir, "The All-Aware."

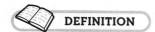 **DEFINITION**

> **Dhikr** means "remembrance of God," and refers both to a meditative practice and to a state of mind. As a practice, it usually involves the recitation of names of God.

Dhikr can be done alone or in groups, with simple versions of the prayer or elaborate dhikr rituals. Depending on the Sufi order, dhikr may involve music or meditative dancing. (The most famous dhikr is probably the trancelike whirling of the Sufis in the order established by Rumi.) The practice may involve hundreds of recitations and may also incorporate verses of praise and other lines from the Qur'an or Islamic scripture. The most important aspect of the practice is the deep state of absorption and devotion with which it's done; ideally, the practitioner affirms the presence of God to the exclusion of all else.

The Theory Behind the Meditation

The remembrance of God in dhikr is seen as the fulfillment of a Sufi's covenant with God. Essentially, if you do your part in remembering Him with the appropriate devotion and presence of mind, He will respond. There are a number of Qur'anic passages in which God commands this process. In one, He says "So remember Me; I will remember you." (Qur'an 2:152, Haleem 2004) He also says to "remember your Lord inwardly, in all humility and awe, without raising your voice, in the mornings and in the evenings" (Qur'an 7:205, Haleem 2004) and "remembering God is greater: God knows everything you are doing." (Qur'an 29:46, Haleem 2004).

While it's the single-minded devotion of remembrance that's essential, remembering God through recitation of His names is especially effective, because His names have power. In Islam and Sufism, the names—written and pronounced in Arabic—are considered to be actual manifestations of God. Dhikr works on your unconscious; by inviting God into yourself in the form of His names, you're asking to be transformed and touched by Him. In the Sufi love affair with God as Beloved, it's understood your own love and longing arise only in response to His—so through your practice you prepare yourself for Him, and He will come to you when He wills.

Beginner's Meditation Instructions

The dhikr practice I share here is a very simple one. As mentioned earlier, the form of this meditative practice varies widely depending on the order of Sufism in which it's done and the setting in which you're doing it (privately or with a group). This is a fairly short and simple—but still traditional—version of dhikr. Keep in mind that if you explore dhikr further, you'll encounter many different instructions for what to recite, how many times, and how to keep count of your recitations.

Setting and Posture

Choose a quiet place where you won't be disturbed. It should be a clean place in order to demonstrate respect for God. Set aside time for dhikr with the full intention of devoting your mind and heart solely to God; don't allow yourself to think about other things or to anticipate when you'll be finished with the practice and can go on to other things.

While you can perform dhikr in any of the seated postures described in Chapter 2, it's not necessary to sit on the floor. If you're seated in a chair, sit up respectfully and attentively and rest both feet on the ground. Close your eyes and imagine closing off your ears to any sound (while you'll still hear things, the idea is not to let your attention be drawn to sounds). Place your hands on your thighs, relax your body, and turn your awareness inward.

POINT OF CLARIFICATION

Because you want to be turned inward during dhikr, you should be minimally distracted by thoughts about your body or posture, or by too many physical sensations. Take a position that's as comfortable as possible—but one in which you still manage to stay awake.

Basic Practice

In this dhikr, you end up reciting brief phrases of praise to Allah, including His name, 100 times. Keep in mind that *Allah* simply means "The God," and He is formless and absolute. So you can practice this dhikr as long as you have—or want—a relationship with God, even if you aren't a Muslim or Sufi.

The three phrases of praise are each repeated 33 times, and these repetitions are traditionally counted using the joints of the fingers on your right hand. First, you use your index finger to touch the tip of your thumb (1), the inside of your thumb knuckle (2), and the base of your thumb (3). You then use your thumb to touch the inside of your index finger at its three joints—your top knuckle, the middle of your finger, and the base of your finger—for 4, 5, and 6. Continue this process with your middle, ring, and pinkie fingers, which will bring you up to the count of 15. You then start over with your pinky finger and continue to your ring, middle, and index fingers, bringing you to 27. Finally, use your index finger to count on your thumb again (tip, middle, and base), and finish with a count of three moving up the thumb (base, middle, and tip). This brings you to a count of 33.

As you perform this dhikr, you can recite silently or out loud, and you can use the Arabic (recommended, because it's believed to carry special power) or the English translation (you can find an audio version of this meditation on idiotsguides.com/meditation):

1. Before beginning the recitations to remember God, take a moment of silence and search within for a sense of His presence. If you feel Him near, perform the dhikr as a song of praise. If you don't feel Him near, perform the dhikr as a call to your Beloved.

2. Recite *Subhan Allah,* or "Glory be to God," 33 times. As you recite, summon a feeling of great love and longing for God. Try to mean each and every recitation. Contemplate how God is perfect, all-seeing, and the creator of the universe.

3. Recite *Alhamdulillah,* or "Praise be to God," 33 times. Again, mean every repetition. Contemplate how everything you have comes from God, and think of His kindness in sending you spiritual instruction and guides.

4. Recite *Allahu Akbar,* or "God is the Greatest," 33 times. Contemplate how nothing compares to God and how He is perfection itself.

5. Finish with one more recitation in order to have recited God's name 100 times: *La Ilaha Illa Allah,* or "There is no God but God."

You may find you're inclined to chant or even sing the verses in this dhikr, and that's fine. Whatever helps you awaken a devotional and concentrated state of mind during the practice is beneficial. Let go of the suggestions about what to contemplate as you recite if, instead, you're able to stay with a feeling of love and devotion.

Additional Guidance and Encouragement

What if you try remembrance of God but don't end up feeling any closer to Him? What if you adopt a practice like dhikr, but it doesn't seem to give you much access to a sense of deep love and devotion or to awaken in you your original self—the one who supposedly already knows your unity with God? The following are a couple ways that could help you through any mental blocks in your meditation.

Opening to Longing

While it may seem counterintuitive, you may need to explore your inner experiences of dissatisfaction and isolation before you seek rewarding experiences of love and connection. As discussed earlier in this chapter, an essential part of the process of remembering your connection to God is recognizing your separation from Him. In the Sufi view, most people distract themselves with the things of the world and fail to realize that a veil separates them from God. They also fail to intuit the divinity that lies behind the veil. Therefore, they dwell in forgetfulness.

 **WATCH OUT**

Longing is a good sign in Sufi practice. Therefore, be aware of any resistance you have to allowing yourself to become dissatisfied with your life as it is. While it's true this could become a slippery slope in which you allow depression or anxiety to take over, if you're careful to translate this dissatisfaction into love and longing for God, the outcome can be positive.

When you first awaken to a vague memory of God and of having been one with Him, it can be painful and disturbing. In contrast to this memory, your life may seem bleak and meaningless. It requires strength and courage to face this stage of spiritual development—to admit your longing. As Sufi scholar Al-Qushayri (986–1072 C.E.) wrote, "Longing is a state of commotion in the heart hoping for meeting the Beloved. [The depth of] longing is commensurate with the servant's love of God." Basically, the more you long, the more you love. Sufi teacher Llewellyn Vaughan-Lee calls this *divine discontent*—and while it can be painful to experience at times, the promise of God and Sufi teachers alike is that allowing yourself to feel it deeply leads to reunion with God.

Allowing Yourself to Be Transformed

It's typical to approach spiritual practice with the same effort to achieve something that you apply to other aspects of your life. Of course, attaining reunion with God is a different kind of undertaking. In Sufi meditation, you try to let go of any willful attempt at anything. Instead, you cultivate a willingness to allow yourself to be transformed.

The names of God, as mentioned earlier, have power. As you recite them, He influences you. The more concentrated and devoted you are while practicing remembrance, the more open you are to His influence. You might think of this as a sort of positive, voluntary brainwashing. You perform an activity others have proven to be transformative over and over, until you forget why you're doing it and let go of any concepts about it (such as "I feel separate from God, so I'm performing dhikr to remember Him"). Ideally, you end up completely absorbed in your meditative practice, the veil of separation created by your own mind falls away, and God reveals Himself within you.

Deepening Your Sufi Meditation

You can deepen your dhikr practice by doing it regularly—it's recommended you do it at least twice a day—and by trying to do it more and more wholeheartedly. You can also spend time contemplating your love for God, to awaken the longing within you and to shift your motivation for meditation from your own desires toward pure love of God. In addition, you can explore the rich Sufi tradition of teachings, practices, and community in order to give your dhikr context and to receive additional guidance about the Sufi way.

Other Supportive Sufi Practices

Strong emphasis is placed in Sufism on having a teacher. In fact, many Sufi practices are only taught to you if you've established a committed relationship with a teacher through a process of initiation. A Sufi teacher has thoroughly studied and mastered the teachings and practices within a particular Sufi order and is therefore able to transmit them to others appropriately. The teacher becomes your spiritual friend and guide, giving you specific practices and assignments suited to your character and needs. Sufis believe every person's path is unique, and in order to navigate your way through potential pitfalls and find your way to God, you benefit greatly from wise, individualized spiritual direction.

> **POINT OF CLARIFICATION**
>
> Ultimately, a Sufi teacher is viewed as the external teacher who guides you toward your internal teacher. While teachers are considered invaluable—because it's unlikely you can break free of ego on your own—they don't give you anything you don't already have. You're already one with God; you just need to see through the veil that hides Him from your sight.

Sufis also deepen their spiritual life by studying teachings and by striving to apply them in their everyday lives. The ideal is holding the love of God first and foremost in your mind at all times, and consequently renouncing anything that distracts you from loving God. Sufis describe this as "inner poverty" undertaken not as a penance but as an act of love. Some Sufi orders offer retreats for deepening your meditative practices and your understanding of Sufism. These range from 3 to 40 days and may be individually or in a group. Retreats may involve Sufi teachings or be entirely focused on solitude, silence, remembrance, and meditation. In either case, they are led by a Sufi teacher who offers personal guidance to participants.

Learning More

There's a lot more you can learn about Sufism, dhikr, and forms of Sufi meditation besides dhikr. Useful books include *Sufism: The Transformation of the Heart* by Llewellyn Vaughan-Lee, *Sufi Light: The Secret of Meditation* by Ahmad Javid, MD, and *Essential Sufism* by Robert Frager and James Fadiman. You may also want to investigate the teachings of Hazrat Inayat Khan, the founder of Universal Sufism, in *The Heart of Sufism: Essential Writings of Hazrat Inayat Khan.*

Sufis also deepen their meditative practices by performing them together. Both silent and audibly chanted dhikr are performed in groups, and sometimes music and sacred movement are added. These group rituals can be profoundly moving and inspiring. You may be able to find a Sufi group in your area to practice with. The following websites, representing different orders of

Sufism, generally have listings of their affiliated groups throughout the world, as well as resource materials about the order's teachings and practices:

- **Golden Sufi Center:** goldensufi.org
- **Naqshbandi Sufi Way:** naqshbandi.org
- **Nimatullahi Sufi Order:** nimatullahi.org
- **Shadhiliyya Sufi Communities:** suficommunities.org
- **Sufi Order International:** sufiorder.org

Sufi Meditation Over a Lifetime

Like many meditative practices, you can devote as much time and energy to deepening your Sufi meditation as you want! It's understood that true mastery takes a long time. However, Sufism isn't a monastic tradition. Although ancient Sufi masters practiced literal renunciation in order to concentrate on their spiritual practice, over time the ideal has become a balanced life. When you have a balanced life, you devote yourself to deepening your inward experience of connection to God, as well as manifesting that love outwardly in the midst of ordinary, daily life.

"Ideal" Sufi Meditation

There's an arc of development in the Sufi practice of dhikr that progresses from the obvious to the subtle. At first, you recite God's names as words. These words have power, as mentioned earlier, but they're also tools to help you focus on God. After a while, the words can drop away, and your dhikr becomes a wordless turning of the heart. Finally, even the practice of dhikr itself falls away, and there's only an invitation to God.

The ideal of Sufi meditation—in dhikr, as well as other forms of meditation within the tradition—is called the *annihilation of the self in God*. While this may sound drastic or negative, that's not the Sufi experience. Instead, this annihilation simply refers to the final, complete letting go of the ego or lower self in surrender to God. The only thing that gets annihilated is your sense of separateness, which is an illusion. In the deepest experience of meditation, you realize there's no one who is becoming united with God because there has never been any real separation to begin with.

The Ultimate Goal

When you fully realize oneness with God, you recognize He is you, and you're nothing but Him. This gives you a profound sense of relief and groundedness, because you realize that death will not be the end for you—you'll continue as God continues. You also see how all things and beings are God, and you become filled with gratitude and love.

CONTEMPLATE THIS

Ideally, in Sufi practice, you learn to live in two worlds—the inner world of unity with God, and the outer world in which the activities of life tend to pull a veil between you and God. Although you may long for oneness with God, He created human beings to love and worship Him—and this requires some degree of separateness. Therefore, out of love, you accept the tension between the two worlds and don't seek one over the other.

After experiencing reunion with God, you live out your life in an outwardly normal way, taking joy in your opportunity to live according to God's will and to constantly deepen your relationship with Him. Part of God's will is you continue to participate in life and fulfill your responsibilities (which, remember, would have been prescribed for a traditional Sufi by Islamic law). While it can be challenging to balance your longing for intimate spiritual experiences of God's presence with keeping up the activities of daily life, this is part of the sacrifice you make for Him. After death, you'll be completely and permanently reunited with God. In the meantime, you can allow yourself to be sustained by the sense of fullness from having remembered He resides within you.

The Least You Need to Know

- In the Sufi view, the purpose of human life is to worship God.
- While you aren't actually separate from God, your ego and attachments to the world create a veil that hides His presence from you.
- The Sufi path is one of love, in which you awaken to and acknowledge your illusory but painful sense of separation from God and long to return to Him.
- Meditative practices that focus on God eventually let you to see past the veil that hides Him from you. They allow you to experience union with God directly, in this lifetime.

Native American Meditative Practices

The spiritual traditions of the indigenous peoples of North America are rich and varied. While it's difficult to generalize about the spiritual practices of hundreds of different tribes that speak hundreds of different languages, it's safe to say all Native American traditions make significant use of meditative ritual. Religious ritual involves prescribed and careful sets of actions, done in a particular order with clear intention, that either fulfill a divine requirement or affect a participant's state of mind (or both). Meditative ritual happens when you deliberately direct your mind toward the experience of ritual.

In this chapter, I introduce you to some of the important themes common in most Native American spiritual traditions—themes that give context to meditative ritual and explain why it's effective and valuable. I explain more about meditative ritual and its benefits, and I suggest a way you can create your own ritual based on the Vision Quest that's part of many native cultures. I also give you some ways to deepen your practice of meditative ritual, describe some other important Native American practices, and tell you how to learn more.

In This Chapter

- Native American spirituality and non-natives
- The circle of life, the spirit world, and the importance of maintaining relationships
- The importance of meditative ritual in native practice
- How to do a meditative ritual on your own
- Deepening your connection to the natural world and to the sacred

Overview of Native American Spirituality

The indigenous peoples of North America are believed to have migrated there when the continent was connected to Asia by the Bering Straits land bridge. These migrations began as early as 30,000 years ago (the Stone Age). By 12,000 B.C.E., human settlements could be found in all areas of North America that were not covered by glaciers.

CONTEMPLATE THIS

Many people are unaware that there were large, highly developed cities in North America long before the arrival of Europeans. The Mississipian culture built a city at the confluence of the Mississippi and Missouri rivers that had a population of about 40,000 people by the year 900 C.E. Other major developments included a city on the site of present-day Phoenix, Arizona, with hundreds of miles of irrigation canals—some of which are still in use today—and a pueblo in Chaco Canyon, New Mexico, completed in 1067, which had over 2,500 rooms and was surrounded by 500 miles of roads connecting it to outlying settlements.

These early cultures eventually developed sophisticated agriculture, permanent settlements, specialized methods of hunting and fishing, and elaborate religious practices, as evidenced by artifacts, burial mounds, and the remains of worship spaces. Large settlements were established throughout the continent, some with highly developed architecture, city planning, irrigation systems, and roads. It's thought the native population of the Americas reached its height around 1300 B.C.E., when an estimated 12 to 15 million people lived in North America alone (not including Central America, which had an estimated 30 million people).

After the fourteenth century, most large Native American settlements either contracted or were abandoned, perhaps because of widespread disease (which was a big problem on other continents about the same time). Tribal migrations, climate changes, and intertribal warfare led to the tribal structure and distribution Europeans encountered when they arrived in 1492.

Given that Native American history before the arrival of Europeans includes the rise and fall of dozens of civilizations and thousands of tribes over the course of 10,000 years, it's extremely difficult to generalize about Native American religion or spirituality. However, in his book *Teaching Spirits: Understanding Native American Religious Traditions*, professor Joseph Epes Brown suggested the common themes in native spirituality include different senses of time (cyclic and mythical), the importance of a sacred place, emphasis on the power of language and oral transmission, a metaphysical view of nature and the spirit world, and the transformative power of ritual.

Contact with Europeans

Any discussion of the cultures of indigenous peoples has to acknowledge the way these cultures have been devastated by colonialism. With the arrival of Europeans, Native Americans died by the thousands, primarily because they were exposed to diseases to which they had no immunity, but also because of various forms of exploitation. Europeans sought to expel natives from their ancestral lands, in some cases in the face of violent opposition. In all cases, the Europeans eventually prevailed. Within a few centuries, the estimated native population of North America had decreased to around 250,000.

The American Revolution accelerated the process of systematic displacement of the native population westward. Natives unwilling to assimilate and give up rights to their native lands were forced onto reservations without regard for their tribal differences, connection to their homelands, or sources of livelihood. In part because spiritual and religious practices tended to unite and empower Native Americans, many of these practices were suppressed or outlawed.

Revival of Native Spirituality

There have always been native traditionalists who struggled to keep their spiritual traditions alive, but for a long period of time, they had to operate in secret and watch their children be educated in Christian boarding schools. In these schools, children were forbidden to carry on any native practices or use their native languages. Starting in the 1950s and 1960s, Native American efforts to revive their traditions and regain the right to practice them began to gain momentum.

In addition to growing interest among Native Americans in remembering and maintaining their traditions, non-natives have started to discover the deep wisdom and healing to be found in them. As many people become disenchanted with modern society and concerned about intensifying environmental and social problems, they recognize the possibility for an alternative way to live embodied in the Native American spiritual teachings and practices. While some natives disagree with sharing their traditional practices and ceremonies with non-natives, others feel it's their responsibility to share what they have in order to help influence modern society.

 **WATCH OUT**

It's important to adopt a humble and respectful attitude when studying Native American culture and practices. Many oversimplified or overgeneralized aspects of native spirituality have been appropriated and used without being fully understood. It's fine to be interested and inspired—and even investigate or do some native practices yourself. But remember, there are hundreds of distinct native cultures, and their practices can ultimately only be fully appreciated if you study them in person with a Native American who's experienced with them.

The Essence of Native Traditions

Currently, the U.S. government recognizes over 550 distinct Native American tribes, so it's important to remember the great variety in native ways of life, language, and culture when attempting to identify the "essence" of native traditions. In addition, Joseph Epes Brown points out in his book *Teaching Spirits* that Native Americans experience their spiritual practice as a whole and rarely engage in philosophical analysis of it. Even more importantly, natives tend to make no distinction between religion (or spirituality) and everyday life. Your spirituality *is* your way of life—it's doing what's supposed to be done in all of your daily activities. Still, some common features are shared by most—if not all—of Native American traditions. These features are remarkable in large part because of how different they are from non-native spiritual traditions and cultures.

The Circle of Life and the Spirit World

Generally speaking, native traditions see both time and natural processes as being cyclical or circular. Until modern exposure to the non-native concept of linear time, there was little sense within native cultures that the course of life is one of constant improvement and development, and that the further you progress in time, the further you get from the past (which should be left behind anyway, because it's old and outdated). Instead, the native view is that everything is going to come around again. You live out your life in four stages—birth, adolescence, adulthood, and old age/death—with the understanding you'll return to the earth so the cycle can start again.

An important implication of seeing time as cyclical is it opens up the possibility of mythic time. Because you're not constantly moving away from the past, in some ways the past is always near. Beings and events from the past, recent or distant, can be summoned in a literal way to appear in the present. Native ways of doing this include the telling of stories, the identification of real physical places with past events, and ritual.

All things, animate and inanimate, are seen as arising from the Great Spirit—a vast, incomprehensible source of life. Therefore, all things have a spirit of their own and a place in the grand scheme of creation. It's not so much that Native Americans perceive of a special, separate spirit realm with which humans can commune. It's more that they don't differentiate between humans and everything else, or between spirits that exist now and ones that exist in the past or future. It's perfectly natural, therefore, that you would speak to spirits, thank them, appease them, and ask them for help. It's also perfectly natural that they would respond, sometimes in signs and visions.

CONTEMPLATE THIS

The Native American sense of time as cyclical is connected to the fact that, for millennia, they were dependent on the cycles of nature for survival—seasons, periods of growth, the migrations of animals, and so on. Therefore, they also have a sense that things can't and shouldn't be rushed, especially because of human greed.

Relationship and Reciprocity

A unique aspect of much Native American spirituality is a deep sense of relationship and reciprocity with all beings, the land, the Great Spirit, and the cycles of life. This is often expressed with terms of kinship that extend beyond people you're literally related to. People, animals, features of the landscape, and natural forces are referred to as *father, mother, sister, brother, aunt,* or *uncle.* Because of this kinship, you have a responsibility to take care of things and beings far beyond your immediate family. To maintain harmonious relationships, you don't ask too much. You remember to express gratitude and to fulfill promises.

Each person, ideally, has a sense they belong and are an important part of the whole. That whole was designed by the Great Spirit and requires the appropriate participation of every part in order to keep functioning in a healthy, sustainable way. When you make an effort to fulfill your responsibilities in life, act appropriately, and keep up your end of your relationships, you do so not simply to keep getting what you want. Instead, your effort is integral to the continued functioning of the whole world. The world system is dependent on humans, just as humans are dependent on the world.

Some of the ways humans help keep the world functioning in a harmonious way is through the performance of particular rituals and ceremonies. Some of these ceremonies were prescribed by powerful spirits and are done in the spirit of thanks or reciprocity. Some are done to restore balance in the world, within an individual, or within a particular system. Other rituals are considered a necessary part of the cycle of life—if they aren't done, the essential processes on which all of life depends might stop or be thrown off-kilter.

The Role of Meditative Ritual

Although some Native American rituals may be done to influence things in the physical or spirit world, it would be incorrect to assume they are done for external as opposed to internal reasons—for example, to appease spirits outside you as opposed to deepening your own sense of connection to the sacred. No such distinction between internal and external is actually made in native traditions. You're part of the world; your experience of ritual and the changes it might cause in you are included in the ritual's overall purpose. In general, native rituals inspire awe, respect, gratitude, humility, and a sense of connection to all life.

POINT OF CLARIFICATION

When Native Americans view a ritual as being essential for the successful continuation of the cycle of life, they generally believe the ritual actually has an effect on the world around them. However, if the idea of supernatural effects and forces don't appeal to you, you can think of this in purely psychological or spiritual terms. For example, when you hear a ceremony is done "so the people may live," you can reflect on how the ritual affects, informs, and inspires the people doing it. It may be very true the continued life of a culture, a people, or the ecosystems of our planet may depend on aligning our minds and hearts in particular way.

The meditative aspects of Native American ritual, for the purposes of our discussion, are those which ask you to direct your mind in particular way and which end up affecting it in some positive way. Few native practices—with the exception of specialized techniques employed only by highly trained holy men or women of the community—involve the kind of prescribed systems of introspection featured in many of the other meditative traditions in this book.

Instead, meditative experience in Native American traditions is usually achieved through ritual elements that engage your whole body and mind. These elements encourage you to drop below the level of ordinary, discriminatory thinking, and open up to a deeper, intuitive level of experience. In native rituals and ceremonies, a meditative state is often produced through dance, drumming, spontaneous prayer, fasting, tests of endurance, and ritual movements.

Three Benefits of Native Practices

The meditative rituals of Native Americans are done for many reasons: for the sake of the community, to remind participants of how to live appropriately and correctly, for health and good fortune, and for self-improvement so you'll be of greater benefit within the community. At times, an elder might prescribe a certain practice for you to help you overcome a particular problem, or to develop you further on your spiritual path. For the most part, however, almost all native spiritual practices—meditative and otherwise—have a generally beneficial effect in the ways I describe here.

Deeper Appreciation for the Natural World

Most native spiritual practices take place in natural settings. The proximity of the natural world is considered an essential aspect of most rituals, and the land itself is believed to hold special power. For Native Americans, the connection to nature and the land has traditionally been very specific, not generic. They formed relationships with particular mountains, bluffs, rivers, rocks, and valleys. Many times, significant things were supposed to have happened at these locations, or someone in the tribe will have had a significant vision about the place. In any case, the native connection with nature and the land has traditionally been very personal (which means, of course, displacement from—or destruction of—ancestral lands is devastating to Native Americans).

So you'll very likely end up with a greater appreciation for nature and your surrounding landscape if you participate in native spiritual practices. Part of it will simply be due to the fact you have to get out in nature—or at least outside—to do most of them. In addition, Native American rituals usually involve natural objects like sticks, stones, and feathers, and prayers are addressed to natural spirits like Mother Earth and Father Sky. The effect of these rituals is to make you notice and appreciate the natural world and to awaken gratitude for the support you receive from it.

CONTEMPLATE THIS

In modern life, it's common for people to have little connection with the natural world—even nearby landscapes or the rivers and farmlands on which their lives depend. If you're interested in feeling more of a connection with where you live, consider researching the places near you that Native Americans have traditionally considered significant (there will definitely be some), and then visit them.

A Greater Sense of Interdependence

The lessons of interdependence and reciprocity are found in most native rituals and practices. There's a social and spiritual dimension to these lessons, as well as a physical one. As mentioned earlier, all manifestations are part of the Great Spirit, and therefore everything and everyone—from the tiniest ant to the largest whale, from your mother to a stranger from the other side of the world, and from the tomato you've just picked to a magnificent mountain—are your relatives. You have a role to play in the world, as does every other being, and your relatives support you in your efforts to fulfill that role.

Native American rituals take these lovely ideas about interdependence and connection from the realm of pure concepts (which have little transformative power) into the realm of your actual, present experience. It may not seem like it would make a big difference to enact gratitude with a gesture or a prayer, to seek connection by sitting on the earth side-by-side with others in a sweat lodge, or to ask for the eagle spirit to give you courage by touching an eagle feather, but it does. In the Native American view, ordinarily intangible realities are made manifest in ritual though language, place, objects, and actions. It's not just that rituals serve as symbols or reminders of an ideal of interdependence; enactment gives you a direct experience of interdependence with all things, and this experience is deeply healing, inspiring, and motivating.

Perceiving the Sacred in Everyday Life

While ritual can momentarily intensify your experience of the sacred, or what is divine or worthy of reverence, ultimately it should also increase your sense that everything you encounter and do in your daily life is sacred. After all, the Great Spirit is in all things. Your relatives take the shape of people, animals, plants, objects, places, life processes, forces, and energies. All of you are participating in the functioning of the universe—and this isn't just the case during ritual, or during a time designated for religious or spiritual activity.

The perception that everything in your life is sacred—whether or not you're aware of it at any given moment—leads to a sense of meaning and purpose in your life. This purpose doesn't have to be based on achieving something in the future. Instead, it's about the role you play in the world at this moment—manifesting care, respect, and appreciation as you interact with various aspects of the Great Spirit.

CONTEMPLATE THIS

You might say the Native Americans were among the world's first ecologists. Many of their traditions reflect a deep understanding of how interdependent each being is with its environment and with all other beings, and how intricately connected all life processes are to one another. This wisdom was probably hard-won by the Native Americans who established these ways of viewing and relating to the world. There's evidence that large Native American settlements throughout the millennia went through repeated cycles of growth and collapse as they exhausted their local natural resources and had to abandon their magnificent cities.

Vision Quest as Meditative Practice

Many Native American meditative rituals, such as the Sweat Lodge Ceremony, require group participation. If you're interested in such practice, I encourage you to see if you can find a group where you can learn the traditional ways and participate with others. The Vision Quest—a practice found in one form or another in many native cultures—is generally done alone, however, so I've chosen that as the practice to share with you that you can try on your own. (Note, however, that intensive Vision Quests are still done with the support of others who help you prepare and who stand by for the duration.)

General Description of the Method

The traditional Native American Vision Quest typically involves spending time alone in nature—preferably in the wilderness, away from the comforts and distractions of home and civilization. It lasts two or more days, including at least one overnight (although I present the option for a shortened version in this chapter). Traditionally, a Vision Quest began with purification through fasting and participation in a sweat lodge, and it was often undertaken at significant points in your life, such as the transition from adolescence to adulthood, the beginning of a new task or responsibility, or during a time of spiritual questioning or doubt.

After preparation, you start on your journey to the place you've chosen for your Vision Quest. Someone might accompany you a certain distance, but eventually you press on alone until you find a place that seems appropriate for your meditation. Such places are often high up on hills or in the mountains, although any beautiful spot that invites spiritual reflection will do. You then settle in, paying careful attention to everything around you, both living and inanimate. Nothing should be ignored; after all, you're asking for vision—some kind of insight into yourself, your life, and your role in the world—and you don't know when it will come or from where. The Great Spirit is present in everything, so it may be a grasshopper that conveys to you the message you need to hear! You try to keep up this attentive effort, along with your internal request for a vision, as long as your Vision Quest lasts—even through the night.

WATCH OUT

If you do a Vision Quest, try not to ruin your experience with too many expectations. The visions in Vision Quests may occasionally be literal visions in the sense that you see something that isn't physically present, have an incredibly vivid dream, or witness a remarkable occurrence in the natural world. In other instances, the visions may simply be insights—less dramatic in their unfolding, but potentially just as transformative.

The Theory Behind the Meditation

A few techniques are associated with a Vision Quest. Like many other Native American meditative rituals, it relies on your actions and setting to support a meditative state of mind. In the case of a Vision Quest, these are the physical enactment of your intention, the silence and vastness of the natural setting, and your isolation. While Native Americans don't generally theorize about why Vision Quests work, it's probably safe to say this particular form of practice puts you in a very sensitive, open state of mind that allows you to see the answers you need.

To deepen your experience, you direct your mind in two ways. First, you try to remain as alert, attentive, and open as possible. Second, you continually ask for a vision. Asking requires an attitude of faith and humility, so some natives prefer to call this *beseeching* the spirit world for assistance and insight. An essential aspect of this practice is to acknowledge you aren't seeking to achieve wisdom all of your own accord; you're connected to all beings and things, and can't achieve anything without that support. Traditionally, asking for a vision is also a fairly open-handed request. While you may have a particular issue or question in mind, you remain open to any kind of vision the spirits choose to send you—and generally, the wisdom of their choice will become clear with time.

Beginner's Meditation Instructions

In his book *Mother Earth Spirituality: Native American Paths to Healing Ourselves and Our World*, Ed McGaa (Eagle Man) recommends against making your first Vision Quest longer than one day and night or two days and nights at the most. If you don't want to (or aren't able to) spend that amount of time on your Vision Quest, at least the first time you do one, you can simply dedicate one day or even a few hours. McGaa also suggests fasting the entire time—drinking only water or juice—which is traditional (but optional, of course). In any case, during this dedicated time, you shouldn't read, write, listen to music, talk to anyone, or distract yourself in any way.

Setting and Posture

Ideally, you'll go to a secluded spot in nature for your Vision Quest. It doesn't have to be in the middle of real wilderness, although generally speaking, the farther you go from human habitation and activity, the more still and quiet you'll be able to become during your practice. (If you do go out in the wilderness, be sure someone knows where you are and what you're doing.) Preferably, you should not be able to see other people, and no one should be able to see you. Another feature of a good location is being up on a hill so you have an expansive view. Of course, you may have to compromise these ideals depending on your circumstances, but try to find the most beautiful, inspiring, and secluded spot you can.

There's no particular posture associated with a Vision Quest; however, the hope is you'll be able to remain as alert and attentive as possible, so sitting upright whenever you can is good. Depending on how long your Vision Quest is, you may need to lie down, and whether you're sitting or lying down, you may doze off. Your dreams are included in the Vision Quest, so you should try to carry your intention to receive a vision even as you're falling asleep.

CONTEMPLATE THIS

While a shorter time won't take you as deeply into a meditative space, it can still be a very significant thing for a modern person to do! Have you ever gone somewhere in nature to sit by all by yourself without any distractions—even the distraction of hiking? If you only do this practice for a few hours, you might want to call it something less dramatic, like *Vision Time* or even just *Vision Quest–inspired meditation*.

Ritual Objects to Bring

You can bring a few ritual objects with you on your Vision Quest in order to help you cultivate the right frame of mind and to create a ritual space for your practice. The first of these are four small pieces of fabric you can use as flags—one red, one yellow, one black, and one white. These represent the natural powers in the four directions: red is for the east, sunrise, and knowledge; yellow is for the south, warmth, abundance, and connection; black is for the west, the setting sun, and the spirit world; white is for the north, cleansing, endurance, renewal, and dreams. You'll place these flags in a square around your Vision Quest place, each in the appropriate direction (so bring sticks to tie them to if necessary and perhaps a compass).

The other ritual object you might want to bring is a special stone. In some native traditions, people search for a stone that holds special significance and power for them, often because of images suggested in the patterns on the stone. You may already have a special stone, or you can search for one (Ed McGaa has suggestions for this process in his book). Alternatively, you can look for one on the way to your Vision Quest place. The stone is involved in the basic practice I describe next.

Basic Practice

As soon as you start preparing for your Vision Quest in a practical way, also start preparing yourself mentally. Try to be reverent and careful in each part of the process. Allow yourself to anticipate your experience, and acknowledge how precious this opportunity is to ask for guidance from the spirits, God, or the Divine. Once you've finally arrived in your Vision Quest place, follow these instructions:

1. Put down whatever you're carrying. Take several minutes to look around you, and listen to whatever sounds you hear. Open up your awareness as much as possible, trying not to miss anything. Maintain this kind of awareness as much as possible throughout your Vision Quest.

2. Slowly and reverently, place your colored flags in the appropriate directions around you, either tying them to trees or to sticks you push into the ground. The flags delineate your meditative and ritual space.

3. Holding up your stone in both hands in front of you, ask the spirits of each direction for assistance and vision. Refer to the meanings of the directions discussed previously, and offer a spontaneous prayer to each (spontaneity being the traditional native way).

4. Settle down on the ground in a way that's comfortable but allows you to stay alert. Call to mind your deepest aspirations, and ask whatever powers you believe in to show you whatever it is you most need to see. Cultivate a willingness to "look" spiritually, even if the message is difficult to understand or accept.

5. As energetically as possible, for as long as your Vision Quest lasts, maintain both your open awareness of your environment, as well as your longing for a vision.

6. When it's time to end the Vision Quest, hold up your stone and thank each of the four directions for their support. Carefully take down your flags, and then spend another few minutes contemplating your meditation place before leaving.

After your Vision Quest or Vision Quest–inspired meditation time is over, be gentle with yourself as you return to the world. Even if the experience didn't seem remarkable to you, it will have had an effect. Follow it up with mellow activities and try to relish any sense of calm, connection, or insight you're feeling.

Additional Guidance and Encouragement

Even if your Vision Quest was very short or didn't seem to result in any remarkable experiences, it's important to acknowledge how significant it was. You took time out of your life to spend it in solitude and silence with the sole purpose of making yourself receptive to whatever the Divine had to say to you. Beyond that, the following are some pieces of advice and inspiration to help you with Vision Quests.

Balancing Hope and Acceptance

There's tension in a Vision Quest between longing for a vision and accepting whatever happens. If you're too caught up in hope and expectation, you'll actually inhibit the whole process. You may end up striving too hard (making it all about you) or constantly evaluating your experience to see if the spirits have come through for you yet (again, making it all about you). On the other hand, if you don't really want a vision—an experience beyond the everyday that tells you how to live better—you won't be very motivated to stay concentrated on your Vision Quest or to spend one, two, or three days and nights all alone doing nothing.

CONTEMPLATE THIS

Many of us who are only familiar with modern Western culture expect explicit instructions when we try something. You may want to know exactly what to expect on a Vision Quest, and how to do it "correctly." However, in *Mother Earth Spirituality: Native American Paths to Healing Ourselves and Our World*, Ed McGaa (Eagle Man) writes, "In the end, the quest is very personal. It is you and your thoughts and your prayers to the Great Spirit. There is no blueprint for vision questing, no checklist of do's and don'ts. Just you, the powers, and isolation."

Learning how to live with this tension is part of the Vision Quest process. How do you *really* ask for a vision? Can you ask and hope for a vision with all your heart, but not demand one? Are you preventing a vision because you have too much of an idea about the kind of vision you want? Are you looking for hallucinations and bright lights and missing the fact that a butterfly is emerging from its chrysalis right in front of you? With time, you can find a way to remain fully receptive without having any agenda at all. That's when a vision tends to come.

Challenging Yourself

It's important not to bite off more than you can chew in terms of a Vision Quest. If you're not used to solitude or isolation, don't go off for a seven-day solo wilderness trek with nothing to entertain you! Too much isolation too fast can be surprisingly distressing.

Start with a reasonable amount of time, and don't judge yourself for deciding that a reasonable amount of time for you is only an hour. What's valuable is challenging yourself—spending a little longer in complete solitude, without any distraction, than you feel comfortable doing, or going to a slightly more isolated place than you feel comfortable going. It's *your* point of feeling challenged that makes you open and sensitive to Vision Quest practice.

Deepening Your Practice

If you find the initial experience of a Vision Quest rewarding or intriguing, you might work up gradually to spending a couple days and nights alone in nature doing nothing the whole time except meditating or praying. You may even want to fast or try to avoid sleeping as much as possible, the time-honored way of inviting visions. (Just be reasonable and challenge yourself a little at a time, as described previously.) You may also want to see if you can plan a quest with any experienced Vision Quest leaders or guides or try some other Native American meditative rituals (especially the one described next).

Participating in a Sweat Lodge Ceremony

Full Vision Quests, in many native traditions, are preceded by a ritual purification like a Sweat Lodge Ceremony. Such a ceremony is led by at least one very experienced person who is either a Native American or who has received personal instruction from one. A small, simple lodge is built, usually by bending down saplings and covering them with thick blankets or a tarp until the space inside is completely dark. A fire is built outside the lodge, and large stones are heated on the fire.

POINT OF CLARIFICATION

Each native tradition is different, so if you explore the practices of a tribe near you, you may encounter different teachings, approaches, and rituals than I've shared in this chapter. Keep an open mind and learn by watching and listening carefully.

In the sweat lodge, a group of people—often 8 to 12 or so—assemble and sit on the earthen floor. After prescribed opening rituals, stones are brought into the center of the lodge—sometimes sitting only inches from people's feet. There are more prayers, and at certain times water is poured over the stones, causing steam to permeate the lodge. The whole experience tends to have a powerful effect on people, sometimes evoking strong emotions, visions, or just a deepened sense of connection with the spiritual world. If you're interested in participating in this kind of ceremony, simply search online for "sweat lodge." Many groups hold regular—often monthly— sweat lodges, and many are open to anyone who wants to attend.

Learning More

An essential part of all Native American traditions is oral transmission of teachings, so there's a severe limit on what you can learn about native practices from a book. If you're sincerely interested in learning more, seek out Native Americans in your area. You may be near a reservation or an urban American Indian center that holds some events for the public—attend these and try to make some personal connections. Ask questions, especially about how else you can learn more and get involved. You may be able to attend activities like powwows (social dances) or drumming circles. Over time, you'll get a sense of who the holy men and women are in a particular community, and they may be willing to guide you in your exploration of their native tradition.

In the meantime, useful books include the ones I've already cited in this chapter: *Teaching Spirits: Understanding Native American Religious Traditions* by Joseph Epes Brown and *Mother Earth Spirituality: Native American Paths to Healing Ourselves and Our World* by Ed McGaa (Eagle Man). You may also want to read *Medicine Seeker: A Beginner's Walk on the Pathway to Native American Spirituality* by Stan E. Hughes, and find out more about the history of Native American peoples from *Native American History* by Judith Nies. You can also learn more on the Native Languages of the Americas website (native-languages.org), and access a directory of American tribes on the Bureau of Indian Affairs website (bia.gov).

Native Spiritual Practice Over a Lifetime

In traditional Native American cultures, elders are deeply valued and respected. It's understood it takes a lifetime of experience and practice to find one's appropriate role in the world and establish a deep connection with the spirit world. While each tribe usually has *Medicine Men* or *Women* who have undergone extensive spiritual and ritual training and are empowered to lead ceremonies and guide others, they aren't held up as the ideal for all. They have their roles as Medicine Men or Women, and you have your role—you just need to recognize what it is an embrace it.

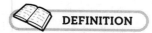

> A **Medicine Man** or **Woman** is a term sometimes used for Native American spiritual experts, teachers, or healers. They undergo extensive apprenticeship training and are tested before they're allowed to practice independently, and their special responsibility is learning and performing the esoteric aspects of a spiritual tradition so they can perform important ceremonial functions.

"Ideal" Meditative Ritual

In terms of meditative ritual, the Native American ideal is complete absorption into the experience. Self-consciousness falls away along with any inhibition or agenda. Natives traditionally believe the ritual space is prescribed by the spirits themselves in order to be effective, and the end result is a communion with those spirits in mythic time. In this experience of time, as described earlier in the chapter, the past or future can become manifest in the present. In this absorption, also, the illusion of separation from all life and all beings falls away, so you're left with an entirely sincere sense of kinship and mutual communication.

Still, as profound as any deep meditative ritual experience might be, its value lies in how it changes the way you live. Profound spiritual or philosophical understanding divorced from your personal experience might be fascinating, but in Native American spirituality, it's considered largely irrelevant. Special states, insights, powers, or visions are given to you by the spirits, and were you to simply rest in your satisfaction at having attained them, you would fail to express the appropriate gratitude and humility. It's only when you practice reciprocity and give something back to the world—when you make use of what you've experienced or learned—that the cycle will be completed.

The Ultimate Goal

The ultimate goal is not just that you find your role in the world, but that the world continues to function in a way that supports all life and that the systems and cycles on which life depends continue into the future. Therefore, the goal of Native American spirituality is very practical and outwardly focused. It includes healthy communities and social structures, strong spiritual traditions, a cultural appreciation for nature, and the restraint of arrogance and greed. In this era of environmental crisis, it also includes a connection to the land and a consciousness of how to participate in the circle of life in a sustainable way.

Whatever spiritual practices you do in a Native American tradition are then meant to prepare you to better serve your community and the world. You seek a deeper sense of connection with all of life so your selfishness will drop away and you'll be motivated by compassion. You ask for visions in order to grow in wisdom, which allows you to fulfill your responsibilities more skillfully and to teach others. You do practices that tie you to the land so you'll recognize how you depend on it and fight to protect it. The ultimate goal is nothing other than harmonious, sustainable life within your family—and given that all beings are your relatives, your family includes the whole planet and everything on it.

The Least You Need to Know

- Because there are hundreds of different native tribes, an enormous variety of Native American spiritual ideas and practices exist. Many modern ideas about those practices are erroneous and based on idealized views or overgeneralizations.

- Some of the common themes of Native American spirituality are a sense that time and natural processes are cyclical, all things and beings are imbued with spirit, and you exist within an intricate web of relationships.

- Ritual plays a central role in Native American spirituality as a way to access the spirit world. Meditative ritual affects your state of mind and encourages you to drop ordinary thinking and use a more direct, intuitive way of knowing.

- The Native American Vision Quest is a meditative ritual you can try on your own, although if you want to take it deeper, it's a good idea to find a guide or mentor.

- While some Native Americans focus on sharing their spiritual traditions within their own communities, others are willing to share some of them with non-natives in the hope they will positively influence the world.

Secular Meditation

In this part of the book, I feature secular approaches to meditation that have been developed to make the benefits of meditation more accessible to everyone. While each of these methods has a basic philosophical basis explaining why it works, for the most part they are free of any association with religious or spiritual teachings, traditions, or communities. You can practice these secular methods purely for their benefits to your health and quality of life. (While this is also the case with the other forms of meditation covered in this book, you may prefer a clearly secular approach).

I first offer a chapter on what I call *modern-day mindfulness meditation* in order to distinguish it from the Buddhist tradition from which it arose. If you study mindfulness, you may encounter mentions of Buddha or Buddhist ways of viewing the mind, but mindfulness practice doesn't require you to know, understand, or accept anything about Buddhism. I explain how mindfulness developed, discuss some of its well-documented benefits, and tell you how to practice it.

I then cover a number of other secular meditation techniques you may want to investigate, including the relaxation response and progressive muscle relaxation. While each of these techniques has a particular focus and flavor, they were all designed to be fairly simple, straight-forward, and easily incorporated into busy modern lives to improve health and wellness.

Mindfulness Meditation

Over the last 35 years, mindfulness—deliberately cultivating greater awareness of your present experience—has gained wide acceptance as a tool for improving your mental and physical well-being. At first glance, mindfulness may appear simple, but this appearance is deceptive. While it's simple to do, the effects of doing it can be profound. Practiced in a completely secular way that's compatible with any religion or with no religion at all, it's both a method of meditation and a way to approach your everyday experience outside of meditation. Mindfulness can be practiced by anyone, and is designed to be accessible and relevant to people living typical modern lives.

In this chapter, I introduce you to mindfulness as presented by the modern mindfulness movement, a growing network of health-care professionals, researchers, mindfulness teachers, and practitioners who recognize that strengthening your faculty of awareness is beneficial to your physical and mental health and happiness. I also explain how, within the mindfulness movement, awareness is defined and deliberately cultivated, the role formal meditation plays, and how you can apply mindfulness practice to everyday activities. And as usual, I offer a practice you can do, and suggest ways to deepen your meditation over time.

In This Chapter

- The modern, secular practice of mindfulness
- How awareness is viewed in mindfulness and why it's important
- The benefits of becoming more mindful
- How to do mindfulness meditation
- Ways to bring more awareness into everyday life

Overview of Mindfulness

The term *mindfulness* is sometimes used synonymously with *awareness,* but it also refers to deliberately cultivating greater awareness. *Mindfulness* is a translation of an ancient Buddhist term *sati,* which can also be translated as "memory." Essentially, it means remembering whatever it is you've decided you want to pay attention to. Mindfulness can also mean the ability to remain aware of something—once you've remembered to pay attention to it—without forgetting or getting distracted.

> **POINT OF CLARIFICATION**
>
> Mindfulness is a prerequisite for concentration but is different. Concentration has to do with the intensity with which you can focus on something, while mindfulness is about turning your mind toward an object so focus is possible.

While mindfulness has always been an important aspect of Buddhist practice, it developed its modern, secular form within the last 35 years. In the 1970s, a Buddhist practitioner and micro-biologist named Jon Kabat-Zinn become interested in how practicing mindfulness might affect the physical recovery and sense of well-being of people receiving typical medical care. In 1979, he developed a program of mindfulness training that eventually became known as mindfulness-based stress reduction (MBSR). He then proceeded to conduct scientific research into various effects on the people who completed the course.

Over the years, Kabat-Zinn and others have been able to demonstrate many positive benefits of learning mindfulness. Because MBSR is a standardized eight-week course always taught by trained and certified teachers, it is an ideal subject for research (you can test people before, during, and after the course, and compare different studies on MBSR to each other). It's now widely accepted by the scientific establishment that mindfulness can—among other things—reduce stress, help with emotional regulation, increase your sense of well-being, decrease symptoms of medical problems, and increase rates of healing (more on such benefits later in this chapter).

Mindfulness is now used in a wide variety of settings to address all kinds of issues. A growing number of psychotherapeutic programs include mindfulness, such as dialectical behavior therapy (DBT) for addressing harmful behaviors, and mindfulness-based cognitive therapy (MBCT) for treatment of depression. Mindfulness is also taught to people facing medical issues as a complementary treatment to aid the healing process or to help them deal with pain. It's even used in schools to help kids focus and deal with their emotions (and thus reduce acting out and truancy), by the military to help soldiers cope with trauma and stress (and thus allow them to make wiser choices in the field), and by corporations to increase well-being and decrease stress in employees (and also reduce medical costs).

The Essence of Mindfulness Practice

In his book *Mindfulness for Beginners,* Kabat-Zinn defines *mindfulness* as "awareness, cultivated by paying attention in a sustained and particular way: on purpose, in the present moment, and nonjudgmentally." He says that mindfulness is "all about awareness"—what it is, how it's different from ordinary thinking, why it's so valuable, and how to strengthen it. The central message of a mindfulness approach is this: You can learn to use your mind in a more effective, beneficial way.

The Nature of Awareness

Awareness is a faculty of mind you already have, and you use it all the time—probably without ever thinking about what awareness is. Essentially, it's your capacity to be conscious of everything that's going on around you and within you—sights, sounds, smells, tastes, touches, sensations within your own body, and your thoughts and emotions. Awareness doesn't have anything to do with thinking. In fact, you might say it's bigger than thinking. You can be aware of thoughts coming and going, and you can even be aware of being without thoughts!

 POINT OF CLARIFICATION

Another way to define *awareness* as compared to thinking is that awareness is about what's happening right here, right now, while thinking is always about the past, the future, or an abstraction. Even if you're thinking about something going on right here, right now, you're comparing it to something that happened in the past, deciding whether you want it to happen again in the future and making plans accordingly, or categorizing it (you like it, don't like it, or feel neutral about it). While it's obviously very useful at times, thinking essentially puts a filter between you and your experience, while awareness is a direct experience.

Most of us are identified primarily with our thoughts and emotions or the content of our minds. Therefore, our happiness or distress is more or less determined by what we're thinking and feeling. If, instead, you're able to rest in your sense of awareness, you can gain some distance from the content of your mind. No matter what's going on, your awareness is unperturbed—it's just aware. This doesn't involve denial of your thoughts and feelings in any way; it just lets you identify with something bigger. This allows you to see how the content of your mind is part of who you are, but it's not your entire reality.

Cultivating Greater Awareness

Fortunately, it's possible to become centered in your awareness more often, and for longer periods, and to become more identified with your faculty of awareness. This is the goal of mindfulness practice. As discussed previously, mindfulness is remembering to be aware. It's noticing you're caught up in the content of your mind and then opening up your awareness again (you may continue to be aware of the content of your mind but not be completely absorbed in it). Once you're aware, mindfulness involves staying that way for as long as you can.

You can strengthen your mindfulness (and thereby cultivate greater awareness) with practice. Essentially, the more you practice it, the better you get at it. The effort itself is very simple: repeatedly choosing to be aware. This builds up a habit, and you find yourself remembering to be aware more often (that is, you get more mindful). The experience of awareness itself is usually rewarding, so each time you choose awareness, you get positive reinforcement for doing it. That's not to say it's always easy, but generally speaking, you can cultivate more awareness if you want to.

To some extent, mindfulness isn't as much about developing a skill as it is about learning to make different choices about how to *be*. It may seem strange that such a simple activity as choosing to be aware isn't something you do naturally. Of course, it *is* something you do naturally (at some level you're constantly aware of something), but you tend to give your faculty of awareness much less emphasis than your thinking faculty. Moments when you spontaneously rest in awareness—which is below the level of thoughts, concepts, and judgments—are probably rare. You tend to get drawn into thinking the moment a slightly interesting thought or feeling pops into your head. In mindfulness practice, you learn to spend more time relating to life with the open receptivity of awareness.

 CONTEMPLATE THIS

In *Mindfulness for Beginners*, Kabat-Zinn describes mindfulness practice as the "cultivation of moment-to-moment awareness through careful, systematic, and disciplined attending." *Attending* means paying attention, which is what you do when you consciously direct your mind toward something. It may seem like *mindfulness*, *awareness*, and *attention* all mean the same thing, and it's true that the terms are often used interchangeably. However, you can think of awareness as a natural state that becomes obvious as soon as you let go of thinking, attention as the conscious act of directing your mind (which may allow awareness to manifest), and mindfulness as your ability to notice these different faculties of mind and make choices about them.

Suspending Judgment

Part of the process of learning to relate to life in an open, mindful way is temporarily suspending judgment. Once you've remembered the present, the idea is to rest in awareness instead of getting drawn back into active thinking—and this means refraining from commentary on the present. If you're like many people, you may find this is the hardest aspect of mindfulness practice. After all, you're in the habit of using your discriminating faculty of mind to continually evaluate what's happening to you and around you: good or bad, pleasant or unpleasant, interesting or boring, beautiful or ugly, beneficial or threatening, and so on.

The only way to stay with awareness is to set aside your discriminations for the time being. You don't have to refrain from judgment forever—that would make mindfulness a very unreasonable and ineffective practice! Instead, you "let the jury stay out" for the moment and, as much as you can, continue with simple, receptive awareness. If a judgment arises in your mind, you become aware of that; you don't have to decide whether it's true or false, or judge yourself for judging. The judgment simply becomes part of your experience of the moment; it's rather like your awareness responds to it by saying, "Hmmm. Interesting. We'll see."

The purpose of the practice is to balance your discriminating faculty with mindfulness. While we usually rely on the first almost entirely, mindfulness has a lot to offer our lives. Suspending judgment not only keeps you from getting caught up in your thoughts and emotions again, it helps you stay clear-headed. Instead of seizing on an evaluation about what's happening, you remain aware and open, continuing to collect more data. Sometimes a clear decision or course of action will arise in your mind at some point without a lot of conscious effort on your part, and if it does, it will probably be a wiser one than you would have come up with if you hadn't spent some time in mindfulness of the situation.

The Role of Meditation in Mindfulness

Mindfulness practice is divided into two areas of emphasis: informal, which takes place moment to moment in your daily life, and formal, which is meditation. Even though most mindfulness takes place away from the meditation seat, the meditation is what deepens your mindfulness. Remember all of those research studies about the positive effects of MBSR? When you take that eight-week course, you commit to 45 minutes a day of formal practice, and at least half of that time is spent meditating (the rest of the time is spent doing simple, mindful yoga, which is really like a slow, moving meditation). While it's impossible to say how many of the benefits of mindfulness are due to formal versus informal practice, most people agree the meditation is a substantial factor.

WATCH OUT

While you can practice mindfulness in the midst of your everyday activities, try not to let that be an excuse not to meditate. While it can be challenging to find time for meditation and to discipline yourself to actually do it, you'll find meditation informs and transforms your informal mindfulness practice.

Devoting time to meditation is crucial to becoming more familiar with your faculty of awareness and how to work with your mind. Because it's a focused activity with minimal distraction, it gives you the opportunity to practice aiming your mind where you want it to be and keeping it there. As your mind inevitably wanders, you can then bring it back to your chosen object of meditation again and again while refraining from judgment about your meditation. The relative stillness of meditation allows you to become aware of this entire process and see in a deep way how your thoughts and emotions arise and pass away and don't define you. While many of these lessons can also occur in the midst of activity, it can be harder to perceive them there. Meditation is like your mindfulness gym or laboratory—it's where you work out your mind or study it intensely.

Three Benefits of Mindfulness Meditation

As you read about the benefits of mindfulness meditation, keep in mind that this practice is fundamentally a very natural one. It's not a special technique you adopt in order to achieve positive results. Mindfulness is about learning to use your mind in a more effective way, and this way is available and accessible to anyone. Chances are, many of the other beneficial activities in your life also happen to increase your mindfulness!

Reduced Stress and Improved Physical Health

I'm discussing stress and physical health in the same section because mindfulness can improve your physical health; this is in large part *because* it reduces your stress. Many physical illnesses and disorders are stress-related, and all of them can be made worse by stress.

It may help to take a moment and talk about what stress is. Basically, it's a physiological response in your body that happens in reaction to a perceived threat to your survival or well-being. This response involves a cascade of hormones through your body, plus other physical, mental, and emotional changes. All of this is meant to prepare you to put all of your energy into fighting, fleeing, or freezing in the face of danger. The problem is, your brain doesn't differentiate between physical danger and other relatively minor potential threats to your well-being. So it can trigger a stress response in you when you're slowed down in traffic or perceive an insult from a coworker.

CONTEMPLATE THIS

Mindfulness has been associated with improved cardiovascular health, increased rates of healing for psoriasis patients, and a decrease in the reported intensity of pain for chronic pain patients.

Basically, in modern life, most of us experience at least a low level of stress all the time. This has a negative effect on our bodies and minds, especially after experiencing stress for decades. When your body is stressed—gearing up to fight, flee, or freeze in response to a perceived threat— it isn't devoting as much energy to healing as it otherwise would. By reducing stress, you allow your brain and body to focus more on healing and healthy functioning.

As discussed in Chapter 1, meditation triggers a relaxation response in you that's essentially the opposite of the stress response. Basically, then, you have some choice about whether to remain stressed all the time! In mindfulness meditation, you also develop greater awareness of your thoughts, feelings, states of mind, and physical sensations, so you're much more likely to notice when you're stressed. You then have the option to do something about it—meditate, practice mindfulness of your breathing, or maybe just take a walk. Often, simply recognizing stress is helpful; as discussed earlier, you can be aware of thoughts, feelings, and sensations without having to believe them or be completely caught up in them.

Freedom Around the Content of Your Mind

As mentioned earlier in the section on the nature of awareness, you tend to be identified with your thoughts and emotions or the content of your mind. Thinking and feeling tends to dominate your experience in a way that seems to define it completely. When the content of your mind is pleasant—you're thinking interesting, positive thoughts or feeling positive emotions—you're happy. When the content is negative—you're thinking negative thoughts or feeling unpleasant emotions—you're distressed. For example, if you're worrying about something and feeling anxious, you probably say you *are* anxious.

If, alternatively, you can identify with your awareness, your whole sense of the situation changes. In the example of anxiety, you become aware of your anxious thoughts and feelings, and aware that this is a state of mind that arose at some point and will change at some point. Your awareness itself is not anxious; it's simply aware. In a sense, you gain some distance from the content of your mind not by trying to push it away, but simply by identifying with a part of your mind that's not synonymous with the content. While it's aware of the content, it's also aware of the time of day, the sound of the clock ticking, and whether you're warm or cold.

CONTEMPLATE THIS

Relating differently to your thoughts and emotions through mindfulness may not seem like a big deal, but it is. Mindfulness is successfully used in the treatment of many serious mental health issues, such as obsessive-compulsive disorder and post-traumatic stress. Research has also demonstrated an association between mindfulness practice and reductions in the severity and/or frequency of episodes of anxiety and depression, a reduction in emotional eating habits related to psychological distress, and a decrease in rumination (thinking repeatedly or obsessively about a particular distressing subject). In addition, studies indicate mindfulness may cause structural changes in your brain associated with greater emotional balance and a decrease in fear-based reactions.

This distance from the content of your mind essentially gives you more freedom around it. It gives you a more balanced way to relate to your thoughts and emotions because you're less likely to see them as defining your whole reality. Because part of you remains aware that mental content comes and goes, you're better able to tolerate disturbing thoughts and painful emotions without entirely believing them or acting on them. Eventually, you can even weather emotional storms more easily.

Seeing Reality More Clearly

Mindfulness also lets you see things more clearly, because you're actually paying attention to what's going on rather than being completely absorbed in what you're thinking and feeling (reliving memories, creating arguments, rehearsing future actions, and so on). Also, when you let go of your attachment to thinking and rest in awareness instead, you experience things more directly, and thus more clearly. As discussed earlier, thinking can create a sort of filter between you and your experience. As you evaluate and judge something relative to your self-concern, you think you're seeing reality, but you're actually seeing your own version of it, colored by your ideas and agendas. You therefore may end up paying much more attention to the stories and narratives you've created about your life than you do to what's actually happening.

When you see the reality of your life more clearly, of course, you're able to make much better choices. You can see what really matters or recognize dysfunctional patterns. When you're more aware, you also notice a whole lot more, both inside and outside you. This can lead—among many other things—to a greater appreciation for your life; more harmonious relationships; and the reawakening of inner qualities you may have been neglecting, like generosity and compassion.

The Practice of Mindfulness Meditation

The formal part of mindfulness practice—meditation—requires you to set aside time to focus entirely on awareness of the present. You temporarily opt out of your "doing" mode in favor of your "being" mode. It's helpful to let go even of any agendas you have about meditation and how it might improve your life. It might, indeed, improve your life. But while you're meditating, the point is to simply be aware of right here, right now, just for its own sake.

General Description of the Method

When you first start a mindfulness practice, you're generally encouraged to use guided meditations. These are recordings that last 10 to 40 minutes in which someone verbally leads you through the steps of a particular meditation. They can be very relaxing, and listening to guidance tends to help you stay focused. Many people continue to use guided meditations even after many years of mindfulness practice.

POINT OF CLARIFICATION

To obtain a guided meditation, you can take a mindfulness class or find recordings online by searching for "guided meditation." You can also order a set of classic meditations narrated by Jon Kabat-Zinn at mindfulnesscds.com.

Mindfulness meditation, whether guided or on your own, generally begins with awareness of your breathing. There are many different approaches to this kind of awareness, and you're invited to be creative in any way that encourages you to remain aware of the present. These creative efforts could include simple visualizations (such as imagining you're inhaling and exhaling air from the far corners of the earth) or an emotional component (embracing the inhalation with compassion). Typically, mindfulness students will progress over time through somewhat more challenging meditations on physical sensations, sounds, thoughts, and emotions; eventually, they get to "choiceless" awareness, in which there's no specific meditative object.

The Theory Behind the Meditation

The emphasis in mindfulness meditation is always on the act of paying attention and maintaining awareness, rather than on the meditative object itself. The important thing is the process of meditation, which strengthens your ability and willingness to rest in your awareness. Naturally, during meditation you try to concentrate on your chosen technique as opposed to just letting your mind wander. But achieving intense concentration on your meditative object isn't as important as patiently, diligently, and repeatedly bringing your mind back to it. Over time, you become much more familiar with how your own mind works—where it tends to wander, the most effective way to bring it back to the present, and the nature of attention and awareness—and you get better at meditating.

If you meditate enough, it can actually cause positive changes in your brain structure and function. Neuroscientists call this kind of phenomenon *neuroplasticity,* and it's basically physical changes in the brain resulting from how you use it. Without any training or effort, most of your mental activity—particularly when you aren't engaged in a task or being entertained—takes place in what neuroscientists call the *narrative focus* network (or the default network, because that's the one you tend to end up using most of the time). Activity in this network is associated with processing narratives about your life, especially self-referential ones. When you're engaging this network, you're usually thinking stimulus-independent thoughts unrelated to anything happening in the present, such as worrying about the future or ruminating on the past.

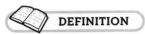

> **DEFINITION**
>
> **Neuroplasticity** refers to changes in the synaptic connections and neural pathways in the brain in response to your experiences, what you think and feel, how you use your mind, or injury. The discovery of neuroplasticity contrasts with the now-outdated view of the adult brain as being more or less fixed in its structure and function.

Research has shown that people trained in mindfulness show less activity in the narrative focus network, and more activity in what's called the *experiential focus* network. When this network is engaged, you're paying attention to what's going on around and within you in the present moment. You're grounded in your physical experience and are using your faculty of awareness, which gives you more freedom around the content of your mind. In summary, by deliberately practicing awareness in meditation, you build up your ability and tendency to be aware.

Beginner's Meditation Instructions

While all of the beginner's meditations offered in this book are easy to try and are designed to be accessible to anyone, you may find mindfulness meditation particularly attractive if you're looking for a completely secular, evidence-based approach. The mindfulness movement has sought over the last 35 years to appeal to people who might never try meditation otherwise. Mindfulness meditation has been adapted for use in medical facilities, corporations, the military, and schools, so it's clearly appropriate for practice in a wide variety of settings. Here, I give instructions for a very simple and classic mindfulness meditation: the body scan.

Setting and Posture

Choose a quiet place where you won't be interrupted. Turn off your phone and dedicate a certain amount of time to mindfulness of the present moment. The advice in Chapter 3 about a good setting for meditation applies well to mindfulness meditation.

In terms of posture, mindfulness meditation is quite flexible. The bottom line is to take a posture that allows you to stay awake and alert. It's possible to lie down (if you can stay awake), stand, or walk (within a contained area; see Chapter 15 for instructions for walking meditation). However, most people take a seated posture because it offers a nice balance between physical stillness and comfort. You can sit in any of the seated postures described in Chapter 2, including in a chair (if you sit in a chair, however, just remember not to cross your legs; instead, sit with your feet flat on the floor).

Basic Practice

Once you're in your meditation posture, take a few moments to relax. Breathe deeply and bring your awareness to your body. When you're ready, follow these instructions (you can find an audio version of this meditation on idiotsguides.com/meditation):

1. Close your eyes.

2. Become aware of the very top of your head, and allow your awareness to rest there. Notice any tension you might be holding in this area. Relax this area more and more deeply. In a sense, there's always more tension, so this process of relaxation can continue indefinitely. Once the top of your head feels relaxed, imagine a sense of warmth filling it.

3. Move your awareness down to your forehead. Again, check for tension. If there's any, first notice it and then release it if you can. If the tension doesn't release, simply notice it and invite it to melt away.

4. Move your awareness down to your eyes. Notice any tension, and invite any tension to melt away. Imagine your eyes feel warm. Repeat this process for your cheeks, nose and nasal passages, mouth, neck, and shoulders.

5. When you reach your chest, instead of continuing down your torso, take a detour to your upper arms. Notice any tension, and invite any tension to melt away. Imagine your upper arms feel warm. Repeat this process for your elbows, lower arms, wrists, palms, and fingers.

6. Move your awareness to your chest. Notice any tension, and invite any tension to melt away. Imagine your chest feels warm. Repeat this process for your back, abdomen, pelvic area, hips, thighs, knees, calves, ankles, feet, and toes.

7. Simply rest in awareness of your whole body. Enjoy any relaxation or calm that has resulted from your meditation.

This simple meditation may help you relax your body, and that's great. However, as mentioned earlier, the main point of it is to simply practice being aware. It doesn't matter so much how technically you follow these instructions, as long as you use your meditation time to pay attention to something that requires you to use your experiential network and let go of using your narrative network.

Additional Guidance and Encouragement

Mindfulness meditation can be difficult at times. You may find your mind wanders all over the place. You may find yourself bored and wondering why on Earth you're doing this or concerned the meditation isn't working. Maybe you'd like to be able to meditate without listening to a guided meditation but feel you lose track of the point of the meditation if you don't. Fortunately, in mindfulness meditation, as long as you try, you're doing a great job; you're likely to see positive results in your life, even if meditation feels challenging. The following are a couple helpful tips to help you with any mindfulness meditation challenges.

Letting Go of "Doing It Right"

Mindfulness teachers emphasize that your attitude during meditation is very important—and the best attitude is pretty much the opposite of worrying about whether you're doing it right. The meditative process is much smoother and more effective if you can engage it with an open mind, patience, acceptance of whatever's going on, trust that the meditation is helpful, and an attitude of "nonstriving."

CONTEMPLATE THIS

You'll probably be surprised how much the process of meditation takes care of itself, without requiring a lot of willful struggle on your part. For example, as Bob Stahl and Elisha Goldstein write in *A Mindfulness-Based Stress Reduction Workbook,* "The moment you see that you've been trapped by your thoughts, you gain the freedom to step out of the trap." Simply stepping out of the trap is a natural next step!

The good thing is, even if your mind wanders over and over from your chosen meditative technique, you probably aren't doing as badly as you think. The moment you become aware your mind has wandered, *you* are aware. You don't have to do anything extra at this point; you don't have to wrestle your mind back into the present or berate yourself for having lost your concentration. All you have to do is acknowledge your awareness and try to rest in it—try to allow it to continue. If you get caught up in trying to meditate "right"—which requires judgment—you're just getting caught up in thinking again. So relax and enjoy your meditation, and be grateful for each moment you become aware.

Taking a Gentle, Compassionate Approach

You'll often hear mindfulness teachers talking about kindness and compassion. What does this have to do with mindfulness and meditation? As discussed previously, your attitude is important. It not only helps to keep an open, relaxed mind and avoid getting caught up in judgment, it also helps to go a little further and bring some warm, positive feelings to your practice.

Basically, the effort to be mindful can be hard sometimes. It's not what you're used to, and it requires some self-discipline. If you approach this task in a hard, clinical way, it won't be as fulfilling and, more importantly, your mind isn't as likely to cooperate. You might want to think of your mind, with its strong habits and tendency to get lost in thought, as a child you're trying to teach. If you're harsh and demanding, a child is going to react negatively. Alternatively, you can ask a great deal of a child if you do so creatively and compassionately, making it clear at all times that you have the child's best interests in mind. If you similarly treat your own mind with gentleness and compassion, you'll end up getting the best results.

Deepening Your Mindfulness Meditation

You can deepen your mindfulness meditation by doing it often but also by practicing mindfulness throughout the day. As I mentioned earlier in this chapter, meditation is considered the formal part of mindfulness practice, and cultivating awareness moment by moment in your daily life is your informal practice. While you're likely to have more focus during meditation, you spend more time going about your other activities, so the effects of practicing mindfulness while eating, talking, exercising, driving, and working will be cumulative and significant.

You can do all kinds of mindfulness exercises throughout your day. Books and classes on mindfulness offer many exercises. For example, in her book *How to Train a Wild Elephant: And Other Adventures in Mindfulness,* Jan Chozen Bays suggests you spend a day using your nondominant hand as much as possible, or concentrating on eating during meals instead of doing anything else, or taking several deep breaths before you answer the phone. Basically, anything works that opens up your awareness of what's going on around and within you in the present moment, so you're welcome to get creative with mindfulness exercises. Let's take a look at some other things you can do to deepen your meditation.

Taking a Mindfulness Meditation Class

Perhaps the most significant thing you can do to deepen your mindfulness meditation is to take a class. While you can find many different kinds of classes out there, the most typical is the eight-week MBSR course. In order to offer this class, an instructor has to undergo hundreds of hours of training; do a number of long meditation retreats; and receive certification through the Center for Mindfulness in Medicine, Health Care, and Society.

POINT OF CLARIFICATION

The regular inclusion of simple yoga in mindfulness practice is an innovation by Jon Kabat-Zinn. It consists of very basic, easy stretches and postures inspired by Hatha Yoga, and it is generally done with verbal guidance from a teacher or a recording. The idea is continue your mindfulness practice in the midst of slow, simple movement. You keep your awareness centered on your body and the sensations of stretching. Many people find this guided, meditative movement very helpful, especially as a complement to still, seated meditation, which can get physically uncomfortable after a while.

The MBSR course has to follow a fairly standardized format and is quite rigorous and supportive. It meets for 1½ to 2 hours a week for 8 weeks, and ends with a day-long retreat. During the course, you commit to 45 minutes a day of formal practice, which includes meditation and mindful yoga. While this commitment is substantial, many people find the experience life-changing, in part because of the personal advice from a teacher and the moral support of other people taking the course.

Learning More

Two books already mentioned in this chapter are great resources for learning more about mindfulness: *Mindfulness for Beginners* by Jon Kabat-Zinn, and *A Mindfulness-Based Stress Reduction Workbook* by Bob Stahl and Elisha Goldstein. To read about the history of MBSR and learn more about mindfulness in the context of medicine and health care, visit the website of the University of Massachusetts Medical School's Center for Mindfulness in Medicine, Health Care, and Society (umassmed.edu/cfm).

To find a mindfulness class in your area, simply type "mindfulness class" into your favorite internet search engine. Keep in mind that classes on the resulting list may not be MBSR courses (if you want to find one of those, be sure to search for "mindfulness-based stress reduction"). You can also find a number of options for taking a mindfulness class online, including through Mindful Schools (mindfulschools.org) and Palouse Mindfulness (palousemindfulness.com).

Mindfulness Meditation Over a Lifetime

Mindfulness practice is very down-to-earth and practical, and it's useful no matter how often you do it or how intensely you engage the practice. Still, that doesn't mean it can't make a big difference in your life. Many people who practice mindfulness find that over time, resting in awareness becomes fairly natural and easy. They find they spontaneously choose to be aware of their present experience more and more often.

"Ideal" Mindfulness Meditation

As discussed earlier, the moment you notice you're not aware of the present moment, you *are* aware of the present moment! In a sense, ideal mindfulness meditation is simply allowing that remembering process to happen over and over. Still, there's always a way to make your meditation deeper—although in the case of mindfulness, that really means making it more natural and wholehearted.

To really surrender into awareness of the present moment, you're required to put aside all of the efforts you usually make to push away things you don't like and grasp after (or hold on to) things you like. It's this very process of engaging in grasping and aversion that causes you extra suffering. Basically, things may be difficult and painful at any given moment, but your resistance to the situation only makes things worse. In deep mindfulness meditation, you let go of grasping and aversion and settle into a kind of open contentedness that can be very profound and healing. No matter what your meditative object is, you allow your mind to become simple enough that the object fills it completely.

The Ultimate Goal

Mindfulness can become a way of being. If you think about the people you know, you can probably tell which ones are mindful. They're the ones who will notice you're not feeling well or know when there's something they can do to help. They're more likely to be thoughtful and careful when they do a task, understand clearly what's said to them, adapt their behavior appropriately depending on the circumstances, and know what they're thinking and feeling. Mindful people don't act this way because they're trying really hard to be nice, smart, or agreeable; they're simply acting naturally in response to what's happening around and within them. It's just that they're aware. They're actually paying attention, instead of being wrapped up in their own internal world.

 CONTEMPLATE THIS

If you improve your mindfulness, it may feel as if your luck has improved as well! However, it's really just that you're better able to recognize opportunities when they arise.

From the inside, the ultimate goal of mindfulness is a sense of direct engagement with life. After a while, it stops feeling like you're making an effort to be aware of what's going on, which presumes a separation between "you" and "what's going on." Instead, awareness becomes your default mode—less a state you're trying to achieve and more of a way of being. Kabat-Zinn calls this *awarenessing* in order to point to the fact that a mindful life is a dynamic one in which you meet each moment with as much attention and appreciation as you can.

The Least You Need to Know

- Mindfulness means remembering the present moment. It's when you become aware of what's going on around and within you—and once you're aware, mindfulness involves staying aware.

- Most people tend to be identified with their thinking faculty of mind rather than their awareness. This means their sense of well-being is largely determined by the content of their minds (what they're thinking or feeling at a given time).

- In mindfulness practice, you strengthen your identification with your awareness faculty. Because your awareness is simply aware and not affected by the content of your mind, this gives you a sense of distance from—and greater freedom around—the content of your mind.

- Mindfulness meditation works by building up your ability, willingness, and tendency to rest in your awareness rather than get caught up in your thinking. You do this by patiently returning your mind to the present over and over. Doing this can eventually change the structure and function of your brain!

- The ultimate goal of mindfulness is to be fully present for your life as it unfolds, moment by moment.

Other Secular Meditation Techniques

In this chapter, I introduce you to four secular meditative techniques that, like mindfulness, have been developed over the last 100 years by health-care professionals. These practices have been the subject of research studies that prove they can be beneficial to your mental and physical health. You'll probably find this chapter especially interesting if you're looking for a simple, practical meditative technique that's completely detached from any established tradition or even from related teachings and practices.

Like all the meditative practices in this book, the techniques featured in this chapter ask you to direct your mind in beneficial way for a time. The first three techniques—autogenic training, progressive muscle relaxation, and the relaxation response—are all what you could call *meditative relaxation methods*. Such methods tend to affect what's happening in the part of your nervous system that regulates unconscious activity in your body. They generally decrease activity in the part of your nervous system associated with your stress response (fight, flight, or freeze) and increase activity in the parts responsible for regulating digestion, eliminating waste, healing, and regenerating tissue.

In This Chapter

- Meditative approaches created and used by health-care professionals
- Using autogenic training to self-induce a relaxed, recuperative state
- Learning to consciously relax through progressive muscle relaxation
- Using any basic meditative technique to bring about your relaxation response
- Focusing to gain insight into what you're really thinking and feeling

The fourth method, focusing, is a method developed for use in psychotherapy but which can also be useful outside that setting. While it also involves directing your mind in a particular way, in this case, it's not in order to relax and relieve stress in a direct way. Instead, it allows you to achieve insight into your own thoughts and feelings. Learning about all four of these meditative techniques will give you new tools for taking care of your life.

Autogenic Training

Autogenic training was developed in the early 1900s by Johannes Heinrich Schultz (1884–1970), a German neuropsychiatrist. He and his colleagues had noticed that certain *psychophysiological states* promoted the natural healing processes of the body and mind. At first, they associated these states with hypnosis. Later, however, they discovered that what they termed the "autogenic" state was unique and could be brought about consciously by a patient without any external support or guidance from a therapist, as long as the patient followed certain simple procedures.

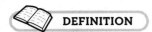 **DEFINITION**

> **Autogenic training** is a method of learning how to promote your own mental and physical healing from within; *auto* refers to "self" or "from within," and *genic* refers to "generating" or "developing." A **psychophysiological state** is a replicable, identifiable state that has typical psychological characteristics as well as physiological ones—in other words, the mental and physical characteristics tend to happen together.

Since autogenic training was introduced in Germany in the 1920s, it has gained widespread acceptance and use throughout Europe, as well as in Japan. It has been the subject of hundreds of peer-reviewed studies that suggest it can help reduce the severity and symptoms of many physical and emotional problems, including chronic pain, headaches, hypertension, sleep disorders, anxiety, and irritable bowel syndrome (IBS).

In autogenic training, you're taught a series of simple exercises that allow you to self-induce a relaxed, recuperative state. While it's recommended you learn autogenic training methods from a qualified teacher so you can be sure you're doing them correctly, the methods themselves are quite simple. Once you know them, you're encouraged to continue to practice on your own two or three times a day for 15 minutes each time indefinitely. Teachers of the method emphasize you'll be unlikely to feel the full benefits of the training unless you continue daily practice for weeks or months.

Basic Practice

In order to do this autogenic exercise, find a place that's very quiet and free of distractions. Ideally, it won't be too bright, and you won't be disturbed throughout your practice. Go ahead and lie down on a bed, couch, or soft rug, or even in a recliner. Use pillows as necessary to prevent strain on any part of your body. If you find yourself getting too sleepy while reclining, you can sit up in a comfortable chair, preferably one with arms and a high back, so you can rest your head and arms on the chair.

As you practice, don't try to make anything happen (even relaxation), and refrain from judging your experience. These activities only increase stress and tension. Try to trust the process and cultivate what's called *passive concentration* in autogenic training.

When you're ready, follow these simple steps:

1. Close your eyes.

2. Make mental contact with your right arm in whatever way works best for you: imagine you're looking at your arm with your eyes closed, or bring your awareness to the position of your arm or to your arm's sensations.

3. Say silently to yourself, "My right arm feels heavy." Imagine this to be the case in whatever way works for you—visualize it or feel it. Repeat the phrase about heaviness slowly, five to seven times.

4. Say, "My left arm feels heavy," and make mental contact with your left arm. Follow the same process as you did with your right arm, repeating the phrase five to seven times.

5. Follow the same process for your right leg, left leg, and then for your entire body.

6. When you're finished, gently stretch your limbs and then open your eyes.

Ideally, give yourself several minutes just to sit or lie there afterward, enjoying any relaxation you've cultivated, and then stand up carefully.

Exploring Autogenic Training Further

You can find variations on the heaviness exercises in more advanced autogenic training, as well as exercises that involve imagining warmth instead of heaviness. All such exercises are meant to deepen your state of recuperative relaxation and the ease with which you can enter it. To learn more, read *Autogenic Training: A Mind-Body Approach to the Treatment of Chronic Pain Syndrome and Stress-Related Disorders* by Micah R. Sadigh.

While there aren't many American therapists focusing on autogenic training, if you visit the website of the British Autogenic Society (autogenic-therapy.org.uk), you can find a list of therapists who do (and some are willing to work with you online). You can also find information about autogenic training courses on that website.

> **WATCH OUT**
>
> If you practice autogenic training for a while, it's possible you might experience "autogenic discharge," or involuntary twitches or other physical sensations. These may be the body releasing built-up tension from past traumatic or difficult experiences. Most of the time, these discharges aren't a problem; however, you may want to consult a professional about them.

Progressive Muscle Relaxation

Progressive muscle relaxation was developed by Edmund Jacobson, a physician in Chicago, Illinois. In 1929, he published his first book on the technique, *Progressive Relaxation: A Physiological & Clinical Investigation of Muscular States & Their Significance in Psychology & Medical Practice.* Progressive muscle relaxation involves the deliberate and systematic tensing and relaxing of muscle groups throughout the body. Jacobson's theory was psychological tension and distress cause muscles to tense, and the tension in the muscles results in a negative feedback loop with the brain, which causes even more stress. Alternatively, a relaxed muscle sends a message to the brain to relax as well. Whatever the exact mechanism, progressive muscle relaxation has been associated with a decrease in the symptoms of anxiety, phobias, depression, insomnia, fatigue, and muscle pain.

The idea behind tensing your muscles before trying to relax them comes from the fact that many people are unaware of the tension in their muscles—and even if they are aware of such tension, they often aren't very good at deliberately relaxing. Through the process of tensing muscles and then immediately releasing all tension, you learn what tension and relaxation feel like and how to influence the process. If you keep working on the practice, eventually it's possible to release only, without having to go through the tensing process.

It's important when doing progressive muscle relaxation that you tense each group of muscles as tightly as you can—*but without hurting yourself.* If you have any areas that are typically tense, sore, or injured, tense them slowly and stop before you cause yourself any pain. However, if an area is without these problems, go ahead and tense the muscles energetically for five full seconds. When it comes time to relax (typically for 20 to 30 seconds), you then release all of the tension immediately and quickly. Your muscles should ideally feel completely limp after the release.

Basic Practice

To do this progressive relaxation exercise, take a comfortable position either sitting or lying down. A quiet, private place is good, especially when you're first learning how to do this kind of practice; however, it can be done in any kind of circumstance. You can keep your eyes open if you need to in order to refer to these instructions. Take a moment to settle, and then do the following (you can find an audio version of this meditation on idiotsguides.com/meditation):

1. Close your eyes.

2. Tense all the muscles in your face for five seconds. Squeeze your eyes shut; tighten your lips; and scrunch up your forehead, nose, and cheeks. After five seconds, suddenly release with an exhalation.

3. For 20 seconds, pay close attention to all of the sensations of relaxation in your face, allowing it to become completely limp.

4. Repeat the action of tensing your face for five seconds, releasing quickly with an exhalation, and relaxing with awareness for 20 seconds.

5. Tense your neck and shoulder muscles, bringing your shoulders up near your ears. After five seconds, release quickly with an exhalation, and maintain awareness of relaxation in these muscles for 20 seconds. Repeat the tension, release, and awareness process for your neck and shoulders.

6. Perform two repetitions each of the tension, release, and awareness process for your upper arms (squeezing your arms to your sides), fists and lower arms (bending your arms), and chest.

7. Perform two repetitions each of the tension, release, and awareness process for your abdomen, back, glutes, thighs, calves (curling your toes upward), and feet (curling your toes downward).

8. To finish, tense your whole body for five seconds, release, and then rest in relaxation for as long as you like.

It's recommended you practice this technique for a total of about 15 minutes a day, twice a day, in order to deepen your physical experience of tension and relaxation.

Exploring Progressive Relaxation Further

You can develop your practice of progressive muscle relaxation in a number of ways. You can pay closer and closer attention to isolating certain muscle groups during the process. Try to carefully tense and relax muscle groups independently and to deepen your awareness of how relaxation in the area feels. This will give you valuable information about where you tend to hold tension and teach you how to release it. You can also tense larger groups of muscles together (such as glutes with lower limbs; chest with stomach; and arms with shoulders, neck, and face) in order to condense the practice and use it throughout your day.

> **POINT OF CLARIFICATION**
>
> The progressive muscle relaxation method originally developed by Edmund Jacobson is much more involved than the simple process explained here; he suggested it could take months (or longer) to learn how to do the process in a way that would provide maximum benefit. However, simplified versions of the technique are still useful. Plus, simplified forms are what you'll probably encounter online and in various therapeutic settings, where the method tends to be taught fairly informally.

You can become even more aware of and familiar with your muscular tension and relaxation by experimenting with the amount of tension you use during the practice. In *The Relaxation and Stress Reduction Workbook,* Martha Davis, Elizabeth Robbins Eshelman, and Matthew McKay call the normal type of tensing "active" and also describe "threshold" tension (still tensing, but without obvious physical movement) and "passive" tension, where you simply notice any tension that already exists within a muscle group. They suggest it can be very calming to follow a session using active or threshold tension with a session using passive tension.

The Relaxation Response

The *relaxation response* is not so much the name of a technique as it is a way to refer to the result of most meditative techniques. The term was coined by Dr. Herbert Benson, a cardiologist who was one of the first people to research the connection between hypertension (or high blood pressure) and stress. Taking note of his research, practitioners of Transcendental Meditation (TM; see Chapter 14) suggested Benson study them. He did and found their blood pressure was significantly lower than that of the general population.

With more research, Benson identified a relaxation response induced by meditative activities. It involves decreased respiration, heart rate, and metabolism—basically all reactions that are the opposite of the stress response. The stress response had been identified decades earlier as your body's physiological preparation for responding to danger by fighting, fleeing, or freezing. Benson proposed the human body had also evolved a relaxation response in order to focus the body's energies back on maintenance and healing activities in the absence of danger.

Benson and his colleagues demonstrated the relaxation response could be induced with any basic meditative technique. It happens when you consciously decide to direct your mind toward a meditative object—a word, sound, prayer, image, simple activity, and so on—while maintaining what Benson calls a "passive attitude." This entails letting go of distracting thoughts and returning your attention to your meditative object, but without worrying about how well you're doing or trying to achieve any particular thing through your effort.

Basic Practice

It's actually not necessary to be in a quiet environment or a comfortable position in order to self-induce the relaxation response. You can do this during meditative movement or activities as well (see Chapters 15 and 16). However, initially it helps you to concentrate and maintain a passive attitude if you sit comfortably in a place with few distractions. You can then follow these very simple instructions:

1. Choose something as an object of your meditation that's consistent with your beliefs, interests, or aspirations. It can be a word, phrase, prayer, image, object, or even a simple movement—anything you can pay attention to in a sustained way that isn't stimulating or entertaining (nothing that encourages you to think).

2. Close your eyes or keep them open, as you like, and introduce your meditative object. Keep your awareness on it as much as possible. When you find your mind has wandered from the meditative object, patiently return your attention to it.

3. Let go of any evaluation of how you're doing or any sense of impatience or frustration about a wandering mind.

4. Continue this process until your meditation period is over.

> **POINT OF CLARIFICATION**
>
> Unfortunately, the relaxation response can only be induced deliberately—it's not something that happens by itself while you're engaged in leisure activities. As Dr. Herbert Benson writes, "Unlike the fight-or-flight response, which is repeatedly brought forth as a response to our difficult everyday situations and is elicited without conscious effort, the relaxation response can be evoked only if time is set aside and a conscious effort is made." (From *The Relaxation Response* by Herbert Benson, MD.)

You can practice the relaxation response for any amount of time, but generally speaking, 10 to 20 minutes is recommended. It can take a while to get used to meditation, so be patient. As long as you're making an effort, it will have some effect.

Exploring the Relaxation Response Further

Of course, in a sense, you're practicing the relaxation response if you're doing any of the meditative exercises in this book. If you've chosen one type of meditation to focus on, you're exploring the relaxation response further by deepening your experience with that kind of meditation. If you want to keep it simple and stick with the straightforward instructions given by Benson, the best way to explore this practice further is to do it regularly—daily, if possible. While the technique doesn't change over time, you'll experience the cumulative effects of inducing your body's relaxation response.

If you want to learn more, read Benson's classic book *The Relaxation Response.* You can also visit the website of the Benson-Henry Institute for Mind Body Medicine, which was founded by Benson at Massachusetts General Hospital (bensonhenryinstitute.org). The website includes a history of the Institute and the relaxation response, plus recordings of guided meditations and further instructions. The site also has an exhaustive list of research publications focusing on the technique and the various benefits it has on mental and physical health.

Focusing

Eugene Gendlin, PhD, is a philosopher and psychologist who "created" focusing and introduced it to the public in 1978 with a book by that name. He often explains that he didn't *create* focusing; he simply described a process many people intuitively use and then outlined a series of steps people can follow to engage focusing in a deliberate way. Focusing is now practiced worldwide, often in therapeutic settings but also in peer groups or individually.

Focusing asks you to turn your awareness toward your "felt sense" of something—such as how your life is going or a particular issue you're dealing with. You focus on a physical sense of knowing within your body, below the level of thinking. For example, you might notice a sinking feeling in your stomach or a sense of tension in your chest. The idea behind the technique is to bring this felt sense into awareness, briefly describe its overall quality, and investigate it more closely—but always in a direct, experiential way as opposed to an analytical, thought-based way. Through this process, you often bring into consciousness things you're thinking or feeling. You also open up to the possibility of things shifting in a significant way as you become more familiar with what's going on for you.

 POINT OF CLARIFICATION

In Chapter 1, I discussed how meditation has two main functions: calming the mind and cultivating insight. The first three meditative techniques described in this chapter are primarily about the calming aspect of meditation, while focusing is more about insight—particularly, insight into your own internal experience. While practitioners of focusing don't generally call it meditation, it fits the definition of this book because it involves directing your mind in a deliberate way in order to bring about positive effects in your mind (and body).

Basic Practice

Focusing is a personal process, so even though these are the steps for the technique as described by Gendlin's Focusing Institute, the Institute encourages you to do what works for you and not get too caught up in following them exactly. Find a quiet, private, comfortable place where you can concentrate, and let these steps guide your process:

1. **Clearing a space:** Close your eyes, turn inward, and invite a felt sense to arise by asking yourself how you feel. Do you feel fine? Is there anything preventing you from feeling completely fine? As concerns arise, just notice they're present without getting drawn into thinking about them.

2. **Engaging a felt sense:** Choose one concern to focus on. Notice how your body senses or responds to this concern. Look for feelings of tension, tightness, heaviness, lightness, energy, and so on. Allow yourself to feel your body's experience of the concern.

3. **Finding a handle:** Find a word that describes or fits your felt sense (it doesn't have to be an adjective). Try to allow the word to arise from within your felt sense.

4. **Resonating:** Go back and forth between the handle and your felt sense, allowing the handle or the felt sense to change as seems appropriate.

5. **Asking:** Ask whatever questions seem appropriate in order to learn more from your felt sense, such as "What's happening here? What is needed? What makes this unpleasant?" Don't answer in words or analyze. Simply ask and allow your felt sense to respond.

6. **Receiving:** Accept whatever has happened in your focusing session, and recognize any awareness of a felt sense as a positive result.

You may find an inquiry into one felt sense leading into another. Go ahead and repeat this process if it feels appropriate, allowing yourself to explore your inner experience. However, try to stay with a felt sense long enough to be sure you're not just avoiding a deeper experience of it.

Exploring Focusing Further

You can further explore focusing in many ways. Many people find it helpful to get live instruction from a certified focusing teacher. The website of the Focusing Institute (focusing.org) provides a searchable international listing of certified teachers, some of whom are psychotherapists and some of whom are not. The website also includes a listing of focusing workshops (some of which can be taken online), as well as opportunities for one-on-one phone sessions with certified focusing teachers. Of course, you can also read Eugene Gendlin's classic book, *Focusing,* which includes detailed explanations of how to work through the six steps given previously, as well as how to deal with various challenges you might encounter in the process.

CONTEMPLATE THIS

Sometimes a deep focusing session can result in what's termed a *felt shift*. Through the process of bringing into consciousness and exploring your felt sense about a particular concern, you can potentially bring about a new relationship to the concern or a new understanding of what's happening for you. A deep sense of relief, resolution, or change can result—and is something you can experience in your body as well as in your mind.

People often also find it helpful to practice focusing with another person, and the other person doesn't have to be a therapist or even a trained focusing teacher. The Focusing Institute helps coordinate partnerships between people who spend one hour a week doing focusing together, in person or on the phone. For the first half-hour, the first person speaks and—if they choose—goes through a focusing process, while the other person simply listens or provides nonintrusive observations or questions. For the second half-hour, the roles switch. If you're interested in such a partnership, you may be able to find someone near you willing to participate, or you can make a request for a partner through the Focusing Institute website.

The Least You Need to Know

- A number of completely secular, relatively straightforward meditative techniques are available for improving your physical and mental health, and their effectiveness has been proven by modern scientific research.

- In autogenic training, you self-induce a deep state of relaxation by taking a completely relaxed physical position, making mental contact with different parts of your body, and repeating phrases to yourself in order to suggest sensations of heaviness or warmth in the body part you're focusing on.

- Progressive muscle relaxation teaches you to recognize and release tension by having you systematically tense and relax muscle groups throughout your body.

- The relaxation response is essentially the opposite of your instinctual stress response. It can be deliberately cultivated by concentrating on any kind of meditative object with a nonjudgmental, open attitude.

- Focusing involves introspection to locate your felt sense about some aspect of your life. You can then gradually call that subverbal felt sense into consciousness and explore it in a direct, experiential way.

More Ways to Meditate

Forms of meditation are many and varied, and in this part of the book, I describe some important meditative traditions not covered in previous chapters. I also introduce all kinds of general meditative practices you can use in your everyday life, including walking meditation, meditative work, chanting, ritual, and the use of artistic expression as a meditation. While all of these practices are inspired by ancient, traditional forms of meditation, they can be easily adapted in ways that make them interesting and useful to you.

In this part of the book, I also suggest some simple meditation exercises for dealing with specific challenges in your life, such as anxiety, anger, depression, pain, and loss. A regular meditation practice will increase your overall mental and emotional health, strength, and resilience. However, it can still be helpful to apply appropriate exercises to particular ills, like meditative "medicine." You also find a chapter on how to share meditation with children, including kid-friendly meditation exercises.

More Meditation Traditions

In this chapter, I discuss four more practices that deserve to be mentioned in a book on meditation, but for which I can't offer you a beginner's version of them to do on your own. The reasons for this vary: you can only do the practice in a group, there's no representative technique to offer, or the practice can only be learned from a certified teacher. However, for each kind of meditative practice, I describe the basic method and its benefits, and I tell you how you can find out more if you want to try it. I think you'll find that simply reading a little about each of these meditative forms will give you a better sense of the wide variety of ways in which meditative practices are used in the world.

In This Chapter

- The meditative experience of unprogrammed Quaker meetings
- Meditation in the Bahá'í faith
- Varieties of meditative techniques employed in traditional Taoism
- An introduction to Transcendental Meditation

Unprogrammed Quaker Meeting

Quakerism developed as a Christian movement in England in the seventeenth century. At the time, the founders of Quakerism were disillusioned with the way they saw Christianity being practiced. They became convinced that Christians needed to return to the simplicity of the early church—that is, the Christian church shortly after the death and resurrection of Christ—and do away with the use of clergy, elaborate ceremonies, and other things that distract people from a direct relationship with Christ. While Quakers have been repeatedly persecuted by mainstream Christian sects throughout their history, the movement—formally called the Religious Society of Friends—has continued to this day.

> **POINT OF CLARIFICATION**
>
> There's great diversity in Quaker beliefs and practices, and not all Quaker groups practice the unprogrammed meetings discussed here. Those groups that do are generally called *meetings,* while Quaker groups that call themselves *churches* have usually adopted "programmed" worship (the kind typical of other Protestant Christian denominations, with bible readings, sermons, songs, and so on).

One of the traditional practices of Quakers is "unprogrammed" worship or meetings, in which people sit together in silence and cultivate receptivity to the presence and teaching of Christ. In the Christian Bible, Jesus Christ assured his followers, "For where two or three are gathered together in My name, I am there among them." (Matthew 18:20, HSCB) Because of this, Quakers believe Christ is present in their meetings and that each person is capable of perceiving the Light of Christ within them. It's a Quaker's responsibility to look for that light because it lets them know God's will, discerns between good and evil, and allows them to see the unity of all humanity.

Description of the Method

By definition, an unprogrammed Quaker meeting takes place in a group. Within that group, no one has a special role or status; even beginners and non-Quakers participate like everyone else. Worshippers sit facing one another in a circle or rectangle on chairs or benches, with no prescribed ways to sit or place your hands. You can also choose whether or not to close your eyes; it's up to you to find what works best for you.

An unprogrammed Quaker meeting lasts between 30 minutes and 1 hour. Once the meeting has begun, everyone sits together in silence. Internally, you work on what some Quakers call *centering down,* or settling your body and mind. There are no set instructions for how to do this; generally, each person centers in their own way. The idea is to become receptive to your Inner Light (the presence of Christ within you), so obviously, thinking about other things isn't the point. At the same time, willful concentration—as if you can make God speak to you through your effort—is discouraged. Instead, you're asked to cultivate an attitude of patient and humble but expectant waiting. The meeting is called to a close when a designated person stands and shakes hands with someone next to him.

Exploring Quaker Worship Further

Attending an unprogrammed Quaker meeting is the best way to explore this practice further. The full benefits of this practice are intimately tied to the presence of a group. The effort of others to be receptive to the Inner Light tends to be supportive of your own effort, and people's spontaneous vocal ministries help build a sense of communal experience. When a meeting coalesces in a powerful way, the effects can be profound, leading to insights and shifts in individual participants, as well as to a deep sense of connection with others.

POINT OF CLARIFICATION

Unprogrammed Quaker meetings may also have moments of vocal ministry, when participants feel moved to speak something out loud that has arisen from their Inner Light. The expression is meant to be spontaneous, short, offered for the good of all, and (ideally) free of egotistical concerns. Also, each person generally only speaks once in a meeting, if at all, and waits several minutes after the last vocal ministry before offering something. Some meetings end up having no vocal ministry at all.

Quaker groups that do this kind of worship don't proselytize, so you'll be able to try this kind of practice with a group without feeling any pressure to do so again or to become a Quaker. To find a group near you (always called a *meeting*) in the United States, use the searchable list on the website of the Friends General Conference (fgcquaker.org). For meetings elsewhere in the world, see the Quaker Information Center website (quakerinfo.org). These sites also offer information, resources, and links related to Quaker practice. If you prefer learning more from or supplementing your experiences with a book, read *Encounter with Silence: Reflections from the Quaker Tradition* by John Punshon.

Bahá'í Meditation

The Bahá'í faith is a monotheistic faith and a growing world religion. It was established by Bahá'u'lláh (1817–1892), who was born in Persia (present-day Iran). Bahá'u'lláh is viewed by Bahá'ís as a "Manifestation of God," or a prophet, in a long line of prophets that includes Moses, Jesus, Muhammad, and holy men from non-Abrahamic faiths (such as Krishna and Buddha). Bahá'u'lláh established a new religion that Bahá'ís believe better meets the needs of the modern world than previous ones, in part because of its emphasis on the unity of all religions and peoples, social justice and service, and world peace.

Bahá'u'lláh left many writings, as did his successors Abdu'l-Bahá (his son) and Shoghi Effendi (his great-grandson). These writings form the basis of the Bahá'í faith, including its guidelines for practice and daily life, spiritual teachings, and prayers. According to the foundational Bahá'í teachings, the purpose of human life is to know God and attain His presence. Bahá'ís do this in many ways—including service, devotion to family, fasting, and pilgrimage—but one of the important ones is through self-development. Each person is seen to possess an immortal soul, and through spiritual practice and devotion, you can prepare that soul to know God and to reunite with Him after death.

Description of the Method

Throughout Bahá'í scriptures and modern writings, you frequently encounter the phrase *prayer and meditation* when referring to the important daily practices of Bahá'ís. While prayer and meditation are seen to be two separate things, there's a clear emphasis on how you should include both in your life.

Bahá'í prayer is seen as a direct supplication to God, and Bahá'ís do prescribed daily prayers, as well as more informal prayers. Bahá'í meditation, on the other hand, is a way to gain deeper understanding of both personal matters—which helps you improve yourself and prepare your soul to know God—and heavenly matters, depending on where you put your attention. While the exact techniques employed in meditation are left up to the individual, the value placed on meditation is made very clear in the Bahá'í scriptures. For example, Bahá'u'lláh wrote, "One hour's reflection is preferable to seventy years of pious worship." (*The Kitáb-i-Íqán*, Bahá'í Reference Library, bahai.org.)

 CONTEMPLATE THIS

Although there aren't explicit instructions in Bahá'í meditation, you can find clear descriptions of the meditative state in Bahá'í scriptures. In a long passage on meditation, for example, Abdu'l-Bahá explained, "Meditation is the key for opening the doors of mysteries. In that state man abstracts himself: in that state man withdraws himself from all outside objects; in that subjective mood he is immersed in the ocean of spiritual life and can unfold the secrets of things-in-themselves ... This faculty of meditation frees man from the animal nature, discerns the reality of things, puts man in touch with God." (Paris Talks, Bahá'í Reference Library, bahai.org.)

While Bahá'í meditation commonly focuses on a scriptural passage or prayer, it can take anything as its object. Despite the importance of meditation in the religion, however, Shoghi Effendi made it clear in his writings that in the Bahá'í faith, there are no set techniques for meditation; individuals decide for themselves how they want to undertake this practice.

Exploring Bahá'í Meditation Further

You'll definitely get a clearer sense of what Bahá'í meditation is and the role it's meant to play in your spiritual life if you visit a Bahá'í temple. You can try to find one near you by using a search engine (look for "Bahá'í temple") or visiting the Bahá'í Faith website (bahai.org; search for the link at the bottom of the homepage that says "A Global Community").

The Bahá'í Faith website also has the information about the religion, including Bahá'í beliefs, practices, and activities within the church. You can access many of the main Bahá'í scriptures there as well, in the online Bahá'í Reference Library. You may also want to read *God Speaks Again: An Introduction to the Bahai Faith* by Kenneth E. Bowers.

Taoist Meditation

Taoism is a rich and ancient Chinese religious tradition. Many westerners are familiar with the classic Taoist text, Lao Tzu's *Tao Te Ching,* which dates from the third or fourth century B.C.E. and beautifully describes the concept of the *Tao,* or the primordial, impersonal, natural order of the universe. While the Tao is an unnamable mystery beyond verbal description or conceptual understanding, it's possible to perceive its functioning and to live in greater harmony with it. To live in accord with the Tao leads to stability, strength, health, well-being, and other kinds of positive results, while acting out of accord with it is the source of human suffering.

Western affinity for the ideas found in the *Tao Te Ching* has led to a modern conception of there being two Taoisms: one, a pure philosophy, and the other, a religious Taoism. Philosophical Taoism tends to focus on ideas and Taoist literature, divorced from religious practices or participation in a Taoist community. Religious Taoism, on the other hand, is deeply rooted in traditional Chinese culture and often includes elaborate rituals conducted by priests, scriptural study, practices for health and longevity, attention to the flow of *Qi* (energy or life force) within the body, and devotion to celestial deities and immortals. Quite naturally, westerners often find these aspects of Taoism more difficult to access or relate to; however, there's a movement to introduce the full range of traditional Taoist practices to people outside of China.

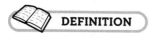 **DEFINITION**

Tao, a Chinese Taoist term sometimes translated as "way" or "path," refers to natural order of the universe, as well as to the path of perceiving and living in accord with that order. **Qi,** another Chinese term, refers to the vital life force, energy, or "subtle breath" that flows through the human body, as well as through all of creation.

Description of the Method

When discussing Taoist meditation, it's important to note that the more involved and intensive practices of Taoism have traditionally been practiced by priests or monastics. In fact, Taoism was intimately woven into the Chinese cultural landscape, and it was usually only priests who were formally called *Taoists;* laypeople primarily relied upon the priests as ritual specialists to address what was perceived as ill effects of being out of harmony with Tao, or of having blocked or imbalanced Qi within the body. This isn't to say laypeople didn't sometimes do intensive Taoist practice; in fact, the tradition as a whole is complex, and it's difficult to generalize.

There's also no single method of Taoist meditation. In fact, several major categories of meditative techniques exist (including lineage-based variations within those techniques). Each major type of meditation is practiced for different, although overlapping, purposes. The first kind of technique—a silent, introspective method sometimes called *sitting and forgetting*—is meant to empty your mind of all content and eventually allow the dropping away of self-identity in order to achieve unity with the Tao. The second technique is an elaborate visualization meditation that's employed to affect the balance and flow of Qi in your body and, at a deeper level, to perceive the manifestation of the Tao within your body in a deeply experiential, physical way.

The third meditative technique, internal alchemy, is a complex psychophysiological process aimed at uniting the disparate parts of yourself—physical and spiritual, worldly and heavenly—into a transcendent spirit that can become immortal (a very involved, difficult process). After death and dissolution of the physical body, this transcendent spirit would persist. However, such a spirit would also transcend self and return to the source, or Tao, so this isn't immortality in a self-aggrandizing sense. Internal alchemy involves the previous two kinds of meditation, as well as other Taoist practices, and is only undertaken under the close guidance of a qualified teacher.

Exploring Taoist Meditation Further

Chances are the nearest center or group to you that identifies itself as Taoist is going to focus primarily on Chinese body practices, such as Tai Chi or Qi Gong. These practices—emphasizing physical movement, energy flow, and health—are somewhat related to Taoism and can certainly be approached in a Taoist way. However, these body practices developed in China somewhat in parallel with Taoism, and such practices are only a small part of the full Taoist tradition.

If you're interested in the kinds of Taoist meditation described previously, you'll probably want to look for a fairly traditional Taoist group. While these can be a little hard to find, the Daoist Foundation maintains a list of groups, along with information on their leadership and tradition, so you can make an informed decision (daoistcenter.org/organizations.pdf). Additional useful websites include the Daoist Foundation (daoistfoundation.org) and Daoist Studies (daoiststudies. org), and a good book to start with is *The Daoist Tradition: An Introduction* by Louis Komjathy.

CONTEMPLATE THIS

Taoism suffered intense persecution during the Cultural Revolution in China (1966–1976), when religious sites were destroyed or closed down, and overt practice of religion was banned. Since then, however, Taoism has been experiencing revitalization. The two largest Taoist schools or sects are Quanzhen (Complete Perfection Taoism), a primarily monastic branch headquartered at White Cloud Monastery in Beijing, and Zhengyi (Orthodox Unity Taoism), a liturgical branch centered at Dragon Tiger Mountain in Yintan Kiangsi. Look for references to these schools in the lineage accounts of a group if you want to know how traditional they are.

Transcendental Meditation

Before the advent of the mindfulness movement in the last 30 years, probably the type of meditation best known to westerners was Transcendental Meditation (TM). Maharishi Mahesh Yogi (1918–2008), an Indian and student of a Vedic religious tradition, traveled the world throughout his life teaching TM and training teachers to further spread the practice. He had already gained a significant following in the United Kingdom and elsewhere when the Beatles and various other celebrities began to study with him, which of course further increased the number of people aware of TM. It's estimated by the TM organization that about 6 million people have learned the technique worldwide.

The Maharishi presented TM as a simple and easy-to-practice but highly effective method of personal growth and spiritual development. Although the technique arose out of his Vedic training and can be explained using Vedic principles, it's taught independent of dogmas or other religious practices. In fact, the Maharishi called TM a spiritual "technology" that was perfectly compatible with other religions or with having no religion at all. Doing it relieves stress, improves health, increases happiness and effectiveness, and potentially allows you to experience a profound transcendence of self. TM is the most-studied form of meditation, and hundreds research papers have been published on its practical benefits.

Description of the Method

The basic premise of TM is that your habitual way of operating uses only a fraction of your potential as a human being. This is because the stressful demands of modern life cause your active, external functioning to be out of sync with the deepest level of your being. This deepest level is pure consciousness—an undifferentiated field of "Being" that's below thought, full of potential, and the source from which all thinking and activity arises. It's only by turning to this inner field that you can attain true and lasting happiness. The purpose of TM is to connect your inner field of Being with your outer field of activity.

However, you don't need to understand or believe any of the philosophical explanations behind the TM method in order to do it or to benefit from it. In fact, TM teachers emphasize it will work even if you're completely skeptical about it. The technique involves sitting in a comfortable position and "thinking" a mantra or special sound. The mantra is assigned to you by a qualified TM teacher who chooses it based on your individual needs. You spend 20 minutes twice a day sitting and thinking your mantra—but without striving to achieve anything, including concentration on the mantra. As long as you do the practice, your mind will be naturally drawn toward the happiness of experiencing more and more subtle levels of thinking.

Exploring TM Further

You have to learn TM from a qualified teacher. When asked why, teachers will point out that you can't learn how to be a good golf player entirely from a book or a video—you need to actually do it and have your actions guided by a real person. In addition, the TM teacher assigns you a personal mantra, and considerable weight is given to the importance of this sound in the effectiveness of the meditation.

TM courses are offered all over the world. The cost of a course varies by area but is usually around $1,000 and includes a standardized seven-step training with about 10 hours total instruction. After the course, you're able to practice on your own indefinitely, but for the rest of your life you can contact a TM teacher for a personal consultation about your meditation for free. To learn more about TM in general, read Jack Forem's *Transcendental Meditation: The Essential Teachings of Maharishi Mahesh Yogi.* The TM organization also maintains a website (tm.org) with resource materials, introductory videos, testimonials, and a search feature for finding a certified TM teacher in your area.

The Least You Need to Know

- While unprogrammed Quaker worship can only be done in a group, it can be a powerful shared experience of perceiving your Inner Light—the presence of Christ—in silence.
- Bahá'í meditation involves no fixed techniques; each person finds his own way to reflect deeply and immerse himself in the ocean of spiritual life.
- There are many involved and specific types of Taoist meditation, and they are best practiced under the guidance of a qualified teacher.
- Transcendental Meditation (TM) is extremely simple and easy to do, and hundreds of research studies suggest it has practical benefits.

Meditative Movement

Meditative movement can be a very useful and rewarding practice. Just about any physical activity—such as walking, running, working out, bowing, or doing simple physical tasks—can be done meditatively if you make the effort to do so. Meditative movement helps you take what you've learned in still or seated meditation and apply it in the midst of activity. After all, you spend most of your day engaged in activity, so being able to make at least some of it meditative will increase the benefits your experience from meditation practice. It's also good to have meditative movement as an alternative to seated meditation, in case you find yourself physically or emotionally unable to sit still for prolonged periods.

In this chapter, I explain how to make any kind of movement meditative. I also introduce you to a number of forms of meditative movement that are either traditional or growing in popularity, and I give you an exercise you can try for each kind of movement.

In This Chapter

* The benefits of meditative movement
* How to make a simple movement meditative
* Traditional walking and bowing meditations
* Bringing meditation to running and other physical workouts
* How to turn a simple task into a meditation

Still vs. Active Meditation

Some people use the term *mindfulness* (as you learned about with Insight Meditation in Chapter 5) when talking about bringing a meditative approach to movement or activity and reserve the word *meditation* for focused, formal practices in which you don't move the body (or move it in a very slow or minimal way). In this book, however, I'm using a very general definition of meditation that I believe covers what's usually meant by mindfulness: conscious direction of your mind for a period of time in order to affect the mind itself. You can do this when you're sitting still in silent meditation, praying, or engaging in a practice of meditative movement.

CONTEMPLATE THIS

If you do physically still or focused formal meditation, meditative movement can be a wonderful way to bridge the gap between the quiet, calm space of meditation and the busy, active space of everyday life. Meditative movement lets you practice applying the skills and lessons you learn in formal meditation in the midst of activity.

I highly recommend doing still, seated meditation, even if you also enjoy meditative movement. There's great value in getting to know the workings of your own mind in the simplified space of formal meditation practice, without even the minor distraction of simple physical movement. However, you may find that sitting still is physically or mentally too uncomfortable—in general or at certain times in your life. For example, some people find it very difficult to do still, focused meditation when they're experiencing trauma or unusually strong anxiety or depression. When this is the case, it's very helpful to try meditative movement or a meditative activity instead (see Chapter 16).

What Makes Movement Meditative?

People often say their chosen form of exercise—such as running, working out, or stretching—is their meditation. This is because many forms of movement naturally encourage you to "get out of your head" and focus on the here and now. When you're paying close attention to your breathing, the movements of your limbs, or keeping your balance, you're directing your mind in a grounding and calming way very similar to meditation.

However, it's easy for any kind of movement to become mostly physical rather than a conscious effort involving both your body and mind. When this happens, the movement ceases being meditative. For example, once you're familiar with a particular physical activity, your mind will tend to wander out of boredom. You may start engaging in the movement mostly for its physical and emotional benefits, so it becomes another sort of chore to be performed. At this point, you might try to make the time go by more quickly by entertaining yourself with music, television, or daydreaming.

Of course, exercise and simple tasks can be beneficial and useful even if they're not done meditatively, but you might want to make your activity into a meditation for a number of reasons. For one, you'll add the benefits of meditating to the list of rewards from your movement. You'll also probably find meditative concentration increases your physical performance—your stamina, precision, balance, and ability to move through discomfort, among other things—and your sense of appreciation and enjoyment of whatever physical activity you're doing. So how do you incorporate meditation into movement?

Doing Only One Thing

The key to making movement meditative is to do only one thing at a time—in this case, the movement itself. Of course, any activity is made up of countless sensations, perceptions, decisions, and activities. For example, as you walk, you're maintaining a particular posture and pace; moving your legs, feet, and toes; perceiving things with your eyes and ears; breathing; and noticing any discomfort or pain in the body. Any and all of these things are part of the "one" activity of walking—and as long as you direct your mind to something within that sphere of experience, you're making your movement meditative.

 POINT OF CLARIFICATION

If you try to concentrate just on your physical activity, you're likely to find it as challenging as concentrating during seated meditation. In fact, you might find it more difficult because you're not used to directing your mind in a meditative way while moving around or while encountering lots of potential distractions. The practice of meditation is the same whether you're physically still or moving: you just gently return your mind to the object of your meditation whenever you find it has wandered.

In order to encourage making your movement meditative, it's best to forgo listening to music while doing it, unless your movement is coordinated with the music—that is, unless you're dancing or maybe working out in time with the beat. If you can't do the activity without your music, you might try listening to something without lyrics or something that doesn't affect your emotional state too much. The idea is to minimize distraction from the direct and full experience of your chosen physical activity. This means meditative movement is also incompatible with carrying on a conversation, reading a book, or watching television. While you may anticipate that just doing the physical movement would be boring, if you try it, you'll probably find it's engaging and rewarding in and of itself, even apart from any benefits from meditation.

The Experience vs. the Results

Another thing that makes a movement meditative is why you're doing it. You may recall that meditation is "conscious direction of your mind for a period of time in order to affect the mind itself." You may have other motivations for your movement as well—increased physical fitness, pleasure, or completing a simple task—and that's fine. But it's important to set aside the effort to achieve some result in order to focus on the experience of the movement itself. By doing so, you involve your mind as well as your body in the activity, which is why it will have a deeper impact on your whole being than moving or exercising while your mind wanders.

As you engage in your physical movement of choice, pay attention to the sensations you feel in your body. How is your breathing? Can you feel the effects of strenuous movement in your muscles? Notice what you see, hear, and smell without fixating on any of it; just observe, as if you're watching a movie. You can even notice your thoughts as if they're passing clouds. After all, wondering, "How much longer do I have to go?" is part of your whole experience! As long as you don't get caught up in a train of thought as a result, your meditation continues. You're paying attention to your present activity for its own sake, something that most of us rarely do in our daily lives.

Slow and Fast Walking Meditation

One of the most traditional forms of meditation in movement is walking. In his book *Walking Meditation,* Zen master Thich Nhat Hanh explains, "In Buddhism, there is a word, 'apranihita.' It means wishlessness or aimlessness. The idea is that we do not put anything ahead of ourselves and run after it. When we practice walking meditation, we walk in this spirit. We just enjoy the walking, with no particular aim or destination." Because it's so beneficial, walking meditation is done every day in Zen monasteries and practice centers all over the world.

General Approach

To engage in meditative walking, you first need to choose an environment that won't be too distracting. If you're able to concentrate on the physical experience of walking while wending your way down a busy city street packed with pedestrians, well—congratulations! You have amazing powers of concentration.

Most of us need a less stimulating setting in order to keep our minds on our meditation, at least at first. You can find such a setting in solitude or nature, or within a constrained area—a room indoors, your backyard, or a longer course that you keep repeating. The point is you won't be constantly encountering new stimulation, which naturally draws your attention. You might walk slowly back and forth between two spots 10 to 30 feet apart, or you could walk around your city block or a running track.

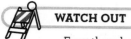 **WATCH OUT**

Even though you intend to make a physical movement meditative, it may not be so easy at first. You're probably used to doing other things, or at least *thinking* about other things, while you walk, run, work out, and so on. Be patient with yourself, and with any sense of resistance or boredom that may arise. These feelings are natural; they aren't a sign that you're not meditating "right." Just notice whatever's going on—including feelings of boredom or a wandering mind—and gently return your awareness to your physical activity.

You can do slow or fast walking meditation, but in either case, you'll want to anchor your awareness on the sensations in your legs or feet. Keep your eyes lowered, looking at the ground in front of you. Just walk—and try to enjoy just walking! Go ahead and use any technique that helps you keep your mind directed toward your movement: count steps, coordinate your steps with your breathing, or chant to yourself one word or syllable per step, such as "Here-and-now-walk-ing-here-and-now."

Walking Practice

To do this walking meditation, find a quiet place where you can practice undisturbed—it can be indoors or outdoors. Decide on a straight course for walking that's between 10 and 20 feet long; you might want to walk the length of a room and then turn back, or walk between two trees. If it's feasible, walk barefoot in order to be better able to concentrate on the sensations on the bottoms of your feet.

Keeping your hands clasped together in front of you, take very small steps that are coordinated with your breathing. With your first exhalation, move one of your feet forward about 6 inches or so, taking a small-enough step that you can easily keep your balance. As you exhale, shift your weight gradually and slowly onto your front foot. As you then inhale, continue shifting weight off your rear foot until it lifts gently off the ground. Move this foot about 6 inches in front of the other, and shift your weight to it as you exhale.

As you walk, keep these movements continuous and fluid. Set the length of your meditation based on distance walked or time, and if you'd like, end your meditation in a deliberate way (for example, with a small bow, or by bringing your feet together and closing your eyes for a few moments).

Meditative Running

Many books and training courses recommend increasing your mindfulness while running. Runners observe that bringing a meditative approach to running transforms the experience—running fills their consciousness, and not only does it provide benefits similar to other forms of meditation, it also increases their stamina and helps them be a better runner.

CONTEMPLATE THIS

If you already run but are daunted by the prospect of seated meditation, take encouragement from the fact that both activities require similar things: self-discipline, determination, and the ability to endure some discomfort (even if it's primarily mental). You're already a step ahead by having worked on these things in your running practice!

There's a strong tradition of combining running with meditation. For instance, a group of Buddhist monks in Japan are popularly known as the "marathon monks." An established part of their training is running—sometimes more than 50 miles a day for months at a time—in the mountains where their monastery is located. (See *The Marathon Monks of Mount Hiei* by John Stevens.) Also, Sakyong Mipham, Tibetan Buddhist teacher, spiritual leader of the international Shambala organization, and author of *Running with the Mind of Meditation: Lessons for Training Body and Mind,* is an avid runner. Training programs based on his teachings around running are regularly offered at the Shambala Mountain Center in Colorado.

General Approach

Like all forms of meditative movement, running primarily requires you to keep your awareness on the experience of running. It's particularly important to pay attention to your breathing, but without judgment. The idea is that your mind and body will naturally function at their best if you simply bring your full awareness to the process. Of course, you have lots of things to pay attention to while running—the pounding rhythm of your feet, the breeze on your skin, or the beating of your heart, just to name a few. Some people report feeling especially aware of their surroundings once they've settled into their running and allowed their thinking to subside.

What's particularly fascinating (and potentially fruitful) about meditative running is how it invites you to witness the workings of your own mind as you come up against obstacles like pain, heat, exhaustion, or a sense of being overwhelmed based on how far you still have to go. Bringing extra awareness to how you push through or deal with these obstacles helps you integrate what you learn while running into your everyday life (consciously or unconsciously). You may also find that deliberately "turning toward" your pain and discomfort—rather than distracting yourself from them—actually ends up making them less distressing or limiting. This meditative "turning toward" involves allowing discomfort to be part of your larger experience, as opposed to obsessing or worrying about it.

Running Practice

This practice assumes that you already run; if you don't, consult another book or a trainer about how to get started. If you do run, however, you can practice this running meditation no matter how far or how fast you tend to run.

First, decide how long you want to run in a meditative way. If you're just starting this practice, don't make it too long—maybe just 5 to 10 minutes. Run in a meditative way long enough to challenge yourself but not so long that you start to resent and fight it, in which case you'll be much less likely to try it again. After you've run a certain length of time or a certain distance, go ahead and turn your music back on or let your mind wander.

> **POINT OF CLARIFICATION**
>
> Even if you adopt a practice of meditative movement like running, it can still be beneficial for you to do a more formal and introspective kind of meditation. In fact, the two practices can be very complementary. Concentrated—usually physically still—meditation can help you learn to direct your mind more effectively, while meditative movement teaches you how to be more present in all of your activities.

During the meditative part of your running, remind yourself that you're running just for the sake of the experience (that is, put aside your health and fitness goals for the time being, as best you can). Coordinate your breathing with your steps, without forcing anything. Your inhalation may be shorter—and therefore fewer steps—than your exhalation. Whenever your mind wanders, turn your awareness back to the amazing experience of running: all the different parts of your body moving in a coordinated way without you having to consciously direct them. If resistance or discomfort arises, simply notice this. Concentrate on the miracle of being alive and the good fortune of being healthy enough to run.

Yoga, Stretching, or Weight Lifting

Focused physical activity aimed at increasing your strength, flexibility, or balance—such as body-oriented yoga, stretching exercises, or weight lifting—are great opportunities for meditation. Of course, as described in the previous sections on walking and running, in order to make these activities meditative, you need to shift your awareness from future goals to your direct, immediate experience. The amazing thing is you're more likely to achieve your short-term and long-term goals by keeping your whole mind focused on the present—not because you're striving, but because you move more effectively and carefully.

General Approach

So how do you transform a session at the gym or yoga studio into a meditation? As described earlier, you do this essentially by making an effort to do *only* your physical activity. For instance, you've probably noticed you have plenty of mental "bandwidth" to stretch and plan dinner at the same time! It can be very tempting to plan, analyze, and fantasize while doing a physical activity with which you're fairly familiar. But if you actually watch your mind as it wanders from topic to topic, you'll notice how rarely it's doing anything useful. Even if you're thinking about something important, it's probably something you can put your mind to *after* your session of meditative movement.

As you move your body, allow yourself to become completely absorbed in your movements. Put aside listening to music, and if you're at the gym, try to avoid facing a television that's playing something you're interested in. Pay attention to the whole process of your movement, including the times between postures, stretches, or sets. Keep the thread of your awareness going as you prepare for and come out of a strenuous posture or exercise. Notice everything you can that's associated with your movements at the points of greatest exertion. For example, notice not just the fact that you've managed to lift a certain amount of weight or get into a difficult yoga pose, but the position of and feeling in all parts of your body—including those that aren't directly involved with the effort.

Meditative Workout

During one of your regular sessions of yoga, stretching, weight lifting, or some similar workout, dedicate 10 minutes to meditative movement. This can be at the beginning or end of your workout. During this period, don't expect yourself to be able to concentrate on your movement nonstop; however, whenever you find your mind wandering, bring it back to the question, "How is my body right now?" Check in with your physical position; your sense of energy; and any sensations of warmth, coolness, discomfort, or exhilaration.

WATCH OUT

Don't let your aspiration to be mindful during your exercise routine turn you off of doing it. While it's great to up the ante and make your movement meditative, if you need to entertain yourself in some way during exercise in order to make yourself do it, go ahead and indulge!

In order to hold your attention on your movement for longer periods, go ahead and create little mental games for yourself. You might count how many seconds you're able to hold a position, or count repetitions of a movement. You might see if you can notice the arising and passing away of any pain or discomfort you experience, and try to locate and describe it (if you do this with open curiosity, you'll usually find it makes the discomfort recede or seem less important). You might imagine you're performing an elaborate dance that lasts the entire meditation period (so all of your movements count). Pretty much anything works as long as it keeps your awareness centered in the present moment in a nonjudgmental way.

Bowing

Another traditional meditative movement that can be very rewarding is bowing. You may wonder why bowing would be relevant to you if you aren't part of a religion or culture that includes the practice. It's a valid question! After all, don't you have to bow *to* someone or something? The short answer is no. Plenty of people actively engage in bowing practice simply because of the humbling and grounding effects of the practice, not because they're bowing to something or someone they believe is superior to themselves.

General Approach

Of course, traditionally bowing is done either to God or to some aspect of the universe that is, in a sense, superior to you. Observant Muslims bow as they pray five times a day, setting aside their worldly activities in order to align themselves with what is most important—God. Buddhists bow to remind themselves of each person's ability to awaken spiritually or out of devotion to universal ideals, such as compassion. Regardless of what you might feel like bowing to, the physical act has an effect on you. A Zen teacher I knew once observed, "It's pretty much impossible to bow when you're angry!" If you try, you'll probably find some of your anger dissipating.

Bowing as a practice unto itself—as opposed to bowing as an occasional sign of devotion or greeting—usually involves a series of full prostrations. In a full prostration, you start in a standing position, bow down to the floor (kneeling or lying down on the ground), and stand back up. Practitioners of Seon Buddhism (the Korean form of Zen) start their morning practice with 108 of these full bows every day. This is great exercise, plus the repetitive quality of it encourages a meditative mental space.

Bowing Practice

When practicing this bowing meditation, call to mind something that inspires you—something that gives you a larger perspective or makes life seem worthwhile. If you'd like, you can keep this inspiration in mind as you bow, or you can let it go and simply perform the motion. You can set a number of bows to do (traditionally Buddhists do bows in sets of nine) or bow for a certain length of time. To start out, I recommend trying nine bows in a row, done as slowly or quickly as you like. Try to keep your awareness on your motion and make it as wholehearted and sincere as possible.

In Tibetan Buddhism, a traditional form of pilgrimage involves endless bowing. Pilgrims make a full prostration, stand up, take a few small steps, and then make another prostration—sometimes for hundreds of miles! Keep in mind that in Tibetan Buddhism, a full prostration requires you to end up lying prone on your stomach, with your arms extended in front of you, your legs stretched out behind you, and your whole body in contact with the ground.

For each full bow, start standing with your hands pressed palm to palm in front of you. When you're ready, bend at the waist and sink down gently to your knees. You can keep your toes curled under you or point them out behind you. Allow yourself to sink as low to the ground as you can and then bend over and touch your forehead to the floor. In one form of Buddhist bow, you lay your hands palm up on the floor at this point, on either side of your head, and then raise them slightly. Alternatively, you can simply place them palms down on the ground. You then reverse this whole process, standing back up as gracefully as you can. Pause and then repeat! Notice whether you feel any different afterward, mentally or physically.

Simple Work as Meditation

It may strike you as a little strange that work can be meditative. When something qualifies as work, we tend to mentally or emotionally "check out" while we're doing it as much as possible. Work is usually, by definition, *not* something we're choosing to do, and often we look at a particular task as boring or onerous—just something to get through. Alternatively, maybe we enjoy a task but are eager to finish it to achieve some result. If we approach work as an opportunity for meditation, we can appreciate our experience more, let go of hurrying, and use our work time to de-stress.

General Approach

To make work meditative—you guessed it!—you concentrate on the experience of doing the work rather than on a particular outcome, or on just getting the work done. You adopt a completely different orientation toward your task than you typically do: you want to be present for each and every moment of this experience for its own sake.

It's best to use very simple, physical tasks for meditation, such as weeding the garden, chopping vegetables, washing dishes, or sweeping the floor. This allows you to turn your awareness to the simple sensations, internal and external, that arise as you work. When your mind wanders, you simply return your attention to the movements of your hands or feet, the sound of the knife hitting the cutting board, or the feeling of the breeze on your cheek. If you ever visit a Zen monastery, you'll witness periods of communal, silent "work practice," where everyone engages in simple tasks in this meditative way.

Work Practice

To practice work as meditation, choose a very simple, repetitive physical task, and decide to do it mindfully for 10 minutes. You might want to set a timer so you don't keep looking at a clock as you work. For the duration of your meditative work, try to do this simple task wholeheartedly. Imagine there's nothing on Earth you'd rather do than scrub this dish or rake these leaves. Try to let go of all worries about not having enough time to get things done, or about whether the task could be done better another way. Let go of planning related projects and thinking about your next task.

 POINT OF CLARIFICATION

It's possible to weave a more meditative quality into work that's complicated and largely mental, but only by inserting moments of mindfulness into it. At these moments, you set aside your mental task and bring your awareness to your breathing or basic physical sensations. When you need your mind for your work, however, you work wholeheartedly, without trying to meditate at the same time.

When you find yourself thinking about things other than your work (which you will), take a moment to be grateful you've noticed this. As soon as you become aware of your thinking, you've already returned your awareness to the present moment! Take this opportunity of having "remembered" the present to shift your awareness back to your physical movements and sensations as you work.

The Least You Need to Know

- Meditative movement is a great alternative if you find forms of meditation that require physical stillness or intense focus too uncomfortable.

- Even if you do seated meditation, engaging in meditative movement can be beneficial, because it helps you learn to bring the mind of meditation into everyday activity.

- You bring the same approach and intention to meditative movement as you do to still or formal meditation: a conscious direction of your mind for a period of time in order to affect the mind itself.

- To make your movement meditative, you turn the movement itself into the object of your meditation. You concentrate on doing the movement for its own sake, and return your mind to the movement whenever it wanders.

- Traditional forms of meditative movement include walking, bowing, and performing simple physical tasks. But activities like running, yoga, stretching, and weight lifting can also be done meditatively.

Meditative Activities

In the last chapter, I described how you can bring the mind of meditation into various kinds of physical movement, and in this chapter, I introduce some meditative activities you can try. While meditative activities are similar to meditative movement in that you maintain an awareness of your physical motions while you do them, meditative activities are different in that they're carefully chosen because of the effects they have on your mind.

In the first part of this chapter, I explain what makes an activity a good meditation. I then discuss a number of traditional meditative activities, including how they're done and what makes them rewarding. Although these practices—chanting, hand copying texts, fingering a string of beads, performing simple rituals, and artistic expression—may sound either religious or specialized, they can be easily adapted for use in a way that feels comfortable to you, and I suggest ways to do so. For each type of meditative activity, I also offer a practice you can try.

In This Chapter

- What qualifies as a meditative activity?
- The value of meditative activities
- Classic meditative practices
- Adapting activities for secular use
- Simple meditative activities you can try

What Makes an Activity Meditative?

It's a little hard to put your finger on what makes a meditative activity different from a regular activity. You usually know when something is meditative when you experience it though—it calms you down and gets you out of your head and into your body. It defies intellectual analysis and ambition, so it requires you to switch into a different mode of operation than you use in much of your daily life. Perhaps for this reason, a meditative activity can help you access nonverbal parts of yourself that are often neglected or unnoticed. Such nonverbal parts include deep inner experiences of devotion, conviction, unconditional strength, intuition, and creativity. So how does an activity qualify as meditative?

Focusing on Doing One Thing

Like all forms of meditation, a meditative activity asks you to direct your mind in deliberate way—in this case, toward the activity itself. In many ways, this is similar to what you do in a movement meditation, such as walking or bowing (as discussed in the previous chapter), but meditative activities generally give you a little more to focus on. They're designed to fully engage your body, mind, and heart in a way that potentially allows you to pour everything you've got into the activity, and yet remain somewhat concentrated, because you're doing *one* thing.

 CONTEMPLATE THIS

Like the forms of meditation discussed earlier in this book, meditative activities generally have no purpose—or for the time being, you set aside whatever purpose they may have. While you engage an activity as a meditative practice, you do it simply because of the effect the practice has on your mind and body.

At an even deeper level of engagement in a meditative activity, you also try to allow the separation between yourself and the activity to dissolve. Your sense of "I am concentrating very hard on this meditative activity" gradually dissolves into a pure experience of the activity itself. There's *just* chanting, *just* copying, or *just* performing a simple ritual. The activity fills your awareness; you let go of evaluating how well you're doing, whether you're enjoying yourself, or how much longer you're going to do it. When you're completely absorbed in a meditative activity, your pervasive sense of self drops away and, for the time being, you're able to experience full, intimate engagement with life.

A Positive Effect on Your Mind

When I describe wholeheartedly doing something until you forget yourself, you may wonder why your favorite pastimes—reading books, watching movies, talking with good friends, or strolling through the neighborhood—aren't considered meditative activities. Of course, some of the things you do may indeed be somewhat meditative, and that may be part of the reason you enjoy them. However, two things have to be true in order for an activity to be truly meditative instead of just pleasant:

- You deliberately keep your mind on the activity and that activity only (bringing your mind back whenever it wanders).

- Doing the activity in a meditative way has a positive effect on your mind (your mental functioning, emotional state, and so on).

While it's true that doing an activity you enjoy can have a positive effect on you just because it makes you happy or gives you a break, this is different from the benefits of a meditative activity. Consciously engaging a meditative practice tends to have deeper and subtler impacts on your mental and emotional state than simple pleasure does. After meditation, you often find yourself less stressed, even though you can't explain why intellectually. Chances are you feel less reactive and agitated, and not just because you're in a good mood. You may also feel inspired or connected to something deeper in your life in a way that's not usually associated with leisure activity.

A meditative activity will generally *not* be something that requires you to use the intellectual part of your mind. While activities that require complex thought can be enjoyable and beneficial for other reasons, they don't allow you to direct your mind in a meditative way. Just to clarify, though, during a meditative activity, your mind is still involved—it's just involved in a way that's rooted in your present, embodied experience. You make decisions as you go based on skill, intuition, or creative impulses, such how to move your pen as you do hand copying, how long to pause before beginning the next line of a chant, or what to write next as you're doing calligraphy. All of these are ways your mind is responding spontaneously in the moment to the activity itself. You make a decision and then move on—you don't analyze it, criticize it, or plan future decisions.

 POINT OF CLARIFICATION

If you're anything like most other people, some of your favorite ways of taking a break include reading or watching television or movies. While these can be wonderful and rewarding activities, they aren't meditative. As discussed in Chapter 1, the meditative state is triggered by consciously directing your mind in a particular way; when you get caught up in a narrative, you allow your mind to be drawn along with that story or explanation. That's part of what makes reading and watching television enjoyable and provides a sense of escape—you've essentially given up conscious control of your mind (temporarily, of course).

It's entirely possible that one of the things you already do meets the previous criteria and is a meditative activity. It may be cooking, building models, fishing, bird watching, listening to music, or gardening—as long as you make a conscious effort to concentrate on just that one thing, engage it as completely as you can for its own sake, and forgo thinking about anything else. If you already have a somewhat meditative activity you like to do, you might find it very beneficial to recognize it as such, and make more of an effort to do that one thing completely.

Secular vs. Religious Practices

I introduce five classic meditative activities in this chapter, and all but one of them are things you might associate with religious practice. Indeed, for the most part, these activities were created and evolved in religious traditions. However, you can engage them in useful and meaningful ways, regardless of your religious or spiritual leanings (including no leaning at all). If you practice a religious or spiritual tradition that doesn't include these kinds of meditative activities, you can adapt the content and focus of the activities to be consistent with your tradition. For example, you can make a practice of hand copying whatever texts are sacred to you or create rituals consistent with your beliefs.

If you're not interested in religious or even spiritual practice, you can still find value in the meditative activities described in this chapter. The practices suggested at the end of each discussion about a particular type of activity will be general and accessible, and will suggest ways you can adapt particular activities to your needs. For example, instead of hand copying a religious text you find sacred, you could copy an essay or poem that's deeply inspirational to you. It's not so much the content involved in the activity that's important; it's the *doing* of the activity that's meditative. Besides, some traditional meditative activities are practiced independent of any religion. The Japanese tea ceremony is an excellent example of a completely secular form of ritual that can be very meditative (more on that later).

Chanting

Chanting basically involves reciting something out loud. Generally speaking, you chant something that's of significance to you—something inspirational, sacred, or a piece of important teaching. Chants can be short (a few repeated phrases) or long (30 minutes or more). They can be simple recitations done in a normal tone of voice at the pace of regular speech, or they can be rhythmic, musical, or intoned (while a prolonged tone is produced, it's not necessarily sweet or musical). Chanting can be done alone or in groups, loudly and energetically, or very softly.

What Makes It Meditative

How does chanting—particularly more musical forms of chanting—compare to singing? In some cases, it's a subtle difference, but essentially, chanting produces a more meditative effect than singing. Consider the second criteria for a meditative activity (doing the activity in a meditative way has a positive effect on your mind): sometimes singing is done in part to produce benefits in the singer—an increase in the singer's sense of devotion, an elevation of mood, and so on. However, much of the time singing is done for pleasure or in order to enter into the narrative of the song or its melody. Just as reading or watching television isn't meditative (even if it's relaxing) because your mind gets drawn into the narrative, singing is usually more of an experience unto itself than a meditation. Most songs have content that draws you into a particular story or mood.

 CONTEMPLATE THIS

Once you know a chant, you'll even find yourself chanting without any conscious effort involved, raising the question: Who is chanting? This is an opportunity for spiritual reflection because usually we connect our speech to our conscious will.

Chants, on the other hand, are either a) fairly unexciting in terms of content, or b) pointedly turn your attention toward deeper aspects of your experience as a human being. In the case of unexciting content, consider that many chants are very repetitive, and in some traditions, people even chant sounds that have no explicit meaning or have a meaning that was forgotten centuries ago. Limited content or meaning in a chant points to the fact that the most important thing is the act of chanting itself—breathing, producing sound, feeling the sound resonate in your body, and experiencing the strange phenomenon of creating sound without any self-expression involved. All of this centers your awareness on your immediate experience in a meditative way.

In the case of chants that deliberately turn your attention toward important aspects of your human experience, these are usually recitations of important teachings, principles, aspirations, or hymns of praise. They are not, you might say, entertaining, although you might enjoy them. They don't give you a narrative to get caught up in. Instead, they remind you of fundamental human issues, such as deepening your relationship to the Divine, living a meaningful life, appreciating things because life is short, generating more compassion, or striving to fulfill your full potential as a human being. As you chant, you don't analyze the meaning of the chant intellectually; you allow the words to move through you and impact you at a subverbal level. Later, you'll often find that words from the chant pop into your head at appropriate moments, and you'll realize you've gained a certain understanding or appreciation of them without deliberately trying.

Traditional Examples of Chanting

Every spiritual and religious tradition involves chanting of some kind. In the Indian Vedanta tradition, groups of practitioners worship together by chanting with calming rhythms and musical accompaniment. They're usually reciting passages from their scriptures or verses of praise for God or prominent spiritual teachers. Chanting is also a central practice in most forms of Buddhism and takes many different forms. For example, in one type of Buddhism, only one phrase is chanted repeatedly to the exclusion of all others (paying homage to a particular Buddhist scripture) because this practice is believed to be so effective at producing spiritual salvation that no other practice is needed. In other types of Buddhism, long, complex teachings are chanted fairly atonally along with percussive instruments.

 WATCH OUT

While intoned or musical chanting tends to be associated with religious practice, don't think the value of reciting things out loud is limited to religious spheres! There are many secular settings in which people speak or sing prescribed things out loud—alone or together—because of the power of audibly verbalizing something. They may make vows and pledges (like the U.S. Pledge of Allegiance), review guidelines (such as the 12 steps in Alcoholics Anonymous), or state aspirations (like verbalizing self-affirmations).

Chanting is also valued in Western traditions. Throughout the history of Christianity, there have always been hymns that encourage quiet devotion and introspection. The most famous of these may be Gregorian chants, which were devised by monks in order to put scriptures to melody in a beautiful and inspirational but still meditative way (the melodies are very repetitive, and are sung at a stately pace). And as described in Chapter 8, observant Jews pray aloud several times a day—in most cases, a recitation in a normal tone of voice. However, especially when praying together, traditional melodies may be used. Daily and group Islamic prayers, similarly, have standardized content and are chanted out loud to simple, beautiful melodies. In some forms of Sufi prayer, physical movements like swaying and whirling are added to the chanting to help induce complete absorption in the practitioner.

Chanting Practice

The simplest form of chanting is reciting (or reading) something out loud. You can do this in a normal tone of voice, or you can produce a prolonged tone (intoning) without worrying about what note you pick or staying in tune. Of course, as with all forms of meditation, you should try to keep your awareness on your chosen object—in this case, the act of chanting—and let go of other thoughts when you notice they're getting in the way of your full experience of the chanting.

Pick something of deep significance to you—something that reminds you of your deepest aspirations. Ideally, it will be something you'd like to keep in mind all the time; chanting it out loud will help lodge it in your brain, and reciting it regularly (say, on a daily basis) will keep bringing you back to what you find most inspiring or helpful.

Choose a time and place for the chanting in which you can complete it without being disturbed. When you're ready to start, take a deliberate posture. It doesn't matter if you sit or stand, but don't just slouch in a spot where you're used to doing all kinds of other activities. Take a deep breath or two and then chant your chosen passage out loud. Don't go too quickly—let the chant find its own rhythm, and go ahead and lengthen the words so they're much longer than ordinary speech, if that seems appropriate. You might add a very simple musical quality to your chanting by intoning one line on a particular note, raising or lowering the tone for the next line, and returning to the first note for the line after that. When you're finished, spend a moment in silence before going about your other activities.

Hand Copying Texts

In the age of computers and easily available printed material, most of us rarely have to write anything by hand beyond making out checks or jotting down brief notes. This is somewhat unfortunate because writing carefully by hand can be a soothing and satisfying activity. Copying something makes handwriting—already a calming thing to do—a meditative activity because you don't have to think about what to write. You simply concentrate on the simple act of creating the written word on paper.

What Makes It Meditative

A number of things make hand copying into a meditation. One is copying a text that's meaningful to you. It could be something that describes what you aspire to, offers an encouraging view of the world, or contains deep teaching or thinking you would like to understand. The process of hand copying is a way to engage this text with both your body and mind. It's much slower than simply reading, so it makes you spend time with each and every word. As you copy, you not only benefit from the fact that you're inducing a relaxed, meditative state in yourself, you also have the opportunity to understand the text you're copying in a new way. As I explained in Chapter 1, the state of meditation is conducive to insight, or "knowing" in ways that don't directly involve the intellect.

Second, hand copying becomes meditative when you set aside a certain amount of time for it and do it in a clean, uncluttered, comfortable place with minimal distractions. You might be amazed to feel how relaxed you instantly get when you sit down to this simple task, knowing you have the next 20 to 30 minutes to simply let your awareness rest on the process of handwriting inspirational words.

Finally, although it's entirely optional, the meditative quality of hand copying can be enhanced by taking special care with your writing. You might want to choose beautiful paper or a bound journal you use just for this purpose. You can use a nice pen—perhaps even a special kind you don't usually use, like a fountain pen or a pen with a nib that you dip into a bottle of ink (which requires extra thoughtfulness and care so you don't drip ink anywhere). You can write slowly and carefully, trying to make your script both legible and aesthetically pleasing. You might even want to use calligraphy.

Traditional Examples of Copying Text

One of the best-known examples of copying important texts by hand is, of course, the production of illuminated manuscripts before widespread use of the printing press. People, usually monks, created beautiful works of art as they copied, often illustrating the texts as they went with ornamental lettering and pictures. You can find not only illuminated manuscripts of religious texts from many different traditions, but also manuscripts of scientific treatises, chronicles, literature, and other secular works. While we can't be sure that creators of these texts engaged their task in a meditative way, chances are it was a very absorbing activity and, in the case of monks copying religious texts, it was probably also something done with care and reverence.

In the Buddhist tradition, the practice of hand copying scriptures continues today. It's a Japanese tradition called *shakyo*, or tracing the scriptures, and is around 1,000 years old. When you do shakyo, you not only copy the words of the text but also actually trace the Japanese characters. Japanese characters are complicated, and skillfully writing them by hand is an art. In shakyo, you start with a beautifully calligraphed version of the scripture you're copying, cover it with a sheet of semitransparent paper, and slowly trace the characters with a pen or brush. Whenever you make a mistake, you put a small dot above the error and then write a correction in the margin of the paper. You maintain a good posture throughout the practice, begin and end with a short prayer, and treat the copied text with reverence.

 **DEFINITION**

> **Shakyo** is a Japanese Buddhist tradition of tracing Buddhist scriptures, in which a beautifully calligraphed version of the scripture, or *sutra*, is traced reverently and meditatively on a thin piece of fine paper.

Text-Copying Practice

To do this practice, choose a text that's important to you in some way. It may be something inspirational, something you want to remember, or something you want to understand more deeply. You can copy a long text over the course of many sessions or copy a significant shorter text over and over. Set up a clean space for copying where you won't be disturbed for the duration of your meditation. You can add any rituals you feel are appropriate, such as arranging your materials carefully, writing in a special journal, carefully washing your hands before you start, or beginning with a prayer.

As you sit and copy, try to maintain some awareness of your posture. Allow yourself to let go of thinking about anything except for your task. Feel the pen in your fingers and the paper under your hand. Write in a deliberate way—slowly enough to make your writing as legible and beautiful and possible or, if you prefer, quickly enough to be able to follow the meaning more smoothly. Try to put all of your attention and energy into the writing; think of your whole body as being involved, even the parts that aren't moving, and keep in mind why the text matters to you. As you write the words, allow their meaning to arise in your mind, but don't put any deliberate thought into them. In a sense, just let them "move through" you. When you're finished—you've copied a whole text or section, or spent a certain amount of time copying—put down your pen and finish with a few moments of silence or with a short closing statement or prayer.

Fingering a String of Beads

There must be something universally beneficial about the act of holding beads between your fingers because almost all religious and spiritual traditions include the use of a string of beads in prayer, meditation, or ritual. Modern secular traditions of mindfulness and psychotherapy have also recognized the value of taking a moment to become aware of holding something like a bead between your fingers. It's a very simple thing, but it offers a very quick, simple, and easy way for you to disrupt dysfunctional trains of thought, center yourself in your body, and return your awareness to the present moment. A string of beads also allows you to maintain that awareness for a time, as you pass one bead after another through your fingers.

What Makes It Meditative

What's meditative about holding a string of beads? Essentially, you're giving yourself an excellent object for your meditation. You experience the sensations in your hands as they touch the beads and the movements you make as you pass the beads through your fingers. This meditation object is very simple—it's not exciting, it doesn't trigger thinking, and it's happening right here, right now. It brings both body and mind together in action.

> **CONTEMPLATE THIS**
>
> When you regularly use beads in meditation or prayer, the beads themselves often end up becoming a source of calm and reassurance, even when they're not being actively used. Many people carry their beads with them and hold them during times of stress or challenge.

The moment you become aware of the beads in your hands, you remember why you're holding them. So you can tie just about any kind of meditative practice to the beads. For example, you may wear beads on your wrist, and whenever you become aware of them, you touch them, take a deep breath, and try to let go of worry. You may carry a long string of beads in your pocket and periodically take them out and use them to focus your recitation of a short verse, passing one bead between thumb and forefinger with each repetition of the verse. You can also use beads in formal, seated meditation, passing one bead through your finger with each breath. The change in sensations as beads move through your fingers provides something for you to focus on.

Traditional Examples of the Use of Beads

In most religious and spiritual traditions, beads are used as an aid to concentration. The oldest evidence of the use of such beads is in India, where images over 2,000 years old have been found showing figures holding strings of 108 beads. The number 108 is symbolic of the cosmos, or everything, in the Vedic religious traditions (Hinduism, Vedanta, and Yoga) and in Buddhism. In these religions, strings of beads can be used to focus on and keep track of repetitions of prayers, or to count breaths. Indian and Buddhist prayer beads can also be found with other multiples of 9 beads, typically 27 or 54. They're treated with reverence and not worn merely as jewelry.

Beads are also used in Catholicism and some forms of Islam. The classic Catholic rosary is a string of 59 to 60 beads and a crucifix, divided by spacers into groups of 1, 3, and 10. Particular prayers are said or repeated as someone handles each part of the rosary, and there are also prescribed religious subjects they're supposed to reflect on while they do so. Although some Muslim sects view the use of beads as inappropriate, other sects regularly pray using a set of 33 or 99 beads. They touch a bead for each recitation of a way of referring to Allah, or God, such as "Glory to Allah." It's common to recite one way of addressing Allah 33 times, and cycle through 3 different addresses.

Bead Practice

To try this form of meditation, choose or make a string of beads appropriate to your beliefs. If none of the traditional beads—Hindu, Buddhist, Catholic, or Muslim—appeal to you, you might investigate some of the prayer beads created more recently by the Anglican church, or by some Protestant Christians (see *A Bead and a Prayer: A Beginner's Guide to Protestant Prayer Beads* by Kristen E. Vincent). If you want to make this a secular practice, chances are religious practitioners wouldn't mind if you used their style of beads, as long as you treat them with respect and don't just wear them as a fashion statement. Alternatively, you can simply find or make something to use that has at least a dozen or so beads at least ¼ inch in diameter—preferably something natural or beautiful and that feels good in your hands.

POINT OF CLARIFICATION

Whatever you decide to do during your bead meditation, you have several ways you can work it into your life. You can designate a time and place for this meditative activity, like you would other forms of meditation. You can also do a few minutes of meditation whenever you get the chance—just carry the string with you, and when you find yourself alone in the break room at work, you can work through a few beads. You might even find it helpful to keep your beads in your pocket or purse, and secretly do your meditation or prayer while you're waiting in line, riding on the bus, or sitting through a difficult meeting.

Next, choose a list of three to seven significant words to recite as you finger each bead on the string (ideally, you should be able to remember them all). The words should refer to things or relationships that you want to recall regularly and make a priority in your life. You could use a list of your moral guidelines, spiritual ideals, or aspirations. You could also work your way through a list of words that remind you of important lessons you've learned or relationships you value.

When you have your list, take your beads in your hand, hanging the string so it passes over your palm. Take a bead between your thumb and forefinger and silently say the first word on your list. Reflect on the word, letting the meaning and associated feelings and thoughts pass through you without analyzing them. Linger on the word as long as you like, going on to the next bead (and next word) once your mind wanders. Alternatively, go through one bead and word per breath. Finish your meditation when you're done with your list, or go ahead and repeat the list if you have time.

Ritual

At the most basic level, a ritual is a deliberate, thoughtful way of going about something that helps you recognize the significance and value of the activity. The ritual aspects of something are almost never necessary; instead, they're extra things—motions, words, or objects—you incorporate into an activity. These extra things require you to pay attention, and they typically express care, enhance your appreciation, help you process what's going on, or encourage you to relax and open up emotionally.

Like many of the meditative activities already discussed in this chapter, ritual is something that can be religious or secular. Rituals vary from extremely elaborate to very simple, and they can be traditional or improvised, communal or private, special or mundane. Everyone is familiar with rituals around important transitions in life—births, deaths, graduations, and so on—but you probably have more ritual in your life than you realize. For example, you may have a ritual around your morning coffee or tea if you always drink it at about the same time, before or after other particular activities, or using a special mug you hold with both hands as you lean against the kitchen counter and contemplate your upcoming day.

What Makes It Meditative

There's something meditative about rituals, even when you aren't consciously engaging them as such. This is because, by their very nature, rituals direct your attention in a particular way. You may recall our working definition of meditation refers to deliberately directing your mind in a particular way for the purpose of affecting it; however, you may not realize a ritual is *causing* you to direct your mind in a beneficial way. But ultimately, that's why you're doing it—it positively affects your mind, body, and experience.

Several important aspects of ritual encourage a meditative state:

- **Ritual actions or preparations require an unusual degree of care and attention.** Ideally, you can't do them on autopilot. For example, when you bring out the fine China for a special dinner, you're going to pay much more attention to setting the table than you usually do.

- **Rituals encourage you to slow down.** They're either performed for a set period of time or it takes a while to complete them. While you're doing them, you might as well engage them completely and let go of other worries and concerns.

- **The ritual actions, words, and objects incorporated into an activity are "extra."** The only purpose they serve is to positively affect your mind in some way. This fact naturally brings your attention not just to the activity you're doing, but also to your experience of it.

- **As you do a ritual, you enact some deeper truth of your life.** Even if you don't feel relaxed, reverent, connected, celebratory, and so on at the moment, you go through actions or say words that express these things either because you *want* to feel them or because you know at some level you already do.

Of course, like all of the meditative techniques and activities described in this book, the benefits of ritual are enhanced when you consciously engage them as a meditative activity. This deliberate direction of your mind is what induces the state of relaxation associated with meditation (a state which is the opposite of the stress response, as discussed in Chapter 1). All you have to do is try to pay more attention to your rituals while you do them, returning your mind to what you're doing whenever it wanders.

Traditional Examples of Ritual

Traditional examples of ritual are everywhere. The ceremonies surrounding important life events like weddings, funerals, baptisms, and graduations are elaborate rituals we do as communities to help us recognize and process important transitions. They're actually a whole series of rituals in a package! For example, marriage is one of the most significant events in a person's life, and months of preparations for ritual aspects like special clothing, decorations, and meals help direct your attention to the fact that something important is going to happen!

CONTEMPLATE THIS

You'll probably notice that if you create a little ceremony or ritual around something, you'll find yourself appreciating it more. In her book *Tea and Ceremony: Experiencing Tranquility,* Japanese tea ceremony teacher Diana Saltoon explains: "Ceremony creates a special climate in which we explore the subtler dimensions of existence ... Too often we are not cognizant of such dimensions, or have no way to appreciate them when we discover them."

More meditative rituals include many things you do to relax, appreciate your life, and improve the mental and emotional well-being of yourself and your family. Almost any set of activities you do regularly, in a careful and prescribed order, ends up having aspects of ritual to it. Traditional home rituals include sitting down with family to dinner at a particular time, maintaining a vase of fresh flowers on the mantelpiece, and greeting people as they arrive or leave with a kiss or a hug. All of these things are "extra" in a sense, but they help direct your mind in a positive way.

One of the most beautiful and fascinating examples of traditional ritual is a Japanese tea ceremony. You can make a lifelong study of this ritual, but even if you don't want to study tea, you can take inspiration from the ceremony in designing your own rituals. In the tea ceremony, a small group of guests are served powdered green tea by their host. Each serving is prepared one at a time in front of the guests and then passed to them in a ritual manner.

Absolutely every detail of the gathering is carefully planned: the spare, enclosed room; the choice of guests invited to the same ceremony; the single flower arrangement in the alcove; the hand-made tea bowls used; and the sound of the hot water simmering in the pot. Even the conversation is ritual, as guests discuss the beauty of the tea bowls, the meaning of the calligraphy hanging in the alcove, and the flavor of the sweets served with the tea. The effect is profound. For a whole hour or so, you forget about everything else in the world and enter completely into the simple, aesthetic, communal experience of drinking tea.

Simple Ritual Practice

Many of us have difficulty putting down our work or projects at the end of the day without simply distracting ourselves with television, reading, or some other form of entertainment. While there's nothing wrong with entertainment, of course, a small ritual may help you spend some time being more relaxed, present, and appreciative of your life (and the people around you) *before* you go for the entertainment.

You can perform this simple ritual to bring more awareness to when you begin and end work for the day and to help you let go of thinking about work-related things when you want to. Choose something to symbolize your work, like a book, a relevant award, or a tool. It might even be your clothing or shoes, if you change into and out of special ones just for work! If the symbolic object isn't something you wear or carry, choose a special place to put it during the day while you're working. It might be a mantelpiece, table, or shelf—anywhere that's fairly free of clutter (the more special, the better!).

As you put on your work clothes or place your symbolic object in its designated place, say a short verse to yourself, like "As I go to work, I dedicate the benefit of what I do to the people I love." When you get home, take off your work clothes or move your work item into a drawer in an unhurried, thoughtful way, saying to yourself, "My work is done for the day, so I put away my concerns about it." If you make these actions into short meditations (instead of allowing them to become automatic), you'll probably find this short ritual will help you let go of work concerns when you'd rather be focused on another aspect of your life.

Artistic Expression

Most artistic expression can be meditative, as long as you deliberately keep your mind on the activity and don't let it wander. One of the neat things about artistic expression as a meditative activity is that if you *do* let your mind wander, your artistic expression is going to noticeably suffer! You won't be as inspired, skilled, creative, or spontaneous, and you'll be less likely to connect with your intended audience. If you use artistic expression as a meditative activity, this feedback is very helpful for encouraging you to concentrate.

What Makes It Meditative

Artistic expression comes from a nonverbal part of you, and it requires you to let go of your usual discriminative thinking in order to allow the expression to flow. You need to attend to that quiet, subtle voice or source of artistic creativity within you. Little or no conscious thought is involved, as that wordless inspiration becomes a brush stroke, shape, texture, or sound. As long as you're engaged in your art in this meditative way, you're aware of your present experience. You're not caught up in stress and worry. Your mind is deliberately directed in a positive way.

 WATCH OUT

> Unfortunately, as a writer I have to tell you that writing nonfiction isn't meditative. It's a creative activity, but one that involves lots of use of your discriminating mind as you try to produce a coherent and linear flow of ideas. That doesn't leave bandwidth for you to direct your mind toward your present, embodied experience. On the other hand, writing poetry—and, perhaps to a lesser extent, writing fiction—can be meditative as you center yourself and try to connect with your inner source of inspiration.

It's possible to lose the meditative quality of artistic expression if you get too caught up in producing a final product. While creativity will still be involved, the activity itself will start to get future-oriented and involve lots of evaluation and critique (getting the ordinary thinking mind involved again). One of the best ways to know whether this is happening as you engage in artistic expression is to look at the results of spending time doing it. Remember, one of the definitions of meditative activity is that it has a positive effect on your mind (your mental functioning, emotional state, and so on). If you find yourself exhausted or frustrated after having spent time absorbed in your chosen form of artistic expression, you may want to find ways to let go of the effort to finish something or achieve a particular result.

Not all forms of artistic expression are equally meditative, of course. While it may be rewarding or therapeutic to express anger or sadness through music, or paint something that calls attention to injustice, engaging an activity in a concentrated way is going to have more of a positive effect on your mind if the activity was actually designed to do so. That said, you could aim for countless positive effects by doing meditative art, including calm, joy, insight into your emotions, a sense of connection with nature, or increasing your ability to concentrate.

Traditional Examples of Meditative Arts

Zen has been the source of most of the traditional forms of artistic expression designed specifically as an aid to meditation. In meditative calligraphy, you prepare your materials, calm your mind, and then write a Chinese or Japanese character on paper with brush and ink. Characters beautifully and expertly executed in this manner have a dynamic, flowing quality to them, and it helps if an artist coordinates their movements with their breathing. If you're thinking too much, you inhibit your brushwork, and your characters end up looking somewhat stiff and awkward. If you deliberately try to be "dynamic and flowing," you end up with sloppy- or pretentious-looking characters. Only the right state of mind produces the characters you're looking for, so this is a great meditative practice.

Another traditional meditative activity is creating pottery on a wheel. It helps that the process is straightforward, earthy, and tactile. It's also helpful to your meditation that it's very challenging to produce beautiful and functional pieces if you don't maintain the right state of mind. If you push too hard, you end up with pottery that's too thin and fragile, or that breaks right on the wheel. If you don't engage the process fully—just doing it halfheartedly, with your mind wandering—you'll end up with thick or uninspired pieces. To make the best piece of pottery you can, you have to maintain an ongoing awareness of your hands, the consistency and thickness of the clay, the speed of the wheel, and the shape of the pot; there's no room for stress, worry, or depression.

Meditative Art Practice

If you already have a form of artistic expression you do, you can make it more meditative in several ways. First, decide how long you're going to work on your art. This is the designated period of time that helps mark something as a meditation. Don't go any longer than this, but keep to your original intention. Second, don't listen to music while you work (assuming your expression isn't musical), or at least work in silence for part of the time. Third, do the art just for the sake of doing it, trying as much as possible to let go of wanting to produce anything, improve your skill, or even make anything beautiful (don't worry, you probably will anyway).

POINT OF CLARIFICATION

Sometimes the most difficult part of a meditation technique or activity is simply making the time to do it! However, this is also the single most important aspect of any meditative practice: setting aside time to benefit your mind in a positive way. No matter what practice you do, you're halfway there as soon as you start—you've put down all your other activities and turned your attention to your own mind.

If you don't have an artistic practice, a very sweet and simple way for you to enjoy the benefits of this meditative activity is coloring. Yes, that's right, coloring—that thing you used to do as a kid! While it doesn't require any artistic skill, as you color, you can appreciate the beauty of the image you're coloring, concentrate on the motions of your hands, and express your creativity with the care you take and the colors you choose. Many coloring books have been published for adults, some of them specifically designed to be meditative. You can also download some beautiful black-and-white drawings online that work great for coloring (just search for "meditative coloring"). Get yourself a good set of markers, designate a time and place, and settle into this soothing, meditative activity.

The Least You Need to Know

- Meditative activities can be very useful because they help you direct your mind and give you plenty to focus on.

- An activity qualifies as meditative if you do only that activity, if you keep bringing your mind back to the activity when it wanders, and if the process has a positive effect on your mind (your mental health and emotional well-being).

- Traditional meditative activities are designed to have positive effects, such as evoking a sense of calm, reminding you of what matters to you most deeply, or giving you the ability to access a deeper, nonverbal part of yourself.

- Chanting, copying texts by hand, meditating with a string of beads, performing simple rituals, and doing meditative art are all effective forms of meditative activity that can be adapted and used by anyone, regardless of their religious affiliation, knowledge, or skill.

- The most important aspect of a meditative activity is simply taking the time to put all of your other activities down in order to do something that benefits your mind.

Meditations for Specific Challenges

It's useful to maintain a regular meditation practice in which you use a basic, consistent technique, because that will improve your overall mental health and your ability to meditate. Occasionally, however, you may find your mind filled with troubling emotions or thoughts that need to be acknowledged and addressed. When you're facing challenges in your daily life, you can do particular meditations to stabilize your emotions, ground yourself in the present moment, and cultivate a more positive state of mind. You might think of these practices as particular medicines for particular ills.

In this chapter, I offer a dozen meditation exercises you can do when you're dealing with stress, anxiety, anger, depression, physical pain or illness, and loss or trauma. In each one, you direct your mind in a way that helps you notice and accept what's going on, and points you toward a different, more constructive and healthy way to relate to things.

In This Chapter

- Dealing with physical, mental, and emotional challenges

- The value of a "maintenance" regimen of meditation

- When to try a special meditation to address particular issues

- Alleviating stress, anxiety, anger, and depression

- Additional meditations for facing pain, illness, loss, or trauma

Meditations for Stress

Stress is a physical and psychological reaction to your perception that something in your environment needs to be dealt with or your safety and well-being will be at stake. We all experience stress to some degree. It causes an increase in your blood pressure and metabolism, and is associated with the release of certain hormones. While it prepares you for the primal responses of fighting, fleeing, or freezing, it's not helpful as a baseline mode of operation—which is the way many of us experience stress in the modern world. (After all, there's always something we need to deal with, right?)

How can meditation help relieve stress? As discussed in Chapter 1, the simple act of meditation—consciously directing your mind to some otherwise unproductive object or activity for a time—relaxes you. So the best remedy for stress is to make time for meditation, and it doesn't really matter what kind of meditation you do. However, a couple techniques are particularly helpful in breaking you out of the stress response.

Awareness of Your Breathing

Your breath is always available as a meditative object. Awareness of your breathing is beneficial whether you turn your attention toward one deep breath as you go about your daily life, or concentrate on the breath as a formal meditation. This practice is especially effective as a way to de-stress because it shifts your sense of identification with your mind (which has lots of ideas about what needs to be dealt with) to identification with your body (which is doing just fine at the moment). You're still breathing, and chances are you're not in any actual danger. Taking note of this fact sends messages to your body to relax.

 WATCH OUT

If you try to follow your breath for a prolonged period of time, you may get bored or restless. Try acknowledging how incredibly simple this activity is and then try to think of it as a well-deserved vacation for your mind. Rather than thinking, "I can't think of anything except my breathing," try to think, "Ah, how nice—all I have to do is sit here and breathe."

When you want to de-stress by grounding yourself in your breathing, take anywhere from a moment to a half hour to let your breath fill your awareness. Don't try to get rid of stressful thoughts; just gently return your attention to your breathing whenever they arise. And don't argue with the stressful thoughts or try to convince yourself not to worry; this is still engaging the thoughts. The point of the breath meditation is to momentarily operate in a different mode—one in which your stressful thoughts and feelings aren't directly relevant (in this moment, you're okay).

Disidentifying with Your Stress

Another meditation you can do for stress is a little more creative. It also requires more meditative skill—that is, a greater ability to direct your mind the way you want to within the context of a meditation. If you can manage it, this can be a very effective practice.

You start out by doing a breath meditation as described in the previous section. This time, however, whenever thoughts arise, you try to watch them in a detached, objective way. Instead of immediately returning your full awareness to your breathing, allow part of your attention to remain on your breathing (a subtle, background kind of awareness) while you turn the rest of your mind toward your thoughts and emotions. Simply notice them, perhaps even verbalizing your observations like "Wondering if I'm going to get that project done on time" or "Worrying about money again." Try not to get drawn into involvement with the thought; if you find yourself analyzing it or planning how to deal with its subject matter, gently return your awareness to your breathing.

During the in-between moments where you're observing a thought or feeling but are not yet caught up in it, you can learn to disidentify somewhat with your stress. During meditation, "you"—your sense of agency and will—are trying to meditate, while thoughts and feelings arise all on their own. You should notice you're not the same as your thoughts and gain some objective distance from them. This doesn't mean you discount them or pretend there's actually nothing in your life that needs to be dealt with. Instead, you become better able to evaluate and prioritize stressors, make wiser decisions about what to pay attention to, and decide how much you're going to allow things to stress you out.

Meditations for Anxiety

Anxiety can be a powerful and distressing experience. You can find yourself in the clutches of a deep sense of fear, harboring a pessimistic anticipation that something terrible is going to happen. It ends up creating a negative feedback loop in your body and mind, because your initial experience of anxiety—which may very well be unjustified—tells you something's wrong. It's like your mind and body can't believe their alarm could be groundless, so they take your anxiety as evidence that you should get *more* anxious. However, meditation in the form of movement or activity, or using meditation exercises to relate to how you're feeling differently, can help you deal with your anxiety.

Meditative Movement or Activity

Sometimes it can be very difficult to concentrate on a still, introspective form of meditation when you're feeling anxious. To whatever extent you can keep up your regular meditation practice, try to do so; this will help, and eventually you'll feel less anxiety, and your regular practice will have remained strong throughout the time when anxiety was bothering you. However, be kind to yourself as well, and consider engaging in a meditative activity of some kind as an alternative to still or introspective techniques.

> **POINT OF CLARIFICATION**
>
> When you're facing challenges, you may find you resist meditating at all. It may seem like you can't spare the time or energy, and then even when you do meditate, the results are unsatisfying. It's important to keep in mind that this is exactly when meditation is going to be *most* beneficial to you. Even though it may not seem like your meditation is very "good" when you're stressed or troubled, the effort you're making is extremely valuable. When things are going well again, you're likely to find your meditative skill has improved significantly because you've meditated through challenging times.

A meditative movement or activity gives you something to do with your restless, anxious energy, but it also encourages a simpler mindset and invites you to let go of dysfunctional trains of thought. Chapter 15 includes various forms of meditative movement, and Chapter 16 has suggestions for meditative activities; you can choose a practice from these chapters you'll enjoy and naturally find calming.

Whatever you choose—walking, yoga, chanting, artistic expression, and so on—try to avoid engaging the activity with an anxious energy. Put whatever potentially productive aspects the activity has aside (such as fitness, or the creation of something beautiful), and keep your awareness on the simple doing of it. While exercise can be beneficial in and of itself, you might also consider doing something completely useless, like coloring in a book made for adults. As in the case of breath awareness discussed previously, this sends a message to your body and mind that things are okay because you can spare the time and energy to do something utterly impractical.

Drawing Boundaries with Your Anxiety

This meditation exercise involves using your imagination to relate to your anxiety differently. When you start having anxious thoughts and feelings, first notice them. You can then ground yourself in a basic meditative support, like awareness of your breathing. Once you've turned the moment into meditation, try to imagine the anxious thoughts and feelings are coming from a source outside you—one that's trying to undermine you. Go ahead and use any kind of creative story or visualization that helps make this seem real to you. Maybe someone in your past encouraged your anxiety and sense of helplessness, so you can imagine your anxious thoughts being expressed in her voice. Alternatively, you might want to use the Buddhist imagery of Mara the tempter, who in Buddhist mythology sought to stop the Buddha from gaining enlightenment by sending him painful doubts.

You probably already appreciate intellectually that your anxiety doesn't do you any good, even when it's based on legitimate concerns. This meditation takes that one step further and can turn an intellectual understanding into something experiential. As you imagine anxious emotions and thoughts being sent from outside, you can "draw the line" and refuse to be overwhelmed by them. All you've got to do is recognize the anxiety as something that undermines you (and it does), and you're already somewhat free of it. This allows you to draw a boundary with the anxiety without arguing with it or getting too caught up in it.

Meditations for Anger

Few things are as disruptive and agitating as anger or irritability, and generally speaking, it doesn't help much when you simply try not to feel it. A habit of anger can compromise relationships, damage health, and be a source of stress and shame. There are so many reasons to want to be "above" anger! And yet it seems to persist and even get stronger no matter how much you struggle against it, suppress it, hide it, or argue with it. Meditation can help because it's a different way to relate to your anger. It doesn't deny anger; however, it gives you some measure of choice about how you respond to it.

Just Noticing Without Judgment

Instead of fighting your anger, you can first notice it, and then ask yourself, "What's going on here? What's upsetting me? Is there something I need to do?" A meditative approach lets you ask these questions without simply getting caught up in the anger. Instead of being angry and reviewing all the justifications for your feelings, you simply notice anger is present. Just doing this will give you a measure of objectivity about it. To stay grounded meditatively, direct your mind toward the feeling of anger and its associated sensations—a tightened jaw, a clenched stomach, or the heat in your face.

 CONTEMPLATE THIS

At the most basic level, anger arises when you feel threatened. Somehow you're getting the impression that you, or someone or something you care about, needs protection. Anger is simply information about how you perceive a certain situation. Any attempt to squash it is likely to cause the anger to get inflamed, because now something needs protection and you're denying it!

Next, notice the content of your angry thoughts. Observe them without judgment—don't argue with them, even if you know intellectually your anger isn't justified, or there's nothing you can do about the situation anyway, or the anger is petty and useless (and the last thing you want is to be an angry person). It can help if you silently verbalize what you're thinking without any censoring at all: "People are so inconsiderate" or "She never cares what I think." Chances are when you observe your thoughts and feelings in a meditative way, your mind is naturally going to put things into a more appropriate perspective for you and make the anger a little less compelling.

For example, if you manage to state to yourself, "People are so inconsiderate" in a meditative way—without justifying the idea but also without arguing against it—you simply acknowledge that's what you're thinking at the moment. Instead of this being an all-consuming conclusion, it's just a thought you're having. Maybe it's true. But as you generalize about how inconsiderate people are, other thoughts and feelings are also free to arise. Spontaneously, thoughts may arise in your mind about the *considerate* people in your life, or about how stressed these inconsiderate people look, or about how someone has called you inconsiderate in the past. These thoughts can mitigate your anger, and because you aren't deliberately fighting it, it doesn't make the anger more entrenched or inflamed.

Loving-Kindness Practice

A classic meditation to deal with feelings of anger or ill will toward people is loving-kindness meditation. It's a Vajrayana Buddhist technique, and it's also useful for cultivating compassion and a greater sense of connection with others. In this form of meditation, you call to mind a living being or a group of beings and "send" them loving-kindness. It's recommended you start with someone you already feel unconditional love for to get yourself warmed up (you can find an audio version of this meditation on idiotsguides.com/meditation).

You then bring this person or animal to mind, and say silently to yourself, "May you be free from fear and anxiety. May you be at ease. May you be happy." You can pause after each phrase and try to sincerely feel what you're saying, taking as long you like or repeating the series of phrases. Once you're ready, you can move on to beings for whom you don't feel quite such unconditional love, beings about whom you feel neutral, and eventually people you hold resentment toward. (An audio recording that guides you through loving-kindness meditation is included along with this book.)

 WATCH OUT

Sometimes the most challenging person to do loving-kindness meditation for is yourself. Lack of acceptance and goodwill for yourself tends to make you more irritable with others, so when you're struggling with anger, be sure to try sending loving-kindness your own direction. Sometimes, trying to sincerely wish yourself well can highlight those areas where you deny yourself peace and happiness. Watch for little additions you make in your mind as you say "May I be happy," such as "as soon as I ..." or "as long as I ...." If you can, soften those conditions you have for yourself, and you'll probably find yourself softening toward others.

Whether or not you're able to bring yourself to do sincere loving-kindness meditation for some-one you're upset with, the practice can be beneficial. It gets your mind out of an angry and resentful rut and awakens the mind of compassion. While I don't know of any scientific research on this form of meditation, I'd be willing to bet it causes a physiological change in you—perhaps even the release of hormones associated with trust and intimacy. In any case, loving-kindness practice generally has a positive effect. If you're able to do it for a person you're angry with, one of the most effective aspects of the practice is how it invites you to think of the person as being free from fear and anxiety. This naturally suggests the likelihood that if they're acting inconsid-erately, it's probably because they're experiencing fear and anxiety at some level, even if it isn't obvious.

Meditations for Depression

Depression is essentially about getting stuck in a negative view of the world or way of operating in it. The unfortunate thing is how self-perpetuating this state can be. When you're in the midst of depression or despair, everywhere you look you can find evidence to support your view that everything is hopeless, bleak, or meaningless. Your ability to enjoy life is compromised, so you're likely to sink further into depression unless something jolts you out of it. This is where medita-tion movement and activity, as well as recitation of an inspirational text, come in.

Meditative Movement and Activity

Physically still or introspective meditation isn't always a good idea when you're depressed. Watch carefully to see what effects a particular form of meditation has on your mood and ability to function in a healthy way. If you're essentially spending your meditation ruminating on all the things that depress you, this can be harmful. Meditation that draws you inward or encourages you to shut out the world can also be a bad idea. When you're in a healthy state, this kind of technique can encourage calm and insight; however, when you're depressed, it can get twisted into another manifestation of your depression.

What you probably want when you're depressed is some kind meditative movement or activity (see Chapters 15 and 16). This will encourage some exercise or engagement with the world, which is useful in and of itself. An activity will also allow you to direct your mind in a meditative way toward something that runs completely contrary to your depressed view or mode of operating.

When you're depressed, your mind is probably telling you it's not worth doing anything. But if you can manage to make yourself do a meditative movement or activity *anyway*, it starts sending different information to your body and mind. Instead of letting the depression self-perpetuate, you're enacting the belief that life *is* worth it and that you're not depressed. Even if this doesn't change your conscious view right away, it has a positive effect over time. Pick a meditative activity you feel up to doing; don't pick something so involved or demanding that you just end up avoiding it. Just doing *something* will be enough.

Recitation of an Inspirational Text

A particular meditative activity you might use to alleviate depression is the recitation of an inspirational text. In Chapter 16, I discussed the tradition of meditative chanting, so you can refer to that chapter for details on this kind of meditation. When you're adapting this practice for depression, make sure to choose a passage, poem, or text to recite out loud that turns your mind in a positive direction. It should express gratitude, love, hope, or strength. However, it should be something you actually believe in or resonate with at some level—or at least something that resonated with you before you got depressed. Avoid anything that sounds too trite or naïve to you, because it won't affect you as deeply.

 CONTEMPLATE THIS

An inspirational text you might consider reciting when you're struggling with depression is Zen master Thich Nhat Hanh's poem "Call Me by My True Names" in his book *Peace Is Every Step: The Path of Mindfulness in Everyday Life*. It's a beautiful and sobering but hopeful poem. Here are a few lines:

"My joy is like spring, so warm it makes flowers bloom in all walks of life. My pain is like a river of tears, so full it fills the four oceans. Please call me by my true names, so I can hear all my cries and laughs at once, so I can see that my joy and pain are one."

When you choose your text, recite it out loud to yourself. Ideally, it will take you at least a few minutes to recite; if it's something short, you can read very slowly and pause between sentences to reflect. When you mind wanders from the recitation, bring it back to words and the sensations associated with speaking them. It may help to anchor part of your awareness in your breathing. When you recite the words, you may want to try to mean them or believe them as best you can. However, if you feel resistance to doing this, go ahead and read in a neutral way. Pay attention, but let go of trying to evaluate the meaning or truth of the text. Let the words wash over you, and trust that directing your mind in this way is having a positive effect, however small.

Meditations for Physical Pain and Illness

There's some evidence that meditation can increase your tolerance for pain and discomfort in a measurable way, at least based on self-reports of subjects in studies about the effects of meditation on pain (see Chapter 1). Of course, your tolerance for pain is naturally subjective, and such tolerance depends a great deal on your state of mind. This is where meditation can be of the greatest benefit: improving your general mental health and helping you disidentify with your physical distress.

As you meditate, no matter what technique you use, you notice you're bigger than your pain or illness—there's "you" trying to meditate and observing your discomfort and then there's the discomfort. While this may not sound like it would make much of a difference, it definitely can. One of the most discouraging things about pain and illness is how all-consuming it can feel, as if it's taking over your life and there's not much you can enjoy that makes life worth living. In meditation, you deliberately turn your mind toward doing something positive; even though you may still be aware of your pain or illness, you're refusing to let it dictate your thoughts and feelings entirely.

What Part of You Doesn't Hurt?

One useful meditation when you're experiencing physical difficulties is turning your awareness to the parts of your body that don't hurt, or that aren't affected by your illness. It's easy to dwell on what hurts, or what isn't functioning properly, until it seems like your discomfort is intense and endless. If you look carefully with a meditative mindset, however, you usually find plenty of places in your body that feel just fine. Even if you have a painful disorder that affects your entire body, such as rheumatoid arthritis, chances are your skin doesn't hurt. Your heart, eyes, and tongue probably don't hurt either. Shifting your attention to these parts of your body with gratitude can give you a few moments of relief.

POINT OF CLARIFICATION

If you're struggling with pain or illness, be sure to meditate in a comfortable position. Go ahead and lie down, if that's how you feel best, or sit in a stuffed chair. You don't want to add to your discomfort by taking a difficult or rigid meditation posture.

To meditate on the parts of your body that don't hurt, try to relax your body completely. Next, do a check-in of the most painful or compromised parts of your body. Maybe your back hurts, or your head is throbbing with congestion from a cold. Allow your awareness to rest on these uncomfortable places without worrying about how to get rid of the pain. Just notice, and try to be curious: Is the pain constant, or does it wax and wane? Is it acute or dull? Can you find the edges of your discomfort—the place where it fades away and your body feels normal?

Once you've given some awareness to the physical discomfort in a meditative way, shift your attention to other parts of your body. If you'd like, start a body scan from the top of your head. As you go, notice whether a particular place contains any pain or any symptoms of illness: scalp, brain, eyes, cheeks, teeth, chin, neck, ears, and so on. When you find a part of you that feels fine, linger there. Allow your awareness to linger there, and become conscious of yourself as someone without pain or illness (at least in places). Continue working your way down your body all the way to your fingertips and toes.

Enduring Physical Challenges with Dignity

You may be afflicted by a prolonged condition of ill health or chronic pain. If this is the case, your energy is probably limited, and "ordinary" forms of meditation may seem daunting. It's also possible that introspective types of meditation can encourage depression or a heightened awareness of your pain. If you can do a regular meditation practice, that's great! But if you can't, you may need a practice tailored to your particular challenge.

One of the most discouraging aspects of a chronic illness is feeling helpless or useless because almost all of your time and energy are devoted to simply coping with your physical condition. All the things other people enjoy—exercise, trips, socializing, and so on—may be out of your reach most of the time. In meditation, you need to shift your mind from ruminating on discouraging things to finding a sense of dignity in your own experience. This isn't about thinking happy thoughts and hoping to feel better (although that may help!); instead, it's about fully embodying your life for a few moments and giving yourself credit for what you endure on a daily basis.

To make this into a meditation, take a comfortable position and ground your awareness in your breathing for a few minutes. Once you do that, call to mind one of the aspects of your pain or physical condition, such as your aching ankles, your nausea, or your inability to move as you would like to. As you do this, allow any associated thoughts and emotions, if any, to arise spontaneously, including those of frustration, discouragement, or sadness. Don't analyze; just notice.

 CONTEMPLATE THIS

Research has proven that that putting up with pain and illness draws on the same reserve of energy as concentration, self-discipline, and making decisions! (See Roy Baumeister and John Tierney's book, *Willpower: Rediscovering Our Greatest Strength*.) In other words, simply enduring pain and illness takes work—real work. You deserve a great deal of admiration if you experience pain and illness every day and still manage to maintain some reverence for life, concern for others, and a sense of humor. That's not to say you're expected to be happy, compassionate, or funny all the time—it's just that you should acknowledge the effort you make to remain positive.

After spending a few moments contemplating your experience, say something to yourself like "Facing this difficulty, I bring all of my patience and strength to bear. I acknowledge that this challenges me, and I make it my work to keep finding joy in my life despite my physical experience." As you say this, try to feel compassion for yourself in your strenuous and mostly invisible work of enduring your pain or illness. See if you can instill some dignity into what usually may seem like a difficult and pointless endurance test. Your ability to accept and enjoy your life not only helps you, it helps those around you!

Meditations for Loss and Trauma

Trauma and significant loss—of a loved one, a job, a home, and so on—are related. In both cases, you've experienced something very painful or disruptive. The negative experience tends to feature in your thoughts and emotions frequently—through painful memories, regrets, anxiety about the future, and a whole host of other things. Sometimes when you've lost a loved one, you don't actually want to stop thinking about them; however, in many cases of loss or trauma, your mind can feel like a broken record, playing one tune over and over. It can feel like you'll never experience anything else, or at least not without your thoughts about your loss or trauma running in the background at the same time.

If you're recovering from loss or trauma, certain kinds of meditation may cause you to sink into even more perseveration on the difficult experience you've had, or even trigger episodes of post-traumatic stress. As is always the case when you meditate, watch carefully the effects a particular technique has on you. If you find yourself feeling even more sad, depressed, anxious, or paranoid during or after meditation, get some professional advice on whether you should continue, and, if so, what kind of meditation you should do. Note that meditative movement and activities (see Chapters 15 and 16) are usually always safe if still, introspective meditation in the following ways doesn't seem to help.

Acknowledgment and Acceptance Practice

One kind of meditation you might want to try if you've experienced significant loss or trauma is acknowledgment and acceptance practice. When you do this, you carefully call to mind your loss or trauma, but not in great detail. That is, try not to replay events in your mind, dwell on the negative impacts on your life, or plan how you're going to get rid of your grief or traumatic stress.

Instead, as you take a comfortable position and center yourself in your breathing, direct your mind toward how your loss or trauma is affecting your body and mind in the present moment. The impacts of all of your experiences, especially significant and painful ones, are carried in your physical and mental being. You don't have to think about the past in order to touch your internal injury, just as it is right now, as you meditate. You might sense this injury as an ache in the heart, a sinking feeling in the pit of your stomach, or an emotion like grief or loneliness.

WATCH OUT

It can be difficult to meditate (or do anything else, like exercise or therapy, for that matter) without having an agenda. It's natural to want to feel better and to get free of painful memories or feelings. However, the very desire to get rid of particular thoughts or emotions can make them stronger (or more painful, if only because you're still experiencing them). When you meditate, try to set aside any agendas and trust that your efforts will help your body and mind to heal eventually.

Whatever form your current, embodied experience of your loss or trauma takes, turn your awareness toward it in a gentle, compassionate way. For the time being, don't struggle against it or wish it away. Simply acknowledge it and accept it for what it is—a symptom of emotional injury. For at least a few minutes, spend time with your immediate physical and emotional experience. When you inhale, you can imagine embracing your own pain; when you exhale, you can imagine sending warmth and compassion to it, encouraging it to heal in time.

A Ritual of Healing

Rituals were described in Chapter 16, where I discussed meditative activities. They can be powerful meditative tools, especially for emotional healing. Doing your own rituals is very valuable in the case of loss or trauma for two reasons:

- Any community rituals after loss, such as a funeral, are often brief and insufficient for acknowledging and processing someone's passing if they were a big part of your life.

- There's often a complete lack of community ritual around extremely significant and painful events like the loss of a job, intimate relationship, or unborn child, or the traumatic experiences of war or assault.

Ritual meditations tend to be underused, because people don't realize they can create and do their own rituals instead of relying only on culturally provided ones. All you have to do in order to create your own ritual is to remember that ritual takes place in a meditative space. What this means is that during the ritual, you direct your mind to the experience of the ritual (the movements, objects, or words involved) and allow it to have a subverbal, nonintellectual effect on you. If a ritual is well-designed, it will evoke important thoughts and emotions without any conscious effort on your part (although you may have consciously designed the ritual, while you're actually doing it, you just let it work its magic).

A ritual can be simple or complex, short or long, private or done in a group, done once or repeated many times. If you're stuck on what to do, you can refer back to Chapter 16 for more advice on creating a ritual, including ways to make it meditative. When creating a ritual around loss or trauma, make sure it contains an acknowledgment of your difficulty. Incorporate a picture or words that, for at least a moment, touch your injured place. For example, in the case of a divorce, you might include a picture of you and your former spouse when you were happy or a copy of your wedding vows.

In the overall ritual, create an enactment of what you would like to see happen. Again using the example of divorce, let's assume you want to honor the value of the relationship you were in but also let go and move on. You might choose something to symbolize the relationship and then burn it during the ritual, or read aloud a poem that says good-bye. Even if you aren't yet ready to heal, let go, move on, or whatever it is you're hoping for, the ritual enactment of this will help facilitate that process over time.

The Least You Need to Know

- A regular, basic meditation practice can increase your general mental health, strength, and flexibility. That way, when you face challenges, you can deal with them more effectively.

- When things are difficult, it's still worth trying to do your regular meditation. However, if you can't or your issue just won't go away, you can do special meditations to address particular challenges.

- Depending on how you direct your mind in meditation, you can learn to identify less with your troubling thoughts and emotions by realizing "you" are meditating, while the thoughts and emotions are arising all by themselves. Those thoughts and emotions are just part of your experience, not the entire truth.

- Meditatively turning the mind in a particular way—toward kindness instead of anger, inspiration instead of depression, or healing instead of trauma—can have a positive effect on your body and mind, even when you don't (yet) identify with the positive instead of the negative.

CHAPTER 18

Meditation for Children

Few children naturally gravitate toward a focused and disciplined activity like meditation. But if you can convince them to try it, they are well-suited for it in some ways. While it won't be any easier for children to concentrate than it is for adults, they're very unlikely to add any extra agenda to meditation the way adults do. For instance, if you tell a kid to quietly move a pebble from one pile to another with each breath they take, that's what they'll try to do. They won't be distracted with evaluations of how well they're meditating or how they hope it will make them into a better person! While you have to be careful about how you introduce meditation to children, it can be one of the most important things you ever share with them.

In this chapter, I discuss the benefits kids in particular get from meditating. I then give you advice on how to introduce kids to meditation so they'll actually like it, and describe ways to adapt meditative exercises for children. Finally, I offer four kid-friendly meditations you can do with the kids in your life—whether you do that one-on-one, in a small group, or in a classroom setting.

In This Chapter

* How meditation benefits children
* Ways to encourage kids to try meditation—and then keep doing it
* Adapting meditation so it's accessible and useful for children
* How to hold a meditative space that still has room for kid energy
* Four particularly kid-friendly meditations you can use

The Value of Meditation for Children

We teach kids all kinds of things—how to take care of their bodies, get along with other people, understand the world around them, and perform the various tasks required of them. One thing we rarely teach kids is how to reflect on and relate to their own minds. For some reason, we assume they'll just figure that out as they go along and will end up mentally and emotionally well-adjusted adults. Or maybe we assume a child's genetics and life circumstances determine how well-adjusted they'll be. Fortunately, a child's long-term mental health doesn't have to be left up to chance.

When children learn meditation, they also learn incredibly valuable lessons—ones you were probably never explicitly taught as a child. They learn it's possible and useful to turn their awareness toward their own mind and its processes. They discover meditative self-awareness, in which they observe their thoughts and emotions and realize they don't have to be defined or controlled by the content of their mind. When they meditate, children get better at consciously directing their attention, and they gain tools to managing stress and difficult emotions on their own. In short, meditation can help young people learn to use and relate to their own minds in a healthy, sustainable way.

Empowering Kids to Deal with Their Minds

Adults give plenty of guidance to children about what kind of behavior is appropriate, and they also tend to communicate—directly or indirectly—that certain thoughts and emotions are undesirable or even shameful. This leaves kids more or less at the mercy of their own minds. They're responsible for how they express or act out their thoughts and emotions, but no one tends to give them guidance about how to deal with the content of their minds when they feel full of anger, resentment, fear, and so on. Even if they can manage to refrain from "bad" behavior when they're feeling troubled, they're likely to start bad habits. This could be anything from suppressing or denying what they're thinking and feeling (even to themselves) to using unhealthy methods of coping, such as numbing out in front of the television or seeking distraction by acting out.

 CONTEMPLATE THIS

Just in case you find it difficult to imagine the kids in your life choosing to meditate, I'll share a sweet story. A young girl at my Zen center had spent several years in our children's program. During the school year, this child had meditated for about 5 to 10 minutes at the beginning of our classes, which were held every two weeks. When she was diagnosed with childhood diabetes around the age of 6 or 7, her parents explained how it was going to impact her life, and she responded, "I'm going to go meditate now." She meditated alone for about five minutes and then returned, ready to continue the discussion about what needed to happen next to address her illness.

Now imagine a different scenario, in which children are regularly taught meditation from an early age (and this is actually starting to happen more widely). Essentially, by teaching meditation, an adult tells a child, "Yeah, there's a lot of stuff going on in your mind and heart. Don't be ashamed or worried; that happens to all of us. The good thing is, there are things you can do to help calm yourself down and feel better." Adults can share various meditations like the ones described in this book, choosing ones that are particularly appropriate for a child's needs and character. Sometimes all a kid will need is a basic meditation that triggers the body's relaxation response (as discussed in Chapter 1), while at other times they may benefit from simplified versions of meditations designed for specific challenges (like those in Chapter 17).

As they're being taught meditation—even if they don't end up liking it or doing it regularly— a child is being given the message they can have some control over their own mind. Their mental and emotional states don't have to be entirely determined by their circumstances (such as whether they get what they want, whether people like them, or even the weather). Do you remember the emotional roller coaster of young adulthood? While meditation doesn't necessarily prevent that from happening, it can give kids some hope and objectivity about their internal processes. This is very empowering.

A Tool for Calming Down

It's hard enough for adults to calm down—to release stress and anxiety, or to let troubling emotions subside. Kids have it even harder, because they don't have as much of an ability to "talk themselves out of it" as adults do. The great thing is that the simple act of meditation is relaxing. As described in Chapter 1, directing your mind in a meditative way induces a unique physiological state, which is the opposite of stress. So kids don't have to understand anything about meditation—or anything else in the world, for that matter—in order for it to have a calming effect.

If you can just get kids to meditate for a while, it's pretty much guaranteed to calm them down, at least a little. If you get kids familiar with meditation, they'll have a tool for calming themselves down for life. Of course, as the saying goes, you can lead a horse to water, but you can't make it drink. In the case of having kids meditate, you can instruct them and get them into some kind of meditation position or posture, but you can't control what they do with their minds. And it's what they do with their minds that matters in meditation. Fortunately, there are ways to encourage kids to actively engage in meditating to gain the benefit of a calmer state, and I'll discuss them later in this chapter.

Increased Self-Awareness

Especially with some additional guidance from adults, meditation can also allow children to increase their self-awareness. This includes awareness about their thoughts, emotions, and tendencies. You can point a child toward meditative observation of their internal experience by encouraging them to notice what's going on in their minds during meditation—and by reminding them not to be judgmental or to try to figure anything out while they're meditating. If you encourage a little reflection after meditation, you might find a child spontaneously reporting they feel calmer, less worried, or less upset. You don't have to say anything else; the child will just have become more aware of their mental and emotional states, and will notice that meditation affected it.

 WATCH OUT

As you guide children in learning to reflect on their own thoughts and emotions, be aware they're watching your reactions very carefully. They might want to please you, or they might want to deny you what you're looking for. But if you convey expectations—about the content of their inner experience, or their ability to perceive or talk about it—you're less likely to get sincere and truthful answers. Try to maintain an open-minded curiosity about a child's experience, and be patient if they aren't able to verbalize it when asked.

Meditation is especially effective at increasing self-awareness because it provides a background against which the phenomena in the mind and body become more obvious. When kids are trying to direct their mind in a particular way—toward their breathing, a prayer, or a meditative activity—they tend to notice when they're *not* concentrating on their meditation. While this can make it easier for anyone to become aware of what's going on in their minds, it's especially helpful for children, who usually aren't used to objectively reflecting inward.

Let's say, for example, you want to encourage a child's emotional self-awareness. It's probably not that helpful to ask them to reflect on their emotional state at random times (they'll probably just tell you they aren't feeling anything) or to reflect on their internal process when they're upset (it will be difficult for them to avoid being completely caught up in their emotions). However, if you ask a child to reflect on what emotions arose during his meditation, you might get a meaningful answer. The situation during meditation is fairly neutral and not upsetting, and any kind of emotion—positive, negative, or neither—is fair game for noticing and reporting. Chances are the child will have felt or thought *something* over the course of a meditation, and encouraging meditative observation of this is a great opportunity for increasing his self-awareness.

Getting Kids to Meditate

How on Earth can you get kids to meditate? Meditation is pretty much the opposite of a kid's activity—physically still or restrained, disciplined, repetitive, and deliberately unexciting. Also, as mentioned earlier, you can't make children meditate by simply ensuring they go through the motions. Meditation is something you do with your mind, so you need a child's willing participation. Fortunately, you can make the practice accessible and attractive to kids in different ways.

Making Sure Children Don't Hate Meditation

First of all, you have to make sure you don't turn kids off of meditation from the get-go. While you don't have to wait to introduce the practice to them until they're thrilled with the idea, you can take the lead in a positive, low-pressure way. Tell them you're going to do a new and cool thing together, give them the instructions, and then do it with them. Don't burden kids with too much explanation about the purpose of meditation, how it's going to help their problems, or how this is going to be something they need to do forever. The experience of meditation will speak for itself.

Definitely don't start children off with a kind of meditation that's too difficult for them, or that lasts too long. (Later in this chapter, I discuss ways to design and adapt meditation for children, and I also offer some kid-friendly meditations.) Basically, children should have a more or less positive, or at least neutral, experience. It can border on painful for a child to have to sit too still or too long, or fight boredom and restlessness for what seems—to them—to be no good reason. Keep an eye on kids when you're introducing meditation to them—push them a little further than their comfort zones but not so far they end up hating the practice.

Letting Them See Others Do It

One of the most powerful ways to interest kids in meditation is to do it yourself and to let them see you do it. Whether you sit silently, pray, or do a meditative activity, find ways to work your practice into the experience of any children in your life. Many times it's tempting to meditate only when children aren't around because it's less distracting for you. However, this is depriving kids of witnessing a significant part of your life—one they may want to adopt someday.

 CONTEMPLATE THIS

Many parents who regularly meditate report their kids get used to this quirky habit of theirs and will naturally calm down at the same time, even if they just continue going about their normal activities. Sometimes kids—without being asked—will remind one another to be quiet because Mom or Dad is meditating and will occasionally even join in for a few minutes.

Probably just as influential is introducing children to meditation in groups, so they can watch one another doing it. You might consider this positive peer pressure—a particular kid may hate the idea of sitting still for five minutes, but when she sees several other kids meditating quietly, it challenges her to stick it out. Inevitably, in any group of kids, there will be one or two who resist and act out slightly; however, there will usually also be one or two who want to follow instructions and meditate "right." As long as the meditation is appropriate for the ages of the children, those who embrace it usually end up carrying the others along.

Establishing a Ritual

When getting kids to meditate, it helps immensely to create some kind of ritual around the process. Make meditation something you always do at a particular time—first thing in the morning, before bed, at 10 A.M., at the beginning of a class, or whenever they first arrive at Grandma's house. The practice then becomes a habit that doesn't require anyone to stop and think, "Do I *want* to do this?" Even adults will neglect their meditation practice sometimes if they always stop and think about whether they feel like doing it, and kids are especially likely to prefer to go do something fun or entertaining instead of meditate if given the choice. However, almost everyone is happy they took time for meditation once they've done it, and kids also thrive on routine, so this can be a clever way to work meditation into their life.

Additional ritual can also help kids get into the right frame of mind for meditation. You might meditate in a particular place and have kids help you prepare it by spreading out a nice blanket on the floor, lighting a candle, or getting the prayer books. It's also important that meditation happen in a particular posture, whether that's sitting on the floor, standing for prayer, or seated in a chair facing the wall or the other people who are meditating. Don't just let kids slouch in a chair in a casual way; you can't control what they do in their heads during meditation, but you can try to create conducive circumstances by asking them to sit or stand upright.

Ignoring a Certain Amount of Resistance

While most parents will be familiar with this approach, if you're introducing meditation to children, it's very important to keep this in mind: don't let kids discourage your effort to share something valuable with them just because they resist it or don't seem interested. If there's too much resistance, of course, kids won't actually meditate (even though they're going through the motions). But if you can get even a little bit of participation, meditation will have an effect on kids whether they're aware of it or not.

 POINT OF CLARIFICATION

Ultimately, meditation is a maintenance activity like exercise, eating well, and brushing your teeth. It supports your mental, emotional, and spiritual health. Sometimes meditation is pleasant, calming, inspirational, or enjoyable, but sometimes it's not. What's important is what it does for your life, not how you feel about it during any given meditation session. If you can convey this attitude to kids—that meditation is just this thing you do because it's good for you—you have a better chance of establishing meditation as a regular part of a kid's life.

If you can only manage to get children to meditate a few times and then they refuse to participate, don't lose heart. You've planted a seed in them that may lay dormant for many years before sprouting. Kids are naturally full of excitement and hope about the future and the things they're going to do or get that will make them happy or solve their problems. They don't have the insight, based on personal experience, that adults do: namely, that external things—even if you get what you want—rarely provide lasting happiness. Sometimes it isn't until kids hit a rough patch in young adulthood that they start to wonder if there's a different way to achieve happiness and inner peace, and consider turning inward. Far in the future, they may be going through difficult times and suddenly think, "What was that meditation thing so-and-so taught me that time?" When they need it, they'll know meditation exists and basically what it's for, and then they can do more research on it and maybe even try it again.

Adapting Meditation for Children

Children's brains are still developing. They have shorter attention spans and more difficulty tolerating physical or emotional discomfort without restlessness. Therefore, it's important to adapt adult forms of meditation to make them suitable for children, or to design unique and engaging meditations just for kids (although adults can always do them, too). In general, the meditation or meditative activity shouldn't be too long, perfect behavior shouldn't be expected, and the practice should be engaging enough to hold kids' interest.

The Right Length of Time for Children

Individual children will vary widely in terms of how long they can do meditation. One kid may not seem to be able to concentrate for more than a few seconds, while another of the same age is ready to meditate for 15 minutes. Go ahead and determine what length of time for meditation is good for a particular child, if you have that option. You can meditate with kids for 30 seconds or for as long as a half hour if they're willing.

Generally speaking, however, kids under the age of 3 or 4 shouldn't be asked to concentrate on a still or disciplined form of meditation for more than a minute or two at time. Making it any longer can feel like a confusing punishment to them. Kids around kindergarten age can graduate to five minutes, especially if you make them feel proud of meditating that long. Time can gradually be increased as kids grow, to around 10 or 15 minutes by middle school, and 20 minutes by high school (although some high schoolers are ready for adult meditation).

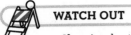

WATCH OUT

If you're sharing meditation with a group of grade school-age kids that includes both boys and girls, be careful not to make kids of either gender ashamed or frustrated. There are always exceptions, but generally speaking, it's much easier for girls to sit still and concentrate on instructions at this age. They might want to meditate quietly for 10 minutes, while most of the boys find more than a few minutes excruciating. At my Zen center, for instance, we separated the genders in our kids' meditation classes only at the grade school age so we could better tailor the meditations to the kids' needs and abilities. By junior high, this was no longer necessary.

Of course, a physically restrained or introspective form of meditation can be followed by a meditative activity of some kind, and many kids enjoy these very much. Most of the meditative activities described in Chapter 16 can be easily adapted for children, and I'll offer a few more particularly kid-friendly ones in this chapter. Meditative activities still require children to direct their minds in a particular way for a set period of time, and they have similar benefits to introspective forms of meditation. However, they offer children something more engaging to concentrate on and give them an outlet for their physical energy. Kids can generally spend much longer doing a meditative activity than they can sitting silently.

Setting Parameters with Room for Wiggling

There needs to be at least some formality around meditation or meditative activities or they won't actually qualify as meditation! So set some rules and boundaries for meditation with children. Make it clear that for however long the meditation period lasts, no one should talk (except as part of the meditation, if speaking is involved) or touch anyone else. It's also helpful if each kid has a small space within which he has to stay, such as in his chair, at his desk, on a meditation mat, or on a particular spot on the carpet.

Once the parameters for meditation are set, silently tolerate wiggling. This includes physical wiggling, but also slight violations of rules or boundaries. Don't invite it, but don't point it out or forbid it. You should be meditating along with the kids, so you can set the tone by not reacting when one of them lets out a long sigh, pokes his friend's arm, or rolls his eyes. (While meditating with kids can actually be quite entertaining, be sure not to laugh!) If the stillness or formality of the meditation is more or less held, it eventually influences even the kids who initially resist it.

Making It Fun and Interesting

Finally, you can make meditation more attractive to kids by having fun with it. Of course, meditative fun is not the rambunctious kind of fun many kids are used to, but that can be part of the lesson. Introducing the aspect of a game—or mild competition with yourself—can help, such as "Let's see if we can count to 100 breaths" or "Last time we meditated for five minutes. Do you think we can do six?" Even without a deliberate effort to make meditation fun, most young kids are intrigued, at least initially, by doing a new activity with an adult. You can add to the sense of drama by not explaining much ahead of time but instead just leading the child through the meditative experience. You'll probably be surprised how few kids will ask why they just meditated. Somehow, it just makes sense to them, even if they didn't really like it.

You can also invite kids to participate in aspects of any ritual you set up around meditation. They can help arrange the space or watch a clock and ring a bell to begin and end the meditation. Some meditations involve items or prayers that kids can help select, making the whole activity into a collaborative process. Alternatively, you can make the point that you're initiating kids into an important adult activity, and that by doing so, you show respect for their maturity.

 POINT OF CLARIFICATION

You may find yourself wanting to ask kids how their meditation went, in order to find out whether they enjoyed it or benefited from it. Of course, while you may encourage kids to reflect to increase their self-awareness, do so only if they seem ready for it. If they aren't or if they don't like verbalizing their experience to you, they may come to associate meditation with being grilled about their thoughts and feelings and start resisting it. Trust that the meditation is having a positive effect, even if it isn't obvious, and try to help kids enjoy doing it!

Some Kid-Friendly Meditations

Some meditations are particularly well-suited to kids. These are generally meditative activities, or meditations that involve some kind small movement or sensory interaction. Other than the basic instructions for how to do the meditation and setting simple parameters for holding the meditative space, you usually don't have to give any additional explanation or instruction. While some meditative activities have a natural beginning and end, if the meditation doesn't, find a way to mark the time. Decide how long the meditation is going to be, communicate this to everyone, and ideally begin and end with the pleasant sound of a bell. Let's go through some of the different meditations you can try with children.

Pebble Meditation

For pebble meditation, have the kids follow these instructions:

1. Take a seated posture, ideally on the floor.

2. Place a small pile of stones in front of you—as few as 3 but as many as 20, if you want. Become aware of your body and your breathing, and try to let go of all of your extra thinking.

3. When you're ready, pick up one of the stones *just* as you're breathing in, and set it down a few inches away as you breathe out. This is the start of a new pile of pebbles.

4. Go back to the first pile and pick up a pebble as you breathe in and then move it to the second pile as you breathe out.

5. Keep doing this until all the pebbles have been moved to the new pile. If you want to keep meditating, start over—move one of the stones back to where it started, and start piling pebbles up there.

You can deepen the pebble meditation for you and the kids in a number of ways. You can use very nice stones—beautiful ones or ones that feel cool, smooth, or heavy in your hands. You might want to make the meditation feel more special by carefully choosing or collecting pebbles to use or finding a nice bag to hold them in. (You may want to use these pebbles *only* for meditation.) You can also make sure that yours and the kids' hands move perfectly in time with your breathing: move in slow motion as you lift a stone and breathe in, pause in the middle—at the highest point—as you hold your breath for a moment, and then let your hand sink slowly toward the second pile of stones as you breathe out. (Note to adults: This slow-motion movement isn't necessary—just moving pebbles from one pile to another in a businesslike way is fine, too.)

Heed the Bell Meditation

Heed the bell meditation is a gentle and fun way to introduce kids to silent, still, introspective meditation. The following walks you through how it's done:

1. Take a seated, upright posture that lets you be comfortable but keeps you alert and awake.

2. Choose some simple thing to meditate on, like your breathing or the sounds you can hear in the room. Whenever your mind wanders, gently return it to awareness of your breath, or sound, or whatever is your object of meditation.

3. Every so often, someone is going to softly ring a bell. This will happen every minute or so, but sometimes sooner or later than that, so you'll never know exactly when the bell's going to ring.

4. When you hear the bell, touch something that makes you feel calm—maybe the floor, your heart, or your head.

5. Ask yourself what you were just thinking or feeling right as the bell rang and then say goodbye to that thought or feeling and become aware of your meditation again.

6. Have someone ring the bell twice to end the meditation.

Altar Ritual

An altar ritual can be meaningful whether or not you or the children you're working with are religious. You can actually find nonreligious altars in all kinds of homes and public places— they're essentially just elevated, special places where people put symbols of things that are important to them. For some people, an altar will contain a symbol of their God or religion, but for others it will have trophies, mementos of important times or experiences, or photos of loved ones. Whatever is on them, generally speaking, altars are kept clean and uncluttered and are often decorated with objects of beauty like flowers or candles.

To do an altar meditation, you assemble an altar, perform some gesture of respect, and then take it down again. (Very small children *love* this meditation!) You need a table or shelf that's clean and can be easily reached, a pretty cloth to put over it, and a box containing many different small objects of beauty or importance to you. You'll obviously need to collect some things ahead of time; you might want to include lots of little animals, pictures of people or things you care about, dried flowers, or pretty rocks—anything you want.

Once you've done this, complete the altar meditation by following these steps:

1. Put the cloth over the altar.

2. Go to the box and pick something to put on the altar.

3. Carry the item with both hands, decide where to put it, and then set it down carefully. If there's more than one person doing this ritual, you should take turns putting items on the altar.

4. Keep doing this, without talking at all, until all the items in the box have been placed.

5. Do something that shows how much you care about the important things on the altar, like bowing or saying a verse of gratitude.

6. One by one, take each thing off the altar and put it carefully back in the box.

Chanting

Chanting as a meditative activity—and how it differs from singing—was discussed in detail in Chapter 16; you can adapt this technique for children by making it fun. Many kids love chanting, especially if it's energetic, rhythmic, and involves percussion instruments or bells they can learn to play. Generally speaking, a mere recitation isn't going to be as engaging for kids, so you'll probably want to intone whatever it is you decide to chant (using a sustained tone like singing, except without trying to sound pretty or stay on any particular note). You can chant something that's meaningful to you or contains an aspiration or teaching—a prayer, a scripture, a poem, a song (without the melody), or maybe something you write yourself.

For the chanting meditation, use the following steps to guide you:

1. Have someone ring a bell to begin the meditation.

2. Have one person chant the title and then have everyone else join in.

3. With each syllable, have someone hit a percussion instrument of some kind—a drum, or two drumsticks together, or one of the little wooden "percussion frog" instruments you can buy online for $10 to $20 (which sound very resonant and are designed to accompany chanting).

4. As you chant, keep time with the percussion and concentrate on the sensations of chanting—your breath, the way the sound feels in your chest, and what you can hear. Don't worry about thinking about what you're chanting; just let the words wash over you.

5. At the end of the chant, have someone ring a bell twice to signal it's the end of the meditation.

The Least You Need to Know

- Simply sharing meditation with children—even if they don't want to keep doing it regularly—is valuable. It introduces kids to the practice and lets them know there are ways to acknowledge the content of their minds without being controlled by it.

- If they meditate with some regularity (even once a week or so), meditation can help kids calm down, develop a healthier relationship to their thoughts and emotions, and gain self-awareness.

- To help kids enjoy meditation, make sure the session isn't too long, do it with them, and involve more than one kid if you can.

- Meditation is more attractive to children when it's always done at a particular time, in a particular place, and has some amount of ritual around it.

Taking It Deeper

In this part of the book, I discuss how you can further develop and maintain a meditation practice once you've decided what kind of meditation you want to do. Like any healthy habit, it can be challenging to establish a regular pattern of meditating and to keep up the momentum of the habit over time. I offer tips for how to do this, as well as for how to deal with some issues unique to meditation, such as physical restlessness, sleepiness, and experiences of unusual states of consciousness. In case you're interested in meditating with a teacher or a community, I also explain the benefits of doing so and how to go about it.

Finally, I describe the ways you can allow meditation to transform your life. Just as exercise may be a simple 10-minute walk, but may also involve intensive athletic training or even a lifelong dedication to mastering a discipline, the practice of meditation can vary widely in terms of how much time and energy you devote to it. I discuss four levels at which you can engage meditation—from improving your everyday life to reuniting with the ultimate—and how each one can be valuable.

Developing a Meditation Practice Over Time

So now you've tried meditation and decided you'd like to make it a regular part of your life. How do you go about doing that? It can be difficult to work meditation into a busy schedule and to create a strong habit of doing it. Meditation also tends to present a number of challenges, regardless of the type you're doing; while you may not face all of them, you're probably going to face at least a few!

In this chapter, I offer recommendations for how to deal with common difficulties encountered in meditation, including frustration with how you're doing, trouble concentrating, boredom, sleepiness, and unpleasant thoughts and feelings. I also talk about the best ways to deal with any remarkable insights or experiences that might happen in your meditation, and the value of practicing with a group. By the end of this chapter, you should have many of the tools you need to strengthen your meditation practice and keep it up for a long time.

In This Chapter

- Ways to strengthen and sustain a practice of meditation
- Avoiding the trap of judging your meditation
- Effective ways to face common meditative challenges
- How to relate to unusual experiences or insights
- Why you might want to meditate with others

Making Meditation a Routine

Throughout this book, I've compared meditation to exercise, and it particularly applies when talking about getting into a routine. While exercise is good for you and usually makes you feel better, it can be hard to make yourself do it regularly—that is, unless you've developed your exercise into a strong habit. Once you're on a roll with an exercise routine, you just do it without even thinking about it. You even *want* to do it. But if your routine gets broken for some reason— such as illness or the holidays—it can be very hard to start exercising again.

The same pattern applies to a meditation practice. The very best motivation for meditating is, well, meditating. Most people find that even a short meditation period transforms their whole day. They feel calmer, more able to deal with challenges, and generally more aware and appreciative. On a day you've meditated, you'll probably wonder why you don't do it every day! But then, of course, another busy day arrives, and meditation may or may not make it into your schedule.

 CONTEMPLATE THIS

> While a strong habit of meditation will improve your everyday life, one of the greatest benefits of it will be how it serves you in times of crisis. When everything else in your life is turned upside down—relationships, work, schedule, health, and so on—you'll probably find yourself turning to your meditation practice for grounding and relief more than at any other time.

Just like when you're trying to kick-start an exercise routine, if you haven't been meditating much, you simply have to make yourself do it. Try to move yourself toward the activity without reflecting on whether you want to do it or not. It will probably help to remind yourself that it won't always be a struggle. Meditation will be rewarding, and your habit of doing it will gain momentum.

It Helps, Even If You Aren't "Good" at It

Every form of meditation or meditative activity encourages you to work on your concentration. Whether you're focused on your breathing, following a guided meditation, or chanting a prayer, the idea is to put your awareness on your meditative object or technique and let go of extraneous thoughts. Ideally, you eventually become very wholehearted in your meditation, until you're completely absorbed in it—so there's *just* breathing, listening, or praying, rather than a sense of separation between you and your meditation.

It can be difficult to meditate according to these ideals, and it's important not to let that fact discourage you. Your meditation has a positive effect on your mind, body, and life regardless of how well you're able to concentrate, summon devotion, or achieve any other meditative goals. The essential thing is that you try. And I'm not just saying this to make you feel better; it's true! Many people report a sense that their meditation "isn't very good," but somehow it still has a profound effect on their lives. So what are some ways you can see how a meditation routine is helping you without worrying about whether you're doing it correctly?

Looking for the Results in Your Life

Meditation affects you in many different ways (physical, emotional, psychological, and spiritual) and at many different levels (conscious, subconscious, and unconscious). Immediate effects on the conscious level are the only ones you can perceive directly during meditation, and therefore these are likely to be the basis of any evaluation you make about your meditation. However, relying only on assessments of your conscious meditative experience is like judging a book by its cover. Meditation affects your body and mind in a lot of ways you aren't aware of.

When deciding whether your meditation is working for you or whether you're doing a good-enough job at it, look for positive results in the rest of your life. How does meditation affect your state of mind the rest of the day? Do you feel any calmer, less reactive, or more compassionate? Have you suddenly gained any insights about your life since you started meditating? Have your relationships improved? Have any health issues subsided a little? Have any negative habits started to drop away? When you look around for these signs that meditation is helping, keep an open mind; something may be shifting that you didn't expect.

Recognizing and Letting Go of Judgments

You can interfere with your own meditation by judging it too much. It may seem to make sense to continually evaluate whether you're doing it right or whether you're successful. However, judging your meditation is just getting caught up in mental elaboration and defeats the whole purpose. When you're meditating and you notice your mind is wandering or you're distracted by emotions, simply notice this. In a sense, your awareness has already returned to your meditation as soon as you've noticed the state of your own mind. Gently and patiently shift your mind back toward your meditative object or technique, and try to refrain from any additional commentary on your meditation. Who cares what was happening a minute ago? Just start over and allow every moment to be a clean slate.

> **POINT OF CLARIFICATION**
>
> Part of the issue around judging your meditation is connected to the fact that you've probably identified with your conscious sense of self. This means that when you meditate, you assume it's a process controlled and dictated by the part of your mind that discriminates and judges good and bad. However, meditation is meant to engage your whole being; your conscious, discriminating self has to participate, but it isn't in charge the way it thinks it is. Try trusting the overall process, regardless of what your conscious mind is telling you.

Sometimes, however, you may need to acknowledge your judgments or frustrations about meditation and simply include them within your meditative experience. It's possible to make "lack of judgment" just another ideal you use to assess the quality of your meditation, and this is counterproductive. Simply notice that you're thinking "Oh man, I can't concentrate today at all" or "I've been meditating for a year and I don't think I've made any progress." You can relate to these thoughts as if they're just the scenery of your mind, or as if they're insubstantial passing phenomena like clouds. If you don't believe or reject the thoughts, they'll subside more quickly.

Common Challenges in All Meditation Forms

One of the drawbacks of meditation is that it takes place within your own mind, so you really don't know anything about other peoples' meditation, and they can't know anything for sure about yours. This means it's easy to assume other people have it together in their meditation. From the outside, it usually looks like they're calm and peaceful or concentrated and mindful.

You might assume you're the only one who struggles with challenges like a wandering mind, fantasies, resistance, or sleepiness. Trust me, you're not! Many people find it encouraging just knowing they aren't alone in their struggles with meditation and that there are ways to deal with the difficulties you might face. In this section, I discuss mental challenges typical to just about any form of meditation (for more information about physical discomfort, see Chapter 2).

Difficulty Concentrating

Generally speaking, the more you can concentrate during your meditation, the more effective it will be. Concentration is the power behind your meditation. You can compare concentrating your intention and awareness during meditation to concentrating sunlight with a lens so it focuses on one spot and gets very hot. While it's not always necessary to have lots of "power and heat" during your meditation (depending partly on the type it is), it's necessary to have some. All the attention and awareness in the world isn't going to amount to much if it's dispersed all over the place.

In the course of daily life, your mind tends to concentrate only when you're interested in something. Your interest is naturally drawn to things that are new, entertaining, pleasurable, potentially advantageous or threatening, or that hold a special fascination for you personally. When there's nothing around that fits one of those descriptions, your mind most likely wanders. This is what psychologists call your *default mode;* when you're not engaged in something of particular interest, you process all kinds of self-referential stuff—memories, plans, worries, fantasies, and so on. (See Chapter 12 for more discussion of your default network.) It's like the brain uses your spare mental bandwidth to figure stuff out and maximize your future happiness.

CONTEMPLATE THIS

Research on meditation has proven that you shift out of default mode while meditating, as long as you're concentrating. This has been shown through functional magnetic resonance imaging (fMRI), which essentially allows researchers to take a video of brain function in order to watch how activity changes in the brain over time. In default mode, there's lots of activity in the self-referential processing areas of the brain. During meditation, this activity shifts into areas associated with receptivity and attention to the present.

While there's nothing wrong with your default mode, it's not the mode you want to be in when you're meditating. Remember, the benefits of meditation come only when your mind is directed in a deliberate way (see Chapter 1). Meditation, then, requires a strong effort to opt out of your default mode in order to concentrate on your object or technique, and this isn't easy! Time and time again, your mind will slip into default mode.

You can really help your mind settle down if you don't get upset by this process. Simply recognize the default mode for what it is; recall that you want to meditate; and patiently, gently return your mind to its meditative object. You want this return to meditation to be pleasant and positively reinforcing for your mind! If you get frustrated and lecture yourself every time you remember your meditation, your mind is likely to start resisting, because meditation will become a negative experience. You're welcome to try other things to intensify your concentration, such as summoning your willpower or reminding yourself of your deepest aspirations; in the end, however, there's no shortcut to concentration. It requires a patient, nearly infinite repetition of shifting your mind back to your chosen object.

No Time to Meditate

Do you keep meaning to meditate but it just doesn't happen? Chances are you just get carried away with other things, and then putting everything aside to meditate—or, by definition, to engage in something that's not outwardly rewarding or productive—seems unattractive, wasteful, or just impossible. (Who's got the time?) There may always seem to be something else that needs attention in your life, so taking time for meditation may even seem self-indulgent.

You can get yourself to make time for meditation in a number of ways, such as the following:

- Bargain with yourself using this argument: "Meditation generally makes me more effective and efficient at everything I do. So 20 to 30 minutes of meditation won't actually result in accomplishing less." (Try it; it's true.)

- Deliberately try to think of meditation as self-indulgent. Imagine it as a mini-vacation for your mind, because, well, you deserve it.

- Meditate at the same time every day. Work it into your daily routine, so you always meditate right after your morning coffee, before the kids get home from school, or right before bed. This will make meditation much more likely to happen than if you just try to fit it in wherever you can.

- Seek social support for your meditation practice. Just as a regular yoga class or a visit to the gym can support your physical fitness routine, attending a meditation group on a regular basis can inspire you to make meditation more a part of your life.

CONTEMPLATE THIS

If you can't get to a group, try using the free Insight Timer app (insighttimer.com) on your smartphone or tablet. You can use it to signal the beginning and end of your meditation with the pleasant sound of a bell, plus—if you want to—it lets you join the Insight Connect community. This lets you see how many people are currently meditating with the app all over the world, and where they are on a world map (there's sometimes more than 1,000 people meditating at any given time). You can also establish personal connections with friends through Insight Connect, which lets you see when they last meditated and for how long, and vice versa. It helps motivate many people to know they aren't meditating alone.

Boredom and Dullness

Boredom is a conscious sense of disinterest or resistance because you'd rather be elsewhere or doing something else. While you may not know what you'd rather be doing, you know it isn't *this*. Dullness is the opposite of alertness; it's a lack of energy and interest that leaves your mind fuzzy and vacant. When your meditation is dull, it can almost feel as if you're concentrating, because you don't notice any obvious extraneous thoughts or feelings intruding. However, if you pay attention, you'll realize that it's really just that you're not noticing anything at all.

Depending on what kind of meditation you're doing, you may struggle with boredom and dullness right off the bat. However, even meditation techniques that are initially interesting may become boring after time, or you may find your meditation getting dull. It's important to keep on meditating anyway and to try to summon energy, alertness, and interest. This is because meditation is designed to give you very little in the way of entertainment or fuel for active thought. The relaxing, transforming effect of meditation happens precisely because you're directing your mind in a deliberate way toward something that doesn't naturally inspire self-interest or self-concern.

As described earlier in this chapter, you're naturally interested in things that are new, entertaining, pleasurable, potentially advantageous or threatening, or particularly fascinating. It might help to think of these as interests of your small or egoistic self, in contrast to the nobler interests of your deeper or bigger self (such as greater compassion, closeness to God, or self-transcendence). To fight boredom and dullness in meditation, try to remember and connect with the aspirations of your deeper self, and recall how life is short. There's a part of you that wants to be alert and engaged in your meditation, if you can just find it.

WATCH OUT

You may get bored with your meditation because you expect something to happen. At some level, you hope you'll make obvious progress, have pleasant or rewarding experiences, or achieve some particular insight. It can be helpful to notice and acknowledge your expectations around meditation when you're bored or feeling dull, and challenge yourself to appreciate your meditation for what it is, right in the moment you're doing it.

Sleepiness

If you're doing a still, silent form of meditation, you may end up fighting drowsiness at times. Some people never have a problem with this, while others struggle with it often (I did, and I sympathize). If you're drowsy and meditating alone, you might try standing up or doing some walking meditation (described in Chapter 15). You can also try breathing more deeply, sitting at a different time of day, or starting off your meditation period with a recitation of your deepest aspirations (in order to focus and motivate yourself).

If none of these things help, however, don't despair! Sometimes the effort to fight sleepiness just makes it worse. Just keep meditating and try not to worry about it. If you meditate enough, you'll eventually have a session that's wakeful, and this can be positively reinforcing. You might also seriously consider whether you're getting enough sleep; most westerners are sleep-deprived, and a body can't be blamed for taking advantage of a quiet moment to get some rest! If you really can't get anymore sleep, at least give yourself a break from getting drowsy in meditation. If you break up your meditation into two shorter periods with walking meditation in between, you may find you're considerably more alert in the second period, after a little nap in the first.

Unpleasant Feelings and Thoughts

In Chapter 3, I briefly described a bunch of relatively rare stuff that may come up during meditation, and about which you may want to consult a meditation teacher or psychotherapist familiar with meditation. Here, I want to discuss the more typical arising of unpleasant feelings and thoughts during meditation—unpleasant enough to make you resist meditating, but not troubling enough to be disruptive to your life.

During meditation, you shift into a different mode of being. As discussed in Chapter 1, your body goes into a physiological state of relaxation with a lowered metabolism. Your mind also functions differently than it usually does, especially if you're able to concentrate on your meditation fairly well. Feelings and thoughts you haven't even realized you had, or you've been suppressing, will sometimes come bubbling to the surface. By meditating, it's like you're sending a message to yourself that things are okay, which is why you can let go of hypervigilance about your safety and well-being and do something useless like meditation. Your unresolved mental and emotional stuff sees this as a good time to show up.

POINT OF CLARIFICATION

Many people assume you meditate in order to feel better, and in a way that's true. However, meditating doesn't always induce instant calm and happiness. It's more like undergoing a course of treatment for a physical illness or problem; the treatment itself may be unpleasant at times, and you may end up feeling worse before you get better. Over time, meditation should improve your life and sense of well-being. However, at any given time, you may be working through something difficult as a necessary part of the process.

Even though some of the thoughts, emotions, memories, or images you experience in meditation may be sad, upsetting, or otherwise unpleasant, when they arise, you have a great opportunity in front of you. Rather than allowing these things so go unexamined or unresolved for months, years, or decades, you have a chance to acknowledge and study them.

For example, let's say while meditating, you suddenly have a vivid memory of your father criticizing you, and you feel shame and anger arise, even though this event happened in the distant past (so long ago, you'd forgotten about it). The fact that you're still carrying the memory around and that it can evoke such emotion in you tells you that you still have some reactivity around your father and the way he treated you, and/or around being criticized. You may then want to ponder this outside of meditation and there see if you have any related issues in your life you'd like to try to let go of or resolve.

If unpleasant thoughts and feelings occur during meditation without any clear cause, or if you're unable to address the cause, you can practice compassionate endurance. Don't try to get rid of the experiences. Try keep at least part of your mind grounded in your meditative method while you allow the emotions and thoughts to wash through you. This can be a powerful and cathartic practice in which you allow your body and mind to process difficult things, but also maintain some emotional distance from them so they don't completely overwhelm you. If you do this (perhaps repeatedly, depending on what's coming up for you), eventually the intensity of the thoughts and feelings will decrease, and they may even go away.

Remarkable Experiences in Meditation

Remarkable experiences in meditation can include deep states of concentration in which you enter into different levels of consciousness. Thoughts and everyday concerns can truly cease, or it can seem like time slows down so much that you can watch each and every thought and sensation arise in your consciousness and then pass away. You may lose identification with your physical body, and instead feel literally inseparable from all existence. You may have an overwhelming sense of God's immediate presence and intense love. While the nature and content of deep meditative experiences varies, all such experiences present as being very different from the ones you have in everyday life.

With respect to remarkable insights, states, and experiences during meditation, you probably fall into one of two camps: You would like to experience such things, or you don't particularly care about them or even want to avoid them. In any case, I have to be honest and say that meditation does sometimes result in unusual and dramatic experiences. Whether it does depends on the person (their character, psychological makeup, and probably their physiology), the type of meditation they're doing, and the intensity of their effort. Let's look at how each type should approach meditation in regard to remarkable experiences.

 CONTEMPLATE THIS

Shunryu Suzuki was a revered Zen teacher. In Zen, the ultimate remarkable meditative experience is *satori*, or seeing the true nature of the self, and a moment of such awakening is sometimes a dramatic event in someone's life. However, when Suzuki was asked once why he didn't emphasize satori in his teaching, he said, "It's not that satori is unimportant, but it's not the part of Zen that needs to be stressed." (From *Zen Mind, Beginner's Mind.*) Remarkable experiences will happen to you or they won't—what's important is to focus on your meditation practice, rather than on attaining something from it.

Not Seeking Far-Out Experiences

If you would like to have remarkable experiences in meditation (and many of us would), it's important not to get too fixated on them. Generally speaking, deep states of concentration, profound insights, or experiences of closeness with the Divine are achieved through great meditative effort and concentration, but not through striving for the experiences themselves. This can be tricky to understand. Think of it this way: through your meditation, you prepare your body and mind for such experiences, and part of this preparation includes letting go of your self-interest. As long as part of you is eagerly awaiting a cool meditative state, you'll probably prevent it from happening.

However, it's pretty much impossible to make yourself stop wanting the profound and mystical rewards of meditation if you do, in fact, want them. What you can do is recognize your desire and then channel it into your meditative effort. Let it fuel your concentration or devotion, but realize that once you're deep in meditation, you'll need to let your desire go. Ultimately, profound experiences are the result of surrendering your self-concern—even your spiritual self-concern.

Another important thing to know about remarkable meditative experiences is that once you've had them, it's best to let them go. Go ahead and learn from them and appreciate them, but it's generally not useful to try to re-create them. You can continue the diligent meditative effort that led up to them but without getting fixated on having the same experience again.

Accepting Experiences If They Happen

If you don't want to have remarkable experiences in meditation, this may make you avoid doing it, or may prevent you from meditating deeply because you're consciously or unconsciously concerned that something weird will happen. It's true that experiences of alternate ways of being and seeing can be unsettling. Even if they're pleasant or blissful, they may be somewhat disturbing just because they're not what you're used to. However, few people regret having had deep meditative experiences—you usually learn something, and sometimes these experiences are life changing in positive ways.

Try to relax into your meditation and not worry too much about remarkable states. In the grand scheme of a life of meditation practice, these experiences are relatively rare. They usually come only if you spend lots of time and energy on your meditation, and you can generally see them coming. It's almost unheard of for new meditators to suddenly end up in a radically new state of consciousness. If they do, while they usually need to process what has happened with a meditation teacher (see Chapter 3), they're generally just fine and continue meditating and going about their daily lives.

 **WATCH OUT**

Relaxing into your meditation and not worrying about remarkable states is one thing. But if by some chance meditation seems to cause negative or disruptive changes in your life, be sure to use your common sense—seek advice from a meditation teacher or psychotherapist.

Meditating with Others

You may find it easier to sustain your meditation practice over time if you meditate with others. This is also a good way to learn more about your form of meditation and get more of a sense of how to deepen it. Most meditation groups have a teacher or leader of some kind, and I have already discussed how it can be useful to work with a teacher (see Chapter 3).

Meditation groups and communities can offer moral support for your meditation practice. Many people who can't manage to make themselves meditate on their own are easily able to attend a group once a week or more, and they find even this amount of meditation very beneficial. It's helpful to hear about other people's experiences of and struggles with your form of meditation. There are usually also supplementary teachings and practices associated with each style of meditation you'll get exposed to by attending a group. In each chapter in this book that focuses on a particular kind of meditation, I included a section called "Learning More" where you can find information on how to search for a meditation community near you.

Even if you have resistance to participating in a group, you may want to at least visit one or two and see what they're like. Almost all meditation groups (or centers, temples, and so on) are used to having new people join them, especially in this day and age, when more and more people are becoming interested in meditation.

Groups vary widely in terms of openness, friendliness, secular versus religious presentation, formality, and expectations. So if you're fortunate enough to live in an area with multiple meditation groups, you might want to visit them all in order to find the one where you feel most comfortable. While you may not like everything about the group, for the most part, the things presented there should seem helpful and true, and the people should seem kind and authentic. A supportive meditation group can be an incredibly valuable part of your practice—so much so that most experienced meditators consider their community to be central to their lives.

The Least You Need to Know

- Meditation is like exercise in that once you've established a regular habit of it, it will be easy to maintain; however, it can be hard to get that habit started. At first, you may just have to make yourself do it, but eventually it will be rewarding.

- Judgments about your meditation based on your conscious experience of it aren't very helpful. When deciding whether meditation is good for you or if you're doing it right, it's best to look for positive changes in your life.

- It's normal to face challenges in meditation. You may find it difficult to concentrate, stay interested in it, find time to do it, or stay awake for it. Fortunately, there are things you can do to deal with all of these difficulties and make your meditation practice stronger.

- Sometimes meditation can result in remarkable states or insights. Although these experiences can be fascinating or blissful, it's best not to get too fixated on them; doing so will only interfere with your meditation.

- Meditating with others can be a great support to your practice, and you can get involved with many different kinds of groups. There's likely to be one out there with which you'll feel comfortable, so visit a few to see what they're like.

Letting Meditation Transform Your Life

Meditation is beneficial at whatever level you care to engage it. Just as it's always good for you to take a walk and get a little exercise, it's good if you meditate occasionally. If you want to up the ante, you can commit to a regimen of meditation in order to improve your mental and emotional health. Once you feel reasonably healthy, you may be inspired to use meditation to delve deeper into your life and find ways to live more in harmony with your deepest aspirations. Finally, even if your life is profoundly satisfying, the path of meditation can lead you to greater spiritual insights and even to a personal experience of the ultimate goals of the various meditative traditions: transcendence of the self, an experience of nonseparation from all existence, or closeness to God.

In this chapter, I walk you through four different reasons to have a meditation practice, each reason building on the previous one and requiring a deeper level of engagement with your meditation: improving your life, living more fully, gaining spiritual insight, and reuniting with the Ultimate. I also describe what each level entails, the associated rewards and benefits, and ways you can explore it for yourself.

In This Chapter

- Different levels of engagement with meditation and their value
- How to use meditation to improve your life in practical ways
- Ways meditation can help you live more authentically and fully
- Using meditative reflection to gain insight into deeper questions
- Meditation as a way to experience greater connection

Levels of Engagement with Meditation

There's a risk whenever the word *level* is used, as most of us instantly jump to evaluations of better or worse. Hopefully I can prevent this kind of judgment by once again comparing meditation to exercise. If someone takes a fairly slow, 20-minute walk every day because he has had a heart attack and wants to prevent another one, is his exercise inferior to that of a person who runs 2 miles a day? And is our runner inferior to someone training for a marathon who runs 10 miles a day, and is that person in turn inferior to someone who competes in the Olympic triathlon? Of course not. Each person exercises according to his interest, ability, and need. Similarly, everyone engages meditation based on the same parameters.

 WATCH OUT

Assuming you're interested in exploring meditation more intensely, take my levels with a grain of salt. While they describe very real and relevant concerns, practices, and experiences, they shouldn't be taken too literally as categories. One motivation for meditating actually tends to blend into another, and you may feel one for a time but then find another becomes more important. It's also not very helpful to wonder about what level you're on or what level you're capable of. That kind of thinking only gets in the way. Everyone is capable of all levels of meditation, and the process of meditative development is organic and nonlinear—in other words, it can be difficult to know where you are or where you'll be next.

Why talk about levels, then? Simply because you may be interested in getting more deeply into meditation. You certainly don't have to, but at some point, you may be glad to know what the possibilities are. It's somewhat unfortunate that modern innovations have resulted in the use of meditative techniques for therapeutic purposes in secular settings, divorced from the larger-practice contexts surrounding traditional forms of meditation. Of course, while it's great that these techniques benefit people and are gaining wide acceptance, they might give you the impression this is all there is to meditation: simple exercises you do to relieve stress now and then. Because meditation can be so much more than that, however, I refer to levels to discuss how much deeper meditation can go.

Meditation to Improve Your Everyday Life

When you meditate to improve your everyday life, you're looking for tangible or observable results. You may hope for a decrease in stress level, an improvement in mood, or a better ability to manage difficult emotions. Many of the people who have adopted the practice of meditation or mindfulness in the past few decades are at this level of motivation. They started to suffer health problems like high blood pressure, or mental health issues like anxiety or depression, and their doctor suggested they try meditation. Of course, tangible or observable results are the subject of all scientific research on meditation, so there's growing evidence—in addition to the reports of meditators—that meditation can actually improve your everyday life.

You should keep two things in mind when you're meditating for practical, noticeable results. First, you usually have to be patient. Sometimes you'll experience positive changes as soon as you start meditating, but most of the time it takes weeks or months—or more—for something to change. If you give up, meditation definitely won't help.

Second, it's best to stay open-minded about how meditation is going to benefit you. You may be determined to change a particular thing, such as losing your temper, but discover meditation doesn't seem to affect that much. On the other hand, you almost always gain some benefits, so you may find that even if you still lose your temper, your relationships are improving and those momentary bouts of anger aren't causing as much damage as they used to.

Still, even though tangible and observable results are sometimes elusive, you can experience a number of practical benefits from doing just about any kind of meditation. I share a few of them here to help guide and inspire your practice.

Time for a Restorative Reset

Before I instruct new Zen meditators about technique, I always tell them the most important thing about meditation is the simple act of putting everything else down for a time. The mere intention to let work and other activities go is deeply significant, even if you still find thoughts about your responsibilities and concerns intruding on your meditation. Putting everything down to engage in an outwardly unproductive activity sends the message to your subconscious that things are okay—if they weren't, you couldn't afford to get off the hamster wheel of frantic activity! Whether you sit silently, pray, or exercise in a meditative way, you're taking a mental and emotional break that has more of an impact on your attitude throughout the rest of your day than even the most pleasurable leisure activity.

 CONTEMPLATE THIS

> The great thing about this aspect of meditation—how it provides your body and mind with a restorative break—is that you don't have to try to make it happen, and you don't even have to notice that it's happening! All you have to do is concentrate on your meditation as best you can, and your body and mind will naturally take care of the rest.

As you take this break from your everyday concerns, something remarkable happens. As discussed in Chapter 1, when you consciously direct your mind toward a simple, nonproductive object or activity, you trigger a relaxation response in your body and mind. Dr. Herbert Benson's research shows how this response is physiological as well as psychological: your respiration and metabolism slows, and your brain waves change. Essentially, this state is the opposite of the stress response, which is a state of increased metabolism and mental agitation triggered by your daily challenges.

When you enter the meditative state, you reset your body and mind, and counteract the effects of stress. Generally speaking, the more time you spend in meditation, the more substantial the restorative effects will be. This is because, in the state of relative meditative relaxation, your mind and body are allowed to recuperate and heal. Relieved of otherwise pervasive and constant tension and stress, blood and energy flow more freely, muscles relax, stress hormones decrease while immune system function increases—the list goes on. Psychologically, your mind also relaxes. While science doesn't understand healthy brain functioning as well as it does healthy physical functioning, during meditation, it's like your mind is able to do a reboot like a computer does when you turn it off and then on again. When it comes "back online," everything runs more smoothly and efficiently.

Watching Thoughts and Emotions

It's entirely possible for meditation to improve your everyday life without you trying to do anything in your meditation other than the technique or practice you've chosen. The effects of spending time in a relaxed, restorative state, as previously discussed, aren't dependent on your conscious mind. However, your consciousness during meditation can play a role, and can help you access additional benefits.

When you're meditating (or praying, or doing a meditative activity), you'll notice thoughts and emotions appearing in your mind despite your effort to concentrate on your technique or activity. While this can be frustrating, it's actually a great opportunity. The thing is, these thoughts and emotions are always appearing in your mind; you just don't usually notice because you get carried along with them. They're your reality when you're thinking and feeling them. When you meditate, on the other hand, you're trying to direct your mind in a particular way and you notice thoughts and emotions arising and intruding all on their own.

Watching thoughts and emotions arise and pass away during meditation, without getting too caught up in them, results in a process psychologists call *decentering*. Rather than completely identifying with the content of your mind—taking it as irrefutable truth, thinking it defines who you are, or assuming it has to be acted on—you notice how you aren't the same as your thoughts and emotions. After all, *you* are trying to meditate, while content is arising in your mind all on its own! While this observation sounds simple, its effects can be profound. Gaining some distance from dysfunctional, painful, anxious, or depressing thoughts and emotions can allow you to deal with them much more effectively.

 **DEFINITION**

> **Decentering** is a psychological term for how you can learn to center your sense of self somewhere other than in your thoughts and emotions. This helps you relate to the content of your mind differently, so you can deal with it more objectively instead of feeling controlled by it.

Getting to Know Your Own Mind

This way of engaging meditation builds on the previous one: as you meditate, you keep on returning your awareness to your meditative technique but not in an exclusive way. You include your meditative experience as a whole in your awareness. Just as you watched thoughts and emotions arise and pass without getting caught in them (by letting them go and returning to your meditative technique), you can observe the function and content of your mind in a more detailed way.

This effort is perhaps best explained by an example. Let's say you're trying to concentrate wholeheartedly on a prayer or meditative exercise. Throughout your meditation period, you keep returning your mind to your chosen activity when it wanders—but it's wandering *a lot*. You notice that you're worrying about finances again and whether you'll lose your job in the recent round of layoffs at the office. While it may feel like you're failing at your meditation, you're actually getting some valuable information! Sometimes you may not even realize the content and emotional tone of your mind until you meditate. This doesn't mean you allow yourself to get drawn into a prolonged train of thought—you simply notice and then try to let the thinking go.

One of the most amazing benefits of getting to know your own mind through meditation happens when you find the "points of choice" in what's usually a repetitive and dysfunctional pattern of thinking or behavior. It's like you finally spend enough time consciously observing your mind that you find the off switch for a critical part of a pattern. You know how people will give you advice when you're stressed, telling you, "Just don't worry about it"? If you don't know where the off switch for your worry is, this isn't very helpful advice. But when you find it, sometimes you actually can simply opt out of an ingrained habit of body or mind. Of course, this can only happen if you're paying attention, and you may flip the switch back on in five minutes. Over time, however, your insight into your own mind can allow you to change very painful and harmful patterns in your life.

POINT OF CLARIFICATION

When you watch your mind in meditation over the course of hours, weeks, months, and years, you learn a great deal about how it works. You find out where it tends to dwell or get stuck—on particular issues, in the past, or in the future. You notice your mental habits, such as trying to justify, understand, predict, control, or tune out. All of this information is useful because once you see something, you may be able to change it.

Seeking to Live More Fully

What if you're pretty well-adjusted, healthy, and happy already? What can meditation offer you? If you're interested, it can help you realize your full potential as a human being. No one is without limitations, regrets, and fears. Everyone wonders, at times, whether they have fully explored their aspirations, developed their talents, or adequately expressed their love and creativity. Meditation can help you to notice where you're feeling limited or constricted and to understand what's going on, allowing you to find a path toward living more authentically and fully.

Noticing Constriction and Fear

This is the part of meditation that can be pretty challenging. Most people assume you meditate in order to feel better—that when you do it, you feel calm and happy. If you want to use meditation to live more fully, you'll have to let this idea go. You'll need to deliberately turn to face what causes distress or pain during your meditation. You'll also need to stay present with thoughts, feelings, memories, and so on that may be unpleasant, momentarily overwhelming, or scary. Common sense tells you to run away from these things, or to seek distraction or solace in something that will make you feel better. Unless you have all the answers and can fix the problem right away, it's better to avoid it, right?

In meditation, it can be very fruitful to act contrary to common sense and move *toward* difficult things. It starts with a willingness to recognize there's a problem. It's natural to have resistance to this part of the process; you probably have a certain investment and pride in managing your life successfully and in being a fairly happy person. A problem can seem like a failing, or a suggestion that your ways of dealing with life are flawed. Fortunately, you can look at problems in a very different way: as opportunities for growth. Everyone has them, and they don't actually have to be a big deal.

Once you've recognized (and admitted) some issue within yourself—constriction, fear, reactivity, anger, sadness, you name it—you invite it into your meditation. This doesn't mean you think about it or analyze it, although insights about it may arise spontaneously. You simply allow yourself to experience the thoughts, feelings, and sensations that arise. You watch what happens as if you're watching a movie, allowing the plot and scenery to unfold without making an effort to control it. This allows your body and mind to process and work on your issue in the most efficient and effective way possible. While it may also be good to think about your issue in a normal way outside of meditation, you may find that simply being with your discomfort in a meditative way will help things start shifting and changing on their own.

Tracing Back from Symptom to Source

At an even deeper level, you can meditatively investigate your problems in a sustained way in order to see what deeper issues are behind them. In a sense, this is like deep self-psychotherapy, but it uses the mind of meditation instead of discriminative thinking and analysis. Again, you may resist the idea that you need to do this kind of work, and that's fine—if you resist it, you probably don't need to do it. However, if you're seeking to live more fully, this kind of self-investigation is a great opportunity.

Once you've noticed and learned to be present with some kind of difficult or painful issue or experience, you can raise a question, such as "What is this?" (You might also ask, "What's underneath this?" or "What am I afraid of here?") This awakens the spirit of deeper investigation, but in a meditative and receptive way. You ask the question and wait for the answer. However, you don't passively wait; you watch and listen for any possible answers with great attention and energy. Sometimes it takes a while (many meditation sessions, or even months or years) before an answer comes. It may also help to change your question, taking note of whether a particular path of inquiry resonates more than another.

 CONTEMPLATE THIS

When an answer to your question arises due to your meditation, it will often be something you've never thought of before. That's because the space of meditation allows your mind to work in a different way than it usually does. Insights can arise based on intuition or on subtly suppressed feelings, thoughts, and memories. While your ordinary, conscious thought processes often get repetitive and make you unable to "think outside the box," as the saying goes, meditative investigation can help you explore new territory.

While gaining some insight into the immediate causes of some issue you're having can be beneficial, you don't have to stop there. Underneath any constriction or fear is another, deeper one. While this may sound discouraging, if you keep tracing symptoms back to their root causes, it can ultimately be very liberating. At the base of all of our issues are basic, primal concerns about things like survival, happiness, and love. It's possible to keep delving deeper into your issues until you confront your very basic fears and assumptions—and when you do, it can transform your life.

For example, perhaps you notice that you harbor a deep sadness because you don't have an intimate romantic relationship. Upon further meditative investigation, you recognize a concern that you're unworthy of love; underneath that, you notice an intense dread of loneliness; and at an even deeper level, you realize you fear your life has no meaning. Now, it won't be easy to face this root concern or to resolve it; however, once you recognize it, you have a chance of addressing it. If you find a way to discover meaning in your life just as it is, you'll also find yourself liberated from all the issues connected to that concern. To continue with the example, while you may still want a romantic relationship, the lack of one won't cause you anguish.

Greater Insight Into Universal Questions

The previous level of engagement with meditation—seeking to live more fully—leads very naturally into using meditation to gain greater insight into larger, universal questions. If you trace personal concerns back to their source, as described previously, eventually you find yourself asking questions like the following:

- What is the meaning of life?

- How do I face death without fear?

- What is the nature of compassion?

The remarkable thing is that meditation can actually help you answer these kinds of questions. As discussed in Chapter 1, one of the things meditation does is open you up to a different kind of knowing—one that isn't dependent on intellectual thought. If you meditate long enough with a compelling, universal question, you'll discover a new relationship to it. Whatever answer you come up with will be personal and directly relevant to your life. It won't necessarily be something you can explain to others (and until they experience an answer for themselves, it probably won't help them much for you to share yours).

How is it possible for you to find the answers to these ultimate questions? After all, each of us has a limited perspective. We're shaped by our experience and concerns, and few of us have the profound intelligence or vision to create compelling new philosophies about the nature of reality. The thing is, even with our limitations, we have the answers within us. You can ask and answer questions about life because you're alive. You can ask and answer questions about universal experiences like compassion, fear, or joy because you have these experiences yourself. When you turn within and look with the mind of meditation, the answers you need are there. They have nothing to do with your ordinary thinking mind; instead, your answers are clear and lucid observations of truth as it's reflected in your own experience.

Reuniting with the Ultimate

The ultimate goal of almost all spiritual traditions is dissolving the sense of separation you have from other people, from your deepest aspirations, from life in general, and from the Ultimate (God, the Divine, or ultimate reality, whatever description you prefer). This sense of separation seems to have been a universal human conundrum as far back as recorded history goes, because it's described in the most ancient literature and spiritual writings. Your lack of a sense of connection—or of incomplete connection—may be subtle, but it may also be acute and very painful.

 POINT OF CLARIFICATION

"Reuniting with the Ultimate" may sound like a special, far-out experience. Occasionally it is, especially if you've never experienced it before. Once you've understood and integrated what it teaches you, however, you recognize that you're never actually separate, even when you think you are. A sense of connection becomes your new normal—wonderful, but not unusual or special.

Meditation can lead you to a personal experience of reuniting with the Ultimate, and therefore with everything and everyone else. There are many ways this experience is described: transcendence, nonseparation, awakening to the nature of reality, closeness to God, or reunion with the Divine. It may be hard to believe that meditation can actually help you experience this kind of transcendence, or that *you* are capable of such a spiritual or mystical encounter, but it's true—and I'm not the only one who says so! At the end of each of the chapters in this book that focuses on a particular meditation tradition, I included a section called "The Ultimate Goal," which discusses how each tradition approaches this experience of transcendence.

Generally speaking, you're not going to experience a reunion with the Ultimate the first time you meditate. Personal transcendence usually requires you to first engage meditation at the previous three levels discussed in this chapter—meditating to improve your life, seeking to live more fully, and gaining insight into universal questions—for a long time, or quite intensively. Even if you have a profound experience early on in your meditation practice, chances are it will not be something you have reliable access to. After many years of meditation practice, you can not only reliably access a sense of nonseparation, it becomes an underlying truth in your life, as opposed to a special experience you have once in a while.

The important thing to keep in mind is that meditation at all of these levels of engagement is worthwhile and beneficial. Whether you just want to relieve some stress in your life or you want to deepen your sense of closeness to God, meditation can help. There's always more you can learn about meditation, and deeper levels of practice you can do. Hopefully, you can see it as a fascinating journey. Enjoy!

The Least You Need to Know

- Meditation can be beneficial whether you only meditate occasionally or you intensively engage meditation as a lifelong path of self-study and discovery (or anything in between).

- While it's best not to get too caught up in thinking about levels of engagement with meditation, you may find it useful to know how profound and transformative the practice can be.

- Meditation can improve your life in tangible and measurable ways, particularly because it offers your body and mind a period of restorative relaxation, as well as allowing you to observe your thoughts and emotions in useful ways.

- If you want to use meditation to live your life more deeply and authentically, you can engage in a process of self-investigation that can be challenging but very liberating.

- For thousands of years, meditation has been used to gain greater spiritual understanding and a personal experience of transcendence, nonseparation, or closeness to God—and this is a practice anyone can do.

Glossary

Adonai A Hebrew name for God, which can be roughly translated as "Lord."

autogenic training A method of learning how to promote your own mental and physical healing from within; *auto* refers to "self" or "from within," and *genic* refers to "generating" or "developing."

bodhicitta The motivation of a bodhisattva, including both the aspiration for complete enlightenment and buddhahood in order to benefit all beings and infinite, unconditional love and compassion for those beings.

bodhisattva Someone who commits to doing whatever is required to attain buddhahood (full awakening and liberation) for the sake of all beings, even if the process of awakening takes many lifetimes.

buddha A being who has awakened to the true nature of reality and thereby attained freedom from suffering.

Ch'an The Chinese term for the meditation-focused Buddhist school later called *Zen* in Japan.

chakras The seven energy centers of the body. They are located along the spine (just in front of the physical spine) at the base of the spine; at the levels of the sacrum, navel, heart, and throat; at the base of the skull and between the eyebrows (two poles of one chakra); and at the top of the head.

Chenrezig A male, deity-like figure in Vajrayana Buddhism who symbolizes the manifestation of perfect compassion informed by perfect wisdom, or insight, into emptiness. In other Buddhist traditions, this figure is known as Avalokiteśvara, Kuan Yin, Kannon, or Kanzeon, and is sometimes portrayed as female.

decentering   A psychological term for how you can learn to center your sense of self somewhere other than in your thoughts and emotions. This helps you relate to the content of your mind differently, so you can deal with it more objectively instead of feeling controlled by it.

devekut   A Jewish term meaning "cleaving to the Divine," referring either to the practice of holding God's presence in your mind at all times, or to the transcendent experience of your closeness to God.

dhikr   Remembrance of God, referring both to a meditative practice and to a state of mind. As a practice, it usually involves the recitation of names of God.

dukkha   Sometimes translated as "dissatisfaction" or "suffering," a Buddhist term referring to the extra distress you add to your experience when you resist the reality of this moment and wish things were different.

fitra   An Islamic term meaning "nature" or "instinct." In Sufism, it refers to your original, pure nature, which is inclined toward goodness and oriented toward God.

guru   A qualified spiritual teacher with whom you've established a committed teacher-student relationship.

half-lotus position   A crossed-legged meditation posture in which you rest only one of your feet on the opposite thigh.

Hasidism   A movement within Judaism that gained popularity in the 1700s and continues to this day, tending to emphasize the immanent divine in all things, the value of piety and fervor in all activities, and reverence for spiritual leaders who are considered to be especially righteous and spiritually powerful.

Hatha Yoga   One type of practice within the Yoga tradition that involves moving your body through a series of traditional postures.

hesychasm   The Eastern Orthodox Christian contemplative practice of internal silence and continual prayer. It's done with the eyes closed and the mind empty of thoughts but receptive to the presence of God.

Kabbalah   A set of teachings and practices about the relationship between the divine and the everyday world. Kabbalah has traditionally been practiced within the context of various Jewish traditions and doesn't constitute a sect or school in and of itself.

kavanah   A Jewish term referring to directing your consciousness in a deliberate, focused, and devotional way.

koans   Traditional stories of interactions between Zen teachers and their students that are meant to convey an important aspect of Zen teaching.

Kriya Yoga   A particular form of Yoga meditation taught by Paramahansa Yogananda. *Kriya* means "action" or "rite," and *Yoga* refers to union or connection with the Infinite. So Kriya Yoga is bringing about this union through an active process.

lama   The Vajrayana Buddhist term for someone who has been empowered to teach Vajrayana, including the tantras, and to function as a guru in the student-teacher relationship.

Lectio Divina   A Latin term that means "divine reading." It dates back to monastic practices in the fifth century and involves contemplative reading of, reflecting on, responding to, and resting in a passage of scripture, as if you're in a conversation with Christ. The practice of Lectio Divina complements and supports contemplative prayer.

lineage   A spiritual tradition passed from teacher to student through the generations. Lineage is emphasized in spiritual traditions in which someone's practice or realization has to develop to a certain level—and to be confirmed as sufficient by an existing teacher—before he can teach the tradition himself.

lotus position   A meditation posture in which you sit cross-legged on the floor or a small cushion, and rest the outsides of your feet on your thighs.

mantra   A syllable or series of syllables recited silently or audibly for positive spiritual effect. Mantras are usually based on ancient Sanskrit syllables and have accepted meanings and effects, but are rarely translatable.

Medicine Man or **Woman**   A term sometimes used for Native American spiritual experts, teachers, or healers who undergo extensive apprenticeship training and are tested before they're allowed to practice independently. Their special responsibility is learning and performing the esoteric aspects of a spiritual tradition so they can perform important ceremonial functions.

meditation   A practice of deliberately directing your mind in a particular way for a period of time, for the purpose of affecting the mind itself—either your mental or emotional experience, or the way you relate to or use your mind.

nafs   An Arabic word for "self," "ego," or "soul." In Sufism, the word tends to refer in particular to the lower aspects of self that keep you separated from God.

neuroplasticity   Changes in the synaptic connections and neural pathways in the brain in response to your experiences, what you think and feel, how you use your mind, or injury. The discovery of neuroplasticity contrasts with the now-outdated view of the adult brain as being more or less fixed in its structure and function.

psychophysiological state   A replicable, identifiable state that has typical psychological characteristics as well as physiological ones—in other words, the mental and physical characteristics tend to happen together.

Qi   A Chinese term that refers to the vital life force, energy, or "subtle breath" that flows through the human body, as well as through all of creation.

Qur'an   The holy book of Islam, believed to have been revealed by God to his prophet Muhammad and to contain God's definitive teaching and instructions.

Rabbi   A Jewish teacher sufficiently educated in Jewish law and practice to guide a Jewish community.

Rig Veda   An ancient Indian religious text (*Veda* means "knowledge"), dating from as far back as 1500 B.C.E., that formed the basis of the Vedic tradition of religious practice in India.

Rinzai   A sect of Zen Buddhism that often employs contemplation of koans in meditation.

Seon   The Korean term for the meditation-focused Buddhist school called *Zen* in Japan.

Shabbat   The Jewish day of rest and renewal during which all productive work is set aside. Shabbat is observed from sunset on Friday until slightly after sunset on Saturday.

shakyo   A Japanese Buddhist tradition of tracing Buddhist scriptures, in which a beautifully calligraphed version of the scripture, or *sutra,* is traced reverently and meditatively on a thin piece of fine paper.

sharia   Islamic law—a set of rules carefully derived from the Qur'an and other important Islamic scriptures—governing the public, private, religious, and secular lives of a Muslim.

shaykh   An Islamic term meaning "leader." Within Sufism, the head of a tariqa is often referred to as a shaykh.

Shema   A very old, traditional Jewish prayer recited at least twice a day. The first line, "Sh'ma Yisraeil, Adonai Eloheinu, Adonai Echad," is often a focus of special concentration and devotion and can be translated as "Listen, Israel: the Lord our God, the Lord is One."

shikantaza   A kind of Zen meditation known as themeless meditation or "just precisely sitting."

Soto   A school of Zen Buddhism that's the largest sect of Zen in Japan and traditionally employs themeless meditation.

Talmud   An ancient book of commentary on and interpretation of the Torah. It's also widely revered and relied upon in Judaism.

tantra   At the most basic level, an instruction manual. In religious contexts, it refers to texts containing teachings, rituals, and practices that are considered esoteric, or difficult to understand, and therefore taught to a limited number of people.

Tao   A Chinese Taoist term sometimes translated as "way" or "path," it refers to natural order of the universe, as well as to the path of perceiving and living in accord with that order.

tariqa   A Sufi order, doctrine, or path. Tariqas trace their lineage back to a highly realized founding teacher who established the particular practices and emphases of the order.

Theravada   Literally the "way of the elders," the most traditional school of Buddhism. It's practiced primarily in Southeast Asia and is the source of modern Insight Meditation.

Thiên   The Vietnamese term for the meditation-focused Buddhist school called *Zen* in Japan.

tikkun olam   A Hebrew term meaning "world repair," it refers to a Jewish responsibility to fix what's wrong with the world.

Torah   The most sacred scripture in Judaism, traditionally viewed by Jews as being the word of God as communicated directly to the prophet Moses over 3,000 years ago.

Trinity   The Christian view of God as consisting of three people: God the father (ineffable, omniscient, and omnipresent), Jesus Christ (the son of God, who was born as a human, died, and was resurrected), and the Holy Spirit (the invisible spirit of truth, sent by God to abide in the world).

Upanishads   The most recent part of the Vedic literature, consisting of a number of texts composed somewhere between 800 B.C.E. and the beginning of the Common Era.

Vipassana   A Buddhist term meaning "insight" or "clear-seeing," it refers both to a method of meditation and a movement within Buddhism that employs that method.

zazen   Created out of the Japanese characters *za* (meaning "seated") and *zen* (meaning "meditation"), it simply refers to seated Zen meditation.

Zen   The meditation-focused Buddhist school that arose in China as Ch'an.

Resources

In this appendix, you'll find a list of the resources cited in this volume, including those mentioned in the "Learning More" sections associated with each style of meditation.

Articles

Brewer, Judson A., Patrick D. Worhunsky, Jeremy R. Gray, Yi-Yuan Tang, Jochen Weber, and Hedy Kober. Meditation experience is associated with differences in default mode network activity and connectivity. *Proceedings of the National Academy of Sciences,* Volume 108, Number 50, pages 20254–20259, December 2011.

Hasenkamp, Wendy, Christine D. Wilson-Mendenhall, Erica Duncan, and Lawrence W. Barsalou. Mind wandering and attention during focused meditation: A fine-grained temporal analysis of fluctuating cognitive states. *NeuroImage,* Volume 59, pages 750–760, 2012.

Hofmann, Stefan G., Alice T. Sawyer, Ashley A. Witt, and Diana Oh. The Effect of Mindfulness-Based Therapy on Anxiety and Depression: A Meta-Analytic Review. *Journal of Consulting and Clinical Psychology,* American Psychological Association, Volume 78, Number 2, pages 169–183, 2010.

Kabat-Zinn, J., E. Wheeler, T. Light, A. Skillings, M. J. Scharf, T. G. Cropley, D. Hosmer, and J. D. Bernhard. Influence of a mindfulness meditation–based stress reduction intervention on rates of skin clearing in patients with moderate to severe psoriasis undergoing phototherapy (UVB) and photochemotherapy (PUVA). *Psychosomatic Medicine,* Volume 60, Number 5, pages 625–32, 1998.

Killingsworth, Matthew A., and Daniel T. Gilbert. A Wandering Mind Is an Unhappy Mind. *Science,* Volume 330, page 932, November 2010.

Kornfield, Jack. Theravada/Vipassana Practice. *Tricycle Magazine*, tricycle.com/new-buddhism/buddhism/theravada-vipassana-practice.

Pew Research Center. Global Christianity—A Report on the Size and Distribution of the World's Christian Population, December 19, 2011, pewforum.org/2011/12/19/global-christianity-exec/.

Pidgeon, Aileen, Klaire Lacota, and James Champion. The Moderating Effects of Mindfulness on Psychological Distress and Emotional Eating Behaviour. *Australian Psychologist*, Volume 48, Issue 4, pages 262–269, August 2013.

Prazak, Michael, Joseph Critelli, Luci Martin, Vanessa Miranda, Michael Purdum, and Catherine Powers. Mindfulness and its Role in Physical and Psychological Health. *Applied Psychology: Health and Well-Being*, Volume 4, Issue 1, pages 91–105, March 2012.

Reiner Keren, Lee Tibi, and Joshua D. Lipsitz. Do Mindfulness-Based Interventions Reduce Pain Intensity? A Critical Review of the Literature. *Pain Medicine*, Volume 14, Issue 2, pages 230–242, February 2013.

Rocha, Tomas. The Dark Knight of the Soul. *The Atlantic*, June 25, 2014. theatlantic.com/health/archive/2014/06/the-dark-knight-of-the-souls/372766/.

Rossano, Matt J. Did Meditating Make Us Human? *Cambridge Archaeological Journal*, Volume 17, pages 47–58, 2007.

Schwartz, Stephen. How Many Sufis Are There in Islam? HuffPost Religion, July 20, 2011. huffingtonpost.com/stephen-schwartz/how-many-sufis-in-world-i_b_902164.html.

Sheline, Yvette I., Deanna M. Barch, Joseph L. Price, Melissa M. Rundle, S. Neil Vaishnavi, Abraham Z. Snyder, Mark A. Mintun, Suzhi Wang, Rebecca S. Coalson, and Marcus E. Raichle. The default mode network and self-referential processes in depression. *Proceedings of the National Academy of Sciences*, Volume 106, Number 6, pages 1942–1947, February 2009.

Books

Al-Qushayri. *Principles of Sufism*. Trans. B. R. Von Schlegell. Berkeley, CA: Mizan Press, 1990.

Barks, Coleman, and Jalal al-Din Rumi. *The Essential Rumi—Reissue: New Expanded Edition*. New York, NY: HarperCollins, 2004.

Baumeister, Roy F., and John Tierney. *Willpower: Rediscovering Our Greatest Strength*. New York, NY: Penguin Press, 2011.

Bays, Jan Chozen. *How to Train a Wild Elephant: And Other Adventures in Mindfulness*. Boston, MA: Shambhala Publications, 2011.

Beck, Charlotte Joko. *Everyday Zen: Love and Work*. New York, NY: HarperCollins Publishers, 1989.

Benson, Herbert, MD. *The Relaxation Response*. New York, NY: HarperCollins, 1975.

Bokar, Rinpoche. *Chenrezig, Lord of Love: Principles and Methods of Deity Meditation*. San Francisco, CA: ClearPoint Press, 1991.

Bowers, Kenneth E. *God Speaks Again: An Introduction to the Bahai Faith*. Wilmette, IL: Baha'i Publishing, 2004.

Brown, Joseph Epes, with Emily Cousins. *Teaching Spirits: Understanding Native American Religious Traditions*. New York, NY: Oxford University Press, 2001.

Burk, Domyo. *Idiot's Guides: Zen Living*. New York, NY: Alpha Books, 2014.

Buswell, Robert E. Jr., and Donald S. Lopez Jr. *The Princeton Dictionary of Buddhism*. Princeton, NJ: Princeton University Press, 2014.

Chodron, Thubten. *Cultivating a Compassionate Heart: The Yoga Method of Chenrezig*. Ithaca, NY: Snow Lion Publications, 2005.

Cohen, Darlene. *The One Who Is Not Busy: Connecting with Work in a Deeply Satisfying Way*. Salt Lake City, UT: Gibbs Smith, 2004.

Cooper, David. *God Is a Verb: Kabbalah and the Practice of Mystical Judaism*. New York, NY: Riverhead Books, 1997.

Davis, Martha, Elizabeth Robbins Eshelman, and Matthew McKay. *The Relaxation and Stress Reduction Workbook*. Oakland, CA: New Harbinger Publications, 2008.

Forem, Jack. *Transcendental Meditation: The Essential Teachings of Maharishi Mahesh Yogi*. Carlsbad, CA: Hay House, 1973 (Revised edition copyright 2012).

Frager, Robert, and James Fadiman. *Essential Sufism*. San Francisco, CA: HarperSanFrancisco, 1997.

Frenette, David. *The Path of Centering Prayer: Deepening Your Experience of God*. Boulder, CO: Sounds True, 2012.

Fronsdal, Gil. *The Dhammapada: A New Translation of the Buddhist Classic with Annotations*. Boston, MA: Shambala Publications, 2012.

Gefen, Nan Fink. *Discovering Jewish Meditation: Instruction and Guidance for Learning an Ancient Spiritual Practice*. Woodstock, VT: Jewish Lights Publishing, 1999.

Gendlin, Eugene. *Focusing*. New York, NY: Bantam Books, 1978.

Goldstein, Joseph. *Insight Meditation: The Practice of Freedom*. Boston, MA: Shambala Publications, 1993.

Haleem, M. A. S. Abdel. *The Qur'an (Oxford World's Classics)*. New York, NY: Oxford University Press, 2004.

Hanh, Thich Nhat. *The Miracle of Mindfulness: An Introduction to the Practice of Meditation*. Boston, MA: Beacon Press, 1999.

———. *Peace Is Every Step: The Path of Mindfulness in Everyday Life*. New York, NY: Bantam Books, 1991.

———. *Walking Meditation*. Boulder, CO: Sounds True, 2006.

Hartranft, Chip. *The Yoga-Sutra of Patanjali: A New Translation with Commentary*. Boston, MA: Shambala Publications, 2003.

Holman Christian Standard Bible. *The Holy Bible: HCSB Digital Text Edition*. Nashville, TN: B & H Publishing Group, 2010.

Hughes, Stan E. *Medicine Seeker: A Beginner's Walk on the Pathway to Native American Spirituality*. Nashville, IN: NorLightsPress, 2010.

Javid, Ahmad, MD. *Sufi Light: The Secret of Meditation*. Bloomington, IN: Balboa Press, 2011.

Johnson, Willard. *Riding the Ox Home: A History of Meditation from Shamanism to Science*. Boston, MA: Beacon Press, 1987.

Keating, Thomas. *The Method of Centering Prayer (pamphlet)*. Butler, NJ: Contemplative Outreach, Ltd., 2006.

———. *Open Mind, Open Heart: The Contemplative Dimension of the Gospel*. New York, NY: The Continuum International Publishing Group, 1986.

Khan, Hazrat Inayat. *The Heart of Sufism: Essential Writings of Hazrat Inayat Khan*. Boston, MA: Shambala Publications, 1999.

Kornfield, Jack. *A Path with Heart: A Guide through the Perils and Promises of Spiritual Life*. New York, NY: Bantam Books, 1993.

Loori, John Daido, ed. *Sitting with Koans: Essential Writings on Zen Koan Introspection*. Somerville, MA: Wisdom Publications, 2006.

———. *The Zen of Creativity: Cultivating Your Artistic Life*. New York, NY: Ballantine Books, 2005.

Kabat-Zinn, Jon. *Mindfulness for Beginners*. Boulder, CO: Sounds True, 2012.

Kaplan, Aryeh. *Jewish Meditation: A Practical Guide*. New York, NY: Schocken Books, 1985.

Komjathy, Louis. *The Daoist Tradition: An Introduction*. New York, NY: Bloomsbury Academic, 2013.

McGaa, Ed (Eagle Man). *Mother Earth Spirituality: Native American Paths to Healing Ourselves and Our World*. New York, NY: Harpercollins, 1990.

Mipham, Sakyong. *Running with the Mind of Meditation: Lessons for Training Body and Mind.* New York, NY: Three Rivers Press, 2012.

Nies, Judith. *Native American History.* New York, NY: Ballantine Books, 1996.

Novak, Jyotish. *How to Meditate: A Step-by-step Guide to the Art and Science of Meditation.* Nevada City, CA: Crystal Clarity Publishers, 2008.

———. *Lessons in Meditation: Based on the Teachings of Paramahansa Yogananda and His Direct Disciple Swami Kriyananda.* Nevada City, CA: Crystal Clarity Publishers, 2009.

Powers, John. *A Concise Introduction to Tibetan Buddhism.* Ithaca, NY: Snow Lion Publications, 2008.

Punshon, John. *Encounter with Silence: Reflections from the Quaker Tradition.* Richmond, IN: Friends United Press, 1987.

Sadigh, Micah R. *Autogenic Training: A Mind-Body Approach to the Treatment of Chronic Pain Syndrome and Stress-Related Disorders.* Jefferson, NC: McFarland and Company, Inc., Publishers, 2012.

Saltoon, Diana. *Tea and Ceremony: Experiencing Tranquility.* Scappoose, OR: Robert Briggs Associates, 2004.

Sapolsky, Robert M. *Why Zebras Don't Get Ulcers: The Acclaimed Guide to Stress, Stress-Related Diseases, and Coping, Third Edition.* New York, NY: St. Martin's Griffin, 2004.

Schachter-Shalomi, Rabbi Zalman. *Sh'ma': A Concise Weekday Siddur For Praying in English.* Boulder, CO: Albion-Andalus, Inc., 2010.

Schwartz, Stephen. *The Other Islam: Sufism and the Road to Global Harmony.* New York, NY: Harmony Books (Crown Publishing Group), 2008.

Smith, Huston. *Why Religion Matters: The Fate of the Human Spirit in an Age of Disbelief.* New York, NY: HarperCollins, 2001.

Stahl, Bob, and Elisha Goldstein. *A Mindfulness-Based Stress Reduction Workbook.* Oakland, CA: New Harbinger Publications, 2010.

Stevens, John. *The Marathon Monks of Mount Hiei.* Brattleboro, VT: Echo Point Books, 2013.

Suzuki, Shunryu. *Zen Mind, Beginner's Mind.* New York, NY: Weatherhill, 1999.

Vaughan-Lee, Llewellyn. *Sufism: The Transformation of the Heart.* Point Reyes, CA: The Golden Sufi Center, 1995.

Vincent, Kristen E. *A Bead and a Prayer: A Beginner's Guide to Protestant Prayer Beads.* Nashville, TN: Upper Rooms Books, 2013.

Vivekananda, Swami. *Complete Works of Swami Vivekananda.* Calcutta, India: Advaita Ashrama, 1989.

Walters, J. Donald. *The Art and Science of Raja Yoga: Fourteen Steps to Higher Awareness.* Nevada City, CA: Crystal Clarity Publishers, 2002.

Weisman, Arinna, and Jean Smith. *The Beginner's Guide to Insight Meditation.* Somerville, MA: Wisdom Publications, 2010.

Yogananda, Paramahansa. *Man's Eternal Quest: Collected Talks and Essays on Realizing God in Daily Life.* Los Angeles, CA: Self-Realization Fellowship, 1982.

————. *Autobiography of a Yogi.* Los Angeles, CA: Self-Realization Fellowship, 1998 (Thirteenth Edition).

Websites

The following are the websites cited in this book, organized by meditative tradition. If a particular web address no longer works, type the name of the associated organization into a search engine to see if their web address has changed.

Baha'i

Bahá'í Faith: bahai.org

Bahá'ís of the United States: bahai.us

Christian Contemplative Prayer

Contemplative Outreach: contemplativeoutreach.org

World Community for Christian Meditation: wccm.org

Insight Meditation

Buddhist Insight Network: buddhistinsightnetwork.org

Insight Meditation Society: dharma.org

Spirit Rock—An Insight Meditation Center: spiritrock.org

Judaism

Awakened Heart Project for Contemplative Judaism: awakenedheartproject.org

Information on Jewish prayers and other resources: chabad.org

Jewish Virtual Library: jewishvirtuallibrary.org

Judaism 101: jewfaq.org

Mindfulness

Guided Mindfulness Meditation Practices with Jon Kabat-Zinn: mindfulnesscds.com

Massachusetts Medical School's Center for Mindfulness in Medicine, Health Care, and Society: umassmed.edu/cfm/

Mindful Schools: mindfulschools.org

Mindfulness-Based Stress Reduction Workbook website: mbsrworkbook.com

Palouse Mindfulness: palousemindfulness.com

Native American

Directory of Native American tribes: bia.gov/WhoWeAre/BIA/OIS/TribalGovernmentServices/TribalDirectory/index.htm

Native Languages of the Americas (and other resources): native-languages.org

Other Secular Techniques

Benson-Henry Institute for Mind Body Medicine: bensonhenryinstitute.org

British Autogenic Society: autogenic-therapy.org.uk

Focusing Institute: focusing.org

Quaker

Friends General Conference: fgcquaker.org

Quaker Information Center: quakerinfo.org

Sufism

List of Sufi orders in the West by adherence to Islam: islam.uga.edu/sufismwest.html

Naqshbandi Sufi Way: naqshbandi.org

Nimatullahi Sufi Order: nimatullahi.org

Shadhiliyya Sufi Communities: suficommunities.org

Sufi Order International: sufiorder.org

Taoism

Center for Daoist Studies: daoistcenter.org

Daoist Foundation: daoistfoundation.org

Daoist Studies: daoiststudies.org

Transcendental Meditation

Transcendental Meditation official site: tm.org

Vajrayana

Foundation for the Preservation of the Mahayana Tradition: fpmt.org

Kadampa Buddhism: kadampa.org

Kagyu Lineage: kagyu.org

Yoga

Ananda Sangha Worldwide: ananda.org

Self-Realization Fellowship: yogananda-srf.org

Zen

Soto Zen Buddhist Association: szba.org

Sweeping Zen: sweepingzen.com

Index

W-X

Y

Z

seismic shifts

Leading in Times of Change

by
Christopher White

UNITED CHURCH PUBLISHING HOUSE

Seismic Shifts
Leading in Times of Change
Christopher White

Copyright © 2006
The United Church of Canada
L'Église Unie du Canada

All biblical quotations, unless otherwise noted, are from the *New Revised Standard Version Bible*, copyright © 1989, by the Division of Christian Education of
the National Council of the Churches of Christ in the United States of America.
Used by permission.

Care has been taken to trace ownership of copyright material contained in this
text. The publisher will gratefully accept any information that will enable it to
rectify any reference or credit in subsequent printings.

National Library of Canada Catalogue in Publication Data

Library and Archives Canada Cataloguing in Publication

White, Christopher, 1956-
      Seismic shifts : leading in times of change / Christopher White.

Accompanied by a DVD.
Includes bibliographical references.
ISBN-13: 978-1-55134-150-7
ISBN-10: 1-55134-150-6

      1. Christian leadership. I. Title.

BV652.1.W48 2006   262'.1   C2006-902765-X

United Church Publishing House
3250 Bloor St. West, Suite 300
Toronto, ON
Canada M8X 2Y4
1-800-268-3781 or locally 416-231-5931
www.united-church.ca/ucph

Design: Carina Cruz Domingues, Graphics and Print
Cover: Design Pics, Lisa Rebnord

Printed in Canada
5   4   3   2   1   10 09 08 07 06   060023

Dedication

To Wendy and the two present and future leaders we brought into this world, Sarah and Elizabeth White.

And to the people of Westminster United Church in Whitby, Ontario, for their ongoing courage and commitment to faithfully living the Jesus life.

Contents

Preface

I WAS EXTREMELY GLAD to usher last year out the door. It was one of
the most difficult years of my life. Two sets of parents in hospital
who then had to be moved into retirement homes in the same
month; a daughter who had not one but two cardiac procedures;
a sister whose wedding, including a once-in-a-lifetime family
trip to Mexico, was levelled by a hurricane; followed by that
same sister facing emergency surgery. All this while ministering
in a congregation whose demands seem to grow exponentially
and trying to get a book and DVD ready for that fall. I had never
missed a deadline in my life, but I missed that one.

However, all of these experiences shaped this book and it is
richer because of it. When I started this project a couple of years
ago, I wanted to approach it as I had my previous books on the
church, with many interviews and a strong reliance on secondary
sources. But as I worked on it, the book became far more
personal. It grew out of the insights and experiences of almost
20 years in ministry. I suppose if I have a personal manifesto,
this is it.

The issue of leadership is critical at this moment in history.
We are experiencing some of the most seismic changes North
America has ever experienced, and at a rate unparalleled in
history. How we lead and which skills we develop are crucial
to all of our futures.

SEISMIC SHIFTS

All books are a collaboration and I want to thank everyone who spoke to me and who shared their wisdom and experiences. I also want to acknowledge the stellar support from the team at United Church Publishing House and Berkeley Studio.

My church, Westminster United in Whitby, Ontario, continues to be a place of inspiration and challenge and I thank them for their ongoing support, enthusiasm, and courage as we move forward together. In particular, I want to acknowledge the chair of my board, Crystal Smith, who over the past three years has had the unique and at times difficult challenges of leading a congregation in a new building.

I also wish to pay tribute to my good friend the Rev. Robert Thaler. Bob is a person whose life and faith are integrated into a seamless whole. He truly lives out in thought and action what he believes. Bob and his spouse, Ann, have built a life and a family that is Christian in the very best sense of the word.

Last and definitely not least, I could not do this without my supportive spouse, Wendy, who has the courage to read and then improve every manuscript I write. My daughters, Sarah and Elizabeth, have grown up through my writing and are very patient as they see me stare out into space as I think over a sermon or a passage from a book I am working on. Plus, they have converted me into a big fan of the bands Green Day and Yellow Card, whose song "Way Away" eloquently depicts the loneliness of a life without faith. Sarah and Elizabeth continue to be a huge joy in my life as I watch them slowly but surely turn into adults. It is their generation upon whom the mantle of leadership will soon fall and they will be extraordinary at it. The future can indeed be a place of hope.

Figuring It Out Fast

THE YEAR WAS 1987 and I had just been called to ministry in my very first pastoral charge, Springbank United Church, located just outside of Calgary, Alberta. We were still unpacking our boxes from a cross-country move when I attended my very first board meeting. It was a meeting I remember clearly to this day. While everyone looked to me as the minister, I kept looking around for my supervisor to answer their questions. Of course, I didn't have one. It hit me that evening: "Oh my gosh, it's all up to me. I'm on my own." That reality grew on me as the months unfolded—the realization that I was all alone. I would succeed or fail on my own; it was up to me to work with this congregation and try to build something of lasting value together.

In my first year, I was very fortunate to have as my neighbour the Rev. Doug Powell, a tremendous source of wisdom as I struggled through the currents and eddies of congregational life. But the feeling of being alone has stayed with me. Sadly, close to 20 years later, that feeling hasn't changed much. The structures and attitudes of The United Church of Canada create an institutional sense of isolation. I have been blessed with wonderful congregations, terrific colleagues, and great friends who continue to inspire me with their commitment and belief. But I had to learn how to lead on my own, and I had to figure it out fast.

I quickly realized that the models of facilitation and enabling that were held up as the ideal in both my seminary and my denomination would lead to failure in a real parish setting. People expected me to provide spiritual leadership in that church. I was seen as an authority and expected to act as such. So I taught myself leadership through trial and error—and there were plenty of each.

The congregation didn't have time for me to sit back, watch, and reflect over a period of years. Instead, they needed action and life, and they needed it quickly. The result, though not without mistakes, was five years of growth and learning. I worked hard, I loved them with all my heart, and they taught me so much. I feel the same way about Westminster United in Whitby, Ontario, where I have served as ordered minister since 1992. I can honestly say that the people of this congregation have been the best teachers of leadership that I could ever hope to find. This group continues to challenge me to think differently all the time.

With all of these experiences over the years, I can now comfortably say this: *I am a leader*. But it is not always easy to accept, and it is even harder to live out.

The expectations of leadership in my area of work are very confused right now. Over the past two decades, both society and church have moved from rigid, top-down hierarchies to what appeared to be completely egalitarian teams, and have found both wanting. We say we desperately need leaders, but are suspicious and distrustful when someone actually functions in that role. With these mixed messages, those who should function as leaders wear the mantle uneasily. At a time when books are written about Jesus and Moses as archetypical leaders whose examples the secular world should follow, it is ironic that in the church we shy away from those very characteristics that we so desperately need. Yet the challenges that face business, unions, the public service, and other non-profits are very similar. The pace of change is so rapid that it takes our breath away and leaves us running to catch up.

"The future belongs to the fast," one business leader told me recently. He pointed to Asia: at the incredible speed with which that continent is changing, we in North America are going to have to adapt quickly or lose the 21st century. So how do we cope in a time of endless transition? In a time that author Stephen Covey describes as "permanent white water"? How do we deal with a world in which technical expertise is outdated hourly and organizations that have thrived for decades now struggle to survive? How do we lead when we have no clear idea where we are going?

We face a clear choice, to be shaped by the events that are unfolding around us, or to help shape them. Shaping the events will take leadership—leadership that is not authoritarian, but that leads with authentic authority. It will take leadership that helps to create and bring about a vision that will evolve as it unfolds.

Adaptability, tenacity, courage, endurance, humour, tolerance for ambiguity, and the capacity to live in paradox are all needed as we move together into the ever-shifting present. We have to find a way to sprint the marathon, while at the same time rooting ourselves in the values that have withstood the tests of centuries. That is why this book has been written, to reflect upon the vocation of leadership, and to share the insights of other leaders as well as my own thoughts as a person who is still discovering what leadership truly means. My own experiences are as a pastoral leader in The United Church of Canada. But just as the challenges of religious leadership I face are affected by a rapidly shifting global dynamic, so too can the lessons I draw be applied by other leaders in their own contexts. This book invites you to share a journey that preoccupies people in all walks of life, a journey into the heart of authentic leadership.

CHAPTER 1

An Age of Change and Chaos

IF YOU WALK into the business section of any bookstore in the country, you will see rafts of books on leadership. There are parables about mice moving cheese, stories about paradigm-shifting fish markets, and books on how leadership can help you survive if you wind up on the crushing ice of Antarctica. There are how-to books, books on thinking differently and acting differently, books on how to go from "good to great," and even works extolling Jesus or Moses as model CEOs. Workshops and week-long courses are offered on personal mastery, all to answer a hunger for leadership.

But this hunger is not assuaged in spite of all the material that is being produced. Leadership appears to be one of the greatest issues facing us at the dawn of the 21st century. Why? What is missing in our culture that has created such a hunger for genuine, authentic leadership?

To begin, I believe that there is a political dynamic to this question. There is a feeling in our society that no matter who is elected to government, little changes. The same problems endure; the same reasons that things cannot be resolved are brought forward. After each election, the winners toss aside their platform with the same tired excuses: "We didn't know how bad it was" or "Those scoundrels we just threw out left us with a mess we never anticipated." Conversely, politicians act surprised as budget surpluses grow ever larger, resorting to dire warnings of future deficits to excuse their inaction. In Canada, we received the Gomery Report on widespread, systemic corruption in one of our largest political parties. It is no wonder that such a deeply rooted cynicism is directed at our political leadership.

This sense of distrust is reinforced by corporate scandals where companies close or collapse because of the malfeasance of their officers, or relocate overseas in search of lower employee costs. In the church, scandals of sexual impropriety among clergy and the ongoing legacy of the Indian Residential Schools experience make many people wonder who can be trusted any longer. Reinforced with an ingrained postmodern suspicion of authority, it all adds up to a toxic soup of distrust and suspicion.

Yet combined with this reality is a hunger: a hunger for leaders in whom we can invest our trust, for leaders who we genuinely feel have our best interests at heart. A hunger for leaders in whom we want to believe and who want to believe in us, who can communicate clearly, and who act with authority but not authoritarianism. In all sectors of our society, people both seek and want to be those leaders. So how do we as citizens—and as church—move forward into a different future? How can we create, nurture, and be leaders in a century where the pace of change is so rapid that it is becoming a cliché to even acknowledge that profound truth? Let us start this journey together with a look at our situation, on both a global and a local scale.

Global Opportunity; Global Divide

Jeremy Jones (a pseudonym), the Asian manager for a major computer company, has been based in the United States for the past eight years. With the responsibility for creating factories in the Asian market, Jones has watched the world change before his very eyes. "Manufacturing jobs are not coming back to North America. The cost differential is simply too great," he told me. For North America to maintain its standard of living, it is going to have to create "value-added work and new industries that are based not on labour but on creativity and value." Jones believes that in this new century, trade is going to raise all boats—in other words, that all economies stand to benefit from this growth. He believes that there will be huge opportunities to service the Asian economies and benefit locally from their growth, but not without the pain of readjustment. "We are," he asserts, "going to have to think and act differently." We are going to have to focus on meeting needs, not on winning arguments.

Jones tells this story to show the difference. Recently, in China, he was chairing a meeting and began to feel hungry. The meal break was still a while off, so Jones began devouring a bowl of chocolates that was on the table. After a brief, whispered conversation between staff assigned to care for the participants, food instantly appeared, not only for Jones, but for the whole table. The result was an extremely productive and happy meeting, rather than one filled with hungry, cranky people. They saw one person hungry, made the logical assumption that he was not the only one, and responded by creating a productive environment. They instantly identified the need and met it. That, Jones asserts, is happening all over Asia in all sectors of life. Identifying and meeting needs, be it in service or manufacturing, is driving whole economies.

These trends can be seen by anyone who travels or does business in Asia. If the Chinese government wants to enter an industry, it builds the factory itself and then turns the keys over to the consortium that will run it. Asian governments are investing strategically to create work and opportunity.

In his book *The World Is Flat, New York Times* columnist Thomas Friedman asserts that the earth has become so economically interconnected by technology that opportunity has become open to almost everyone on the planet. He calls this phenomenon "globalization 3.0," writing that it has led to a newfound power for individuals to collaborate and compete globally:

> The lever that is enabling individuals and groups to go global so easily and seamlessly is not horsepower, and not hardware but software.... Globalization 3.0 makes it possible for so many people to plug and play, and you are going to see every colour of the human rainbow take part.[1]

In Friedman's view, the collapse of the Berlin Wall, the creation of the Internet, the invention and wide distribution of fibre optic cable, and the open sourcing of software have combined

---

1 From *The World Is Flat: A Brief History of the Twenty-first Century* by Thomas L. Friedman (New York: Farrar, Straus and Giroux , 2005), pp. 10–11. Reprinted with permission.

to create a critical mass of economic opportunity for this planet. Exponential change is occurring all around us; the world has caught up to North America.

With this pace of change, the future may indeed belong to the fast. But will it also belong to the wise? The demand for speed is having a deleterious effect upon our capacity to respond intelligently. A recent study by the University of London cited in the *Toronto Star* showed that text messaging and e-mailing dropped the IQ of men 15 points and women five points, the equivalent of losing a night's sleep. Yet I must acknowledge the blessing of technology as well as the curse.[2] For example, while I wrote the above paragraph I remembered the story on e-mail and text messaging. I simply entered "e-mail makes me stupid" into a search engine on my computer, found the article, printed it out, and voila! In less than a minute, I had the figures I needed.

At the same time, a tremendous gap has developed within our global society between those with technology and those without. This applies to the capacity to afford hardware and software, but also to having the physical infrastructure that makes such technology possible. The world is facing a digital divide, an economic divide, and an infrastructure divide. Even within emerging economies, there are growing divides between those who have access to opportunity and those who do not. While China booms in selected greater urban areas, there is tremendous poverty in the rural communities—a significant gap that is also reflected elsewhere worldwide. Friedman's "globalization 3.0" is only experienced in portions of the world. The impact of the

---

2 Sharda Prashad, "Text Messaging, Emails Not So GR8, Study Finds," *Toronto Star*, April 23, 2005.

AIDS epidemic continues to be felt disproportionately in the global South, especially in parts of Africa. And the ravages of war and terrorism have claimed a worldwide reach.

In her book *50 Facts That Should Change the World*, the BBC's Jessica Williams points out that 70 percent of the world has not yet even heard a dial tone, that one in five people who share this planet with us live on less than a dollar a day, and that the European Union spends $2.50 a day per cow subsidizing their dairy farmers, which is more than 75 percent of people living in African countries have to live on. For one other contrast, imagine Tiger Woods—who earns a cool $148 per second. Think how much he has earned since you started reading this chapter!

A Crisis of Meaning

The constant demands to change and adapt are reducing our capacity to respond. People are not designed physically, emotionally, or even spiritually to deal with the overwhelming pace of change, and the growing rates of clinical depression are a testament to this. Nancy Hopgood, a counsellor who specializes on matters of stress, has a practice largely made up of people in the helping professions. Hopgood is increasingly seeing the impact of this pace of change: "We have created a culture of huge expectations and the belief that we can control everything. We have no preparations for the disappointments and flaws of everyday life. We suffer from magical thinking that there are simple answers to complex questions. We have become so goal-oriented that we have forgotten all about the process. We use 'stuff' to compensate for the empty place inside. All of us need to ask: What are the core beliefs that drive us?"

This point is reinforced in Heather Menzies' book *No Time, Stress and the Crisis of Modern Life*. Menzies makes a compelling case that the pace of life today causes stress on our children and our relationships and creates both chronic fatigue and workaholism. She further believes that our way of life both distracts and disconnects us from our society, leading to an incapacity to act collectively. We are, Menzies states, experiencing a crisis of meaning.

Volatility and crisis are apparent on a national level, too. In Canada, the power and economic base has for generations been located in its manufacturing heart. Our national political and economic debate was long shaped by the Ontario–Quebec axis, but it is now shifting west. British Columbia, as the gateway to the Pacific rim, and Alberta, with its enormous supplies of oil and natural gas, are becoming the new political/economic axis. The increase in the price of oil and the insecurity of world supply have caused tremendous growth, unprecedented prosperity, and even a shortage of skilled workers in Alberta. British Columbia, which is also experiencing economic strength, believes that the 2010 Olympics will catapult it into a new position of economic strength and influence. We are divided in Canada not only into east and west but also into rural and urban—perhaps the new "two solitudes" of our nation—and it could be interesting to watch our country redefine itself over the next decade.

At the 2006 Detroit Auto Show, a Chinese-made car designed for the North American market was unveiled. Its arrival should chill the blood of anyone whose livelihood is tied to this industry here. I live in a community where General Motors has been the primary provider of work and opportunity. You could graduate with a high school diploma, get a job working on the line, and be set for life. Yet now those jobs are disappearing: a major shift in one plant has been cancelled and another whole plant is scheduled for closure in 2008. This is a devastating loss of well-paying jobs, with benefits and pensions, that will not be replaced. Because of the scarcity of these positions, many people commute two-and-a-half hours from St. Catharines, Ontario, to GM Oshawa every day. Folks from St. Therese, Quebec, live in Oshawa during the week and drive home for the weekend. Why? For the precious and increasingly rare GM job.

In the Niagara region of Ontario, manufacturing jobs are vanishing to be replaced with call centre jobs at half the hourly rate. The situation of General Motors is not unique: the Ford Motor Company has announced a massive restructuring with the loss of thousands of jobs, and John Deere and Michelin Tires just closed manufacturing plants eliminating 1,400 well-paying jobs. According to a recent Statistics Canada report, Ontario has lost more than 60,000 manufacturing jobs in the last three years.

As I write this, Hurricane Katrina has just ravaged New Orleans and Hurricane Rita is heading to Texas. From yesterday at lunch to late last night, gas stations were jammed with people in a panic that gas was going to skyrocket in price or run out. Cars spilled out onto the roads, traffic snarled, and a fight that broke out in one station in Toronto sent people to hospital. Yet that was nothing compared to the catastrophe that unfolded in New Orleans, the most fundamental failure of leadership I have witnessed in my lifetime. The line that divides civilization from chaos is exceedingly thin.

Meanwhile, our very world view is being challenged by developments in other disciplines. The Rev. Robert Dalgleish,

who works on congregational development in the General
Council Office of The United Church of Canada, is currently
pursuing his doctorate on the new science and its impact on
faith. He tells me the story of an experiment conducted to study
the properties of electrons and resolve a long-standing debate
as to whether electrons were particles or waves. In testing them,
scientists made a remarkable discovery—the scientists were in
fact in conversation with the electrons. When they tested them
as particles they came across as particles. But then, when they
tested them as waves, they became waves. Who knows what they
became when they turned their machines off? In effect, what the
electrons became depended on a kind of responsiveness to what
the scientists were measuring.

This is quite remarkable as it shows the unbelievable power of
life and energy. Although this experiment was conducted half
a century ago, we are only beginning to see its implications.
We can no longer talk about neutral observation—the very
act of observation has an impact upon what is observed. Life
is not empirical study; life is conversation and community.
But do we have to redefine life? Does an electron have its own
form of consciousness? Are our ideas of God and what God
can or cannot do limited by an outmoded world view? I don't
know, but this strikes me as among the most critical theological
conversations that we have ever had.

The Challenge to the Church

As The United Church of Canada begins its ninth decade, it
is fair to observe that the denomination finds itself in a time
of both crisis and opportunity. Unless we are prepared to deal

13

with the crisis, however, the opportunity will slip through our fingers and we will continue to drift to the margins of society. I believe that it is time to initiate a new conversation, to ask some different questions than we have traditionally raised. What is the role of the church in a world whose axis is shifting, where the age of the American Empire is coming to an end? How do we help a society adapt to rapidly changing contexts, to jobs that are constantly evolving or disappearing? What does it mean to support congregants responding to the stresses of a just-in-time delivery world, and of an era in which they will be required to constantly retrain and reinvent themselves? What institutional pressures do these new realities bring to church administrators? How will we respond to a society mired in debt if a 1980s-style spike in interest rates is accompanied by a return to a 1970s style of inflation? How will we function in a world where there is a danger of an increasing divide based upon education and opportunity? How shall we lead?

In a *Toronto Star* article, David Haskell points out an alarming reality: in 1925 the United Church had 600,000 members; in 2005, while Canada's population had more than tripled, we were on the verge of dropping below that number.[3] While one could quibble with the issue of membership numbers versus participants (a more accurate measurement in my view), there is no question that the United Church is at a crossroads. Either we find new ways to connect to our society or we will fade into irrelevance as a historical curiosity of the 20th century. To explain our decline, Haskell cites the work of American sociologist Rodney Stark, who says that when a faith group—like

---

3 David Haskell, "Easy going Church Turns 80," *Toronto Star*, August 20, 2005, p. L11.

the United Church—positions itself as just one path of many available to a spiritual seeker, it's like a company endorsing the competitor's product because it's just as good.

Haskell writes that faith communities that combine high demands and clarity of purpose are the ones that will grow. This was reinforced by an article in *The Globe and Mail,* in which Alexandra Shimo wrote about two fast-growing multi-ethnic congregations in the Greater Toronto Area.[4] Although incredibly diverse, these charismatic congregations have a personality-driven leadership style and proclaim a fundamentalist theology that would make many United Church members uneasy. But they are meeting the real needs of their growing congregations, feeding the poor, creating street outreach networks, court intervention groups, and schools, and they are even looking at entering banking. These churches have clear beliefs and offer certainty rather than ambiguity. Their theology and practice provide a way of both seeing and living in our world of confusion.

The challenge before the United Church is significant: Can we provide for Canadians a theology and practice that proclaims our values? Can we communicate our theology in all of its diversity and a way of living that helps to navigate our troubled world? Can we lead not in certainties, but through a "clear ambiguity," a place where questions and doubts are not only valued but honoured? And can we be honest enough to recognize the depth of the challenge and the need for ways to lead that go beyond our existing models?

---

4 Alexandra Shimo, "A Gilded Stairway to Heaven," *The Globe and Mail,* August 15, 2005, pp. M1, M5.

SEISMIC SHIFTS

There are two stories happening in North American churches right now. One story is typified by the 16,000-seat arena that a church in Texas just bought and refurbished as its new worship centre. But that is not the United Church's story. The other story is the emergence of high-commitment mainstream congregations that are thriving—even growing—in spite of the gloomy statistics. This includes congregations like All Saints Anglican in Pasadena, a church that Robert Putnam cites in his most recent book *Better Together*. All Saints blends the ritual and tradition of Episcopalianism with political and theological liberalism, radical inclusiveness, and a welcome of ambiguity. The result is a growing, thriving congregation. All Saints' story could and should be the United Church's story. But getting there will require a significant shift.

Churches have a tendency to use the search for meaning as their primary paradigm for responding to the questions humans wrestle with. But I no longer believe that people are only looking for meaning. Rather, they are looking to have a deep experience of life. John Killinger puts it well when he writes in *God, the Devil and Harry Potter* that although people say they are looking for the meaning of life, they are really looking for a deep, numinous experience of life. The challenge to religious leaders is to provide a quality of experience within our congregations that is awe inspiring and life transforming. It is a huge challenge, one worthy of a people called by God to life.

A national United Church official recently told me that we have 10 years to turn things around. He was, I believe, being optimistic. The turnaround needs to start right now—a decade is a luxury we do not have. One of my favourite passages in the Bible comes from the book of Deuteronomy (30:11): "I have set before you life and death, blessings and curses. Choose life so that you and your descendants may live." That is the choice before The United Church of Canada: to choose life, to embrace leadership, or to waste what has been entrusted to us since 1925. Let us learn together what choosing life means. Let us learn to lead not with power, but with authority.

CHAPTER 2

Fixing Our Broken Windows

ONE OF MY FAVOURITE PASTIMES is sitting down with fellow clergy over a beer late at night after one of those United Church "all-day specials." You may know the type of denominational gathering: it starts between 8:30 or 9:00 a.m. and goes straight through until 9:00 p.m. with only the odd break here or there. It's as though, if we are justified by our works as St. Paul says, it is somehow faithful to work ourselves to death. But at the end of the day, eyes drooping, bodies stiff from sitting for long hours, a few brave souls always make their way to a local watering hole and once there, revive like plants receiving rain after a drought.

After about 30 minutes, the guard drops and the real stories start to come out. Stories of struggle, of setback, of the family you poured your life into to get them through a crisis, only to have them leave the church for the most trivial of reasons. Or of the program you were sure would relaunch the congregation's mission only to have you and the chair of the board be the only ones who showed up. Or of the sermon you preached that dropped like a rock just on the other side of the pulpit, and the shame you felt as you faced the congregation at the door as the church emptied. As these stories are told, heads nod and tight smiles are exchanged—all of us have been there, all of us have shared those experiences. Inside, our hearts lighten as we think, "Thank God, I'm not alone. I know exactly what that's like." There are other stories, too—stories of events or ministry that actually worked beyond expectations—and so we exchange business cards and write notes on napkins, followed by phone calls and e-mails the following week.

But at the heart of all of these stories is a question—the question of purpose and religious leadership. I have lost count of the number of colleagues who have told me that they are no longer sure what it is that they are to do. What does it mean to be church in the 21st century? What does it mean to be clergy? The answer is simple: *we do not know*.

The world is shifting so fast that everyone in every sector of society is struggling just to keep up, let alone get ahead of the waves that are engulfing us. Yet if the Irish monasteries saved civilization through the Dark Ages, surely, in today's age of change and chaos, the church can lead by playing a distinctive role. I propose four *C*s for leadership in today's culture: Civility, Community, Conflict Resolution, and the Crucified One.

The Four *C*s of Leadership

Civility

Civility is fast becoming a lost art. Our culture tells us that everything is all about us—about our needs, our wants, and our desires—and that we deserve to have them met, not just immediately but before they are even fully realized. Society is increasingly based not upon gratitude, but instead upon a sense of aggrieved entitlement. True maturity requires the capacity to integrate deferred gratification into our identity. This allows us to plan and at times sacrifice for the future well-being of ourselves, our families, and our community. Instead, we are bombarded by mail from credit card companies and other financial institutions that insist that not only can we have it all now, we deserve it.

A few weeks ago, I received a phone call from my bank giving me the good news that I had been approved for a line of credit for $15,000. I had never applied for that credit, I did not want that credit, but it was sitting there waiting for me—all I had to do was sign on the dotted line. No questions asked about whether I should add that potential debt to my life, no time spent in even meeting with me to develop a financial plan for our family, just a phone call offering me "free money." The banker was shocked and mildly insulted when I started laughing in the middle of her pitch. And then there are the ubiquitous "don't pay a cent" offers for every consumer item imaginable, which go one further than my bank. This scheme gives you the illusion of free washers, dryers, fridges, stoves, furniture—get them now and don't pay for a year, two years, or possibly in the minds of many citizens, ever. But all bills become due.

My eldest daughter is an actor and as I have gone with her to various auditions for film, television, and commercials, I have been struck by the sheer level of effort and complexity that goes into creating 30 seconds of television. The resources invested are enormous and in some cases quite brilliant. We are exposed to a continual stream of the best and the brightest framing the societal conversation around acquisition and creating the need for "more stuff." The problem is that it develops envy and resentment within our society—envy for those who have all the toys and resentment toward them when we do not. Much of consumer culture is based upon coveting the bright and shiny and building a base of anger among those who have no opportunity to participate in the bonanza. This envy and resentment are antithetical to civility.

From road rage to the loss of respect for authority figures (including faith leaders), distrust and an under-the-surface anger seem to permeate much of our world. Civility is a critical component of a healthy society. It allows complex interrelationships to flourish; it provides a process whereby differences can be mediated and potential conflicts negated. Christian civility is based upon the assumption that all people are created in the image of God and as such are worthy of respect. Civility requires that we listen to our neighbours, truly hear our neighbours, and in biblical terms love our neighbours—their hopes and dreams—as we love ourselves. Leading by exercising the ministry of civility is a gift to our churches, our children, and our communities. In an era of increasing dislocation, the art of civility is actually rising in importance as a basic skill to be developed for a healthy society.

Community

In my suburban neighbourhood, one of the most interesting, transformational changes that I have seen in recent years is the reintroduction of the front porch. Residents have become visible, people gather in the evening, and the sounds of conversation and laughter permeate the air, instead of only the sounds of cars driving down the street. The porch opens up the neighbourhood and makes it feel safer. Faces become more familiar; relationships are built. A street formerly filled with nothing but closed garages is evolving into a community.

Community is, I believe, one of the most misunderstood terms in our lexicon. The term often gets appropriated by interest groups and Internet users, but it is more intimate than that. True community is the gathering of multiple generations with differing perspectives, bound together by something bigger than themselves. The bond of community is so deep that it allows individuals to transcend difference, resolve conflict, live in tension, and focus on the meaning and mission of the community. Churches at their best are such a community; at their worst they are caricatures of it.

The gift of a church community is that it models the best of what it is to be human. It lives out caring for the other; it shows faith and resolve in the midst of setback and heartbreak. Church community demonstrates to our children how to live a balanced life based upon values that transcend culture and are focused upon joyful responsibility. It allows the gifts of the young, middle-aged, and old to be valued and cherished. It provides identity and belonging in a world where, as contemporary church writer Len Sweet says, "I have a deeper relationship with my credit card company than with my neighbour three doors down."

How do churches become front porches to our communities, instead of closed garages? Visibility is important. It's easier in a new church building: when Westminster United Church was rebuilt, we were able to introduce floor-to-ceiling glass windows so that people can see into the narthex. I have often said that most people driving by a church have no idea what goes on in the building, but wouldn't be surprised if we were holding eight-hour raves starting at midnight!

Creating front porches means inviting the community in and keeping the doors open. For example, this Advent, Westminster is hosting a community carol sing in December. Using ads and flyers, we are inviting the community to join us to sing Christmas carols on a Sunday afternoon. We'll have our choir and instrumentalists, and share the stories behind the creation of much-loved carols, both sacred and secular. Another "front porch opportunity" is a blessing of the animals service. These are extremely popular and provide direct outreach to the community by bringing in the Humane Society, vets, and animal lovers. By exploring non-threatening ways to invite people in, churches can create opportunities to grow their congregations—and also have a lot of fun. People can be very skittish about church. They can be cautious and sometimes wounded by past experiences. Front porch opportunities are gentle ways of sharing who and what we are.

Personally, I believe in the value of my church community. I believe completely and without reservation that the human experience is enriched and deepened by being part of a worshipping community. I know this to be true because, with all of its flaws, I experience it every day. In a week's time, my daughter Elizabeth is due to undergo a revolutionary cardiac procedure at Toronto's Hospital for Sick Children. On that morning, at 7:00 a.m. our church will be open, and people will arrive to walk the labyrinth and pray for my daughter. I have now lost count of the number of times I have sat in that hospital waiting room, living in fear until the doctor comes out. In each of these times, my family has been held up in prayer. Unless you have experienced something similar, you have no idea how much difference that community presence can make in a family's life. In the church, my daughters have a place of support, a place to both grieve and celebrate, but more importantly, a place where they can be their authentic selves. That is what true Christian community allows—authenticity of the person, grounded in an identity framed by God, informed by the stories of Jesus.

Conflict Resolution

From family to work, to friends, neighbours, and church, conflict is unavoidable. Conflict is a part of life, and it is not in itself bad. A world of uniform agreement would be very boring. The challenge for church leaders is to show how a Christian people resolve conflict appropriately. Two excellent resources on handling conflict within both organizations and families are Kerry Patterson's *Crucial Conversations* and *Crucial Confrontations*. They should be required reading for all involved in church work right now.

The challenge leaders face in the church when it comes to conflict is that we seem to veer between extremes. One extreme is founded in an inherent belief in "niceness" as the primary Christian virtue to protect at all costs. Thus, if a congregation has a person in it who is disruptive and causing problems for leaders at all levels, enormous amounts of energy are expended in coddling or trying to work around that individual. Instead of having the courage to address the person head-on while the issues are still small, leaders often let things build and build into a serious problem.

We fail as congregational leaders to use our own authority.
For clergy, it is difficult to function in that role. In The United
Church of Canada, the reality is that clergy feel alone. We feel we
do not have the support of our denominational bodies, so any
time clergy try to intervene with a difficult person we could be
putting our jobs on the line. Nobody wants to do that, so rather
than having the difficult conversations, there is a tendency to
hope that things will just get better on their own. I believe that
the current movement to unionize clergy in The United Church
of Canada, although a simple response to a complex problem,
is largely driven by an institutional failure to support ministers
who are dealing with conflict. This lack of support explains why
most clergy are allergic to confrontation. We like to keep people
happy; we like to keep churches happy. It's as though we have
been turned into ecclesiastical cruise directors. Until we solve the
underlying structural weaknesses of church governance, church
leaders will continue to fail at handling conflict.

Having had my share of difficult conversations and
confrontations, I've developed a few rules that I do my best to
apply (see box). If we learn to live out the ministry of Jesus in
the way we deal with conflict, we offer an important service to
our communities. Our communities will learn that the Christian
faith has relevance beyond Sunday morning and see that we have
the capacity to not only talk the talk, but walk the walk. If we
walk away from a conflict that does not go our way, the message
we send is huge.

Seven Rules for Dealing with Conflict

1. *Deal with conflict while it is still small.* Don't procrastinate. Deal with it within the week that you hear about it. Because if you are hearing about it, so are others.

2. *Refuse to play "he said, she said."* Get both parties in the same room as soon as possible. While hearing from each side can be helpful, the two parties will want you on their side and may even assume that since they told you, you support their position. Getting the two sides together immediately increases the chances of resolution.

3. *Banish e-mail.* There is no greater way to escalate a conflict than with e-mail. People react rather than reflect, and the temptation to hit Send after writing an injudicious, emotional response is overwhelming. When you receive one of these, your own blood pressure goes up and in an instant you've sent your own missile out into cyberspace. E-mail should be used only to communicate basic information such as meeting times. Content should be saved for face-to-face meetings.

4. *Don't deal with it on your own.* While the initial meeting in a conflict situation may be best dealt with in a face-to-face meeting, other supports—in the United Church, your board chair or Ministry and Personnel Committee—need to be familiar with the situation going in. Otherwise, you put yourself in a vulnerable situation. It may also be appropriate to have one of these people attend meetings with you if you feel the need for a witness or support. It is also important to have someone with whom you can consult about your strategy and what you are planning to say to make sure that you are responding appropriately.

continued

5. *Document, document, document.* Sad to say, but we live in a litigious society. Any time you are in a conflict situation, you need to keep notes and type up memos documenting what happened. It is important to have notes to refer to if the conflict is not easily resolved and requires multiple meetings. You cannot depend upon your memory.

6. *Depersonalize it.* One of the greatest challenges church leaders face is not to take conflict personally. Church is intimate and personal; it deals with issues of the spirit that go to the core of who we are as human beings. Therefore, when we face conflict or disagreement, we can take it very much to heart. In order to deal with conflict effectively, we need to cultivate the skill that allows us to view the whole situation as an observer—watching others' responses dispassionately, not getting our own backs up, avoiding the need to counterpunch or get caught in an emotional vortex. By doing that we are freed from the emotional baggage that gets in our way and blocks us from effective, creative resolution. Staying calm in the midst of crisis is one of the most important disciplines we can exercise.

7. *Pray.* I'm a huge believer in the power of prayer, both as preparation for a meeting and once you are in it. Prayer strengthens us spiritually and gets us in touch with the holy. There are physical results as well: blood pressure drops, bodily tension eases, and we are more able to enter into the moment. Effective prayer changes the spirit of a meeting, allowing appropriate focus and reducing the pressure between people. It reinforces our identity as people of God, reminding us of who we are and how we are to behave. Prayer is a critical component of Christian conflict resolution.

The Crucified One

In a society without a central narrative that binds us together, having a story that roots us is so important to our identity. The stories of Jesus—his ministry, death, and resurrection—provide the Christian community with that identity. We live within these stories and they become part of who we are. Equally, Christian ministry is formed in relationship to these stories. We are to be the prodigal's father and the woman who reaches out in faith to touch Jesus.

Without these narratives as the core of our identity, the church becomes nothing but a mildly inefficient charity. Our stories are the food we share. In relationships with the public, there is no need for the church to focus on converting others to belief: Jesus is present in our outreach, education, mission, and interfaith relationships. Our vocation is to live the Jesus life—a life of passion, compassion, integrity, daring, and risk.

Jesus continues to be of intense interest to our wider culture. From novels to movies to scholarly debates, the person and being of Jesus generate conversation, questions, and controversy. People are curious about what Jesus has to say to us that applies in our current realities. His stories and words continue to find resonance in the human spirit and speak to our human need. The church is the place to engage all of these questions, to ask what it is that lies within people's hearts and to make Jesus alive for our congregations and those outside of the church who yearn to engage in this spiritual quest.

Identifying the Broken Windows

When New York City began its renewal process in the 1990s, it started with a very simple belief—that one broken window leads to a process of decay. In other words, letting the small things slide creates unsafe neighbourhoods and encourages vandalism and crime. If you fix the small things, you by default fix the big things. While in New York this was taken to extremes at the expense of the disadvantaged, the premise itself is sound and has lessons for the church—not only for buildings, but for ministry. If we let one thing slide, from a decaying couch to a dank nursery to a smelly bathroom, we send the message that this place is not valued and it becomes easier to let everything slide. If it is unimportant to the leadership, it will certainly be unimportant to the congregation.

Too often in the church there is an attitude of "it'll do." Because this is the church, it is not valued in the same way that we value other parts of our lives, so we'll settle for what we can get or choose the option that costs us the least in terms of time, money, or effort. Aunt Ida's couch that has been mouldering in the basement for decades is considered good enough for the church, or an old computer with a tiny hard drive is thought to be perfect for the church administrator. This continues on to what is offered in terms of ministry. We settle for the mediocre instead of expecting excellence. God gives us the best—why is it acceptable to return to God only our leftovers?

I fully recognize that we all live in a world of finite resources. That is precisely the point. Do we have the mechanisms to co-operatively vision what ministry within a wider community might look like? What gifts does my congregation have that it can concentrate on? What gifts do each of us possess that we can share? Instead of trying to become all things to all people, why not create areas of excellence within our churches?

Let me give you an example: a congregation may be located in a neighbourhood that is primarily made up of mature and aging families. Instead of trying to beat that demographic and grieving the lack of children, why not create the best, most innovative ministry to seniors that can be imagined? It could include day programs, outreach, food preparation and nutrition, support to caregivers, and respite care. You've heard about Generation X services; how about special worship geared to seniors? Try a weekday morning and include lunch, and I think it could be wildly successful. Look for the opportunities—for example, concentrate on early retirees, a growing segment of our population as our society ages. Or in a young, growing community, concentrate on ministry to young families. The Rev. Cheri DiNovo's church, Emmanuel Howard Park in Toronto, is located in an area with a significant Polish community, so she has added a Wednesday evening service in Polish.

The church is also struggling with issues of development and redevelopment. One of the most pressing realities is that the United Church is primarily a rural church functioning in an increasingly urban world—migration to cities is a global phenomenon. This reality is one that The United Church of Canada is just coming to grips with, as the Greater Toronto Area, Calgary, and Vancouver experience exponential growth. At the same time, the rural areas within a couple of hours' driving distance of these centres are also experiencing an influx of early retirees and others fleeing the urban areas to seek a quieter lifestyle.

SEISMIC SHIFTS

Some denominations are better prepared to respond to this trend than others. The Anglican Diocese of Toronto, for example, maintains a map of churches to be closed, churches to be supported, and new churches to be opened. They can transfer resources from churches that are closing to new churches in growing areas. To support emerging congregations, they will fund a new full-time staff position for up to five years. Because The United Church of Canada's structures prevent this from happening, we are in danger of missing an enormous opportunity to plant churches in emerging neighbourhoods. Churches will be built—perhaps Pentecostal, Anglican, Catholic, or evangelical—but it is an open question as to whether they will be United Church. I genuinely see this as a tragedy. The United Church of Canada brings a unique, rich religious experience to communities and to the civic conversation. If you are part of the United Church, you have an added dimension in your life that is of tremendous value. To miss a whole generation with the unique gifts the United Church offers would be a deep loss, one from which we may never recover. The challenge is significant, but it can be met with congregational and denominational leadership that dares to break down institutional barriers that are inadequate to the task.

We need to identify what the broken windows in our churches are and either repair them so they gleam or close them up altogether. Letting broken windows stay as they are only brings in the snow and the rain. It is time to engage in new ventures. How many times have we seen a United Church in decline sold to an evangelical congregation only to become a thriving community of faith? Instead of closing these churches, should we not give them one more chance by creating "rebirthing teams"? A rebirthing team would have the mandate to go into a church as though it had a blank page and act as though it were a new church development. The team could include clergy, musicians, and lay people with a vocation to build up declining churches. Give them three years' funding, shared among national and local levels of governance, and let them loose.

Let us start using best practices from successful churches and leaders from across the country, pooling excellence so that we can all learn and get better. I want to learn from those who excel. I want to strengthen my church and my own ministry by learning from those who are serving with creativity and imagination and have fun doing it. If the United Church is serious about being a relevant presence in the 21st century, we must cast aside the baggage that strangles us and learn to be light on our feet. We must turn into a permission-giving organization, not one burdened with so much structure that we cannot breathe. One symptom of a declining organization is that more and more rules and bureaucracy are added. Thriving organizations facilitate effective permission.

It will take a tremendous leap of faith and real courage combined with tenacity to create a responsive 21st-century church. But the alternative is too severe to contemplate.

CHAPTER 3

Voices of Leadership

IN SEARCHING FOR ANSWERS to our current challenges, I was
fortunate to be able to speak to a variety of colleagues
representing differing perspectives on leadership. Let us pause
here to listen to their reflections on what leadership means today.

"The problems of poverty are more challenging than when we began" *Gail Brimbecom*

Gail Brimbecom has just retired as the parish nurse for
Westminster United Church in Whitby, Ontario. It is fair to
describe her as the person most responsible for the birthing of
parish nurse ministry in Canada, and in 2006, in recognition of
this pioneering work, she received an honorary doctorate from
Emmanuel College through the University of Toronto. Having
seen Brimbecom at work for over a decade, I have immense
respect for her leadership skills.

Brimbecom strongly believes that we need leaders with vision
who are optimistic and positive. She says that a positive attitude

is "huge," because it means that the person has a positive view of the future and therefore believes and continually thinks that change is possible. She also sees intuition as an essential part of leadership. "Intuition is that inner sense that we are on the right track," she asserts. "An intuitive person feels that which is good, right, and true; it leads to an instant yes." She believes that intuition, our inner wisdom, is the voice of God speaking to us. For example, when Brimbecom first heard about the parish nurse program, she knew inside that this was the right program at just the right time in the church's history. This led her to a missionary journey, establishing a parish nurse ministry ecumenically across Canada and within the United Church.

Another gift that we need to exercise Brimbecom calls "reimagination." This involves first imagining what the work of the church is and then reimagining what the church might become. Brimbecom believes that we are called to a reimagining of the social gospel. "The problems of poverty are more challenging than when we began," she asserts. "The divide between affluence and poverty is greater than ever and we have even greater potential to implement a new social gospel." The charism that we need is one that will return us to our roots and give us new energy to address the issues of the day.

"We need to be ready to bear the wounds" Michael Ward

The Rev. Michael Ward is the minister of Central United Church, located in the heart of downtown Calgary, Alberta. Central United is a church that has experienced a renaissance over the past decade due in large part to the focus and determination that Ward brings to leadership. An unabashed evangelical, Ward sees leadership as Christocentric and believes that to lead in the church, a commitment to Jesus Christ is key. Central United has focused much of its ministry on the addicted and the marginalized and has experienced tremendous growth as a result.

Ward believes that leadership is both influence and enthusiasm: "One enthusiastic flea can worry a whole dog," he declares. He sees Jesus not only as a leader, but as one who had the capacity to create other leaders. "Jesus sent out first the 12 and then the 70 in teams of two, and they probably didn't want to go," he tells me. "But when they came back, Jesus listened to them. He listened to their stories and saw it as a teachable moment."

Ward believes that we need to change the language of the church. "It's not about joining but belonging. It's not about learning but formation, not about membership but discipleship, not about holding hands but seeing them held." Leaders, he believes, need to be ready to pay the price and have a high pain threshold. "We can't be universally liked; we need to be ready to bear the wounds." Ward's advice to other leaders is to lead with your soul and love your people with all your heart.

"We need to wrestle" Mardi Tindal

Mardi Tindal is director of Five Oaks, a United Church education and retreat centre located outside of Paris, Ontario. Tindal illustrates leadership with a story: "Two students are just leaving a church where they have been volunteering at an Out of the Cold program, cooking and serving food to the poor and the hungry. As they round the corner two guys in suits carrying Bibles and tracts bear down upon them. 'Do you know Jesus?' they ask earnestly. 'Sure,' replies one of the students, 'we were just with him.'"

For Tindal, this is an example of the importance of story as a means of communication. As Christians we need to be grounded in the stories of our faith—they form our identity and are the basis from which we lead. A problem is that Christians are currently trapped between two polarities: we seem to see the Bible stories either as fact or as myth. This traps us in paradigms that are not helpful in discerning what God is telling us. Tindal uses the analogy of First Nations stories to illustrate her point. "When we hear the First Nations stories of creation we don't say, 'Well, those are simply mythic stories,' and dismiss them. Nor are they treated as factual—rather, they are seen as *truth*." We need to approach scripture in the same way, as revealed truth.

Tindal sees leadership as a practice that requires spiritual discipline, an attending to God's Spirit, and a commitment to justice, learning, retreat, pattern breaking, and community. Leaders also need "circles of support and accountability," Tindal believes, in order to take risks and deal with the conflict that is an inevitable part of their vocation. "We need to wrestle," she says, "to be honest and open to both conflict and ideas. We need to dare, to risk, and use our imagination and creativity in the face of contemporary challenges."

"It's as if no one is responsible if churches do well or fail" Ed Bentley

The Rev. Ed Bentley has been in ministry at Eastminster United in Belleville, Ontario, since 1983, and has taken it through periods of strong growth, including a brand new building. Bentley feels strongly that the United Church view of leadership has been skewed over the years. "The problem is that there is absolutely no focus on outcomes," he states. "It's as if no one is responsible if churches do well or fail. We need to have job descriptions that are performance based, with annual goal setting, including a built-in evaluation process." Bentley believes that we have not only come to tolerate mediocrity, but "we actually celebrate it. If you are successful, you get shot down," he states. We need to celebrate success and seek it out so that we can learn from it.

The central problem, Bentley feels, is that United Church leaders lack a core message that they can clearly articulate. He tells a story: In his first pastoral charge in Nova Scotia, the town doctor stopped Bentley on the street and asked him what he was going to preach that Sunday. "I realized that I couldn't tell him in one sentence," Bentley remembers, "so I went back to work until I could." For Bentley, leadership is about clarity. Are we clear about what the message is? Are we clear about the totality of the message? These questions are for him the heart of the matter.

Ministry for Bentley is a job that cannot be done by one person—it takes a whole community. Each of us has weaknesses and strengths, and we need to be honest about both of them. This allows churches to focus on their ministers' strengths while filling in the weaknesses with the gifts of others. Bentley also sees consensus decision making as leading to a dysfunctional community. "There is no consensus in a Christian community," he says. "No matter what we do or say, someone will be alienated, but that shouldn't stop us from doing what we need to do." Bentley is concerned about what he sees as a separation between evangelism and social justice: "They are not irreconcilable; each can flow into and from the other." Like Michael Ward, he strongly believes that we are called to love the people we serve. "We are there to serve," he affirms. "We need to love our people with our whole heart."

"We need to revisit what 'call' means" *Evelyn Broadfoot*

The Rev. Evelyn Broadfoot, the Conference Personnel Officer for All Native Circle Conference, works out of Winnipeg. Broadfoot recalls the time when the Elders of a community would lift a person up into ministry. The role of the Elders was to discern leadership within their community, and select the person they felt was called to that role. When Broadfoot's Elders first approached her to enter ministry, she remembers, "I laughed when they first came to me. I had lots of excuses and said 'Not me, not me,' but I entered ministry and it has been a beautiful way of life." Today the Elders play a similar role. They walk a journey with those who are in training for ministry and have a lot to say in supporting them. This ongoing contact keeps students deeply grounded in the community from which they have come.

But Broadfoot is very concerned about the future of ministry today: "We are losing a sense of vocation and it grieves me. We need to revisit what 'call' means in ministry. For too many, it is just a job." For Broadfoot it is time for us to listen again: "We need to listen to our 'Elders,' to our former Moderators. We need to take time to listen, to go and pray for guidance." Broadfoot sees ministry as service: service to God and service to people. "It is not about having people serving you." She believes that we need to reach into our wider communities as we search for leaders.

Broadfoot speaks of her 25-year-old granddaughter—an old soul "who has so much wisdom"—as the kind of person we need in leadership today. Without her own sense of call, Broadfoot does not believe that she could have lasted in the church. It is, in her view, time for a retreat for ministers to focus on their vocation and call from God. "As older people we need at times to say 'no,' to let the Elders say, 'You need to go away for a while, but we'll be here when you are ready.' Ready for God and ready for a life of service."

"What is worth dying for this week?" John Pentland

Since 2000, the Rev. John Pentland has been involved in a unique program called Leadership Calgary. This community development initiative takes one third of its participants from the private sector, one third from government, and one third from non-profit organizations, including churches. The purpose of this curriculum-based program is to equip people to "see what needs to be done and then do it without being asked." Its focus is on raising the bar of leadership. The program believes that we function on two levels: low beam and high beam. Low beam refers to the everyday details; high beam to the long-term vision. Both are needed in order to navigate the road.

Pentland, a United Church minister who recently worked for over two years with the United Way, believes that we have little of either in the church today. "We have no plan for strong churches. There is no appropriate strategic leadership, none, zero, nada," he states. "The expectation of the public is that we are irrelevant, goofy, naïve, and aligned with the political right." He illustrates our lack of strategic thinking with the closing of two churches in Calgary, Alberta. One was located a block from Calgary's upscale Red Mile pedestrian area, the other in the residential neighbourhood of Inglewood. The United Church closed both and they are now booming evangelical congregations. One of them worships three weeks a month and on the fourth goes out and performs community service. "We have handed the ball to the conservative churches," states Pentland. "We need to rethink what we consider church to be and strategically fund our congregations to get the right people in the right place."

For Pentland, our real job is to help people reflect upon the Spirit of God in their community and thoughtfully address the issues that are being discussed outside of church. He strongly believes that we need to get out into the community and make sure that the community is present in our churches. Pentland sees church as a worshipping centre where strong preaching tells the story. In order to tell that story, we need to ask ourselves one central question: "What is worth dying for this week?"

"Whom are we following?" Anthony Bailey

The Rev. Anthony Bailey has served both as a pastor in Canada and overseas in Jamaica. He is currently senior minister at Parkdale United Church in Ottawa, Ontario. Bailey has strong views on where we as a church need to go. Like Gail Brimbecom, he believes that part of our new charism must revolve around social justice. Also like Brimbecom, he believes that we need to reimagine ourselves: we are in the midst of a seismic culture shift and the church is not well positioned to deal with it. "People are experiencing a new postmodern interpretation of reality," says

Bailey. "The promise of progress is over and the old categories are no longer valid."

Part of the church's problem, from Bailey's perspective, is that we continue to appeal to the intellect instead of realizing that what people really want is authentic experience. "Hockey arenas have become the new temples and people find a deep experience of community there, including demands and expectations." In response, all the church has done is to lower expectations and lower the requirements of participation. Bailey believes people want to give themselves to something noble, and we have not articulated that the church is a noble place that undertakes noble work. The appetite for authenticity is not being met in our places of worship. We need to be both more missional and more confessional, that is, both more able to communicate our faith and more grounded in it.

The place for us to begin again, in Bailey's view, lies in worship and preaching. Worship is a place that challenges our ultimate allegiances and contests all other claims upon us. We need to be clear about whom we are following. For Bailey the answer is clear: we are to follow the call of God.

"Are we relevant?" John Joseph Mastandrea

The Rev. John Joseph Mastandrea is part of a team ministry at Metropolitan United Church in the heart of downtown Toronto. Metropolitan, along with many new inner city churches across Canada, can be considered a new church development congregation of the 21st century. The huge number of condominiums being built in the downtown core has led to an influx of new people. Mastandrea and teammate Malcolm

Sinclair have turned Metropolitan into a true 21st century cathedral church, a centre of worship, education, and outreach.

The foremost question in Mastandrea's mind is "Are we relevant?" To be relevant is to offer programs and worship that speak to the culture rather than being defined by it. Among other things, Metropolitan has instituted a program called Sunday Night at the Met, a monthly worship service with dinner led by a youth band that uses an African modality.

The challenge from Mastandrea's perspective is to be relevant, innovative, and contextual all at the same time. As clergy he believes that we are expected to be "jacks of all trades *and* masters of all." The problem is that none of us can be both. He advocates that each of us pick a few areas of expertise and specialize in them. Thus, we can learn from each other and even pool our congregations into clusters, so as to use each other's gifts. But above all, Mastandrea believes we need "an injection of confidence. We have a unique and special perspective on the faith—we need to be less apologetic and more assertive."

Along with that comes a responsibility as leaders to act and look like professionals, which includes a commitment to being informed on a variety of issues. Mastandrea also contends that we need to dress smartly and wisely. "It doesn't have to be expensive, but it is a matter of respect and how we are perceived by the world." We send messages both verbally and nonverbally all the time—we need to be sure that our verbal messages are not compromised before they are even sent.

"How can someone so young as you actually think?" Mary Anne Van Heuvelen

The Rev. Mary Anne Van Heuvelen, as a young clergy person who currently ministers in the northern Ontario community of Sudbury, has strong feelings on the subject of leadership formation and the church. She believes that our current structures do not serve us well. Assigned to minister to three churches at once in a three-point charge, Van Heuvelen felt insufficiently prepared by her seminary experience. "It was great academically, but lousy at preparing you for life in the parish." Van Heuvelen also felt that as a young person she was patronized and stereotyped by her older classmates. "How can someone so young as you actually think?" was a question she often faced in seminary.

Once in a congregation it didn't get much better. Van Heuvelen experienced little support from the local presbytery governance, and felt punished when she asked for help. "There is no support network out there. We need assigned mentors when we first start our work at the congregational level, to help us through those first few years," maintains Van Heuvelen. In preparing people for ministry, we need more courses on conflict management, counselling, finances, and a focus on leadership. "Much of leadership today is refereeing," she says.

In addition, Van Heuvelen is very concerned about the lack of young people in many churches today. "The church is not young-person friendly," she says. "We need to start addressing issues that are pertinent to society as a whole, or we will never attract young people." This means looking at other forms of doing worship to bring young people in the doors. "The church is really dealing with two solitudes, one young, the other old."

"We have to look at the elephant in the room— the church is dying" Cheri DiNovo

The Rev. Cheri DiNovo is the author of *Qu(e)erying Evangelism* and host of the weekly Radical Reverend program on University of Toronto radio. She has succeeded in turning around Emmanuel Howard Park United Church, a congregation in the west end of Toronto that had been in decline, by a profound emphasis on the Christian gospel combined with a belief in social justice as a transformative force in our world. DiNovo, who opened her church to gay, lesbian, and transgendered people, sees all of us as beloved by God. When it comes to leadership, she is frank in her assessment of where we are. "We have to look at the elephant in the room—the church is dying, it's not working. We need to acknowledge this and ask the questions 'Why should it work?' and 'Why should it survive?'" DiNovo says that leaders should lead: "You can't make novel changes by committee; this is what leaders are elected to do. They are to put things into motion. God bless Bill Phipps, for what he said as Moderator got Jesus on the front cover of *Maclean's*." (Phipps had raised questions regarding the resurrection as a literal event.)

DiNovo also contends that we need to stop avoiding difference; there is nothing wrong with healthy disagreement. She agrees with Ed Bentley in disavowing the need for consensus and challenges leaders to act courageously: "Here's an idea: instead of talking about what churches we are going to close this year, why not talk about how many new churches we are going to plant? How many new ethnic ministries can we start? Where are the clergy who speak Hindi and Portuguese? If we don't have them, let's go get them! Let leadership run amuck."

For DiNovo, we only have to agree on two things: that we are a Christian church and that social justice is our way of articulating that to the world. "We are the one church that combines these two in a unique way. That means that 50 percent of Canadians could be part of The United Church of Canada." Now, that's a big goal to shoot for.

"The crucified and risen Jesus draws people to himself" *Robert Thaler*

For the Rev. Robert Thaler, minister of New Hamburg United Church in southwestern Ontario, leadership has everything to do with identity. "We have a business model for the church," he asserts. "We think we need to lead for the greater glory of church growth." Instead, Thaler believes that we should focus on what the church is truly about. "The church is not a building, it is not the people. The church is where the crucified and risen Jesus draws people to himself—everything else is just details." Thaler stresses that if we preach and believe that, then the church works.

Too often, however, we let our own "stuff" get in the way. "We have to let our own egos go and act not out of rights, but out of love," Thaler says. He also points out that we are not leading "a corporate machine, but rather we are drawing people into community." His advice to clergy? "Be calm; walk with people and they will walk with you. At times we become the crucified Christ with them, to allow their resurrection into the community."

"What purpose do we serve?" *Chris Tindal*

Chris Tindal, a young adult and an active United Church member, has just come through a federal election as the Green Party candidate in the riding of Toronto Centre, where he was able to raise the Green Party vote above the national average. Tindal sees the key to leadership as "offering positive and constructive alternatives." People, he believes, are tired of negativity and attacking and criticizing others. Tindal sees parallels between the Green Party and the United Church. "Both work on a model that is more consensus-based and both favour leaders who are reluctant. Look at what we call the spiritual head of our church," he says. "That they are called 'the Moderator' says it all—their main job is to represent the group. They can't be exclusively focused on their own agenda."

For Tindal the question of purpose is central: "What purpose do we serve?" he asks. "Community, directional leadership—we need to help people to live out our creed, living 'with respect in Creation.'" Tindal believes that what we are doing to the planet is an issue of both ethics and theology. "We are headed for some sort of crash," he says. The church for Tindal is a place of both change and stability, a place where we can examine solutions and help people respectfully to make better decisions.

"Ignorance is the worst enemy that we face" Raheel Raza

Raheel Raza is a journalist, author of *Their Jihad, Not My Jihad*, a frequent speaker at United Church gatherings, and a national leader in interfaith discussions. From the perspective of a Muslim committed to multifaith and multicultural leadership, Raza believes that communication skills, mutual respect, and knowledge are vitally important to 21st-century leadership. "The voice of truth and justice, the language of kindness, compassion, tolerance, reason, and equity is the voice we both need to speak and to hear," she says.

Raza also believes in the importance of knowledge of both our own traditions and the traditions of others. "Ignorance is the worst enemy that we face." She points to the Danish cartoons that mocked the Prophet Muhammad and caused a worldwide outcry in 2006 as an example of this. She describes them as a "useless exercise," one that "dehumanized the Muslim faith and spread Islamophobia." Firmly condemning the violence that arose in response to the cartoons, Raza believes that "our job is building bridges, not blowing them up." Leadership, in her view, needs to be positive, with responsibility, and have accountability built into it. Like many other leaders highlighted in this book, Raza places a high value on our ability to listen to others with both sensitivity and respect.

Gender equity remains a significant issue in her view. "Women are the peacemakers and nurturers. If that 50 percent of our population were given leadership roles, we would have a lot fewer problems."

Now What?

This chapter has not been about forging a consensus; rather, it has allowed different voices to add their wisdom. The future lies not in seeking harmony, but in finding music in dissonance, and in that music, both truth and hope. For it is only in facing the truth that we find real hope.

CHAPTER 4

Building Communities

I HAVE RECENTLY had the privilege to witness two dramatic illustrations of leadership in action—one as a close observer of the founding of the University of Ontario Institute of Technology, and the other, almost concurrently, as a member of the team that rebuilt Westminster United Church in Whitby, Ontario.

A Lesson in Practical Leadership

Gary Polonsky, president of both Durham College and the recently formed University of Ontario Institute of Technology, epitomizes for me a best practices example on leadership, one that has many applications for the church's situation. Having known Polonsky for over a decade, I have watched with amazement as he continually sees adversity as opportunity and meets his goals. The impact of his educational initiatives are felt across Durham Region and throughout the province of Ontario, and it was a true privilege to play a very small part in them. Not many people leave a legacy of this magnitude, and it was amazing to watch it unfold.

Fifteen years ago, when Gary Polonsky applied for the job of Durham College president, he undertook a most unusual step to prepare for his job interview. Arriving in town a few days early and walking about the city of Oshawa, Ontario, Polonsky told people he met on the street that he was moving into town and was wondering if they could tell him anything about this Durham College he had heard about. Polonsky collected their responses, the good and the bad, and presented them to the hiring committee when he was interviewed. Needless to say, he got the job.

This type of creative innovation has been the hallmark of Polonsky's tenure at Durham. Committed to serving both students and the community, he has taken a small community-based college and transformed it into a leading-edge institution. He also brought with him a belief that everyone has the right to raise a family in economic dignity and a commitment to offer training that would lead to good jobs, which he supported with a policy that no one would be denied admission because of a lack of money. Polonsky's exemplary leadership has accomplished what many thought was impossible, including the creation of a new high-tech university.

When Cadbury closed its manufacturing plant in Whitby in the early 1990s, laying off workers in the midst of the deepest recession since the Great Depression, Polonsky saw an opportunity for the college. Why not take that manufacturing plant and turn it into a new campus for Durham College, one that would specialize in training for the trades and prepare people for high-tech jobs with a future? Working with provincial and federal governments, business, and the wider community, Polonsky's idea became a reality. In just a few years, I attended the opening of the Whitby Skills Training Centre, a Durham College campus. At the same time, witnessing the devastating effects of unemployment in our region, I approached him with the idea of creating a team of college, government, and church to provide high-quality self-employment training. Polonsky was an enthusiastic partner in launching this initiative.

When Polonsky began at Durham, he met with every staff member through a series of breakfasts to consult with them about how to move the college forward. But it was a meeting with the then president of General Motors Canada that galvanized him into action. When Polonsky arranged to meet with him to see if there were ways that the college could help GM with its training component, he was politely told that Durham just wasn't good enough to provide that level of service to GM. That reaction galvanized Polonsky into making sure that Durham College would never be placed in that position again. Today, many years later, Durham College is a leader in automotive technology training, as is the separately governed institution with which it shares space and a close relationship—the University of Ontario Institute of Technology.

The creation of the University of Ontario Institute of Technology—the "MIT of the north"—will go down as Polonsky's greatest legacy. The first new university in Ontario in over 30 years, which welcomed its first class of students in September 2003, was born in the midst of government cutbacks at a time when everyone said it could never happen. Driven by a deep sense of service—service to students and colleagues, but more centrally service to the wider community—Polonsky made two arguments in support of his vision of the university. First, a community with a population of over 500,000 people that was going to grow to a million in 20 years needed a university so that students would have an affordable local option. Second, the community could not afford to have all of its eggs in one economic basket. The region's future depended upon its capacity to diversify and create new industries, which could only come from a high-tech university. Thus, this new institution would not only add value to the community, but conduct research that would be critical to helping the nation compete globally. Those who graduated from its programs would get jobs that paid well and had a real future.

Leadership has been at the centre of Polonsky's career, and his doctoral thesis at the University of Toronto, "Moving Educational Leaders from Implicit to Explicit Leadership: An Action Research Study" (2003), was completed in the midst of being college president and launching the new university. In his thesis, Polonsky distills a lifetime's experience and insight into leadership, and he has graciously allowed the following discussion to quote from it.

A Model for Educational Leaders

The core of Polonsky's thesis is the creation of the Success-Evoking Leadership Framework (SELF) approach—a model based on three concentric circles. The centre circle can be described as the core of the mission and the strategy for implementing it. For Polonsky, mission and implementation are inseparable—without both components only failure can result. The heart of the vision Polonsky describes—and put into practice—is simple: "Serving students well by serving colleagues well." There is no hierarchy of preference; both constituencies, students and staff, are to be equally served, because the success of both is imperative to the organization's mission.

The middle circle contains the three guiding elements that are the core of leadership: vision, values, and results.

The outer circle contains three aspects necessary to implement leadership: role modelling, recognizing/rewarding, and communicating. Role modelling is defined as "living the shared values of the organization," i.e., walking the talk. Learning from other role models is also stressed. Communication is defined as "listening carefully, speaking with clarity, writing in easy to understand language and being open and available." An important component is not speculating about where other people are on an issue—just pick up the phone and ask them! Polonsky sees effective communication as resting on the word "yes." We should say yes when new ideas or projects are brought forward unless "there is a substantive reason not to say yes."

Polonsky illustrates this decision-making process with the acronym DECIDE:

1. Define the problem or issue to be resolved.

2. Elicit all reasonable options or courses of action.

3. Choose the one(s) that most successfully address the problem.

4. Do it/them.

5. Evaluate the results and adapt the selected options as necessary.

Finally, don't forget to add the *I* into DECIDE, which means involving all the affected people in each step.

Most communication issues are really quite simple, if we bother to do the simple things well. Equally, the task of recognizing and rewarding is not complicated; all it involves is finding ways to say thank you regularly. This, I believe, is a place where churches tend to do the least effective job. We expect a lot from people, we get a lot of volunteer time from them, but do we recognize their contributions adequately? Churches also tend to be strong on vision and values but woefully weak on results, as though measuring effectiveness was somehow unchristian.

Getting to a Win/Win Solution

I learned a tremendous amount about leadership from Polonsky as my church initiated its own building program. At one point, my congregation got into a debate regarding pews versus chairs in our sanctuary. Pew people wanted the tradition and look of pews; chair people wanted the flexibility and lower cost of chairs. There were strong feelings on both sides and I was getting very frustrated trying to find a way to reconcile them. Over breakfast with Polonsky one morning, he told me that I had fallen into the trap of either/or thinking. Either/or thinking, in Polonsky's words, leads to "rigidity between individuals and teams, creates unnecessary conflict and destroys constructive group thinking and decision making." Both/and thinking instead sees polarities not as negatives but as positive opportunities. Polonsky challenged me to find a win/win path that would include both.

That very morning, our organist invited me to go see some "pew chairs" in a church 30 minutes away. Although chairs, they link together to function like a pew, and each row has a pew end attached to it. They were the perfect solution: we got the look and function of a pew, with the comfort and flexibility of a chair. We ordered three as a trial, put them together in the sanctuary, invited people to try them out—and the problem solved itself. Of course, not every problem has a solution as elegant as that one. But the principle is sound. Whenever I have a disagreement, I go to a both/and solution first. It is amazing how often it works.

Leadership Lessons from Gary Polonsky

1. *Tenacity.* No matter how great the odds, believe in your vision and yourself. There will be setbacks: navigate around them and play the long game, not the short one.

2. *Vision.* Once you've got it, never let it go. Use vision as the centre of your strategy and base everything you do around it.

3. *Hard work.* Nothing of value comes easily—be prepared to put in long hours.

4. *Don't be afraid.* Take intelligent risks; don't ever not do something because you are afraid of failing. Discount the naysayers—if you listen to them, nothing will get done.

5. *Share credit, not blame.* Be generous in praise and let others join you on the centre stage. Take responsibility when things go wrong, and fix the problem not the blame.

6. *Have a big goal.* When Polonsky first envisioned the new university, people thought it was an impossible task. It is now the fastest-growing university in Ontario.

A Project of Renewal

At the same time as Polonsky was launching the university initiative, my congregation was involved in a building project of its own. When I reflect upon this process and its results, it is the quality of the leadership I saw that impresses me the most.

Palm Sunday 2003 was one of the best days of my life. In a mere 28 months, our congregation had gone from concept to completion of a 20,000-square-foot building. Gathering with the Christ the King Lutheran congregation in front of our former building, we prayed together, read scripture, passed over the keys from one congregation to the next, and then with bagpipes swirling, our congregation marched north to the very first worship service in our new building. As I looked around, I felt such a sense of accomplishment: we had done it!

Westminster United Church's journey to a new facility began with a board retreat. The only agenda that day was future program planning. A new building was not even on our radar—in fact, quite the opposite. Westminster (founded in 1958 in a postwar baby boom community) had already decided not to move from its existing location. Back in the 1980s, Oshawa Presbytery had commissioned what was called the Lemon Report, outlining demographic trends facing Durham Region—a region just east of Toronto that is the fastest-growing municipal area in Canada—and recommending that either a new church be built in North Whitby or that Westminster move north and be that new, larger church. The presbytery met with Westminster, and the congregation decided to stay put and add an extension to meet its growing needs. It was during this construction that I was called to serve the congregation in 1992, and I was extremely impressed that the congregation would move forward with a project this significant during a time of interim ministry.

Over the next decade, the congregation filled and then overflowed the extension. We developed strategies to cope with our growth: multiple services, off-site worship at a local school during peak times, and the use of a portable and local homes for extra Sunday school space. But we experienced a most frustrating trend: no matter what we did, the church would grow and then shrink again to fit the building. People couldn't get parking spaces, seating became extremely tight, Sunday school space was overcrowded, and as a result, the congregation would contract to fit the space. Once a church hits 80 percent capacity, the rule is that it either moves, adds another service, or shrinks.

After several frustrating years of growing, shrinking, and growing again, the church board had formed a working group to look at building another church. However, we could not find any land close enough at a price we could consider. Nor, having tested the waters, were any buyers interested in purchasing our existing building. After months of exhaustive research, we had voted as a congregation to stay put.

Now, we met as a board to plan for the next year. As we went through both challenges and opportunities, the consultant we had hired helped us to realize that the number one issue that every committee kept bringing forward revolved around our building. By the end of the retreat, we came to the conclusion that we needed to reopen the whole issue. To a congregation that had just the winter before voted to stay in its existing building, this was not going to be seen as good news.

However, two critical components had changed over the year. One kilometre to the north of us a 2.7-acre parcel of land was for sale by the Anglican Church, which it had originally slated as a future church site. The Anglicans, to their everlasting credit, instructed their broker to find a church that was looking for land and to offer it to them. They were having difficulty in fulfilling that goal, but despite numerous commercial offers, the Anglicans stubbornly saw this as a stewardship issue and told their broker to keep looking. At the same time, Christ the King Lutheran Church had come to the difficult decision that the land it owned in Whitby was unsuitable to develop a new church on and was instead seeking an existing building in which to locate its congregation. In one fell swoop, we had both an appropriate site and an interested purchaser. God, we believed, was at work.

Our first step was to secure the land. For that we needed the help of our church extension council, which was entrusted with monies from the sale of church property and bequests. Our board proposed that the council purchase the land immediately to be held for us while we made the decision about whether to build or not. This secured the land, while giving us the breathing room to decide what to do with it. The presbytery acquired an excellent church site for us or for a new congregation, or if everything fell apart, an excellent investment property.

Board and staff together made collective decisions on this project; no single person drove the agenda. With shared leadership, it was not perceived as an ego-driven process, and there were many to carry the burdens. Now we had to discern how to proceed. First we held a meeting to alert the congregation to the changed circumstances. We reviewed the Lemon Report, our own challenges, and the changed environment in which we now found ourselves, and asked permission to spend $40,000 to hire a consultant to do a detailed feasibility study and congregational survey. The congregation was not initially asked to go ahead with the building; it was simply asked to examine it.

It became the task of our congregational leaders to keep the project moving forward. We realized early on that our existing governance was inadequate for such a project, and developed a two-track leadership system. One track, the board, would take care of the ongoing running of the church. The other, which was called the Building Project Council, would run the building project. This council was made up of myself, the chair of the board, our project manager, and the co-chairs of our project committees: building, mission and outreach, and building finance. A process facilitator kept our process clean and effective. We knew that the council would need the trust and authority of the congregation and the board. Decisions involving hundreds of thousands of dollars had to be made, sometimes quickly, and we couldn't keep going back for approval. So when we structured this team, we did it through a congregational meeting that empowered the group to make such decisions. In return, ongoing communication—and consultation, where appropriate—was to be part of the project.

This was possible because of a profound sense of trust—in myself as the spiritual leader, but equally in the lay leadership. This trust had in part been earned by a history of transparency—what you saw was what you got, we had always told the truth. There was no sense of hidden agendas at work or of anyone trying to lead a solo charge up the hill. Rather, we posted for everyone to see the sheets of newsprint from the retreat and reported why we felt it was time to reopen the question well in advance of the congregational meeting. The governance structure we created allowed us to act, to be directive, and not to get bogged down in a typical church-style process, which can strangle new initiatives. There were to be no four-hour meetings about the colour of the kitchen cupboards!

To ensure we had the right people in the right places at the right time, our board chair Joanne Macpherson and I met and recruited each of the key leaders. The most important was the project manager. In his professional life, Hugh Robertson had built plants all over the world, and his knowledge of construction and project management was second to none. As he was retired, he had the time to devote to this job. Robertson also had the ability to make decisions quickly as well as the capacity to make us laugh at ourselves, to forge a consensus where needed, and to act when necessary. Further, he helped us to slow everything down before proceeding.

The mandate of the project council was to exercise leadership for the period of the building project only. Once we were in the new building, the goal was to focus on ministry. Therefore, a mission and outreach group was created to imagine what our ministry would look like as well as deal with the "soft" issues around the move, such as honouring the founders who had built the original church and saying goodbye appropriately to our old building. While a superb job was done of saying goodbye and honouring the founders, the vision piece proved very difficult. In fact, it may have been an impossible task. The building project itself required enormous energy from the congregation. But also, it is extraordinarily difficult for a church coming from a small building to envision how different it will be in a facility that is quadruple its existing space. The new facility opened opportunities that were difficult for us to imagine until we got there. Were I to do it over, I would select a couple of people with leadership potential and ask them to stay on the sidelines of the building project to focus on launching the programming vision once we were in the facility.

As Real as Bricks and Mortar

The experience also showed me how critical it is to make a mission concrete. A building is bricks and mortar: when it is going up, people can see the results. It is much harder when the issue is program. We have to use personal testimony to make it as real as bricks for people. Pictures, stories, and sound all need to be harnessed together to communicate the mission of the church. Ministry needs to speak to people's hopes and dreams for their world.

Let me give you a stewardship example: Bob Stirling is the chair of our Stewardship Committee. Every year, he creates the presentation for our Celebration Sunday stewardship program, and he makes the best use of PowerPoint, sound, and graphics I have ever seen. Stirling has developed a *Jeopardy* theme using that game show's answer-and-question format. Last year, it was Westminster Fact or Fiction questions, complete with soundtrack. When you are carrying a mortgage that costs $10,000 per month to service, the stewardship of money is not a theoretical construct. Stirling's presentations are leadership at its finest. They give congregation members the message without terrifying them or turning them off. The finger is never wagged; guilt is never employed. An invitation is extended to participate in the wonderful things that God is doing at Westminster.

SEISMIC SHIFTS

In looking back, it is important to acknowledge that none of us knows the future here. It's impossible to tell how the enormous risk we took in coming here will eventually turn out. But since opening, Westminster has grown by an average of one new household per week (excepting summer). We have already had to expand our parking. We are on target and working to the plan designed by the project council.

My own role in the building project was to "lead, follow, or get out of the way." I used all three approaches—often in one meeting—as the project unfolded. As the spiritual leader, my job was to help discern that we were proceeding faithfully. As the full-time staff person, there were key components about which I had expertise and where my voice carried more weight than others. This was more than balanced by other parts of the project where my knowledge was extremely limited and I would defer to others. At times, my silence was the most important leadership gift I could exercise.

Leadership requires walking a careful line. Leadership is not domination, filling a room with sound, or monopolizing the floor to keep others' opinions to the side. But neither is facilitation on its own sufficient—no leader should leave his or her light under a bushel. Too long have we in the church confused enabling with leadership; as both clergy and congregations, we have been too afraid of our own authority and of abusing it. But we are called to act bravely and to be champions of new ideas. Authentic leadership means stating clearly what you believe to be the correct course and being prepared to act upon it. This clarity must be tempered by a willingness to listen to other viewpoints and to institute course corrections where necessary. And when mistakes are made, the ability to accept responsibility and apologize is critical.

Obstacles are inevitable; nothing of value is ever accomplished without them, and we have to be ready for things going really, really wrong. My favourite story occurred in the early winter of 2002. Just before Christmas, our building program was broke. The church's cupboard was literally bare, and various creditors were knocking on the door wanting to be paid. There was no possible way for us to access more funds until January, at the very earliest. Much as we wracked our brains, we could see no way out—we had no choice but to close the whole project down and secure the building site until we could accumulate the funds to keep going. This meant that our dream of opening in time for Easter was dead, and worse, that we were going to have to lay off our construction crew just before Christmas. Imagine what this would do to the momentum of the project and the mood of our church.

Hugh Robertson, our project manager, drove up to the site in order to deliver the bad news. At precisely that moment we got a call from our credit union. "We heard you were tight for money," a representative said. "We just deposited $50,000 in your account—hope that helps." Brian Eatok, co-chair of the Building Finance Committee, drove at top speed to the building site to intercept Robertson, who then went into his meeting bearing cheques and ready to pay our creditors. It was a marvellous moment. Christmas came early for many people that year.

Leadership Lessons from the Westminster Building Project Council

1. Communicate with your community (the people you represent). Always consult.

2. Build your team as a sum of its members' best skills.

3. No egos.

4. Analyze the needs of your community. Prepare the best needs assessment you can.

5. Spend money on planning to save money on execution.

6. Slow the process down. Don't get ahead of yourself.

7. Leaders should have (or develop) excellent listening skills.

8. Overcome obstacles by keeping your vision clear. Trust in your team.

9. Give everyone in your community a chance to have a say. They'll feel included if they're heard, even if you don't act on their input.

10. Go about every aspect of your project with faithfulness.

11. Get the right people from outside your team—in the case of a building project, an architect and a builder who knows churches.

12. Manage the trust (within your team and with your community) very carefully: tough to earn; easy to lose.

13. Allow and encourage new leaders to develop—an essential practice, since old leaders get tired.

14. The new leaders should develop a plan for the future in order to put your achievement to good and renewable use.

Responding to Opposition

There were also lessons learned about living in a community with diverse viewpoints. Inevitably, some people opposed the vision we were working toward. In this situation, there are three possible responses: conversion, acceptance, or withdrawal.

Conversion is not the same as convincing. Conversion means engaging in genuinely difficult dialogue that has as its goal the transformation of both parties. It means being honest not just in theory, but in fact. It means opening up your heart to the other, prepared to have it rejected. In any project that is engaged in systemic change, there will be people with valid reasons to resist. It is critical to engage them, to let them be heard so that they do not feel stampeded into acquiescence. My experience is that, if heard, many will feel validated enough to become open to an alternative other than their own. That is when conversion occurs—when they feel comfortable coming on board and offering their gifts and talents. The project is richer for being influenced by these new perspectives.

Acceptance means being able to live with a change that is going to happen, but not endorsing it. It is neither opposition nor participation, it is simply accepting the new reality and finding a way to live within it. Acceptors are genuine in their desire to remain in community; they are not sitting on the sidelines hoping for failure so that they can say "I told you so." They are people who are genuinely struggling and trying to be faithful to their call and traditions.

Withdrawal is a different matter. Withdrawers are so opposed to the change that they withdraw their financial resources and their contributions to community life. The change is too great for them to accept; it goes against who they are as people. They may remain on the margins or form opposition to the change, which can set up a win/lose dynamic that is very difficult to reconcile. When withdrawers lose, they tend to leave the church.

While I personally am saddened when a person chooses to leave a community of faith, it need not be a catastrophe. There are many churches available, and people should feel free to find one that allows them to live out their faith authentically. Too often churches think that having people leave is to be prevented at all costs. However, if people are deeply unhappy and their issues cannot be resolved, why should they feel obligated to stay in a place that no longer fills their soul with meaning? We can grieve that loss or we can recognize that at times each of us may need to be in another place. In my first pastoral charge, I spent an enormous amount of time with an individual who was chronically unhappy with the United Church generally and with my congregation specifically. I could have seen him every day and it wouldn't have been enough. When he left, both he and the congregation were happier.

In the building project, I encountered all three categories of response. I also saw people move from withdrawal to conversion, and those few we lost are happier in a different setting. We have each been in these three places in the past and will be again.

When I look back on the 28 months that I was involved in the building project, I recognize that it was a unique set of circumstances that will not be duplicated again in my life. As I sit in the completed building, I feel an immense sense of satisfaction. So much could have gone wrong; we came so close to failure at different moments. But the result has exceeded expectations and enriched the whole community. The challenges we face now are significant, but my faith in our capacity to meet them is limitless. For through this project, not only did I exercise leadership, I was taught leadership by as fine a group of guides as one could hope to meet.

CHAPTER 5

Time for a Reboot

It is the week after Christmas and I—like every minister of any denomination—am absolutely exhausted. While I dislike the phrase "giving 150 percent," it is the only one that suits the moment. The seasons of Advent and Christmas are all-consuming: this year, my church had a community Christmas carol sing, a Blue Christmas service for those grieving loved ones, a service of lessons and carols, plus four Christmas Eve services and one on Christmas morning. Our Christmas Eve youth play, "A Modern Christmas Carol," was in rehearsal since October, so Sundays had been long indeed. On Boxing Day, I woke up at 5:30 a.m., my mind racing at 100 kilometres per hour, before realizing that I was on break until the New Year.

This past Christmas at Westminster United was the busiest ever. Close to 2,000 people came through our doors on Christmas Eve, adding a big boost to our budget, though not enough to keep us out of deficit. More than 30 teenagers took part in our annual Christmas play, and we're getting ready to mount *Godspell* in the spring. One of my parishioners commented that in a previous life I must have been a Broadway producer.

Frankly, there are days when I feel like either that or a cruise director charged with trying to keep everyone on the good ship *Westminster* content.

But while I felt tremendous satisfaction about Christmas Eve, I now have a nagging feeling in the back of my mind, an alarm bell clanging. That phrase from a show of my childhood, *Lost in Space,* keeps playing in my head: "Danger, Will Robinson! Danger, Will Robinson!" I feel the earth shifting beneath my feet again. The things that have made our congregation successful in the immediate past are the very things that can block future growth. It is time for a "reboot."

Leaning into Danger

Rebooting is a term I use to show that a time for a new beginning is upon us. We all know what it means: Who among us has not sat in front of a frozen computer screen? You whack the mouse, press Enter or Escape, and still the program doesn't budge. So, taking a big gulp, you shut the computer down and turn it back on, hoping that all the work you have done will not be lost or that you are not in the midst of a system-wide hard drive crash. Amazingly enough, rebooting solves an awful lot of problems. It can fix broken fragments and make the system whole again, and with current software, I have never actually lost any work (as long as I had saved it). The term reboot applies well to both congregations and their clergy when we become frozen and need to reinvent ourselves.

For example, my personal life is in the early stages of a reboot. I decided about three months ago that I needed to add more intentionality in my life, that I was in danger of drifting or hanging on to the past rather than focusing on future possibilities. I recognized that I needed some new goals and challenges and that there were things in my ministry that needed to be addressed—and urgently. As I am approaching a significant birthday, it was a good time for an honest assessment of who I am in all phases of my life, physically, spiritually, and as a leader.

I have started to raise my fitness level with a specific goal in mind. I am working out more and increasing my cardiovascular fitness so that I can participate in the Bell Media Canada cross-city race (a day-long Canadian version of *The Amazing Race*) in June 2006 with my 18-year-old daughter, Sarah. I am also taking lessons in the Alexander technique, used by actors, musicians, and athletes to deliver peak performances by channelling the tension within their bodies out into their performance. As a preacher, I am a performer—and I have tension in abundance. I want not only to maintain my capacity to deliver at my current level but to get better. We ministers need to step outside our traditional repertoire to get better at the art of ministry.

I have also taken on the challenge of learning downhill skiing at the same time that my other daughter, Elizabeth, is learning to snowboard. Learning a new skill involves embracing that great Christian virtue: humility. There is nothing like being on the bunny hill with a group of eight-year-olds to give you a sense of perspective. My instructor, Mario, had two pieces of advice that I think apply to the church. "No matter how steep the hill," he told me, "just focus on one turn at a time." That's important to remember when I feel overwhelmed—just take it one Sunday at a time, one meeting at a time, one new initiative at a time, don't hurtle down the hill at full speed. His other piece of advice was completely counterintuitive: "Lean into danger." By that he meant that if I leaned my body back uphill toward imagined safety, I would lose control, fall downhill, and quite possibly crash into the trees. By leaning downhill—into the direction that I feared the most—I actually gained control and was able to manage the hill and banish the fear that was holding me back. In our working lives, we need to lean into and embrace those things that scare us. Embracing the fear conquers it and reduces its power. Every now and then, we may wind up on our behinds staring up into the sky and wondering how it happened—but that's part of the ride.

There is also a set of professional goals that I am challenging myself with—several media projects that I hope to bring to fruition over the next years and some more books. We only get so many chances in this life and we must constantly reinvent or reboot ourselves as professional people. Futurist Alvin Toffler predicted that literacy in the 21st century would be not about reading, but about learning, unlearning, and relearning. Lifelong learning is more than a pat phrase; it's a vital part of being a complete human being.

What I would really love to see is a new professional degree for ordered ministers. Personally, I don't feel like I need a D.Min., but I could sure use an MBA. I have proposed to more than one seminary the creation of an MPM, a Master of Professional Ministry. Business has the MBA; civil servants have the MPA— why not a similar intensive two- to three-year program for clergy in mid-career? Let's team up with a business school or use business leaders from within our congregations and offer a degree with courses on marketing, advertising, and effective communication. Stewardship and financial planning for churches and non-profits would be of immense help to me, as would updates on biblical scholarship, theology, Christian education, and the art of preaching. Just think of the cross-fertilization that would emerge if the degree were created with two streams—one ministry-specific, the other geared to non-profit and non-governmental organizations.

The Fragile but Resilient Church

Those are my personal goals—what about a reboot for the church? One of the realities that church leaders need to accept is the fragility of the 21st-century church. It used to be that congregations were extremely resilient and could cope with just about anything. That is no longer necessarily accurate, and I have experienced this fragility in a number of ways.

Let me tell you a story: Last fall I received a call from an Anglican congregation in Ajax, a fast-growing suburban neighbour to our west that has experienced phenomenal growth as the Greater Toronto Area expands. This congregation has had more than its share of challenges. Its original building was condemned due to structural cracks in both the foundation and walls, and with the congregation relocated into a suburban strip mall, land was secured and a new building project launched. Their building team came to meet with me and Hugh Robertson, Westminster's building project manager.

The meeting was somewhat tense. Their plan was to build first a daycare and then the church, with the idea that the daycare would fund ongoing operations and allow them to build a sanctuary at a later date. We respectfully questioned this strategy. My belief is that people give to a vision of what a church can be. As well, they need to see something tangible when they give that will benefit both themselves and the wider community. I did not believe that a daycare was a compelling vision to which people would donate. Churches need to focus on worshipping God, creating meaningful outreach, and providing challenging, informative Christian education. Daycare may be a side operation, but it should not become a church's purpose. Of course, additional revenue streams can help keep church buildings open, Westminster included. But we did not build a community centre—we built a church, which we now open to the community. That is a critical difference.

Robertson and I urged the Anglicans to recast their vision to include a sanctuary, but they were adamant about moving forward with their original plan. As they left, we agreed to disagree and honestly wished them the best. Unfortunately, when their capital campaign was launched, it fell well short of expectations. The Anglican Diocese of Toronto is now on the verge of closing down the church. This saddens me immeasurably; that church could have been a transformative presence in an area with tremendous potential.

This is not an "I told you so" story, nor do I believe that had they only listened to us everything would now be fine. However, I believe that without a compelling vision, no congregation can survive in the current reality. The vision needs to be refreshed and renewed continually. We must be constantly asking ourselves the question: "What is God calling us to do in this community?" The answers will be very different, but without keeping that pivotal question front and centre, churches will not survive.

The biggest current challenge to the church is that we represent a communal way of life and of responsibility in the face of a culture obsessed with the individual. Everything in our society is geared to individual choice and fulfillment—to being the best you can be, not giving the best of yourself; to individual spiritual fulfillment, not the fulfillment of the community. This is illustrated for me by the trend of personal spirituality gone upscale, which is beginning to be called "metrospirituality." This movement, described well on Beliefnet (www.beliefnet. com), subsumes spiritual and ecological values into a consumer culture. Involving everything from knitting, home altars, and surfing to designer yoga mats and elite tea salons, metrospirituality is a lifestyle driven by the acquisition of high-end virtuous goods. Consumer-driven movements such as a focus on fair trade—assuring fair prices to disadvantaged workers for their goods—have had a positive impact. But metrospirituality, in a marriage of marketing and consumption without guilt, creates a deceptive sense of identity through the consumption of luxury goods with a spiritual component. As Jim Twitchell writes in *Adcult USA*, luxury consumers are seeking the sense of salvation and epiphany that would previously have been associated with church. The challenge churches face is leading congregations of people whose lives have been formulated since birth with the values of consumption and the inevitable debt that goes with it.

Although local congregations can show an amazing strength in their capacity for renewal, the institutional church is bravely rowing against an almost irresistible tide. I am not surprised that churches struggle; frankly, there are days when I am amazed that any of us are still open at all. Churches are a radical symbol whose very existence challenges the mores of our time. This reality is lived out in congregational life in a number of ways.

Attendance patterns, for example, are all over the map. I used to be able to predict that the Sunday after Labour Day would be a big Sunday, then attendance would be a little erratic until another big Sunday after Thanksgiving, and then everything would build up to Christmas. But that was predicated upon a cottage/trailer season that ended in October, which is no longer the norm. Add to that Sunday sports from hockey to soccer to every other activity known to humankind. A colleague asked me if I knew the difference between a boy heading to church and a boy going to play in a hockey game? The answer: the boy going to the hockey game would be wearing a tie. Hockey teams have strong expectations of dress, behaviour, and attendance, and in a choice between hockey and church, I have never known church to win. Further, children in shared custody may spend alternate weekends with each parent. More people are working on Sundays, and more people are absolutely exhausted by Sunday because of the pressure they are under during the week. This was illustrated to me by a child who explained to her Sunday school teacher that she couldn't attend a Christmas pageant rehearsal the following week because it was "do nothing Sunday" in her household. One Sunday a month was set aside by this family to do nothing all day long. They were carving a Sabbath without church for themselves. I confess to being jealous—I too would like a "do nothing" day once a month.

The new reality presents profound challenges of identity and stewardship. How do we link together people whose lives are so scattered? How do we create genuine community for ourselves? With a more tenuous relationship to the church, how will people's levels of financial giving be affected? Given these attendance patterns, it is easier for people to drift in and out, and harder to connect them with programs and fellow congregants.

There is one unexpected surprise—the summer, rather than being a time of inactivity, is getting busier. At Westminster, we had our best attendance ever in July and August and my colleague Gail Brimbecom and I were extremely busy. Not everyone has a trailer or a cottage or takes a holiday all summer long—in fact, quite the opposite. Providing summer content that goes beyond low-season worship is a wonderful niche opportunity just waiting to be discovered. Unfortunately, clergy and key lay leaders are so exhausted by late June that the energy they have to implement anything new is pretty slim. One answer could lie in recruiting a completely different team from among those who are around in the summer months.

Cutting through the Clutter

Our culture is full of noise, and a world of distraction awaits at the touch of a keyboard or the flick of a remote. Part of the challenge for church leaders is to cut through this chatter and find a way of being heard in the marketplace. Think of the apostle Paul wandering through the marketplace in Athens and stopping to preach and you get the idea. There are three groups of people whose attention church leaders need to draw: the members of the congregation, those affiliated with the church but not active, and finally, the dechurched. When the church interacts with the community, congregation members should feel a sense of pride that their church is being noticed. Congregation members are the church's best ambassadors, the primary line of communication. If they are happy with their church experience, they will tell friends and neighbours about it.

For example, when Westminster sent out 10,000 flyers before Christmas, our congregants shared them with other folks they knew. When we sent an e-Christmas card including the times of our services to every household for whom we had an e-mail address, congregants forwarded them across cyberspace to family and colleagues who in turn forwarded them to others. Then we crafted a media release regarding our Christmas Eve camel, Roxie, who was a late addition to our youth pageant cast. Using her image and a humorous touch ("The wise men called: they want their camel back!"), the media release created an opportunity for me to go on radio and television to talk about our upcoming worship services. This intentional communication strategy helped create our busiest Christmas ever—in short, it worked.

During the federal election, Westminster sent out a media release about the all candidates forum we were sponsoring on the future of health care in Canada; another media release announced that Durham Region's new chief of police would be preaching on restorative justice. Each of these keeps our church's profile alive and shows the wider community that our church goes beyond old stereotypes about congregational life. These media releases help to cut through the chatter of contemporary life and get people's attention.

There is also an internal challenge—creating experiences that walk the line between the familiar and the surprising. People need both the comfort of the familiar and the surprise of the innovative to draw them to worship. Every Sunday, they need to make that decision to get out of bed to come to church. Different types of music, like the klezmer band we are having as guest artists in a few weeks, can help inject fresh energy and perspective. Another important emerging trend is themed services, such as an intergenerational service Westminster held on the theme of water last spring involving dialogue, music, and dance.

We have also experimented with hiring a Sunday school coordinator, with sending out "we miss you" cards to children whom we haven't seen in six weeks, and with children's class friendship parties after church. But I increasingly feel that Sunday school as we know it is in its last days. As a model for learning that arises out of the 19th century, it is simply not functional in the 21st. One of the trends that I see is an increasing number of children staying in worship. This is occurring because parents are working longer hours and drop their children off to daycare Monday to Friday. So when Sunday rolls around, the family comes out to church to be together and what happens? The parents are expected to send their children away yet again. This is especially the case with babies; moms and dads who used to happily take their children to the nursery prefer to keep them in church. Every moment families get to spend together is precious and they can't bear to send their children away, knowing that soon their maternity and paternity leaves will be over and their time at home will end.

If we truly believe that church should be a family experience, we are going to have to change our preconceptions about children and Sunday school. Instead of an every-Sunday classroom, the future may consist of monthly multiple-generation worship and separate monthly worship created by the children for the children. This could be enriched by occasional age-appropriate learning experiences. We need to be ready for children to stay in worship, have activities ready for them, and see their presence as a sign of life rather than an intrusion. On their part, parents will need to be sensitive to the needs of the community, taking children to another place in the church if they are being disruptive and beginning to take away from the experience for others.

Attendance is increasingly linked to participation—a feeling that congregants are actively participating in the faith community. Maybe your child is singing in a junior choir or reading the opening prayer. Perhaps you're reading scripture, welcoming people to worship, singing in the choir or band, or participating in a small group. If you're involved, you'll attend. Or perhaps the key is not involvement so much as connection, a sense of being deeply connected to a vibrant faith community. Connection can occur in a variety of ways, primarily through the relationships we form in church. "Holy friendships"—those relationships formed in a congregation that transcend Sunday morning—need to be cultivated. These are the people we not only worship with, but have over to dinner; the friends our children play with and with whom they develop lifelong relationships. Such relationships cannot be artificially created, but the church can set the table for them to be formed. Church should be fun in the best sense of the word—not fun in the sense of expecting constant entertainment, but rather of looking forward to the events that are happening, of looking forward to seeing people in church, of laughing at coffee or during worship. Fun as in seeing a new perspective and viewing the world differently because of what you have experienced. Fun because the holiness of God has embraced and transformed you.

How are we to respond to this context? At Westminster United, after many conversations, we are currently looking at a number of initiatives, from a program of integration for new people to a community of peace movement.

Westminster's Plan for Action

1. *An intentional program of integration.* For the first year of life in our church, we will pair up new people with someone who will befriend them and help them to integrate into the church—answer their questions, invite them to activities, and even sit with them during worship. We hope this will build holy friendships.

2. *A community connections volunteer.* This person's job is to make our community more aware of Westminster.

3. *A more formal program of small groups.* The goal is 30 percent participation by the end of 2007.

4. *More social events that have no fundraising component.* Fun for community's sake should be our motto: more dances, skating, book clubs, or movie outings.

5. *Monthly "focus Sundays."* These worship events will focus on a particular issue or event. They could involve guest musicians, a guest speaker, multiple-generation worship, or all of the above.

6. *Monthly drama in worship and a new music group.* The music group will help the congregation prepare for the release of *More Voices*, the upcoming supplement to the United Church's hymn book *Voices United*, in 2007.

7. *A focus by our new parish nurse on the needs of youth and young families.* The intention is to create support groups and educational events for this demographic.

8. *An every member visitation stewardship program.* This program will target both finances and a commitment toward personal involvement in congregational life.

continued

9. *A working group to research and launch a second worship experience.* We're aiming to launch the second worship by early 2007.

10. *Investigation of a new partnership with one of our partners in the South.* A working group will be assigned to this task.

11. *A community of peace movement.* This initiative involves working with other community partners—including schools, police, and government—in response to growing gang violence in the Greater Toronto Area.

Do I expect us to fulfill every one of them? Why not: we have to aim high, strive to give our best, and learn from what works and what fails. This is a reboot that my congregation needs in order to get to the next level. In response to the question "What is God calling us to do in this community?" this is where we are called to lead.

CHAPTER 6

Responding to the New Realities

IN THIS POST-HIERARCHICAL WORLD, many ask why we should lead. Why should we care? Is leadership not simply an outmoded, elitist concept? My response is that without authentic leadership, all organizations—churches included—would simply perish.

Authentic leadership allows the community to become that which God has called us to be. Good leadership also involves the capacity for good "followership"—authentic leadership is not about personal ego, but about the well-being of the community. It frees us to lift up the gifts of others, to be in the front when appropriate and to be led by others in their turn. If the purpose of the community is clear, then the diverse gifts of its constituents can contribute to its success. Like a flock of Canada geese, sometimes one might be in front, other times supporting the community from the back. But there must be someone who holds up and casts the vision that the community has created. That, I believe, is the critical role that clergy play in their congregations.

Outgoing United Church Moderator Peter Short gave me an image of the minister as the person who stands in the middle of the river holding back the water while the people cross. It is a beautiful image, but I would like to expand it slightly. I believe the minister's job is to stand in the middle of the river while the waters rise, telling the people that they can get across, helping them across, moving back and forth with them across the river and staying in it, wet, cold, and shivering, until everyone who is willing is on the other bank. When everyone is safely across, the minister may well be told that if the crossing had only happened around the bend it would have gone much faster and only people's feet would have gotten wet! But that's the price of leadership. This is the role of authentic leaders: despite the setbacks, to stay up to their necks in the water with their people.

The Challenges Ahead

What are the rivers that we must now cross? I am by nature a hopeful person, but let me outline some concerns—including resource depletion, disaster preparedness, and global economic change—that I believe we need to take seriously as we move forward into this tumultuous century. Although models of the future are often based on the immediate past, the only certainty about the future is that it will not be like the past.

When former Alberta premier Peter Lougheed writes in *The Globe and Mail* that the Americans are coming for our water, we need to pay attention. In a debate with Maude Barlow on the CBC radio program *The Current*, I heard former U.S. ambassador Paul Cellucci speak about Canada's water as a renewable resource and express frustration that it is not for sale. How long will a Canadian government be able to resist the world's only superpower if American communities deplete all their aquifers and the electorally powerful south and southwest run out of water? Water is the oil of the 21st century and we have it. The world will turn its eyes to our abundance—not only of water, but of oil, natural gas, and coal as well. These are the very resources that emerging economic giants seek. The Chinese government is already investing in the Albertan oil sands; oil is their economy's—in fact, the world economy's—Achilles heal.

In the summer of 2005, damage to the refineries in the Gulf of Mexico caused by the most powerful hurricane season in memory made gas prices in my area spike at $1.33 a litre and they have remained volatile ever since. These hurricanes had been supercharged by warmer than normal water in the Gulf of Mexico. Ironically, through the effects of global warming, the use of oil caused the storms that created the disruption in its distribution, and the resulting disaster affected all of North America.

Many people are convinced that the world is beginning to run out of oil. Julian Lee, a senior oil analyst with the Centre for Global Energy Studies in London, England, is not immediately concerned: "From a geological point of view, there is still lots of oil in the ground." However, he says, "it's going to cost billions to get it out." The United States recently announced that it is aiming for major reductions in its imports of foreign oil. This will have a significant impact on the marketplace. "Why should producing countries spend billions on creating more capacity, when their biggest customers are telling them they don't want their product?" Lee asks. In his opinion, oil prices may actually drop over the next five years. Lee does have concerns over the capacity of oil refineries to keep pace with demand and the world's reliance on an increasingly creaky global supply chain. He says new technologies, including renewable resources and high-efficiency engines, could have a positive impact—but only if we start researching and implementing these technologies now.

In these times, church leaders need to be prepared for emergencies, establishing emergency plans and links with local governments and agencies. When Ontario and the Eastern Seaboard states experienced a massive blackout in 2003, were any of the churches ready to assist their congregants or the wider community? Westminster certainly was not. We need to be ready for the next one. This is not alarmist, it is merely prudent. Look at recent floods in Manitoba, ice storms in Ontario and Quebec, and forest fires in British Columbia and into Alberta. In an emergency, does your congregation know how to respond? Do you have a way of contacting each other? Are there emergency supplies of water or food? Can your church be a place of shelter or community gathering? In a time of natural disasters and mounting violence and upheaval, is there a pastoral plan to deal with people suffering genuine distress or shock?

The new realities will put unforeseen pressures on us and offer new opportunities to creatively respond to enhance people's lives. In times of deep cultural stress and uncertainty, we need to have strong bonds to sustain us. It doesn't all have to be doom and gloom: I also believe in the importance of social gatherings and shared meals—anything that will build and maintain community.

Part of church leaders' role in this evolving reality is to help people create adaptations to these new realities in their lifestyles.

In Canada, we are used to having inexpensive food imported from all over the world. But if price increases in the cheap oil on which we have come to depend push up the price of food, that may change. Further, we need to question if the current model is even sustainable for our planet. Instead of asparagus flown in from Peru, the winter vegetable of the future, filled with edgy cachet, may well be the turnip. An excellent book on this subject is *Simply in Season* by Mary Beth Lind and Cathleen Hockman-Wert. This cookbook, written in the same spirit as the 1970s Mennonite classic *More with Less* (a kitchen staple in our home), is a cornucopia of recipes for meals based on locally grown, seasonal produce. Let us support our own farmers by what we purchase, perhaps even helping to save our fast-disappearing farmland. Why not hold a worship service centred on food, perhaps followed by a cooking demonstration featuring seasonal recipes? From there, begin a community kitchen and organize trips to farms and local markets. Rural congregations have a tremendous opportunity to partner with urban congregations. Invite your urban neighbours into your communities, create exchanges, and share stories of your life growing the food we all depend upon. Most urban people (this author included) don't really comprehend the depth of the challenges that rural communities face—help us to understand and show us how we can help each other. Most people in the city don't farm, they garden. So come spring, urban churches could run a gardening seminar on growing vegetables—including in balcony containers—and during the fall, a seminar on preserving them for the winter. Connect to the earth and change the conversation by modelling that which we want our world to become.

When SARS hit my community in 2003, the spread of this new, deadly strain of pneumonia affected everyone. A couple from my church could not attend their own mother's funeral because they had been placed in quarantine. Hand-cleansing stations were installed at church entrances, and we all felt a certain fear that something new had changed our reality. The economic effects were devastating. When I visited the Shakespeare festival held in Stratford, Ontario, this past summer, a local business owner told me that the number of visitors has never recovered. As I write this, Turkey is dealing with an outbreak of avian flu, and we hear continued warnings of a possible global pandemic similar to the 1918 influenza outbreak that killed more people than the First World War. I can't help but wonder if this issue is more like Y2K—the year 2000, when millions made emergency preparations and held their breath in vain, expecting computers to crash and planes to fall out of the sky—or 9/11—the devastating attack on the World Trade Center that despite plenty of signs, no one had foreseen. The rule seems to be that the issue that you worry about the most turns out not to be as bad as feared. The real danger lies in what you do not anticipate.

Leaders can try to discern the future, but we can never know it. Thus leaders must exhibit calm resolve, never giving in to fear or panic, which can be as contagious as any virus. Leaders of any organization set the tone by their very presence. What they say, what they do in a crisis is their true test. If a pandemic or an unforeseen crisis emerges, spiritual leaders will have a role to play. We need to cultivate the discipline of interior calm. People need reassurance and order in times of crisis, and we must live it out as leaders. Of course, there already is a pandemic loose in our world—the social and economic devastation that AIDS is wreaking across vast portions of our planet. On this topic, Stephen Lewis is truly a voice crying in the wilderness about an

ongoing catastrophe that too many of us see, yet pretend not
to notice.

On the economic front, the pressures of global competition are
being felt not only by adults as their businesses struggle to adapt
or move offshore, but by their children as well. The pressure on
children today is enormous. When the character Jeremy in the
cartoon "Zits" tries to explain his vast amounts of homework
to his mother, he tells her of the tremendous competition that
he faces, explaining that "excellence is the new average." Young
people today are expected not only to graduate with outstanding
marks, but to have a resumé filled with activities and hold down
a part-time job. The costs of college and university continue to
escalate, adding financial pressure and in many cases significant
debt upon graduation. And after graduation, landing a full-time
job is difficult for many. Of course, it's just as taxing for their
parents. An attitude of "If you don't want to work the weekend,
don't bother coming in on Monday" is becoming a growing
reality. More is expected of everyone, jobs are disappearing, and
retraining, ongoing research, and innovation are becoming key to
maintaining our standard of living.

While the church is not in any sense an economic powerhouse,
we can have influence. I believe that churches should advocate
on three fronts. First, we should advocate to our governments
for innovation, research, and investment in our public
universities. It is through them that new industries and work
will be created. I have had ongoing correspondence with the
Premier of Ontario on this issue and my views have always been
treated with interest, respect, and courtesy. Second, there must
be opportunities for people to retrain in jobs that will pay them

more than minimum wage; we must advocate for a national strategy that creates dignified, meaningful employment for our citizens. Third, we need to help the growing number of people who are falling through the cracks of our culture.

Congregations can make a difference for such individuals: Mary Taylor (a pseudonym) called me from the hospital just before Christmas. Alone, her children in care, and with nowhere else to turn, she was calling churches from the phone book seeking help. Taylor had an apartment, but no furniture. She was lost. Upon discharge, she arrived without a coat on a cold November day. We got her a coat from another United Church's thrift shop and Gail Brimbecom, our nurse, visited her in her home. Taylor had little but a bed on the floor. We put out a plea for furniture and were stunned by the results. Over the next few weeks, that apartment was filled. On Christmas Eve, I read a poem she had written as a thank-you to our congregation. It was the last stanza that stays with me: "I now have something to offer my children besides a tragic beginning." By now, Taylor has made the transition to a church within walking distance from her refurbished apartment. Thus, three United Churches have been involved in giving her a second chance. It was Mary Taylor who gave the church a great gift—the opportunity to be generous and to help transform a life. The Marys of our world are coming to us in growing numbers and we need to find a way to minister to them.

The Challenge of Violence

In the fall of 2005, during a teenager's funeral at a Seventh-day Adventist Church in Rexdale, Ontario, a gang member shot and killed a rival in a revenge killing. On Boxing Day 2006, gunfire erupted in front of the Eaton Centre in downtown Toronto, and a 15-year-old bystander out shopping was killed and six others wounded. The day before, we in the church had celebrated the birth of the Prince of Peace, but there was no peace to be had on the streets of Canada's largest city. Gun crime and the growth of gangs have been a coalescing issue not only in the Greater Toronto Area but across the country. Some look to Boston, where the Rev. Eugene Rivers helped to create what has been called the Boston Miracle, dramatically reducing the murder rate in that city. His program is a deceptively simple combination of police, churches, and social service agencies working in tandem. The police have been given additional resources to track down and arrest the gangs, while the churches and social service agencies work on the streets with at-risk youth, providing alternatives to the gangs. In Boston, this has included an "adopt a gang" program, crime watch neighbourhood programs, family counselling and support, help for abused women, and local economic development projects.

In looking for solutions to this challenge, the link between crime and income disparity cannot be underestimated. According to the *Toronto Star*, over 40 international studies link income disparity to high levels of homicide.[1] In Toronto, the United Way report "Poverty by Postal Code" showed that for every dollar that the poorest families in Toronto have to spend, the richest have $27. Those with financial resources can afford extracurricular activities for their children that engage them and keep them active. On the other hand, if you are forced to work three part-time jobs at minimum wage—without benefits—just to survive, you can't afford anything extra for your children. The economic

---

1 Leslie Scrivener, "Guns, Crime and Income Disparity," *Toronto Star*, January 15, 2006.

reality means less parental supervision and less energy to devote to children. The consequences are before us daily.

As churches we have two roles. One, to offer our facilities in partnership to minister to these families and truly engage with them. Second, to advocate for social policies that reduce the gap. The cuts to social programs in Ontario in the 1990s have been devastating to community health. Marvyn Novick of Ryerson University, Toronto, calls the circumstances we have inherited as a result of these cuts the children of both former Ontario premier Mike Harris and then prime minister Paul Martin.

In his visit to Toronto, Rivers challenged everyone from all sectors of society to take responsibility for what has happened. In particular, he challenged the churches to work together: "Check egos at the door—make children the bottom line." He believes that churches need to get out of their buildings and into the community and help to offer positive male role models. Without question he has galvanized the wider community into action. Churches need to offer real alternatives that go beyond giving sermons and shaking our heads in dismay.

John Morrison, the principal of Anderson Collegiate in Whitby, Ontario, has made a huge impact during his tenure with the creation of the "culture of peace" program. In this program, students create an intentional culture of peace by addressing issues of violence, racism, and homophobia. Speakers, including Canadian Lieutenant-General Roméo Dallaire, UN Mission Commander to Rwanda during the 1994 genocide, have appeared in the school with searing tales of the truth they have experienced. This program has had a profound impact upon the school community and I believe that we can turn it into a community-wide initiative. Working together with this school, the police, local government, and churches—including Westminster United—have the opportunity to create a community of peace that we hope will prevent what has been happening in nearby jurisdictions. The time for us to act is now, before even more gunfire erupts in our streets.

Every church, no matter where it is located in this country, has a role to play in reducing violence in our culture, but we need to do it in ways that attract youth, rather than sounding like we are simply moralizing and judging. Violence is everywhere—from video games such as *Grand Theft Auto*, to popular television programs such as *24*, where torture is portrayed as a perfectly reasonable course of action. The peace option needs to be equally as persuasive.

One question that plays an important role for churches is that of diversity. Vern White, the police chief for Durham Region, spent 19 years in the far north with the RCMP, where as part of his community involvement, he worked closely with Inuit youth as an athletic coach and mentor. Yet the RCMP was singularly unsuccessful in attracting Inuit youth into the force. White realized that until young people saw themselves in the other RCMP officers, this would never change. So using some recruiting methods that weren't in the textbook, he was able to increase Inuit presence on the force, which in turn led to greater numbers of Inuit applying to the RCMP. If young people don't see themselves in positions of leadership, they will not see leadership as relevant to their lives. Thus we must make sure that our leadership—both clergy and lay—is as diverse as possible. Challenging though it is, diversity is central to the community health of our future.

A Vision of Moral Leadership

As I wrestle with these challenges, I have consulted books on leadership from Heifetz's *Leadership without Easy Answers* to Goleman's *Primal Leadership* to Morrell's *Shackleton's Way*. But it was in the thoughts of the late Ivan Illich—who has been described as an iconoclast Catholic priest—that I found the most pertinent insights. The founder of the Center for Intercultural Documentation in Cuernavaca, Mexico, Illich viewed the world through a unique prism, and his theology continues after his death to challenge our thinking. Illich believed that our society was essentially created as a corruption of the New Testament. For example, we have institutionalized caring as a way of divesting ourselves of the radical gospel claims of compassion and hospitality:

> It is a glorious Western and Christian idea that there should be institutions, preferably not just hotels, but special flop houses, available for people who need a place to sleep. In this way the attempt to be open to all who are in need results in the degradation of hospitality and its replacement by care giving institutions.[1]

For Illich, the most influential biblical paradigm was the parable of the good Samaritan. He saw this parable not as a moralizing tale of goodness, but as a call to radical commitment to the care of the "other," not out of duty, but because of relationship. It is Illich's view that relationship lies at the heart of the Jesus message. The Samaritan "is someone who not only goes

---

1 David Cayley, *The Rivers North of the Future: The Testament of Ivan Illich* (Toronto: The House of Anansi Press, 2005), p. 55. Copyright © David Cayley. Reprinted with the permission of House of Anansi Press.

outside his ethnic preference for taking care of his own kind, but who commits a kind of treason for caring for his enemy."[2] Relationship is a gift, not an obligation based upon societal or cultural expectations or mores. Jesus showed relationship to be a free creation between two people, one that transcends the boundaries we create.

In a world of prescribed boundaries—rich from poor, nation from nation, ethnicity from ethnicity—to lead a gospel community means taking a huge leap of faith. It means focusing on developing not institutions, but relationships between people who might never have even thought to sit at table together. I believe that the moral core of leadership lies in imagination, the imagination to see beyond, to picture a different reality, and to discover ways of bringing that reality to fruition. Any community can create a mission statement and a long-range plan, but can we eat with those who are the Samaritans within our communities?

Many people today are striving for leadership that has at its core a truly moral centre. This type of leadership is even being recognized in the business community. Business writer Nikos Mourkogiannis, in his article "The Realist's Guide to Moral Purpose," writes that without a clearly articulated moral purpose, companies fall sway to amoral expediency.[3] Such companies, with a focus that goes no farther than making money, cannot in the end endure. Moral purpose is a framework around which we build our lives. It is a guide to right behaviour and to success in living a whole life. Leaders in the church should be experts

---

2 *Ibid.*, pp. 50–51.
3 Nikos, Mourkagiannis, "The Realist's Guide to Moral Purpose," *Strategy + business,* Winter 2005.

in moral purpose; it is one of our greatest assets. Yet we have not articulated this purpose clearly, perhaps because of a fear of our imperial past, or of seeming arrogant or superior. Having a truly moral purpose, however, precludes being imperialistic or superior. Instead, it gives leaders and congregations clarity in not only proclaiming our message, but in putting it into practice.

People are hungry for a moral core to their lives. The old narratives in our society no longer have resonance; people are looking for a transcendent story, for a new morality based not on judgment but on right living. We are living in in-between times right now—the past is not yet finished, nor has the future been birthed. When I was trained to do an overseas internship in Sierra Leone, I was taught that in order to adjust to a completely different culture, I would need to cultivate a "tolerance for ambiguity." In this emerging age, that is exactly the skill we all require. The need to respond appropriately in uncertain times is paramount, but it comes without formulas or guaranteed results. We must simply hang on to the hope for a sustainable future.

Chapter 7

Beyond the Big Tent

ONE OF THE MOST IMPORTANT ATTRIBUTES a leader can have is the gift of discernment, an ability to intuit the trends that will affect the organization as it moves forward. Discernment is a way of seeing through the fog, or more accurately, a capacity not to be stopped by the fog. With all the changes that religious leaders must cope with, the temptation to stand still is almost overwhelming. But if we stand still, it is we that will be overwhelmed.

The United Church of Canada is at a critical juncture in its history—whether it will survive as a vital, creative denomination is for me an open question. But I want the United Church to do far more than survive; I want us to thrive. I believe that God has work for us to do and that the church is being challenged to a time of new boldness and creativity. To engage in this journey, we will need to decide what we wish to take with us and what we must leave behind.

One of the leadership characteristics of our age is the capacity to hold two seemingly contradictory ideas together at the same time. Personally, I find it comforting to live in this both/and world, but it takes an ability to live with ambiguity rather than certainty. One challenge is that in a world of increasing uncertainty, people want certainty more than ever. That is captured well for me in a T-shirt slogan that reads "Change is great…you go first." There is so much truth in that—we all tend to be in favour of change as long as it doesn't affect us personally. But we are caught in a whirlwind, a whirlwind in which the world seems to be transformed almost monthly, where certainty is becoming a historical myth. In order for the church to move forward, what do we have to leave behind?

A Collection of Silos

Historically, the United Church has functioned as a "big tent denomination," proclaiming that in our big tent there is room for all types of belief systems—liberal, conservative, and all shades in between and outside. But we need to ask if we are indeed a big tent or merely a collection of silos. Over the last two decades the United Church has seen an increasing detachment from its national governance with an increase in congregationalism, a sort of church-wide cocooning. This trend is celebrated by some and reviled by others, but it is not decreasing. It is exacerbated by the reluctance of both clergy and lay people to invest themselves in the structures of the church.

I am a perfect example. Having spent the first five years of my ministry involved both at the local presbytery level and at the level of the Alberta and Northwest Conference, I have done hardly anything since moving to Bay of Quinte. It comes down to demands on my time: I can focus on the congregation and write, but that is all I can make time for. Other colleagues and lay people are reaching similar conclusions, and the structures have become creaky as we try to staff a 21st-century church with a model of governance created in the early 20th century. It isn't working and I don't believe it can, because its spirit is from another age. Like it or not, I believe that we are going to have to go back to the drawing board and create a new model of governance. The challenge lies in creating a process in which people feel consulted and listened to—just like when Westminster built its new church facility, only on the more challenging national scale. Without that sense of participation, the process will simply fail.

While many people have been quick to criticize the United Church as a structure, let me suggest that the distrust in the national level of our church has emerged in parallel with a society-wide distrust in all authority and institutions. This has been a terribly destructive trend that has eroded the ties that bind us together. It was illustrated for me during the recent debate on restructuring the church's levels of governance. In our presbytery, the debate tended to be framed in terms of "What are they trying to do to us?" That distrust permeated everything. The national level of the church has learned from this and I have noticed tremendous changes in how it communicates with the local level over the past two years.

But one consequence of this distrust has been the emergence in recent decades of a "silo mentality" in many parts of church life, especially in theology. Conservatives sit in one silo, self-identified progressives in another, and the "radical middle" bounces between the two. People migrate in and out of smaller silos that arise depending on the issue—which could be anything from praise bands to same-sex marriage to the identity of Jesus.

The problem with silos is that when we are sitting in one, we hear only ourselves and cannot even see our neighbours. The result is that conservatives have their gatherings and liberals and progressives have theirs. If we cannot even talk with each other, how do we expect to talk with the world?

Diversity in theology is something I would hope the United Church would strive for. Should we not want to have our boundaries pushed and be willing to risk our beliefs? I love the model that Marcus Borg and N.T. Wright have created in their shared writings and workshops. Two outstanding academics with fine minds have reached very different conclusions about the gospel stories and the person of Jesus. But instead of each sitting in a silo of his own ideas, they have created a model of sharing their concepts, lifting up their differences, and inviting readers and listeners to draw their own conclusions. Their differences enrich the dialogue and push the audience in different ways. Does the United Church have that level of diversity in its discussions? When planning events and writing curricula, do we ensure that we have truly diverse theological and biblical content? Or do we simply stay where our comfort level and personal beliefs lead us? True leadership means having the courage to be open to diverse ideas and to the possibility of being changed by them.

Personally, I want it all. I want to read and hear ideas that make me both weep with joy and shout with outrage. I want books that make me feel like tossing them across the room and books that inspire me to highlight every second paragraph. I want to be changed by what I read and learn. I want my faith to grow—I don't just want my own perspective to be reinforced, I need it to be challenged and threatened. Make me work on my faith, make me struggle for what I believe in. Wake me up, make me think, make me mad, change me. True growth comes with struggle; without it, we wind up only talking with those with whom we agree. To paraphrase minister and author Brian McLaren, I would hope that all of us could be progressive, conservative, liberal, eco-spiritual, feminist, orthodox, mystic Christians. But it is not easy; there is comfort in the silo.

Years ago when I was in seminary, my classmates and I studied liberation theology and worked on the assumption that the future would inevitably lead to a liberal, progressive global church that would reflect values that made us comfortable. Instead, we now face a global church that is quite the opposite. In his address to the Associated Church Press Convention in 2004, former *United Church Observer* editor Hugh McCullum pointed out the changes that are affecting the global church:

> I am convinced that there is such a mighty fissure growing within Christianity that will cause such huge mutations that our liberal Northern version of the faith will simply disappear.... The most significant transformation of Christianity of whatever stripe is not the liberal reform so desired here in North America. It is the counter-reformation sweeping in from the global South.[1]

His point is clear. The world church is changing radically, becoming much more conservative, evangelical, and armed with a strong and certain faith. The growing Anglican fissure over the issue of same-sex marriage is but one example of

---

1 Hugh McCullum, "Journalist as Advocate: How We Missed the Biggest Story Going," Associated Church Press Convention 2004. Retrieved March 1, 2005, from www.theacp. org/ACP2005_keynote_mccullum.htm.

this. Across North America, it is the conservative churches whose spokespeople are being heard in the public space and who are shaping the public conversation and perceptions of contemporary Christianity. In a world that is becoming increasingly conservative, what is the future of a denomination that sees itself as primarily liberal?

Adapting to Survive

I suspect the United Church may need to recast its identity more as a niche player, rather than as the biggest Protestant denomination in the country. This may not a bad thing; in fact, becoming smaller and more nimble may allow us to thrive. After all, it was the smaller mammals, not the dinosaurs, that survived extinction.

Jane Armstrong is a senior vice-president at the research firm Environics. In 2006, Environics conducted research for Emerging Spirit, an initiative focused on establishing and nurturing a relationship between the United Church and Canadians aged 30–45. The Environics research probed attitudes of people in this age range about spirituality, religion, and the United Church and things the church might do to be more welcoming. As a member of Richmond Hill United Church, just north of Toronto, Armstrong is keenly aware of the challenges that the church is facing. She believes in the concept of "adaptive navigation" as a leadership model that has something to offer the United Church. Canadians today are both highly educated and highly suspicious of authority figures. The model they are comfortable with is not a "father knows best" hierarchy, but a flatter organizational structure that her firm terms "heterarchy." In this model, leaders are seen as having the capacity to be fluid and to fluctuate with the changes they encounter. They must navigate down the river in a sailboat that depends upon the elements, rather than ploughing ahead in a motorboat that is oblivious to them.

People today have a strong dislike of societal control; they prefer individual control and see community as facilitating their own individual growth. Leadership should enhance their journey by opening the doors of new possibilities for them to consider, by facilitating questions and helping them to draw their own conclusions rather than presenting certainties. People no longer want the prix fixe menu; they want the buffet so that they can make their own choices. For example, with the advent of MP3 players, you can download and create your own playlists of music suited to your individual tastes. Right now, one of my playlists is running, and it is wonderful not to be tied to a whole recording and to have that level of individual control. But if all we do is construct our own personal reality, how do we challenge ourselves? How do we open ourselves to experiences that create possibilities we have not yet considered?

"Don't dumb things down," Armstrong tells me. "Don't speak in code and clichés that no one understands any more." For her, that means terms such as "salvation" and "Jesus as my personal saviour" need to be jettisoned. Instead, Armstrong believes that we should present ideas in plain language that speaks clearly as to who Jesus was and what we believe. "Help people navigate the slalom course that is our lives" is her plea to the church leadership. Armstrong believes that we have an opportunity to not resist but celebrate change, to flow through it and with it.

People are looking for community that is open and ready to enter into dialogue and discussion, community that is comfortable with contradiction. Environics research (in an October 2004 e-mail that Armstrong shared with me) shows the importance of clarity in presenting the message:

> It is becoming tougher to convince Canadians that they need to be led. Canadians are continuing to question leaders in all arenas, and will question leaders' credentials before they will be willing to listen to them. However, in an era of short attention spans, immediate gratification, and decreased social interaction, the only leaders who will be effective are strong ones who capture people's interest and imagination with strong personalities and strong and clear messages.

Armstrong uses former Ontario premier Mike Harris as an example. In his election campaigns he produced clear, understandable messages, and when elected, he did exactly what he said he would do. While we might not see the polarizing Harris government as a model for the church to follow, we miss the point she is making at our peril. The church cannot pierce the chatter of modern life with fuzziness and wishy-washy messages. We need clarity and strength of purpose; we need to formulate an identity that our country will understand.

The United Church is not simply a big tent; it also functions like a department store, a one-stop shop with everything you need under one roof. That worked well in the 20th century, but department stores no longer draw people in the same way. My kids go there only if they cannot find what they want in the specialty stores. In fact, a new mall that opened up west of us in the city of Vaughan, Ontario, has as its anchor tenant a Bass Pro store, not a department store. The future of the department

store does not look very good. So what is a church that has
functioned under a similar model—trying to provide everything
to everyone—to do? I have written earlier about how local
congregations can respond. How can the wider church respond?

A Third Way for the United Church

What is the identity of The United Church of Canada going to be
in this century? The issues are clarity and identity. If we can no
longer be all things to all people, who then are we? As I see it,
we have three choices:

1. Do nothing and continue to stagnate.
2. Specialize.
3. Rebrand ourselves.

The first is not really an option. I don't think that anyone lives
in the denial that everything is just going to be fine if we simply
stay the course.

The second is tempting. We could be the progressive Christian
denomination, the church of activist writers like Tom Harpur
and John Shelby Spong. We could form our identity around
the power of myth and its rediscovery. We could proclaim
a new Christianity for a new century, with new models of
understanding. Certainly that is already happening in many
parts of the church. But in order to specialize in this way, would
we be willing to jettison those parts of the church that are simply
not in that place and will never be? Is that acting in a just,
faithful manner?

I think we need to strive for a third, more complex way. The gift and the challenge we face is the richness of our difference. In any community where there are United Churches, you will experience both similarity and distinctiveness. In some you will find an Alpha course, a conservative introduction to Christianity; in others, *Exploring Faith Questions*, a new United Church faith development program. In mine, you'll find a homegrown combination. Some churches are liturgically traditional, others casual; some clergy preach in jeans, others in robes, and still others in suits. You'll find PowerPoint in some, bands in others, organs in many. While Anglicans, Catholics, and Lutherans are each united by a deep liturgical tradition that transcends the theology of the day, what do we in the United Church have that unites us through our differences?

Back in 1988 when my congregation in Alberta was dealing with the ordination question around sexual orientation, I lost a few families who disagreed with both the national church position and my own on the issue. They left to try other traditions. Over the course of two years, all but one drifted back. When I asked them what caused them to return even though they still disagreed with the church's position, they said at first that it just didn't "feel the same" when they worshipped elsewhere. As I pursued the question, it turned out that the things that drove them away were the very things that brought them back. It was our capacity to question, our openness to others, and our very acceptance that they missed.

This is more than a question of ethos—it is the angel of our denomination, an angel that I have experienced in all the theological ranges in our church. The United Church has a capacity to live in the tension of difference, an acceptance that we are all in unique places, and a willingness to journey together in that. Never underestimate the real God-given power of that reality—it is an incredible gift that we have, one that should never be devalued. It is also a fragile gift that requires nurturing.

That is why I would be saddened if the United Church ever defined who we are doctrinally and theologically with absolute certainty. "Don't like it? Tough, go somewhere else." That is the danger of absolute certainty and one reason that I am happy placing myself in the radical middle. The radical middle does not imply sitting in the midst of the road unsure of which direction to travel in, or being in danger of being hit by traffic coming from both directions. Rather, I want to use the image given to me by my colleague Gail Brimbecom. The United Church is like a river: on one bank is the left, on the other the right, and we flow in between them. Rivers don't flow in a straight line, they bend and curve, sometimes calm and sometimes rocky, fast-running, and filled with rapids and the occasional waterfall. With rivers, you never really know what you are going to find around the next bend, and over a long time they shift and change the landscape and environment all around them. It's a good river to travel; you just have to pay attention to what it is telling you. The radical middle is like that, moving and changing with the seasons, but rooted in a core Christian identity—learning from all, adjusting our faith as we learn, evolving rather than putting a dam in the river or turning it into a canal.

There are many kinds of certainty: liberal certainty, progressive certainty, conservative certainty, orthodox certainty. We need to stay open to the possibility that God's Spirit is blowing in a different direction than we think. We need to stay open to the wisdom of others' experiences of God, especially when they differ from our own. That is the angel of the United Church, which—along with a deep and profound faith in God, an experience of the power of Jesus, and the loving gift of the Holy Spirit—we need to share. The United Church should offer a community that not only welcomes individuals, but welcomes their questions and invites them on the journey, knowing that we will each reach a different destination.

When I speak with young people who worship at Westminster United Church, these are the values they treasure. These values are what has brought them through our doors and will keep them coming back. "Be open-minded," says one such young person, Frank Mah. Open to God, open to the Spirit. Who knows what God has planned for us next? It could very well be the most exciting journey we have ever experienced.

Moderator Peter Short has played an important part in helping the United Church to discern our future. He recognizes how the church needs to proceed on the crucial question of identity and formation. "The founding charism of the United Church has exhausted itself," Short tells me. He believes that the United Church was created to bring a Christian nation into being as a partner with the federal government. "We were founded for Canada and had no being apart from being a part of Canada," he says. This beginning began to fall apart in the 1960s, he says, and during the past decades we have failed to be the church of which our nation would be proud. No longer are we a big player—our world has changed and we are bereft of our founding charism, Short believes. The solution lies not in looking outward, but rather in going inward and "becoming in ourselves that which we long for our country to be." Short, with the soul of a poet, has a profound belief in the church's future, but only if we have the capacity to honestly look at ourselves and create a whole new identity and structure. One thing this means is bringing Aboriginal peoples and multicultural congregations away from the margins and into the centre of who we are.

If the United Church models a truly inclusive community—as a diverse body of Christ, in ethnicity, thought, theology, and community—we will indeed become that for which our country yearns: a church that is the basis for a 21st-century faith, in relationship with a Jesus grounded in both the first and 21st centuries. If we live that community, then our denomination will not just cling to its historic past but thrive in a new, exciting, unique way.

CHAPTER 8

A New Religious Leadership

"WE ARE NOT ALONE, we live in God's world." The words of the United Church's "New Creed" begin with that most reassuring of sentences. In the vastness of space, in the midst of the incomprehensible distances of the universe, we—who inhabit this small, blue planet, as far from the centre of our galaxy as Nazareth was from Rome—are not all there is. God is with us.

But for so many of those who are in leadership in a congregational setting, these words are perceived more as a promise than as a reality. Many feel alone and isolated, confused, and uncertain as to what leadership is in the 21st century. We wonder if we can find a denominational narrative that transcends our individual churches. It seems as though many of us are living within silos that ache with the search for purpose. We hunger for purpose and in the words of Anthony Bailey, one of the voices of leadership we met in Chapter 3, for "a noble life." We need purpose and destiny—not in the Greco-Roman sense where destiny is fixed from birth and individuals become actors delivering prearranged lines, but in the sense of a collective call that transcends our individual lives and congregations. In that sense, we appear to many bereft of destiny—the United Church motto seems to be not "we are one" but "we are ones."

William Butler Yeats's poem "The Second Coming," though written early in the last century, speaks to me with a prescient insight of our current world situation:

> Turning and turning in the widening gyre
> The falcon cannot hear the falconer;
> Things fall apart; the centre cannot hold;
> Mere anarchy is loosed upon the world,
> The blood-dimmed tide is loosed, and everywhere
> The ceremony of innocence is drowned;
> The best lack all conviction, while the worst
> Are full of passionate intensity.[1]

This poem presents the question before us: Can the centre hold or will "things fall apart"?

We should not look to an institution to save us, nor to its structures and councils; rather, we need to look inside, to the deep well of God that rests within. We need to find a leadership that bubbles from the bottom to the top, not the other way around. Top-down leadership is based in institutions, institutions that are in decline and therefore create more rules and regulations. Such institutions become less about freeing creativity and more about demanding obedience to ever-growing binders of procedures and policies, which can never fill the aching void inside. Only a true sense of purpose will do that.

---

1 From "Collected Poems" by William Butler Yeats, A.P. Watt and The Macmillan Company of Canada, 1921.

My purpose as a minister is to reorient people's lives through an encounter with the holy. As a Christian, for me the holy is rooted in God and in the stories and being of Jesus. That is what I believe God created me to do with my life and it is what I attempt to do every day. Undergirding this purpose is a profound belief in the local church as the best vehicle to deliver that encounter. I have always had a strong sense of vocation, a strong belief since I was quite young that there was something specific that I was formed to do. It took me until I was 27 to figure out what it was, but once understood it has given me a profound sense of fulfilling my destiny. It has not always been easy, nor without pain and cost, but it has been the only life that I could imagine. Reorienting means turning toward God. It means shaping the decisions that affect your life and those around you through the lens of the risen Jesus. It involves helping people to discover their vocation and challenging and empowering them to live it out.

The challenges of this century require a new expression of religious leadership. What will its attributes be?

Relationships

Leaders do not function in isolation; they function as part of an interconnected web of relationships. Without high-quality relationships, leadership cannot occur. People choose to give authority to their leaders; it is not given automatically. Leaders without the authority of positive relationships fail. People rarely obey dictates with enthusiasm and will quite often work—passively or actively—to undermine what they are compelled against their will to perform. On the other hand, if leaders have the capacity to develop healthy relationships, those they are leading and their peers will share a sense of ownership in the vision and will work for the greater good. In addition, they will add their own perspectives and thereby strengthen the vision, the organization, and the leader. A leader with good relationships will share the credit when things go well and shoulder blame when they do not.

Leaders must feed their souls with positive, loving relationships outside of the workplace as well, with partners, children, friends, or extended family. Without relationships like these, we do not experience our complete humanity. Friendships are so important to our health—they give us perspective, and a good friend will tell you the truth when no one else will. Good relationships occur only over time and require investing time in people. Being available for conversations and meeting over coffee or a shared meal builds bonds of respect and mutuality.

Good relationships help keep leaders grounded and provide a critical system of support. The 21st century calls for the capacity to both work as part of a team and exercise individual initiative.

Courage

It takes courage to lead—courage to tell people what you really think, courage to stay on the path. This is different from bravery, which exists primarily in the moment: a situation of danger arises, a quick reaction saves those in danger, then the moment passes and life proceeds. If bravery is the sprint, courage is the marathon. Courage means taking the long view and not being overly distracted by opposition. Courage is the capacity to listen to those who agree with you as well as to those who do not. It means admitting openly if you are wrong and when necessary, apologizing for your mistakes. It also involves telling others if you feel they are wrong and, with civility and humility, explaining your reasons. Leading with courage includes the capacity to adjust your plans when the circumstances change. Courage also requires that the motto "peace at any price" is never part of your lexicon; if you give in to everyone, you can't really give anyone anything. We must cultivate the capacity to live with criticism and not be destroyed by it. Courage is daring to open our imaginations to new possibilities that shatter our own preconceptions and prejudices.

Courage is embracing the risk and danger of failure and still moving forward. Courage is being embraced by failure and standing up to it. Courage is accepting success but not being seduced by it. It is looking in the bathroom mirror and liking what you see.

Courage sustains you when you are ready to pack up and go home—it gives you the energy for one more step. Courage means standing up for yourself and for your fundamental values. Courage took Moses to the throne room of Pharaoh, it took Mary to the tomb on Easter morning, it took Paul across ancient Greece. Courage ordained the first woman in The United Church of Canada in 1936, it apologized to First Nations in 1986, it is now working to embrace true diversity. Courage is an angel of the church.

Patience

Patience is a gift that allows leaders not to overreact. Being patient slows us down, so that instead of the innate fight or flight reaction for which we are genetically programmed, we can draw a deep breath and analyze a situation from an emotional distance. Patience also allows us to examine ourselves from that same distance and to judge our own reactions. Patience means that we are not thrown off by setbacks; in fact, we expect them. Patience can be nurtured through prayer and Christian meditation. By learning to observe and control our physiological responses, we can lead without the danger of reactive emotion. We don't counterpunch, we counter-embrace.

Dr. Pandora Bryce is a practitioner of Christian meditation, a form of meditation based upon Christian theology and practice. Having been exposed to quiet worship in her youth through the Anglican tradition of compline, she discovered that it helped to centre and calm her. Later, as a performer, Bryce would do deep-breathing exercises to achieve an inner relaxation that would enable her to deliver optimum performances. But it was a horrific car accident, requiring a seven-year rehabilitation process, that led her to a true appreciation of this tradition. Battling chronic pain and unable to take painkillers other than Tylenol, Bryce went on a journey of discovery so that pain would not define her life. Eventually, she found that imagery meditation helped her in wonderful and unexpected ways. Determined to help others, Bryce did further research on it during her doctoral studies at the University of Toronto. In her own words, she wanted the "chops" to reinforce her anecdotal experience on meditation. For Bryce, Christian meditation is using our faith tradition to "pay attention." The benefits are significant: it trains the mind to be less reactive and to see a thought as a thought; it brings together faith, body, and mind in a way that traditional prayer tends not to; it decreases anxiety and increases resilience;

and it helps us to stay in the moment and concentrate on our inner state.

I too have found Christian meditation to be of great benefit. If you are wondering how it works, let me give you an instant experience: First, start to focus on your breathing. Pay attention to it—is it fast or slow, smooth or ragged? Now take 10 seconds to breathe in and out, one single breath, in and out, paying attention to your physical tension. As you breathe out, breathe out the tension. You can also concentrate on a mental image, a stained glass window, or a scripture passage—anything that brings you closer to the holy.

When Bryce ran a Christian meditation program at our church, we had 30 to 40 people a night for six straight weeks. It was amazing what people carried into that room and what they were able to leave behind.

Patience also understands that the fastest way between two points is not always the best way, that sometimes it is the farthest point that we should pursue. Patience means never giving up; instead, it allows us to understand that when God closes one door, another does opens, even if we cannot yet discern its shape. Patience understands the difference between our time and God's time. It frees us to live within the duality that life is both short and long. Patience is anathema to the culture of quarterly results and instant gratification. It instills delayed gratification and the understanding that what we do shapes not only our lives, but those of our children and grandchildren as well. Patience is the single hardest quality to develop.

Passion and Compassion

Passion is not an emotion. In terms of leadership, it is a complete commitment to, and belief in, what you are doing. It is feeling to the depth of your soul that you are doing what you were created to do with your life. Passion allows focus and creates energy that attracts the interest of others. It builds excitement and commitment. Passion is infectious. It stokes our internal fires when they are fading to greying embers and brings to life a bright, shining flame. Passion is about heat and sometimes friction. No great art was created without passion: no painting, no sculpture, no great novel or piece of music ever came to fruition without an artist's single-minded, passionate belief in its creation. Passion by its very nature is intense and can be selfish.

There is danger in passion, but without it leadership is emotionally empty. I believe that if we are not passionate about our work, if we don't love what we do, if we don't believe to the very fibre of our being that what we do has a transformative, life-changing impact, then we need to examine why we are doing it. No great cause—from the end of slavery to the end of apartheid—was won without passion. All great leaders have passion for what they do. Their passion for their work fuels creativity and imagination. It is what gets leaders up in the morning and keeps them going into the night.

Passion has a companion, compassion. While passion can be selfish, compassion allows us to identify with the other. It gives us the imagination to walk in another's shoes and reach out. Christian compassion is grounded in the words and ministry of Jesus. From the prodigal son and the good Samaritan to the woman at the well and the healing stories, Jesus' ministry was one of crashing through the artificial barriers and social conventions that people erect between themselves. He had the compassion to see into the hearts of both the victims of those barriers and of those who maintained them. His compassion was for all. That is the challenge of leadership, to have compassion not just for those with whom we sympathize, but for those who anger and at times outrage us. To be compassionate is to bring the heart of God into each situation.

Integrity

Integrity is central to leadership. Without it, leadership becomes simply an exercise in power. Power without integrity can become abuse and descend into violence, both personal and institutional. Integrity must exist in us as individuals and in what we do. For organizations from churches to businesses to government, integrity is central to leadership. Integrity and its companion, honesty, must be available for all to see; without them, corrosion sets in to be replaced by self-interest, greed, and ego advancement.

Integrity is a gift that allows us true freedom. It is an important antidote to the cynicism that is engrained in our culture. Integrity creates a climate of authenticity, and the key to authenticity is transparency. From finances to organizational goals, everything must be out there for all to see and to challenge. Integrity insists that we not only speak but live our values. People have a sixth sense about authentic integrity. They know it goes far beyond nice-sounding mission statements. It must be backed up by action and with consequences for those who break faith with an organization's core values.

Integrity allows us to sleep at night; it calls us to truth-telling, especially of the hard truths that we would all like to avoid.

Play

It may seem strange to add play to my list, but I truly believe that the ability to play is central to being an effective leader. Without it, leaders are in danger of becoming humourless workaholics. Play allows us to let go of our serious, sober adult identity and release our angel of fun. It might mean taking salsa lessons, or going to the movies and buying a big bag of chocolate-covered raisins. Perhaps it's playing imaginary games with your grandchildren or going on a date with your partner. Maybe it involves a game, having friends over to dinner, or learning a new skill, playing a sport, or working out in a gym. But it should give pleasure—be it gardening, wakeboarding, or a simple walk in the park. Play frees the mind and allows it to rest or be used in a completely different way. Play blows off stress and renews the spirit. It has the added benefit of bringing value to our other endeavours, not only through the refreshment it provides, but by integrating itself into our daily tasks.

For me, slalom waterskiing is a critical component of summer play. It takes me back to my early years and proves to me that I'm still alive. That, followed by a canoe ride with my fly rod, makes for me the perfect summer day.

Connected to play is rest—as in sleep and as in doing nothing. Too many people today do not take their holidays. They feel pressured to stay on the job, or even worse, take their laptops and cell phones with them so that they can never truly get away from the office. This is a classic example of a false economy.

We need downtime, time to let the mind rest, slow down the rhythms of our lives, and reconnect with friends and family. Without it we burn out or fall prey to a host of stress-related illnesses. Holidays are not frivolous; they are a critical part of being a whole person. It is terrible leadership to stay on the job 24/7; it shows a total lack of trust in your team and it models obsessive, unhealthy behaviour. People look to clergy as models of healthy living, not as people who are constantly overworked and overtired and stay chained to their desks.

Without the time I take in the summer, I simply could not produce as effectively throughout the year. The well runs dry and we need to give it time to refill.

Faith

Of all the components involved in religious leadership, faith is the most important. Faith involves so many aspects of our life. I have faith in God, faith that I walk in the midst of a holy presence. I have faith that when I pray, I am heard and understood, if not always answered within a time frame that makes me happy. I have faith that—though I am filled with imperfections and insecurities—I am loved by God.

Faith is not easy. It is a gift, but one that is tested, sometimes cruelly. Faith is not faith unless it goes through phases of doubt, disbelief, and even despair. The layers of crisis in my life have added to, not diminished, my faith. Faith is hard; it is especially hard when pain is visited upon those we love. But faith also sustains us when we have nothing left and are but a shell of ourselves. Faith can rebuild shattered lives.

I have faith in the traditions and values of the church of which I am a part. I have faith in the people I work with, faith that we share common beliefs and common goals. I have faith that they will stand by me and that I in turn will stand by them. Faith in each other leads to relationships of trust and the ability to take risks, knowing that there are people around to catch you if you fall. Trust allows us to make leaps of faith and enter into unknown territory.

Global Perspective

Leadership today requires a highly adaptive intelligence. The theory of multiple intelligences states that individuals experience knowledge in different ways depending on their learning style and capacity. I propose adding "adaptive intelligence" to that framework. In the 21st century, learning and leading using a global, intercultural approach is critical.

With the Internet and other sources at our fingertips providing such a wealth of information, with discernment there is simply no reason to lack a basic understanding of what is happening beyond the North American context. If the chaos theory states that when a butterfly flaps it wings in Asia, it rains in Red Deer, Alberta, then when there is a shift in the economy in Thailand, it pours in Toronto. We are all interlinked for better or worse and we need to understand these connections.

Equally important, we need to consult with people who reflect a rich experience of diversity that goes beyond our personal ethnocultural and religious background. We need to hear and integrate the stories and perspectives of a variety of people and use their wisdom in our contexts. What are other faith

communities dealing with? On what issues do we share common ground? How can a complete community work together?
I cannot stress strongly enough how important this is. If we stay within one primary cultural/religious silo, we will fail one of the most critical tests of leadership, the test of inclusion. Exercising leadership that is culturally intelligent is a big challenge.
It requires the deliberate building of links both within and outside of the local community in order to reflect the wondrous diversity of the world.

Another form of diversity that is hardly ever mentioned is economic diversity. The church is great at serving the poor, but can we integrate the poor into positions of leadership? Do we actually speak to the people who come to us for help with food, money, or shelter? Are we able to hear their wisdom and experience?

Self-knowledge

Leaders must know themselves; they need to be aware of their own gifts and weaknesses and bring into their circles those who complement their skill set and fill their gaps. In the church, leaders also need to be grounded in our story: we need to fully understand and appreciate our own faith traditions in order to do our work.

Amy-Jill Levine, a professor of New Testament Studies at the Vanderbilt University Divinity School in Nashville, is a practising Jew who attends an Orthodox synagogue. Levine makes a spirited and at times passionate plea to Christians not to dilute the central parts of the Christian story: "The New Testament contains splendid things. Who can read Luke's Christmas story without getting a lump in their throat? Who cannot be challenged by the parables of Jesus? It is inspirational to watch Paul create his Christology while responding to the people in churches in Rome or in Corinth who were at each other's throats." In Levine's opinion, we have domesticated Jesus, resulting in preaching that is "boring, banal, and trite." Jesus is not a "don't worry, be happy kind of guy," she asserts. Rather, Jesus places radical demands on his followers that are very hard to live up to. "He insists that you treat people in your community as blood relatives and you don't upload your own family above others," says Levine. "Don't," she pleads, "jettison your own story, even if it is a struggle for you." Levine sees tremendous value in doctrines like the Trinity: "The Trinity keeps everything in balance. It shows there is relationship within the divine and that the divine is complex. The idea of the Trinity—of the divine as Creator, Redeemer, and Sustainer—keeps every component of the Christian understanding in a delicate balance. It also serves as a check on the church overemphasizing any single one of the three." She notes that if we leave the mystery out of religion, all that is left is secular humanism. Levine also sees Christianity as being remarkably good at adapting to the cultures in which it finds itself. "Christmas in Mexico is not the same as Christmas in Manila," she says.

If, as church leaders, we do not know our own traditions, our own story and doctrines, how can we expect to lead from within, let alone enter into conversation with the wider community? Levine points out that Jesus first explains and then demonstrates his concern in action, and only then does he send the disciples out. That, I believe, is what we need to do. We need to undertake an interior journey so that through knowing ourselves, we will be able to move out from behind our walls and into the world.

But unless we really know who we are, it will be a very short trip indeed.

A New Leadership

Leadership involves holding all of the above-named characteristics in a dynamic tension and exercising them with great care. I recognize that this can at times be a daunting task. But we live in daunting times, times that call upon everything we have and are. Looking at the scope of history, we are in the midst—or coming to the end—of an incredibly peaceful and prosperous moment. The world wars seem a distant memory, and Canadians live in a world that at the dawn of the last century would have seemed to be a science fiction paradise. Yet I do not underestimate how big a challenge we now face. Phyllis Airhart, a history professor at Emmanuel College, Toronto, has written that every generation misjudges its successors' challenges. That is the danger of projecting the present into the future. So it is with humility and trepidation that I have offered my own guesses about the world that is evolving in front of our very eyes.

But no matter what the future looks like, no matter how different it is from the way I or any of us imagine it will be, there is something of which I am certain. God will continue to need and call people into religious leadership. We need to be ready for that call and have the skills with which to respond.

A Light for the World to See

"Nothing that is worth doing can be achieved in our lifetime;
therefore we must be saved by hope."

Reinhold Niebuhr[1]

IN THE CENTRE OF THE FLOOR in Westminster's sanctuary is a
labyrinth. Based on the design from Chartres Cathedral, it was
cut directly into the floor tile by our custodian, Jack Feltham,
and a few volunteers this past summer. A team can pull out the
chairs, and in an hour, the sanctuary is transformed with candles
and music into a place of deep contemplation. I love to walk
the labyrinth because each experience is unique; I feel refreshed
and reconnected to the holy each time. If you come to walk our
labyrinth for the first time, you are invited to participate in a
time of preparation where a guide speaks about the history of
the labyrinth, how to walk it, and what to expect on the journey.
Your guide will walk with you to the start of the labyrinth and be

---

1 From Reinhold Niebuhr, *The Irony of American History* (New York: Charles Scribner's,
   1952), chapter 3. Used with permission of the Estate of Reinhold Niebuhr.

waiting at the end if you have a need to talk about it. This person prepares you, but doesn't tell you what you should experience. There is no judgment, only the offer of companionship of someone who is there to guide you onto the path and to share that moment with you.

I believe that this is an excellent metaphor for leadership in the 21st century. People are not looking for experts, nor to be told what is best for them. Rather they are looking for guides to lead them to a path and walk with them. The time of "one model fits all" is over; it is a time for contextual leadership. The challenge for leaders is to be both local and global at the same time, and it is going to be a difficult balance to keep.

As I have walked through the writing of this book, I have drawn some conclusions: the United Church needs to find a way to celebrate that which makes us unique and the specific gifts that we have to offer our culture. At the same time as we confidently rejoice in who we are, we must honestly assess *where* we are as a church. There can be no resurrection until death has been acknowledged. The Arnprior Assembly on Ministry in 2005, in which Moderator Peter Short gathered over 100 clergy and laity to reflect on what God will require of the United Church in its third generation, was one of the first steps on that journey.

Having talked to people from across the country, it is clear to me that if the United Church is going to rebuild itself, it will need a clear sense of purpose, a purpose that is both particular and national in scope. It will need a unifying ethos that tells people who and where we are. This will not be easy, but it is absolutely necessary if we are to have a future deep into the 21st century.

EPILOGUE

We can disagree theologically while sharing a unifying identity—
that may sound contradictory, but remember that one of the key
concepts of our age is to hold two seemingly opposite ideas in
tension and live with them together.

I deeply believe that a renewed commitment to a reframed social
justice, based upon intentional and profound Christian spiritual
practices, will play a major part in this renewal. Recently, Bill
Hybels of the Willow Creek Association, preaching at the Crystal
Cathedral on the occasion of Robert Schuller's retirement,
challenged the congregation to tackle issues of poverty, AIDS,
and health care. If the evangelical community now sees its
vocation as dealing with issues that in the past got us labelled
as being "too political," then the United Church needs to pay
attention. It's time for the church to stop keeping its light under
a bushel and bring it out for the world to see. But it must be
reflected in practice, not merely words: we must be willing
to walk the talk at a congregational level if we wish to have
influence or be an agent of community transformation.

Chris Tindal, whom we met in Chapter 3 as a Green Party
candidate, told me of being on the board of his church as a
youth, when the church hit a financial roadblock. Its response
was to cut every program that linked the congregation globally
or reached into the community to serve the needs of the poor,
with the result that it "removed all the reasons that people
wanted to come to church in the first place." Another voice of
leadership, Michael Ward, grew Central United in Calgary by
cutting everything that *didn't* have to do with outreach! The path
that congregation chose was a radical commitment to recovery
and opening its doors to those with addictions. At the time, that
path was completely counterintuitive, but that's the gospel and

that's how it works. It takes leaders with courage, willing to bear the burden of answering the call.

The church must be clear what we base our outreach upon. We must proclaim a robust, diverse faith, one that is biblical in the very best sense of the word and proclaims a serious—but not literal—approach to scripture. A faith that is open to different understandings of Jesus and God (including understandings of other faiths) without feeling threatened or superior; one that welcomes difference, while finding common ground. A faith that emerges out of times of contemplation, silence, and prayer. If we can create that kind of church, a place where people of all persuasions can find both unity and difference, then we will have built something extraordinary, not only for the Christian church, but for our nation.

The one common denominator I have found in thriving churches and their leaders is this outward focus. To me, the key to leading in the 21st century is focusing on the needs of our neighbours and communities. Lead by reaching out, not by remaining inside. If a church is in a community with a large population from a different culture than your own, then act as a missionary. Learn their language and their culture: invite them in through your doors. We are all, in the words of Peter Short, "planting churches on the ruins of the ancien régime." He's right, and he's right when he says that simply "maintaining The United Church of Canada is a lost cause." If that is all the vision we possess, the church will die and quickly, as it should.

What we need is a movement as profound as the movement that first drove church union in 1925. We need a sense that God is calling us to do something fresh and new, that the valley of dry bones is getting ready to stand up and run again. I believe that this is possible. I do not believe that The United Church of Canada is destined to be a mere historical footnote; I believe that God is not finished with us yet.

We are not called to be merely a prophetic church; I believe we are called to be an authentic church. Authenticity involves being able to speak to the culture in which we find ourselves in a language that is comprehensible to those who live within it. We must earn the right to speak to this culture, and that means we must serve it. Only through service will people again listen to us; only through service will we have something of value to offer. This goes beyond servant leadership, which has become a fashion in the current literature on leadership—service means a commitment to the authentic transformation of the human spirit. It involves an integration of life and faith on a level that we have not yet offered.

John Morison is one of the patriarchs of my congregation and an extremely wise man. He says that the United Church is both the easiest and the hardest church to belong to. We cannot create a culture of commitment, nor should we try. We can, however, offer a culture of participation—a church that makes such a difference that you feel a hole in your heart if you are not there. What will it look like? What will it offer? I don't know. I think I know what it needs to look like in my context, but to suggest that I know what it would look like in a small town in Saskatchewan or on the coast of Newfoundland would be the height of arrogance.

So let me simply offer you this invitation: an invitation to discover your calling as a leader, to discover your God-given potential to stand in the middle of the river of our church, right up to your neck in the water, not knowing if the water is going to reach up over your head. That, I believe, is the very best place to be and the only place to discover who we really are.

We must let the Spirit of God go free from our constraints, and listen to the voice that is calling us to something as yet beyond our imaginations. We must put our trust not in the destination, but in the journey. Let me end as I ended Chapter 1, with scripture: "I have set before you life and death, blessings and curses. Choose life so that you and your descendants may live" (Deuteronomy 30:11).

It is a choice—a choice of life and death, a choice to lead or to watch the United Church's demise from the sidelines. "Let leadership run amuck," as the Rev. Cheri DiNovo says, and choose life.

Study Guide

Chapter 1: An Age of Change and Chaos

On the DVD: Introduction

1. "The future belongs to the fast," says a business leader (page 3). Is that your current experience in your life and work?

2. Name some of the specific changes mentioned in the chapter and the DVD that are affecting the economy. How should we in North America respond?

3. Economist Thomas Friedman believes that we are in a time of unparalleled opportunity ("globalization 3.0"), yet 70 percent of the world has not even heard a dial tone (pages 8, 10). Which do you think is the dominant reality?

4. A *Toronto Star* article cited in this chapter (page 14) describes a United Church in a system-wide decline that seems irreversible. Do you agree with this assessment? If so, why? If you are in a United Church congregation, what can you do about it?

Chapter 2: Fixing Our Broken Windows

1. Have you experienced a decline in civility in the life of your community? How does that affect the way the members of your community live together?

2. Do you agree with the author's definition of community as "the gathering of multiple generations with differing perspectives, bound together by something bigger than themselves"? How do you experience community in your congregation or neighbourhood?

3. What are some "front porch" experiences that your congregation or organization can offer the wider community?

4. Conflict is an inevitable part of life. How do you deal with it? Are the strategies outlined on pages 27–28 ones that you have employed?

5. One of the pressing issues presented in this chapter (page 31) that the United Church is facing is that of new church development and redevelopment. Do you agree? If so, how should the church be dealing with this challenge?

Chapter 3. Voices of Leadership
On the DVD: Church Leaders' Panel

1. "It's as if no one is responsible if churches do well or fail." (Ed Bentley)
   "We have no plan for strong churches. There is no appropriate strategic leadership, none, zero, nada.... We have handed the ball to the conservative churches." (John Pentland)
   How do you react to these statements of United Church ministers? Are they consistent with your experience?

2. Many of the church leaders quoted put a strong emphasis upon a revived social justice practice and powerful outreach. How do we create and renew passion for these in our congregations?

3. Cheri DiNovo of Emmanuel Howard Park United states that the church is dying. Is she correct? If so, what can be done about it?

4. Green Party candidate Chris Tindal asks the question: "What purpose do we serve?" How would you answer that question?

Chapter 4: Building Communities
On the DVD: Gary Polonsky; Westminster United Church

1. Gary Polonsky has consistently seen setbacks as opportunities. What opportunities are we missing because we currently see them as setbacks?

2. Polonsky advocates both/and thinking as opposed to either/or thinking. In your congregation or organization, which is the dominant paradigm? Give examples.

3. Would any of Polonsky's approaches be applicable in your own context?

4. Review the lessons from the Westminster project council on page 66. Can they be applied in your context? How would you implement them?

Chapter 5: Time for a Reboot

1. What aspects of your personal life need a "reboot"?

2. What aspects of your congregational or organizational context need a reboot?

3. Have you experienced the church more as fragile or as resilient?

4. Review Westminster's congregational list of new initiatives on pages 83–84. Make a list for your own congregation or organization, including timelines.

Chapter 6: Responding to the New Realities

1. The book outlines a number of challenges that we are facing on a global and local level. Make your own list of challenges, and how your community can respond to them.

2. Violence is growing exponentially in communities across Canada. How can your congregation or organization create and become a community of peace?

3. What for you is the definition of moral leadership?

4. Read the parable of the good Samaritan (Luke 10:30–37). What lies at the core of the story that is applicable in your life and the life of your congregation or organization?

Chapter 7: Beyond the Big Tent
On the DVD: Jane Armstrong

1. Has the United Church in fact become a collection of silos? If so, how did we get that way? How can we demolish them and put something else in their place?

2. What is your response to Jane Armstrong's advice to churches to "Help people navigate the slalom course that is our lives"? How might the fluid style of "adaptive navigation" (see page 104) affect congregational leadership styles?

3. If Moderator Peter Short is correct that "the founding charism of the United Church has exhausted itself," then what might our future charism be? What should the future church look like?

Chapter 8: A New Religious Leadership
On the DVD: Next Generation

1. Review each of the components (relationships, courage, patience, passion and compassion, integrity, play, faith, global perspective, and self-knowledge) that the author believes are critical to a new leadership. How can you apply these in your own context?

2. What, in your view, should be added to or subtracted from this list?

3. In the DVD segment "Next Generation," Frank Mah says a leader is "the one who knows when to step in and take a hand in things, but also knows when to step back and let the people who are doing their jobs do their jobs the way they feel they should." What is your concept of a leader?

Epilogue: A Light for the World to See
On the DVD: A Reflection on Leadership

1. What does it mean to be an authentic church?

2. What does it mean to be an authentic leader?

3. Do you agree with the author that a reframed social justice with profound Christian spiritual practices is the way forward for the United Church?

4. The author suggests "guide" as a metaphor for 21st-century leadership. As you reflect upon your own personal and corporate experience of leadership, what metaphor would you use to describe your style of leadership? What do you need to adapt to lead your church or organization into the future?

Selected Bibliography

Adair, John, *The Leadership of Jesus and Its Legacy Today* (Cleveland: The Pilgrim Press, 2002).

Borg, Marcus, and N.T. Wright, *The Meaning of Jesus: Two Visions* (New York: HarperCollins, 1998).

Bornstein, David, *How to Change the World: Social Entrepreneurs and the Power of New Ideas* (New York: Oxford University Press, 2003).

Burke, Spencer, *Making Sense of Church: Eavesdropping on Emerging Conversations about God, Community and Culture* (Grand Rapids: Zondervan, 2003).

Collins, Jim, *Good to Great: Why Some Companies Make the Leap… and Others Don't* (New York: HarperBusiness, 2001).

Covey, Stephen, *The 8th Habit: From Effectiveness to Greatness* (New York: Free Press, 2004).

DiNovo, Cheri, *Qu(e)erying Evangelism: Growing a Community from the Outside In* (Cleveland: Pilgrim Press, 2005).

SEISMIC SHIFTS

Friedman, Thomas L., *The World Is Flat: A Brief History of the Twenty-first Century* (New York: Farrar, Straus and Giroux, 2005).

Goleman, Daniel, Richard Boyatzis, and Annie McKee, *Primal Leadership: Realizing the Power of Emotional Intelligence* (Boston: Harvard Business School Press, 2002).

Heifetz, Ronald A., *Leadership Without Easy Answers* (Cambridge: Harvard University Press, 1994).

Johnson, Spencer, *Who Moved My Cheese?: An Amazing Way to Deal with Change in Your Work and in Your Life* (New York: G.P. Putnam's Sons, 1998).

Kotter, John P., *Leading Change* (Boston: Harvard Business School Press, 1996).

Kouzes, James M., and Barry Z. Posner, *The Leadership Challenge: How to Keep Getting Extraordinary Things Done in Organizations* (San Francisco: Jossey-Bass, 2005).

Morrell, Margot, illus. Stephanie Capparell, *Shackleton's Way: Leadership Lessons from the Great Antarctic Explorer* (New York: Penguin Books, 2001).

Patterson, Kerry, et al, *Crucial Conversations: Tools for Talking When Stakes Are High* (New York: McGraw Hill, 2002).

Patterson, Kerry, et al, *Crucial Confrontations: Tools for Resolving Broken Promises, Violated Expectations and Bad Behaviour* (New York: McGraw Hill, 2004).

BIBLIOGRAPHY

Putnam, Robert D., illus. Lewis M. Feldstein, *Better Together: Restoring the American Community* (New York: Simon and Schuster, 2003).

Sweet, Leonard, *Summoned to Lead* (Grand Rapids: Zondervan, 2004).

Wallis, Jim, *God's Politics: Why the Right Gets It Wrong and the Left Doesn't Get It* (San Francisco: HarperSanFrancisco, 2005).

Wheatley, Margaret J., *Leadership and the New Science: Discovering Order in a Chaotic World* (San Francisco: Berrett-Koehler, 1999).

Williams, Jessica, *50 Facts That Should Change the World* (Cambridge: Icon Books, 2004).